AIR COMBAT

OSPREY PUBLISHING

AIR COMBAT

DOGFIGHTS OF WORLD WAR II

EDITED BY TONY HOLMES

OSPREY PUBLISHING
Bloomsbury Publishing Plc
PO Box 883, Oxford, OX1 9PL, UK
1385 Broadway, 5th Floor, New York, NY 10018, USA
E-mail: info@ospreypublishing.com
www.ospreypublishing.com

OSPREY is a trademark of Osprey Publishing Ltd

First published in Great Britain in 2019
Abridged from the previously published: *Duel 39: La-5/7 vs Fw 190* by Dmitriy Khazanov and Aleksander Medved, Duel 54: *F4F Wildcat vs A6M Zero-sen* by Edward M. Young, Duel 67: *Spitfire II/V vs Bf 109F* by Tony Holmes, and Duel 73: *F4U Corsair vs Ki-84 "Frank"* by Edward M. Young.

A catalogue record for this book is available from the British Library.

ISBN: HB 978 1 4728 3676 2; eBook 978 1 4728 3674 8; ePDF 978 1 4728 3675 5; XML 978 1 4728 3677 9

19 20 21 22 23   10 9 8 7 6 5 4 3 2 1

Maps and formation diagrams by Bounford.com
Index by Zoe Ross
Layouts by Myriam Bell Design, Shrewsbury, UK
Originated by PDQ Digital Media Solutions, Bungay, UK
Printed in Hong Kong through World Print Ltd.

Front cover: Combat between F4U-4s and Ki-84 'Franks' in the Pacific theatre, June 1945. (Artwork by Gareth Hector, © Osprey Publishing)
Back cover: (top left) Three Spitfire VBs from No. 243 Sqn. (Philip Jarret); (bottom left) Oberleutnant Siegfried Schnell's Bf 109F-2. (EN Archive); (centre) Sqn Ldr 'Jamie' Rankin with his Spitfire. (Photo by Chris Ware/Keystone Features/Getty Images); (top right) Several Fw 190A-0 pre-production aircraft at Bremen. (From archives of D. Khazanov and A. Medved); (bottom right) La-5FNs on a snow-covered airfield, 1944. (From archives of D. Khazanov and A. Medved)

Editor's note
For ease of comparison please refer to the following conversion table:
1 mile = 1.6km
1lb = 0.45kg
1yd = 0.9m
1ft = 0.3m
1in = 2.54cm/25.4mm
1 gallon = 4.5 litres

Osprey Publishing supports the Woodland Trust, the UK's leading woodland conservation charity.

To find out more about our authors and books visit **www.ospreypublishing.com**. Here you will find extracts, author interviews, details of forthcoming events and the option to sign up for our newsletter.

The author of Part I: Channel Clashes: Spitfire II/V vs Bf 109F would like to thank historians Donald Caldwell, Peter Caygill, Norman Franks and Donald Nijboer for allowing him to quote from their published works.

CONTENTS

FOREWORD

This richly illustrated volume details the exploits of fighter pilots engaged in air combat on a truly global scale during World War II. The eight aircraft types featured in the book are amongst the most iconic fighters of their generation, flown by some of the leading exponents of the deadly art of air warfare. Spitfires engaging Bf 109s on the Channel Front, Wildcats dicing with Zero-sens over the cool blue waters of the Pacific Ocean, La-5s duelling with Fw 190s against the backdrop of the Kursk battlefront and Corsairs dogfighting with Ki-84s near the outskirts of Tokyo. All of these actions, and many more, are related in *Air Combat*.

The aerial duel between Supermarine Spitfire II/Vs and Messerschmitt Bf 109Fs on the Channel Front in 1940–42 saw a reversal of roles for RAF Fighter Command and the Luftwaffe from the summer of 1940. During the Battle of Britain, Hurricane and Spitfire units had stoutly defended southern England from the Luftwaffe as the latter sought to obtain aerial supremacy as a prelude to invasion. Now it was the RAF fighter squadrons that were on the offensive, charged with protecting vulnerable bombers attacking targets in occupied Europe from marauding German fighters. Spitfire squadrons suffered terribly at the hands of the Luftwaffe's fighter force during this period, when a modest number of Bf 109Fs stoutly defended military and industrial targets in France and the Low Countries from RAF medium bombers.

By early 1942 the RAF was sending dozens of Spitfire V-equipped units over France in 'Circus', 'Ramrod' and 'Rhubarb' operations, which were opposed by just two *Jagdgeschwader* (JG 2 and JG 26) with less than 150 serviceable fighters between them. Yet, these German units claimed four Spitfires destroyed for every Bf 109F lost in return, with high-scoring aces such as Adolf Galland, Werner Mölders, Walter Oesau and Josef 'Pips' Priller enjoying notable success against Spitfire wings led by Douglas Bader, 'Sailor' Malan, Jamie Rankin and Paddy Finucane, amongst others.

ACTION IN THE EAST

The leading German ace in terms of La-5/7 victories was the legendary Walter Nowotny. In this particular action on 14 September, he claimed two La-5s from 286th IAD at low altitude while defending I./JG 54's airfield at Shatalovka-East, on the Kursk front. The base was repeatedly attacked by Il-2 and Pe-2 bombers for 48 hours, and Nowotny claimed 14 kills – five of them escorting La-5s. (Artwork by Gareth Hector, © Osprey Publishing)

Soviet fighter aviation had suffered terribly at the hands of the Luftwaffe in the first year of the war in the East, following the launching of Operation *Barbarossa* in June 1941. With the arrival of JG 51 and its deadly Focke-Wulf Fw 190s on the Stalingrad Front in September 1942, things only got worse for the hard-pressed pilots of the *Voenna-Vozdushniye SIly Krasnoy Armii* (VVS-KA – Red Army Air Force). However, help was on its way in the form of the re-engined LaGG-3 fighter, which was fitted with a powerful air-cooled Shvetsov M-82 radial rated at 1700hp in place of the 1240-hp Klimov M-105. Designated the La-5, the new fighter was capable of withstanding more punishment than the fragile LaGG-3 (hundreds of which had been shot down since the German invasion), and it was also appreciably faster and had a greater rate of climb. The La-5 was more challenging to fly, however, but the new generation of better trained pilots who were led into combat by the survivors of 1941–42 quickly found the La-5 (and, later, the improved La-7) very much to their liking.

Arriving in the front line in August 1942, the new Lavochkin fighters soon found themselves in action on the Central Sector of the front line against the equally new Fw 190As of JG 51. The first engagements took place in November of that year over the frozen ground of the Kalinin Front, and from then on the Focke-Wulf fighter would regularly clash with its counterpart from Lavochkin, particularly during the 50 days of the Battle of Kursk in July–August 1943. More than 3500 VVS-KA aircraft were destroyed in the latter campaign, including 500 La-5s. The Luftwaffe, in turn, had 2419 aircraft destroyed during the same period on the entire Eastern Front, 432 of them Fw 190s.

The sheer scale of these actions between the two types in this theatre led to a handful of pilots claiming astonishing tallies of victories. High-scoring ace Walter Nowotny was credited with 49 La 5/7 kills from a final tally of 258, closely followed by Emil Lang with 45 (from 173) and Otto Kittel with 31 (from 267). Soviet pilots also enjoyed success, albeit on a more modest scale, with Vladimir Serov claiming 21 Fw 190s (from 39 and 6 shared victories) and ranking Allied ace Ivan Kozhedub downing 19 (of 62).

PACIFIC WAR

The Grumman F4F Wildcat and the Mitsubishi A6M Zero-sen were contemporaries, although designed to very different requirements. The second of the US Navy's monoplane fighters, the Wildcat was the fourth naval fighter to emerge from the Grumman stable. Ruggedly built so as to survive the rigours of carrier operations, the Wildcat was superior to the earlier Brewster F2A Buffalo in performance and armament. Indeed, it was the best carrier fighter the Americans had when the nation entered World War II in the wake of the surprise attack on Pearl Harbor by the Imperial Japanese Naval Air Force (IJNAF) on December 7, 1941. It remained the principle fighter for the US Navy and the US Marine Corps well into 1943, operating from aircraft carriers and land bases. The Wildcat held the line until the more capable Grumman F6F Hellcat and Vought F4U Corsair entered service.

As the Spitfire has become the iconic aircraft of the RAF in World War II, so too has the Mitsubishi A6M Zero-sen come to represent all Japanese combat aircraft of that conflict. The fighter was designed to meet a seemingly impossible specification issued by the Imperial Japanese Navy (IJN) for an aeroplane with a speed greater than 300mph, exceptional manoeuvrability, long range and an impressive armament, for the time, of two 7.7mm machine guns and two 20mm cannon. Jiro Horikoshi, the

Zero-sen's principal designer, managed to meet the IJN's requirements and produce an exceptional aeroplane in the A6M, but at the cost of making the Zero-sen structurally as light as possible by doing away with protection for the pilot, engine and fuel tanks.

In the first year of the war such omissions rarely mattered, as Mitsubishi's Zero-sen could out-perform any Allied fighter it encountered. The IJNAF's highly trained pilots took every advantage of the fighter's superiority, cutting a swathe across Southeast Asia and the Pacific. The Wildcat was some 2600lb heavier than its Japanese opponent, with only 250 additional horsepower. In one-on-one combat the Zero-sen was clearly superior, yet the Wildcat pilots had no alternative but to take on their more capable Japanese opponents until superior American aircraft could be put into production. The ensuing battles between the Wildcat and the Zero-sen in the pivotal carrier clashes at Coral Sea, Midway, the Eastern Solomons and Santa Cruz during 1942, and on land during the campaign for the control of Guadalcanal, were classic duels in which pilots flying a nominally inferior fighter successfully developed air combat tactics that negated the strengths of their opponent.

By February 1945, when the bent-winged Vought F4U Corsair clashed with the outstanding Nakajima Ki-84 'Frank' for the first time during US Navy carrier strikes on Tokyo, American fighters were very much in the ascendency following three bitterly fought years of action in the Pacific theatre.

The Corsair was first US-built single-engined fighter to exceed 400mph thanks to it being the first aircraft of its type to be fitted with the powerful 2000-hp Pratt & Whitney R-2800 radial engine. The Corsair was intended to be the US Navy's premier carrier fighter, replacing the F4F. Poor stalling characteristics and other technical problems made the initial models of the Corsair unsuitable, in the US Navy's view, for operating off carriers, however. Instead, the Corsair re-equipped land-based US Marine Corps squadrons in the Southwest Pacific, becoming the mount of all the leading 'Flying Leatherneck' aces of World War II and establishing dominance over the Zero-sen with a kill ratio of greater than ten-to-one. By late 1944 the Corsair, with modifications, had been cleared for carrier operations. In the final months of the war the F4U served with both US Navy and US Marine Corps squadrons aboard the former's large fleet carriers, where its greater speed than the F6F Hellcat proved invaluable in the battles against the *kamikaze*.

From airfields on Okinawa, US Marine Corps squadrons battled with Ki-84s during myriad *kamikaze* attacks against the Allied invasion fleet. In these deadly air battles, the Japanese Army Air Force (JAAF) and IJNAF introduced their own second generation of more capable fighters – aircraft such as the Kawasaki Ki-100, Mitsubishi J2M3, Kawanishi N1K1/2 and, of course, the Ki-84 Hayate. Entering service in the autumn of 1944, the Ki-84 gave the JAAF a fighter that could hold its own in combat with the P-51 Mustang, the F6F and the F4U.

Built in greater numbers – more than 3000 examples completed during 1944–45 – than any other late war Japanese fighter, the Ki-84 saw considerable action in the final months of the Pacific War during the ill-fated defence of the Home Islands and Okinawa. During fighting in the latter campaign, JAAF fighter *sentai* equipped with the 'Frank' battled US Navy and US Marine Corps Corsair units (both carrier-based and flying from newly captured airfields on Okinawa) as they tried to clear a path for the *kamikaze* attacks on Allied vessels offshore supporting the invasion force. Corsair pilots found these newer types to be a greater challenge to shoot down, achieving a combined kill ratio of around six-to-one against their Japanese opponents. They were fortunate that the quality of the average Japanese fighter pilot had declined rapidly since the air battles over the Solomons.

A number of the actions fought by the eight fighter types featured in this book are detailed by both Allied and Axis pilots of the various theatres of war. Supporting the riveting accounts contained in this book are the hard statistical facts chronicling the development of each aircraft, their operational performance, and the weaponry that the pilots relied upon to get the better of their opponents when involved in air combat.

Tony Holmes
Sevenoaks, Kent
June 2018

PART I

BY TONY HOLMES

CHANNEL CLASHES

Spitfire II/V vs Bf 109F

The Battle of Britain had seen the Bf 109E pitted against the Hurricane and increasing numbers of Spitfires as German fighter pilots forlornly tried to protect Heinkel, Dornier and Junkers medium bombers targeting southern England. By early October 1940 it was clear that the hitherto invincible Luftwaffe had for the first time failed to achieve its assigned objective – the neutralization of the Royal Air Force (RAF), which would have allowed the Wehrmacht to invade Britain. With the Luftwaffe forced to switch to a night *Blitz* to reduce the unsustainable losses being suffered by its *Kampfgruppen*, offensive operations during daylight hours began to fall to the Bf 109-equipped *Jagdgeschwader* based along the Channel coast in occupied

Opposite

Three Spitfire IIs were lost on 12 March 1941 when No. 11 Group's units attempted to combat a series of 'Freie Jagd' ('free hunt') sweeps conducted by Bf 109s along the Kent coast. No victories were claimed in return. One of the successful pilots was leading Luftwaffe ace Oberstleutnant Werner Mölders, *Kommodore* of JG 51, who bounced Spitfires from No. 74 Sqn near Dungeness during a late afternoon sweep in his Bf 109F-2. (Artwork by Gareth Hector, © Osprey Publishing)

A fighter pilot from World War I, ACM Sir W Sholto Douglas was initially opposed to the suggestion that Fighter Command should go on the offensive over Occupied Europe following the end of the Battle of Britain. (Tony Holmes Collection)

France. Bomb-equipped Bf 109Es and Bf 110s, escorted by yet more E-model Messerschmitts, continued to take the fight to the RAF long after the battle had officially ended on 31 October – a date observed only by the British.

It was during the autumn that the Luftwaffe introduced a new variant of its standard fighter, the ubiquitous Bf 109E being supplanted – initially in very small numbers only – by the more powerful and aerodynamically refined Bf 109F. Although the first three pre-production examples of the aircraft had been released for service evaluation with JG 51 in early October 1940, many months would pass before the F-model outnumbered the Bf 109E on the Channel Front.

Its main protagonist would, of course, be the Spitfire, initially the Mk I/II and then the Mk V. Like the Messerschmitt, the Supermarine fighter was improved as lessons from the early aerial combat of 1939–40 saw it equipped with a more powerful engine and, eventually, better armament. Most importantly, the RAF would change its tactics as Fighter Command was ordered to go on the offensive from early 1941 once it was clear that Germany had no immediate plans to invade Britain. Its new Commander-in-Chief, Air Chief Marshal (ACM) Sir W. Sholto Douglas, wanted his squadrons 'leaning forward into France'. The first such mission had actually been performed by two pilots from the Spitfire IIA-equipped No. 66 Sqn on 20 December 1940 when they strafed Le Touquet. This was the first time Spitfires had ventured over France since the fall of Dunkirk six months earlier.

Now the roles would effectively be reversed. Fighter Command would be escorting bombers targeting airfields, ports and industrial infrastructure in northern France and Belgium, as well as performing sweeps aimed at tempting the Luftwaffe up for large-scale dogfights. Spitfire pilots involved in these missions had gone from attacking bombers during the Battle of Britain to defending them over Occupied Europe just a few short months later. These operations were codenamed 'Circuses' (fighter sweeps with bombers as bait), 'Ramrods' (escorted bomber missions where the objective was to destroy the target), 'Rhubarbs' (small-scale fighter strafing missions), 'Rodeos' (sweeps by large formations of fighters) and 'Roadsteads' (attacks on German coastal convoys at sea or in port). The growing number of Spitfire units within Fighter Command were in the vanguard of the action on the Channel Front. But losses mounted as German fighters and flak exacted a heavy toll in men and machines.

By the summer of 1941 the 'Circuses' had evolved into large-scale, integrated operations involving up to 300 fighters (primarily Spitfires). These missions were now being generated on a near-daily basis during periods of good weather. Following the German invasion of the Soviet Union in June 1941, the Channel Front was robbed of all but two *Jagdgeschwader* – JG 2 and JG 26. It was the responsibility of these units to defend France and the Low Countries from RAF attacks. Equipped with around 260 Bf 109E/Fs, they achieved a combat score of four-to-one in their favour during the latter half of 1941.

As this chapter will show, although Fighter Command had the numerical strength during the Channel Front campaign, it was the Jagdwaffe that enjoyed the greatest success as scores of Spitfire pilots fell victim to their opponents – or to flak – deep inside enemy-held territory.

THE MACHINES
Supermarine Spitfire II and V

Vickers Supermarine commenced Spitfire construction at its Eastleigh plant in April 1938, although only 306 examples had reached the RAF by the time Britain declared war on Germany on 3 September 1939. As early as May of the previous year it was obvious to the RAF that even with the system of sub-contracting organized by Vickers Supermarine, it was not going to receive anywhere near the number of Spitfire Is required to equip

The finishing touches are applied to Spitfire IIA P8479 as it waits on the ramp at Castle Bromwich for collection by the RAF in early July 1941. Built towards the end of the Mk II production run, this aircraft was paid for by a £5,000 donation from the directors, staff and workers of British Glues and Chemicals Ltd of Welwyn Garden, Hertfordshire. It displays the company emblem just forward of the cockpit. (Philip Jarrett)

a rapidly expanding Fighter Command. A production line similar to that used by the automotive industry was urgently required and the man chosen by the Air Ministry to achieve this was Lord Nuffield, better known as William Morris. Having created the first plant to mass-produce cars for the British market, he was perfectly qualified to establish a new 'Shadow Factory' to build Spitfires.

Although the Air Ministry insisted that the factory be built in Liverpool to help ease unemployment in the area, Lord Nuffield urged that a site at Castle Bromwich be chosen due to the availability of a skilled workforce in Birmingham. Work duly began on the factory in the West Midlands in July 1938 and when finished it had cost more than £4 million to build. Nuffield estimated that the plant would assemble 60 aircraft a week once in full production, the Air Ministry having placed an order for 1,000 Spitfire Is in April 1939. After a series of delays, the first example was delivered on 27 June 1940. The machines emerging from the 'Shadow Factory' were designated Spitfire IIs to differentiate them from the near-identical Vickers Supermarine-built Mk Is when it came to ordering spare parts.

The West Bromwich-built fighters were powered by Merlin XII engines running on 100 octane fuel. They also featured a Coffman cartridge starter system instead of the original electric start of the Mk I's Merlin II, with a small fairing on the left side of the engine cowling housing the new unit.

With the Battle of Britain raging, the first Spitfire IIs to be issued to a front-line unit reached No. 611 Sqn at Digby, in Lincolnshire, in late August 1940. Nos. 19, 74 and 266 Sqns received the new variant the following month, while further units replaced their Mk Is during the late autumn and early winter. Squadrons assigned to No. 11 Group, defending southeast England, were given priority as the fighting was heaviest there. The Castle Bromwich factory was the sole producer of the Spitfire II and 921 had been built by the time the last example rolled off the line in July 1941.

By then the Mk II had been well and truly supplanted in the front line by what would prove to be the most numerous Spitfire variant, the Mk V. Vickers Supermarine had originally intended to replace the Mk I/IIs with the Spitfire III, which featured a re-engineered and strengthened airframe incorporating several key design improvements. Converting production lines in Southampton and West Bromwich to build the new variant would involve considerable retooling, however, and this would take time.

During the winter of 1940–41 the RAF was concerned that it would be forced to fight the Battle of Britain all over again the following summer, possibly against new fighter and bomber types with improved high-altitude performance that were reportedly under development in Germany. The RAF believed that the Luftwaffe's switch to high-altitude operations by small numbers of fighters (including the first examples of the Bf 109F) and bombers in November 1940 was the precursor of a renewed offensive in the spring of 1941. The Hurricane could not intercept the Bf 109F above 20,000ft, let alone fight it, while the Spitfire I/IIs lost much of their advantage over the earlier Bf 109E in terms of manoeuvrability and speed when forced to fight at such altitudes. Although fears of high-altitude combat would ultimately prove to be unfounded, they had a significant impact on the Spitfire's development.

The Mks I and II would be unable to engage enemy aircraft at altitudes exceeding 36,000ft and the RAF demanded a re-engined version capable of enhanced performance. The newly developed Rolls-Royce Merlin XX was intended to provide the Spitfire III with the ability to operate at high altitude. But the engine, which featured a redesigned supercharger with two separate blowers for high- and low-altitude operations, proved to be so complex that Rolls-Royce stated it would be difficult to build in the quantities required by the RAF by the early spring of 1941. Furthermore, Vickers Supermarine made it clear that if these engines were not available it could not guarantee the supply of Spitfire IIIs to the tight production schedule demanded by the RAF.

Fortunately, Rolls-Royce had also been working on a simplified version of the Merlin XX with the low-altitude blower omitted. Known as the Merlin 45, it developed 1,515hp at 11,000ft with more than 16lb of boost. This represented an increase of 500hp over the Merlin III fitted to the

A great deal of the Rolls-Royce Merlin's success during World War II came from the exceptional design of its supercharger, seen at the left-hand end of the engine in this photograph. This Merlin 45 is equipped with a single-stage, single-speed supercharger. The Spitfire V and Seafire IB, IIC and III would be powered by the Merlin 45, 45M, 46, 50, 50A, 50M, 55 and 55M series of engines. (Donald Nijboer)

Spitfire II, despite being no larger and only moderately heavier. The engine also lifted the fighter's service ceiling close to 40,000ft, compared with the Mk II's 34,000ft. Lacking the second blower, the engine was also much easier to mass-produce than the Merlin XX, and thanks to its physical similarity to the Merlin III, the Merlin 45 could be fitted to Spitfire I/II airframes with minimal modification. The new fighter, which was then seen by the RAF as a stop-gap pending resolution of the Mk III's problems, was designated the Spitfire V.

On Christmas Eve 1940 a meeting was held at the Aeroplane and Armament Experimental Establishment at Boscombe Down during which Royal Aircraft Establishment staff joined engineers from Vickers Supermarine and Rolls-Royce and senior pilots from Fighter Command to find a solution to the high-altitude performance problems afflicting the Spitfire. Rolls-Royce admitted that large quantities of Merlin XXs would not be available for many months. But it believed it could quickly modify the production Merlin III to Merlin 45 specification and deliver at least 300 by 1 March 1941, with 200 more to follow by 1 April. Just days after the meeting the Air Ministry contracted Rolls-Royce to convert 500 Merlin IIIs into Merlin 45s.

Several Spitfire Is were quickly modified by Rolls-Royce to accept the new engine and flight trials commenced at Boscombe Down in early January 1941. Most of the aircraft initially converted were cannon-armed Mk IBs, although a few all-machine gun-armed Spitfire IAs were also re-engined. Flight trials soon revealed that the Mk V offered most of the performance advantages of the Spitfire III but without the production delays predicted for that variant. The Chief of Air Staff, ACM Sir Charles Portal, confirmed the abandonment of the Spitfire III in favour of the Mk V during a planning conference on 6 March. The minutes of the meeting stated:

> CAS has decided that the Spitfire V with the Merlin 45 engine with a single-speed blower shall be put into production instead of the Spitfire III. The Spitfire V with improved Merlin 45 [with a slightly larger blower impeller – i.e. the Merlin 46] will give better performance in altitude and ceiling. This will meet the needs of Fighter Command for high-altitude fighters. If the type is a success the Air Staff will want as many as can be produced.

Opposite

Spitfire VB W3312/QJ-J *Moonraker* was delivered new to No. 92 Sqn on 20 June 1941 and it was immediately 'acquired' by the unit's boss, Sqn Ldr 'Jamie' Rankin. He duly claimed 11 and one shared victories, one probable and four damaged (all Bf 109Fs, except for a solitary Fw 190 victory) between mid-June and late October 1941 – his first two victories in W3312 came within 24 hours of the aircraft's arrival at Biggin Hill. (Artwork by Jim Laurier, © Osprey Publishing)

SPITFIRE VB

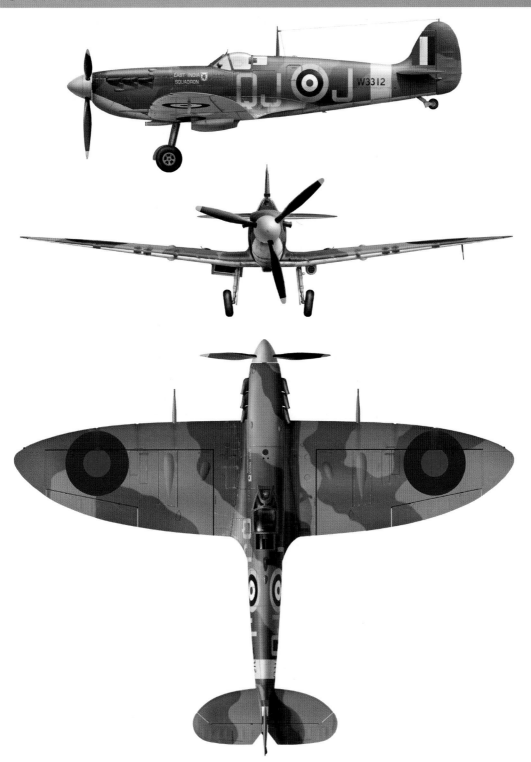

Spitfire IB-equipped No. 92 Sqn at Manston was chosen as the unit to give the Mk V its combat debut. The first converted aircraft arrived at the Kent airfield in mid-February 1941. Over subsequent weeks the squadron sent its remaining Mk IBs to the Rolls-Royce plant at Hucknall for conversion to Mk VB standard. It took up to ten days to replace a Merlin III with a Merlin 45, which meant that for several weeks No. 92 Sqn flew both marks operationally. The first Mk Vs were almost identical to late-production Mk I/IIs, although this soon changed when No. 92 Sqn discovered that the Merlin 45 ran at excessively high oil temperatures and low pressures when at high altitude. Clearly, the fighter's unmodified oil cooling system was not powerful enough to cope with the increased demands placed upon it by the blown Merlin 45. A larger matrix had to be fitted to the cooler, and this in turn meant a larger intake to allow increased airflow through it. The oil cooler intake under the left wing was enlarged and made circular, rather than semi-circular as on the Spitfire I/II – this was an obvious identification feature for the new variant.

Among the No. 92 Sqn pilots giving the Spitfire VB its operational debut was Flg Off Geoffrey Wellum, who recalled one of his early flights with the aircraft in his outstanding autobiography *First Light*:

> Increase in all-round performance is truly tremendous and perhaps most important of all it gives us a much higher ceiling. Only the other day I was a member of the squadron patrolling North Foreland to Dungeness and our entire formation was flying at just a fraction under 40,000 ft. The view was breath-taking. A clear, cold day and I gazed in wonderment at the coastline as it swept right round the bulge of East Anglia to where it curves away westward into the Wash. To the west, the Isle of Wight stood out so plainly that I felt I could put my hand out and almost touch it. Way beyond was Portland Bill. It was a great experience and the sheer beauty had a great and lasting effect on me.

But Wellum's flight was curtailed when he noticed that his oil temperature had climbed alarmingly. This was to be the curse of the early Mk VBs. Five of his squadronmates suffered similar problems during these early sorties, which otherwise proved the Merlin 45's enhanced performance. Wellum recalled, 'The height and results we achieve astound even the boffins, something about the cold winter air giving greater volumetric efficiency.' Yet despite the dramatic results of these flights, No. 92 Sqn received a shock when two German aircraft were spotted *above* them during a patrol:

We were all shattered when a pair of 109s described a couple of wide circles round our formation about 1,000ft above us. We were at the absolute limit of our ceiling and could do sweet damn all about it. I bet they in turn were surprised to see a whole squadron of Spits patrolling in good order at only just below their height. They made no attempt to attack and the thought was that they might have been unarmed photo recce aircraft.

No. 92 Sqn also encountered problems with the Spitfire VB's de Havilland Hydromatic propellers, or, more specifically, failure of the constant speed unit (CSU) that controlled them. This came to a head on 19 March 1941 when three pilots, including the CO, Sqn Ldr James Rankin, were forced to crash-land due to CSU failure during a fruitless high-altitude search for Bf 109s detected at 36,000ft over Kent. Normally, the CSU limited the maximum speed of the Merlin engine to about 3,000rpm, but at the very low temperatures encountered by the No. 92 Sqn fighters the oil in the CSUs congealed and the propeller blades went to full pitch. The engines duly raced to 4,000rpm and threatened to shake themselves apart, forcing the pilots to shut down immediately. All three escaped the ensuing forced landings without injury, although their precious Mk VBs were sufficiently damaged to keep them out of action for several months. Following this incident, pilots flying the Spitfire V at extreme altitude were instructed to make frequent throttle changes to exercise the propeller pitch mechanism. At the same time, as many Mk Vs as possible were fitted with Rotol CSUs until a modification was devised to solve the problem with the de Havilland propeller.

Issues with the Mk VB's 20mm cannon armament and the ballooning of fabric-covered ailerons at speeds in excess of 400mph also afflicted the aircraft in its early service career. Both these problems were inherited from the earlier Spitfire I/II, but were eventually solved as the Spitfire V rapidly matured – this variant was the subject of more than 1,100 modifications during its service life. Far from being a stop-gap, the Mk V proved to be the workhorse of Fighter Command during the Channel Front campaign. A total of 6,479 examples were built between January 1941 and November 1943.

Messerschmidt Bf 109F

Augsburg-based Bayerische Flugzeugwerke began work on what would become the Bf 109F in the autumn of 1938 just as the first Daimler-Benz-engined version of the Messerschmitt fighter, the Bf 109E, was about to enter front-line service with the Luftwaffe. Company founder Professor Willy Messerschmitt and Chief of Project Planning Robert Lusser wanted

The DB 601N of this early-build Bf 109F-1 is exposed for routine maintenance. Whereas the E-model's upper cowling was in one piece, the 'Friedrich's' was split in two halves fastened by two clips on each side. This meant that both cowling sides could be rotated upwards around a common axis, separately or together. As can be seen here, this gave the mechanics improved access to the engine. (EN Archive)

an aircraft that could exceed the performance of previous Bf 109 variants through a combination of airframe aerodynamic refinements and the installation of a more powerful version of Daimler-Benz's DB 601A engine. Designated the DB 601E, the new version utilized direct fuel injection to its inverted V12 cylinders – as had the DB 601A – to give the powerplant a predicted 1,350hp at 17,750ft. This represented an increase of 23 per cent over the DB 601A. The new engine was 17.2 inches longer, which dictated a major redesign of the Bf 109's engine bearers and cowling. The F-model would also feature the streamlined propeller spinner created for the next generation of Messerschmitt single- and twin-engined fighters and inspired by the record-breaking Me 209 racing aircraft.

In a bid to achieve the most streamlined forward fuselage possible, Messerschmitt redesigned the chin-mounted oil cooler intake which was such a recognition feature of the E-model. It also revised the wing-mounted

Opposite

Bf 109F-2 Wk-Nr 9552 was assigned to 9./JG 2's *Staffelkapitän*, Oberleutnant Siegfried Schnell, the leading ace on the Channel Front in terms of Spitfire II/Vs destroyed. Maintained in immaculate condition at the *Gruppe*'s Theville base in the spring of 1942, the aircraft was finished in standard camouflage for the period, with the addition of protective paint on the wing roots and lower fuselage to prevent staining by exhaust deposits. A total of 57 victories were displayed on the rudder. (Artwork by Jim Laurier, © Osprey Publishing)

Bᴘ 109F-2

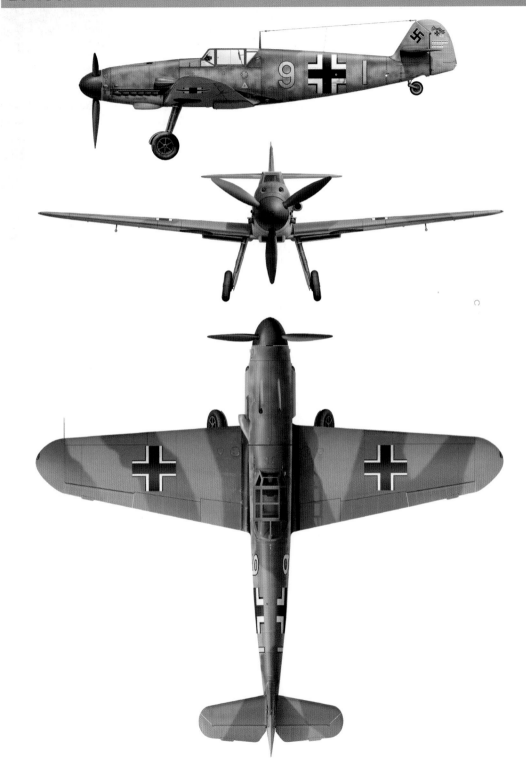

coolant radiators by making them twice as wide and half as deep as those fitted to the Bf 109E. This new design drastically reduced drag. Two-piece airflow flaps were located at the rear of the radiator housings, replacing the single-piece flap of the 'Emil'. The bottom flap both adjusted the airflow and acted as the landing flap. The wings also featured extended semi-elliptical tips rather than the distinctive clipped tips of the Bf 109E. There were also reshaped ailerons, leading edge slats and flaps. To save weight, no wing armament was installed, the F-model featuring a single engine-mounted 15mm or 20mm cannon firing through the propeller hub, supplemented by two MG 17 7.92mm machine guns mounted in the upper cowling.

The tail area of the Bf 109F was also cleaned up to improve the aerodynamics. The most significant of these changes was the removal of the tailplane bracing struts. Although this greatly reduced drag, it also weakened the airframe to the point where several early aircraft were lost in combat when their tail units broke off due to high-speed flutter. The weak point was the tail unit attachment ahead of the tailplanes' leading edges and the tailwheel recess. This problem was cured in early examples by two thin metal strips riveted to the weak point. Definitive modifications were included as part of the production process at Messerschmitt.

The F-model also featured numerous internal improvements. These included a redesigned cooling system with coolant tanks positioned on either side of the engine; a semi-rigid self-sealing fuel tank (on later models only); improved armour to protect the fuel tank and pilot; a new hydraulic system with a reservoir located on the left-hand side of the engine; improved cockpit instrumentation; and electro-mechanical variable pitch control for the VDM 9-11207A or 9-12010A three-bladed metal propeller, the latter modification having been introduced in late-production E-models. Assembly of two experimental prototypes began in the early winter of 1938 once initial research had been completed. The first of these, designated Bf 109 V22, made its maiden flight on 26 January 1939. It was already clear that series production of the DB 601E was behind schedule and the V22 had to be fitted with a DB 601A instead. A second prototype (the V23) flew soon afterwards, fitted with the still experimental DB 601E motor. Both of these aircraft were, in fact, re-engined Bf 109Ds, and during the spring and summer of 1939 they were used for testing the engine, forward fuselage profile, new cooling system and modified wings.

Although the RLM had placed an order for 15 pre-production Bf 109F-0s for delivery between November 1939 and April 1940, progress with the F-model was slow. This was due to ongoing issues with the DB 601E, while Messerschmitt was forced to focus on production of the Bf 109E because of the outbreak of war. It was decided that early aircraft would have to be fitted with the less powerful DB 601N, although it would only be available in modest numbers from mid-1940 due to the Luftwaffe's high demand for the proven DB 601A. Nevertheless, three Bf 109F-0s were assembled during January 1940, these aircraft being regarded as prototypes for the production model. Work was then abruptly halted by order of the Führer himself, as he believed that he could conquer western Europe with the weapons already at his disposal. By then at least two factories had already made preparations for series production of the Bf 109F.

At the end of May 1940 it was decided to restart the 'Friedrich' programme, with a fourth F-0 assembled in late June. By February 1941 14 had been completed, with the final five being built by June of that year. No two F-0s were alike, as Messerschmitt used them to test new systems and equipment in an effort to improve the fighter's performance. Early examples lacked the modified wings with elliptical tips, while others featured differing supercharger air intake shapes – no fewer than ten shapes were tested. All aircraft were initially powered by DB 601A/Ns, although several F-0s and early F-1s were fitted with the definitive DB 601E for flight testing from March 1941. One F-0 served as the series production prototype for the F-1, being fitted with a DB 601N, while another was used as a test bed for the wing slats and radiator flaps unique to the

A pilot is helped on with his straps as he settles into the cockpit of a brand new Bf 109F-2 in early 1941. This is a machine from I./JG 51, and it was among the first 'Friedrichs' to reach the Channel Front in February 1941. Note the fighter's streamlined forward fuselage, Messerschmitt having redesigned the previously protruding chin oil cooler intake that was such a recognition feature of the Bf 109E. (EN Archive)

F-model. Finally, another F-0, fitted with standard E-model wings, tested the 'Friedrich's' engine cooling system.

Despite flight trials with the ever-increasing fleet of Bf 109F-0s still far from completion at Rechlin and elsewhere, the RLM ordered Messerschmitt to start series production of the F-1 at its Regensburg factory from August 1940. The following month the first examples of the Mauser MG 151/15 cannon were delivered to Regensburg for installation in the F-2 variant. Production of this model started shortly thereafter. Assembly of this model commenced at AGO in November, while at the same time F-1 production started at the WNF plant. By spring 1941 the Messerschmitt factories at Regensburg and Augsburg had assembled 157 aircraft – 19 F-0s and 138 F-1s – and the WNF plant 49 F-1s. These numbers fell well short of the 610 planned by the RLM, which meant that the F-model played only a minor role in operations on the Channel Front in the first six months of 1941, with just a single *Jagdgeschwader* (JG 51) fully re-equipping with the fighter.

In January and February 1941 construction of the F-2 commenced at two more plants (including WNF), and the variant would remain in production until September of that year. By then the definitive Bf 109F-4, which at last featured the DB 601E engine and incorporated many of the improvements demanded by the Luftwaffe after early combat with the F-1/2, had been rolling off the assembly lines for four months. F-4s would continue to be built until the summer of 1942, by which time 2,550 'Friedrichs' of all sub-variants had been completed and the fighter's combat career, on the Channel Front at least, was rapidly coming to an end.

TYPE HISTORY
The Spitfire
Spitfire IIA/B

Following a series of delays, the massive 'Shadow Factory' established by Lord Nuffield in Castle Bromwich at last began to produce Spitfires in June 1940. These aircraft were virtually identical to late-production Spitfire Is built elsewhere in the UK but they were fitted with the Merlin XII engine, which produced 110hp more than the Merlin III. Designated the Spitfire IIA, the first examples were delivered to No. 611 Sqn in August 1940, followed by Nos. 19, 74 and 266 Sqns. Towards the end of the aircraft's production run, 170 20mm cannon-armed Spitfire IIBs were constructed at the Castle Bromwich factory, these aircraft also boasting four 0.303-in. machine guns. By the time Spitfire IIA production ended in July 1941, 751 examples had been built.

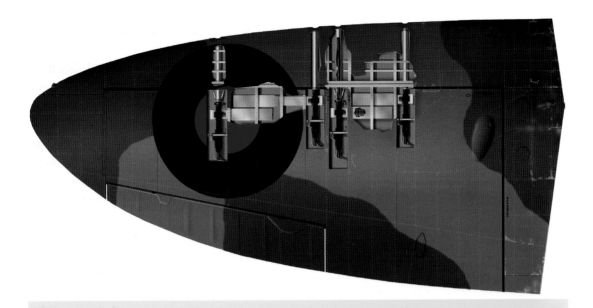

SPITFIRE IIA/VA WING GUNS

The Spitfire IIA and VA was armed with four Browning 0.303-in. machine guns in each wing. This weapons fit was designated the A-type wing with the advent of cannon-armed Spitfire IBs. Rate of fire was 20 rounds per second per gun (160 rounds per second overall) and each cartridge fired ball, armour-piercing, tracer or incendiary bullets weighing around 11.3 grams at a velocity of 2,430ft per second. Total weight of projectiles fired was 4lb per second. Ammunition capacity (350 rounds per gun) was enough for 16 seconds of continuous firing in the Spitfire. Although the Brownings were reliable, they were regularly criticised by RAF pilots for not providing them with sufficient punch when it came to shooting down enemy aircraft. (Artwork by Jim Laurier, © Osprey Publishing)

Spitfire IIA long range

Operations over Dunkirk in May–June 1940 had revealed the Spitfire's limited radius of action, so Vickers Supermarine looked to extend its fighter's range with an external fuel tank. Spitfire I P9565 first flew with a 30-gal tank beneath its port wing in the summer of 1940, but the outbreak of the Battle of Britain stymied development until Fighter Command commenced offensive operations over Europe in early 1941. Eventually, 60 Spitfire IIA Long Range (LR) fighters were built with a 40-gal fixed tank under the port wing, these lop-sided aircraft initially seeing service in the spring of 1941. Although less manoeuvrable and 26mph slower than a standard Spitfire IIA, these fighters carried nearly half as much fuel again, making them ideally suited to bomber escort missions. The Spitfire IIA (LR) was not popular with front-line pilots, one of whom was Sgt Walter 'Johnnie' Johnston of No. 152 Sqn. He recalled, in Peter Caygill's book *Spitfire Mark V in Action*:

When we got the awful long-range Spitfires we all had very narrow escapes. Taking off was full right rudder and stick almost hard over in the same direction. This was due to the extra weight on the port wing only. Flying circuits and bumps to get the feel was dicey as it meant takeoffs and landings with a full wing tank. There was no such thing as a typical curving Spitfire approach to keep the ground in sight – not with about 150–300lb on the inner wing. So we trundled in as if the runway was that of a carrier. Some of us did forget and had hair-raising things happen. We lost two pilots who just undercooked the turn and slipped in.

Overload tanks for the Spitfire V did not appear on the Channel Front until the summer of 1942 (by which time the Bf 109F had all but disappeared from front-line service in this theatre). These tanks were more streamlined and mounted on the aircraft's centre section between the undercarriage legs, thereby eradicating the handling problems associated with the Spitfire IIA (LR). Crucially, the tanks could be jettisoned. Suitably modified Spitfire Vs were initially issued to Nos. 66 and 152 Sqns to replace the last of the Mk IIA (LR)s still in front-line service.

Spitfire V
The Spitfire V was simply a Mk I/II airframe fitted with the new Merlin 45, 46, 50 or 50A engine. The Merlin 45 was the less complex version of the Merlin XX, designed to power the Mk III. The supercharger's second stage (for improved low-altitude performance) was removed and replaced with a new single-speed single-stage supercharger. The Merlin 45 was rated at 1,440hp on take-off and was easy to mass produce. Other engine improvements included a new carburettor that allowed for negative G manoeuvres and prevented interruption of fuel flow to the engine. Pilots soon found the Merlin 45-powered Spitfire V ran at excessively high oil temperatures. The original Spitfire I/II engine cooling system was not powerful enough, so a larger matrix had to be fitted to the cooler. This, in turn, required a larger air intake. The new oil cooler intake was enlarged and made circular in shape. The Spitfire I/II's fabric-covered ailerons were also replaced with examples made from light alloy.

The first Spitfire Vs built were fitted with the A-type wing that housed eight 0.303-in. Browning machine guns. Armour plating was also increased and now weighed 129lb. Top speed for the Spitfire VA was 375mph at 20,800ft. Just 94 were built.

The Spitfire VB would ultimately be the most numerous Mk V variant. It featured the B-type wing, housing two Hispano 20mm cannon, with 60 rounds per weapon, and four 0.303-in. Browning machine guns with 350 rounds per gun. Armour was increased in weight to 152lb. A total of 3,911 Spitfire VBs would be built, 776 by Vickers Supermarine, 2,995 in Castle Bromwich and 140 by Westland.

The Spitfire VC introduced the 'universal' C-type wing first tested on the Spitfire III prototype. The 'universal wing' was designed to reduce manufacturing time and allowed for three different armament options. The 'C' wing featured either eight 0.303-in. machine guns, two 20mm cannon and four 0.303-in. machine guns or four 20mm cannon. The Hispano Mk II cannon were now belt fed from box magazines, doubling the ammunition per weapon to 120 rounds. Early-build Spitfire VCs were delivered with four 20mm cannon but two of these weapons were usually removed once the fighter was in front-line service. Later, production would shift back to the B-type wing with two 20mm cannon and four 0.303-in. machine guns.

The Spitfire VC's airframe was also re-stressed and strengthened. The new laminated windscreen design seen on the Mk III was introduced, as were metal ailerons and a stiffened undercarriage with wheels moved two inches forward. Armour was increased to 193lb.

To increase the Spitfire VC's ferry range, a 29-gal fuel tank was installed behind the pilot. This, combined with a 90-gal slipper tank (rarely seen on the Channel Front), meant that the Mk VC could carry up to 204 gallons of fuel. This gave it a ferry range of approximately 700 miles. When fitted with four 20mm cannon, the Spitfire VC had a top speed of 374mph at 19,000ft. Although some Mk VCs saw combat on the Channel Front, most served in overseas theatres, including the Middle East, Burma and

The only way to distinguish a Spitfire VA from the Mk I or II was by the larger oil cooler fitted to the later mark, with its deeper housing and circular air intake, located under the port wing. This aircraft is R7347, which was one of two early-build Mk VAs sent to Wright Field in Dayton, Ohio, in May 1941 for evaluation by the US Army Air Corps. (Donald Nijboer)

SPITFIRE VB WING GUNS

The Spitfire VB, which was fitted with B-type wings, boasted a powerful armament of four Browning 0.303-in. machine guns and two Hispano Mk II 20mm cannon. The latter (with just 60 rounds per gun) had a useful range of 600 yards, with a total firing time of between 10 and 12 seconds. The machine guns had ammunition for a further five seconds of firing. Plt Off Geoffrey Wellum was suitably impressed with the Mk VB's punch when he flew early examples with No. 92 Sqn in the spring of 1941, noting in his diary at the time, 'The cannons, being new to us, are exciting. The first time I fired them on an air test I was amazed at the noise and the recoil and at the damage the shells did to the ground targets.' (Artwork by Jim Laurier, © Osprey Publishing)

Australia. Some 2,647 Spitfire VCs would be built, 478 by Vickers Supermarine, 1,494 in Castle Bromwich and 495 by Westland.

To improve the Spitfire V's low-level performance, a number of Mk VB airframes were modified and fitted with either the Merlin 45M, 50M or 55M powerplant. The 'M' suffix denoted a Merlin engine equipped with the cropped supercharger blower that worked best at lower altitudes. Indeed, the motor delivered its optimum performance at 6,000ft. The airframe was also modified, with the Spitfire's famous pointed wingtips removed to reduce wingspan to 32ft 6in. The new square-tipped wings gave the LF (low-altitude fighter) V a greater diving speed, better acceleration and faster rate-of-roll compared with the standard Spitfire V. Many LF Vs used Mk VB airframes taken from storage and duly modified.

Due to their previous service, these LF Vs were soon nicknamed 'the clipped, cropped and clapped Spittys' when they reached Channel Front units from early 1943. At low altitude the LF V had a maximum speed of 338.5mph at 2,000ft and 355.5mph at 5,900ft.

The Mk V variant would be built in greater numbers than any other. It would be powered by nine different types of Merlin 45 engine and would see action on every front. The Mk V would also be navalized and transformed into the Seafire IB, IIC and III. The carrier-borne version of the Spitfire took the fight to the enemy over the Atlantic, Mediterranean, Indian and Pacific oceans.

Three Spitfire VBs from newly reformed No. 243 Sqn form up for the Air Ministry photographer during a training flight from Ouston, near Newcastle, in the summer of 1942. EN821 in the foreground was issued new to No. 243 Sqn in late June 1942. (Philip Jarrett)

The Bf 109F

Bf 109F-0

As previously noted, the 19 pre-production F-0s ordered by the RLM on 1 April 1939 served as test and development airframes for the 'Friedrich'. Delivered between January 1940 and June 1941, the F-0s made many flights from Rechlin and elsewhere as Messerschmitt and the Luftwaffe trialled airframe changes, engine upgrades, revised armament and new systems. No two airframes were the same and each example took considerably longer to build than standard production F-models due to their unique configurations. Powered by the DB 601A, N and E, it would appear that none of the F-0s saw operational service.

Bf 109F-1

Constructed between August 1940 and March 1941, the F-1 was built by both Messerschmitt (138 examples, from Regensburg and Augsburg) and WNF (49 examples) before production switched to the F-2. Powered by the DB 601N engine rated at 1,175hp, the fighter's armament comprized a single 20mm MG FF/M cannon firing through the propeller hub and two upper cowling MG 17 7.92mm machine guns. A handful of early examples began to reach JG 51 in northern France in early October 1940 and it was not long before development problems arose. The landing flaps proved prone to damage when lowered at speeds in excess of 250km/h and the control surfaces were shown to 'freeze' in one position when the aeroplane attained high speeds in a dive.

Structural issues also afflicted the F-1. Three examples were lost in fatal accidents during February 1941 after pilots had reported over the radio that the airframe was being violently shaken by engine vibrations at high speed. Examination of the wreckage showed that the fuselage longerons had been deformed by high-speed flutter to such an extent that the tail assembly had broken off. When a fourth aircraft suffered a similar fate, it was found that rivets fastening the aft fuselage skinning had been torn loose or were missing altogether. This had been caused by the insufficient stiffening of joints between the fuselage and empennage, allowing the engine at certain speeds to create a resonant vibration of the non-braced horizontal stabilizer. This literally tore off the tail. Two external stiffeners were added to either side of the affected area and the problem was solved.

The MG FF/M cannon was also prone to jamming due to insufficient cooling and the main landing gear hydraulic braking system frequently failed.

The one-off Bf 109F-2/U1 sits on the airfield at Audembert on 5 December 1941. This aircraft was one of two or three specially modified for Oberst Adolf Galland after he stated that the standard F-model was under-armed. It was amended to carry two MG 131 13mm machine guns in the upper engine cowling in place of the F-2's MG 17 7.92mm weapons. (EN Archive)

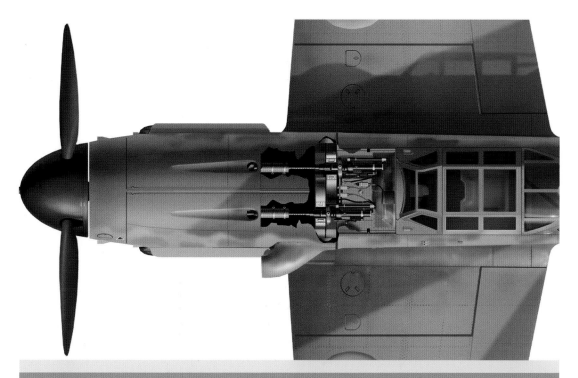

Bf 109F MACHINE GUNS

Designed with aerial combat operations in mind, the Bf 109F had all of its weapons grouped in the nose to give their rounds line-of-flight trajectory. This advantage was somewhat offset by the fact that the aircraft carried just three guns. Like the Bf 109E before it, the 'Friedrich' was armed with a pair of Rheinmetall MG 17 7.92mm machine guns in the nose. Each weapon had a 500-round magazine, mounted forward of the cockpit. The MG 17s were synchronised with the engine to avoid damaging the propeller when they were fired. The weapons were recoil-operated, electrically fired by a solenoid and gas-assisted, with pneumatic charging by means of compressed air bottles housed in the rear fuselage or wings. (Artwork by Jim Laurier, © Osprey Publishing)

Bf 109F-2

Series production of the F-2 began at the WNF plant in November 1940, the factory taking delivery of the first examples of the new MG 151/15 cannon at the same time. Although the Luftwaffe had initially planned to acquire just 120 F-2s, more than 1,350 were eventually delivered by the time production ended in August 1941. The F-1 and F-2 were very similar externally, with both variants being powered by the DB 601N engine due to ongoing supply problems with the DB 601E. The F-2 was, however, fitted with the engine-mounted MG 151/15 15mm cannon. From the early summer of 1941 examples of the fighter-bomber F-2/B began to reach front-line units in the West, and these aircraft were assigned to specially formed *Jabos* (short for *Jagdbombers*) within JG 2 and JG 26. Fitted with an ETC 500/IXb centreline-mounted bomb rack, they could carry a single 250kg SC 250 bomb, or four 50kg SC 50 bombs in combination with an ETC 50/VIId rack.

The F-2 was also the first 'Friedrich' capable of mounting a 300-litre under-belly drop tank, examples of which reached Channel Front units in the late summer of 1941. Bf 109Fs of JG 2 and JG 26 were rarely seen with such tanks fitted, however, as most fighter-only missions flown by these units were short-range operations in defence of local areas being targeted by the RAF.

As with the F-1 before it, the F-2 was plagued with teething troubles. Indeed, these proved to be so serious that the commander of Belgium-based *Luftflotte* 2, Generalfeldmarschall Albert Kesselring, submitted a 24-point report to the RLM in April 1941 detailing what needed fixing. The most pressing problem was the repetition of the tail section failure that had afflicted the F-1. Other areas of concern included inadequate breathing equipment for high-altitude flying; loose ammunition boxes; wing surface deformation; aileron fabric pulled out of shape; excessive tyre wear on concrete runways, resulting in changes after just 20 sorties; widely variable fuel consumption for aircraft from different manufacturers due to poorly tuned engines; supercharger ball-bearing failure after only five hours of engine operation; high wear of DB 601Ns due to leaking valves, resulting in engine changes after just 40 hours; and reduced altitude performance of repaired engines. The majority of the areas highlighted by Kesselring were addressed with the F-4.

Seen at Caen-Carpiquet laden down with an SC 250 bomb on its centreline ETC 500 rack, Bf 109F-4/B Wk-Nr 8352 of 10(*Jabo*)./JG 26 was flown by Feldwebel Otto Görtz during a *Jabo* attack on the Bournemouth area on the evening of 6 June 1942. The fighter was shot down by anti-aircraft fire during the mission, and Görtz was killed. (EN Archive)

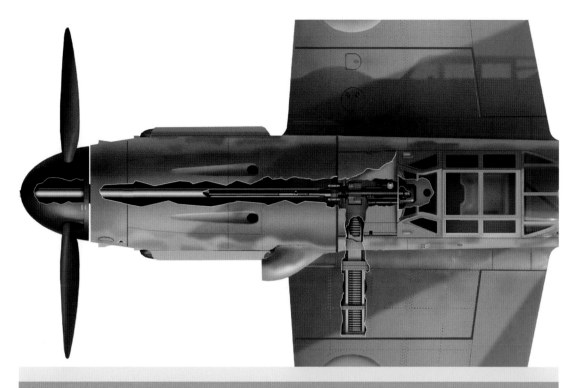

Bf 109F-2/4 CANNON

The Bf 109F's principal weapon was an engine-mounted automatic cannon – the 20mm MG FF/M in the F-1, the 15mm Mauser MG 151/15 in the F-2 and the 20mm MG 151/20 in the definitive F-4. The F-2 and F-4 had a wing root magazine holding 200 rounds of ammunition, while the F-1's MG FF/M had just 60 rounds contained in drums stowed in the cockpit between the pilot's legs. Developed by Mauser, the MG 151 was electrically cocked and fired by electric cartridge detonation and fed by a disintegrating metallic link belt. Boasting a high rate of fire (740 rounds per minute for the MG 151/15 and 750 for the MG 151/20), the MG 151 was one of the best aircraft cannon of World War II. (Artwork by Jim Laurier, © Osprey Publishing)

Bf 109F-3

Just 20 F-3s were assembled by the WNF plant between October 1940 and January 1941, this variant being the first production 'Friedrich' to feature the long-awaited DB 601E engine. It was, however, armed with the older, obsolescent MG FF/M 20mm cannon (along with the standard twin MG 17 7.92mm machine guns) due to a paucity in the supply of MG 151/15s. The MG FF/M proved to be so unreliable in front-line service with the F-1/3 that production of the fighter was soon halted as more F-2s became available.

Bf 109F-4

The most numerous 'Friedrich' variant, the F-4 was in production for exactly a year from May 1941. In that time the Erla and WNF factories had turned out 1,883 examples between them. Almost identical in appearance to the F-2, the F-4 had its internal tail structure redesigned (and external reinforcement strips removed) to eradicate the vibration problems that had plagued earlier aircraft. The fighter also boasted extra armour for the pilot, as well as a bolt-on armoured glass plate for the windscreen. But the F-4's greatest advantage over previous variants was its DB 601E engine rated at 1,350hp. At least 600 aircraft were completed as F-4/Zs, incorporating the GM 1 temporary engine boost system, which enabled nitrous oxide to be directly injected into the DB 601E's cylinders to increase the fighter's high-altitude performance. The GM 1 reportedly improved the F-4's top speed by 12.5mph at altitudes above 19,500ft. GM 1-equipped F-4s were relatively uncommon on the Channel Front, however.

The aeroplane was also armed with an engine-mounted MG 151/20 20mm cannon and two MG 17 7.92mm machine guns.

As with the F-1 and F-3, the F-4 benefited from Messerschmitt's *Rüstzätze* (add-on) programme that saw a variety of equipment kits made available to tailor an aircraft to specific operational requirements. With the earlier variants, four *Rüstzätze* 'R' kits could be used to convert the aeroplane into a fighter-bomber, carrying 24 anti-personnel bombs (Bf 109F-2/R4), four 50kg weapons (Bf 109F-2/R2) or a single 250kg bomb (Bf 109F-2/R1), or give it an extended-range fighter capability through the provision of a 300-litre drop tank (Bf 109F-2/R3).

There were more 'R' kits for the F-4, with the R1 seeing the fighter 'up-gunned' with two MG 151/15 or MG 151/20 cannon mounted in underwing gondolas. These weapons were prone to jamming, however, and only a handful of aircraft were produced by WNF and tested by I./JG 52 on the Eastern Front in May 1942. Five photo-reconnaissance R2s and 36 R3s fitted with a single camera were constructed by the Erla plant. The R5 could be fitted with a 300-litre external tank, while the R4 and R8 were one-off reconnaissance models featuring larger cameras than the R2 and R3. F-4s lacking GM 1 or underwing cannon could perform fighter-bomber missions as F-4/Bs through the installation of the 'R' kits.

Bf 109F-5 and F-6

The F-5 was proposed by Willy Messerschmitt during the summer of 1941 as a dedicated high-altitude interceptor and reconnaissance aircraft based on the F-2. Powered by a GM 1-boosted DB 601N running on 100-octane fuel, it would have been armed with an MG 151/20 20mm cannon. His proposal met with little interest from the RLM, however, and it appears that only one example was completed.

The Luftwaffe had planned to acquire 1,281 F-6s according to its October 1940 production programme. This variant was based on the F-2 and also fitted with a DB 601N running on 100-octane fuel. The F-6 was to be more heavily armed, however, following complaints from pilots (including Oberst Adolf Galland, *Geschwaderkommodore* of JG 26) that the 'Friedrich' was lacking in firepower. The standard F-6 was to be fitted with an engine-mounted MG 151/20 cannon, two cowl-mounted MG 17 7.92mm machine guns and two additional MG FF/M cannon in the wings. As with the F-4/R1, few F-6s were built, as both Messerschmitt and the RLM turned their attention to the follow-on G-model, which incorporated additional weaponry and utilized the more powerful DB 605 engine. One F-6/U, fitted with extra cannon in the wings, was briefly used in combat by Adolf Galland in November 1941 on the Channel Front. The ace also flew a similarly unique Bf 109F-2/U1, which was armed with a single MG 151/15 and two MG 131 13mm machine guns in place of the MG 17s.

SPITFIRE IIA, SPITFIRE VB, Bf 109F-2 AND Bf 109F-4 COMPARISON SPECIFICATIONS				
	Spitfire IIA	Spitfire VB	Bf 109F-2	Bf 109F-4
Powerplant	1,135hp Merlin XII	1,470hp Merlin 45	1,270hp DB 601N	1,350hp DB 601E
Dimensions				
Span	11.23m (36ft 10in)	11.23m (36ft 10in)	9.92m (32ft 5.4in)	9.92m (32ft 5.4in)
Length	9.12m (29ft 11in)	9.12m (29ft 11in)	8.94m (29ft 3.2in)	8.94m (29ft 3.2in)
Height	3.02m (9ft 10in)	3.48m (11ft 5in)	2.6m (8ft 5.3in)	2.6m (8ft 5.3in)
Wing area	22.5 sq m (242.1sq ft)	22.5 sq m (242.1sq ft)	16.1 sq m (173.3sq ft)	16.1 sq m (173.3sq ft)
Weights				
Empty	2,059kg (4,541lb)	2,251kg (4,963lb)	2,355kg (5,190lb)	2,392kg (5,272lb)
Loaded	2,799kg (6,172lb)	3,071kg (6,525lb)	2,780kg (6,127lb)	2,832kg (6,242lb)
Performance				
Maximum speed	570km/h at 5,349m (354mph at 17,550ft)	597km/h at 6,096m (371mph at 20,000ft)	598km/h at 6,100m (371mph at 20,000ft)	610km/h at 6,000m (379mph at 19,680ft)
Range	651km (405 miles)	760km (470 miles)	580km (360 miles)	560km (350 miles)
Service ceiling	11,460m (37,600ft)	10,668m (35,000ft)	11,000m (36,000ft)	12,000m (39,350ft)
Armament	8 × 0.303-in. Brownings	2 × 20mm Hispano IIs 4 × 0.303-in. Brownings	1 × 15mm MG 151/15 2 × 7.92mm MG 17	1 × 20mm MG 151/20 2 × 7.92mm MG 17

THE STRATEGIC SITUATION

When the first Spitfire IIAs began to reach front-line units in late August 1940, the outcome of the Battle of Britain was still very much in the balance. Indeed, initial deliveries to No. 611 Sqn at Digby coincided with the deadliest phase of the campaign as the Luftwaffe concentrated its attacks on Fighter Command's No. 11 Group airfields in southeast England. No. 611 Sqn was part of No. 13 Group, however, and its early operations with the Mk II consisted of patrols with the fledgling Duxford 'Big Wing', led by Sqn Ldr Douglas Bader. By the end of September four more units (Nos. 266, 74, 19 and 66 Sqns, in that order) had replaced their battle-weary Spitfire Is with new 'Shadow factory' Mk IIAs. During the course of that month the Luftwaffe switched its attacks to London in the hope that a killer blow could be dealt to the RAF once and for all. This, of course, proved to be a critical error which ultimately saved Fighter Command from annihilation at the hands of a numerically superior enemy.

In October two more units (Nos. 41 and 603 Sqns) received Spitfire IIAs as the rate of production increased at the West Bromwich plant. By then the terrible losses suffered by the Luftwaffe during raids on London the previous month had forced yet another change in its offensive. German fighters could only secure local air superiority – as they had done earlier in the campaign and during the *Blitzkrieg* in Poland and western Europe – by sending over several *Geschwader* at once. Even then, contrary to Luftwaffe intelligence reports that Fighter Command was on its last legs, Bf 109 and Bf 110 units were sustaining unbearable losses trying to defend bomber formations from attacks from increasing numbers of Spitfires – many of them new Mk IIAs – and Hurricanes.

In early October the Luftwaffe decided that the only way to reduce bomber losses was to switch to nocturnal raids. The result was the start of the night *Blitz*. However, bomb-equipped Bf 109s and Bf 110s (*Jabos*) would carry out nuisance raids by day, while the increasingly combat-weary *Jagdgeschwader* maintained the pressure on an ever-enlarging Fighter Command with frequent 'Freie Jagd' ('free hunt') sweeps over southern England. These missions were both exciting and productive for the more seasoned *Experten* who had survived the previous month's blood-letting. They certainly kept squadrons of Nos. 10 and 11 Groups busy even though they were no more than a nuisance to Fighter Command. Compared with the large formation attacks by fighters and bombers in August and September, they posed no threat to its existence.

With the RAF stronger now than it had been at the start of the Battle of Britain some three months earlier, the *Führer* had no option but to cancel the invasion of Britain (Operation *Sealion*) on 17 October and turn his attention eastwards to the USSR. The Luftwaffe maintained its daily attacks on southern England, however, with escorted *Jabos* appearing more and more frequently in the skies over Kent and Sussex. They would approach at high speed, usually taking advantage of mixed weather conditions and often flying at altitudes exceeding 32,000ft, where the Bf 109E performed better than either the Hurricane or the Spitfire I/II.

In October early production examples of the brand-new Bf109F reached JG 51 at Mardyck, near Dunkirk, to further compound the RAF's problems defeating the high-altitude threat posed by the *Jabos* and their escorts. Although only initially available in small numbers due to production delays, the F-models encountered by Fighter Command proved to be all but untouchable if their pilots chose to remain at altitudes in excess of 32,000ft. Alarmingly for the Spitfire and Hurricane pilots trying to intercept these machines as they flew in from the Channel, the 'Friedrich' was even more capable of operating at such ceilings than the late-model 'Emils' they had been struggling to counter. Fighter Command controllers on the ground were finding it impossible to distinguish 'Freie Jagd' fighter-only sweeps, which posed little threat to southeast England and London, from escorted *Jabo* raids that could still cause damage and civilian deaths due to the inaccuracy of their bombing from high altitude, or from conventional bombers. The RAF had to adopt new tactics. The solution devised by ACM Sir Hugh Dowding, Air Officer Commanding Fighter Command, was to create a specialist fighter unit, No. 421 Flt, manned by experienced pilots and initially equipped with Hurricane Is and eventually Spitfire IIAs. Its task was to patrol the Channel and identify which incoming raids were *Jabos* and which were fighter sweeps. Formed in late September 1940 and based at Hawkinge, on the Kent coast, the unit would send out aircraft alone or in pairs throughout daylight hours.

Although No. 421 Flt proved very successful in this role, the RAF still had to mount standing patrols if it was to have any hope of engaging the high-flying *Jabos*.

With the Spitfire IIA being the only aircraft capable of climbing from patrol height to 30,000ft fast enough to intercept the Bf 109s, the burden fell on the handful of suitably equipped units in No. 11 Group to fly these often costly and ineffective but nevertheless vital missions. When the enemy was encountered, the advantage was definitely with the *Jagdflieger*, who were frequently in a position to surprise their foes by diving out of the sun on climbing British fighters. Yet despite the victories achieved by the Luftwaffe, and the reduced number of casualties it was experiencing due to the change in tactics, the RAF's fighter strength continued to grow to the point where, by December 1940, offensive operations were being considered.

The previous month both ACM Dowding and Air Vice Marshal (AVM) Keith Park, commander of No. 11 Group during the Battle of Britain, had controversially been replaced. Dowding's successor, ACM Sir W. Sholto Douglas, was asked by ACM Sir Charles Portal for his opinion on a suggestion made to him by Viscount Trenchard who had led British air forces in World War I. Always keen to take the fight to the enemy, Trenchard had told Portal in late 1940 that it was perhaps time to take the offensive now that the major daylight raids by the Luftwaffe were seemingly over. 'Lean towards France' was Trenchard's advice. Such missions would invariably involve the squadrons of No. 11 Group, now commanded by AVM Trafford Leigh-Mallory, previously of No. 12 Group, because of their proximity to France.

Douglas initially opposed Trenchard's suggestion. As a fighter unit commander in France during World War I, he was painfully aware of the

This busy scene at I./JG 53's St Omer Arques home in March–April 1941 shows mechanics working on the engines of a number of brand-new Bf 109F-2s. The fighter with *Stab* markings (black chevron and bars) was a reserve machine for the *Kommodore* of JG 53, Major Günther von Maltzahn. (EN Archive)

cost of such offensives both in pilots and aircraft. On the other hand, it would prove to the Germans that the RAF was more than capable of taking the fight to them after many months of purely defensive operations. Douglas reluctantly agreed that incursions across the Channel might well meet with some success. With No. 11 Group in the vanguard of such an offensive, AVM Leigh-Mallory saw that his controversial 'Big Wing' idea could at last prove its worth.

He and his predecessor, AVM Park, had clashed repeatedly during the summer of 1940 over the time it took No. 12 Group to assemble four squadrons into wing formation and then head south to help No. 11 Group defend southern England from Luftwaffe attacks. Leigh-Mallory's squadrons in the quieter No. 12 Group area had time to take off and assemble before searching for enemy aircraft, but Park's units were very much in the front line during the campaign. With their airfields, or nearby London, often the target for approaching German bombers, it was all that the No. 11 Group squadrons could do to get airborne and intercept them before they unleashed their deadly payloads. There was no time to form up in larger wings prior to engaging the Luftwaffe.

Having assumed command of No. 11 Group, Leigh-Mallory was keen to implement his wing concept in support of this new offensive. Without the urgency of engaging approaching Luftwaffe bombers, the squadrons involved in such an operation could take off and form up in good order before heading off to northern France. It was quickly decided that each of the Sector Stations in No. 11 Group – Kenley, Tangmere, Northolt, Biggin Hill, North Weald, Debden and Hornchurch – and Duxford, in No. 12 Group, would create their own wing formations from the squadrons (usually four each) under their control. Each wing would be led by an experienced pilot with known fighting ability and the presence of mind to control up to four squadrons in combat. Officially, the first wing leaders were appointed in early March 1941, although by then a handful of 'Circus' operations had already been mounted, led by the most senior pilot or by the most experienced squadron commander from the Sector Station providing the fighter escort.

Flg Off Hugh Dundas, who was assigned to No. 616 Sqn at Tangmere when the first wing leaders were appointed, recalled their creation in his autobiography *Flying Start*:

His [AVM Leigh-Mallory's] first step was to establish a new post at each Sector Station – the post of 'Wing Commander Flying'. Previously, each individual squadron commander had been responsible directly to the station commander (sometimes, indeed quite often, the station commander was also the sector commander). If more than one squadron flew together as a formation, the senior squadron commander would lead. Now, the new wing commanders flying – or wing leaders, as they came to be called – assumed responsibility for coordinating all flying activities and for leading the wing formations. To Tangmere, for these duties, came Douglas Bader.

The very first offensive operation undertaken by Fighter Command had, in fact, been flown as early as 20 December 1940, when a pair of Spitfire IIAs led by Flt Lt Pat Christie of No. 66 Sqn strafed Le Touquet airfield. This was the first time Spitfires had operated over France since the French surrender. As the new year dawned there was a marked change in operational emphasis, Fighter Command slowly adopting an offensive posture to take the fight to the enemy. Initially, small numbers of Spitfires and Hurricanes flew to France, but soon larger operations in which fighters escorted bombers were being routinely flown. Blenheim IVs and, later, Stirling four-engined heavy bombers were involved in these attempts to draw Luftwaffe fighters into battle. Thus, Pat Christie, a six-victory ace, had paved the way for countless offensive sorties by the RAF over the next three years. The operational codenames of 'Circus', 'Ramrod', 'Rodeo', 'Rhubarb', 'Ranger' and others quickly became achingly familiar to RAF fighter pilots.

A 'Rhubarb' was an offensive sortie by a small section of fighters, usually pairs, to attack targets of opportunity such as trains or fixed targets. 'Circus' denoted an attack by bombers heavily escorted by fighters, the presence of the former being to entice enemy fighters into combat. On a 'Ramrod', bombers, again heavily escorted by fighters, had the primary task of destroying a target. In contrast, a 'Ranger' was a sweep in which a large formation of fighters flew a freelance intrusion over enemy territory with the express aim of destroying German fighters.

The new offensive policy would generally be implemented by units flying from bases in central and southern England assigned to Nos. 10, 11 and 12 Groups. On 1 January 1941 Fighter Command fielded 15 Spitfire squadrons split between No. 11 Group in southern England, No. 12 Group in the Midlands and No. 10 Group in the west. These units were easily reinforced when required.

As with the 'Freie Jagd' sweeps mounted by the Luftwaffe over southern England from October 1940 through to the end of the year, RAF fighters flying 'Rhubarbs' were generally ignored by the Jagdwaffe. The inclusion of light bombers did, however, provoke a response. Fighter Command soon discovered that providing an effective escort for Blenheim IVs was not easy. A large number of fighters ('Ramrods') would eventually be involved, and sometimes as many as 15 squadrons of fighters could be over

France escorting no more than 12 bombers targeting a power station or port facility. It was now the RAF's turn to endure the disadvantages experienced by the Luftwaffe during the Battle of Britain, when its squadrons had to operate at maximum range over hostile territory with a long overwater flight to and from the target.

One of the men charged with implementing this new offensive policy was No. 616 Sqn's Plt Off J. E. 'Johnnie' Johnson, the future ranking ace of Fighter Command. A fighter pilot through and through, he was no fan of the ground-attack oriented 'Rhubarbs' in particular, as he explained in *Winged Victory*:

The 'leaning out' doctrine included low-level flights over France known as 'Rhubarbs'. The idea was to take full advantage of low cloud and poor visibility to slip sections of Spitfires across the coast, then let-down below the cloud to search for opportunity targets, rolling stock, locomotives,

This map shows the location of Fighter Command and Jagdwaffe airfields during the Channel Front campaign. The modest operational range of a standard Spitfire II/V is also shown, as well as the general path flown by Bf 109E/F fighters on offensive patrols over southern England and the Channel from the Pas-de-Calais.

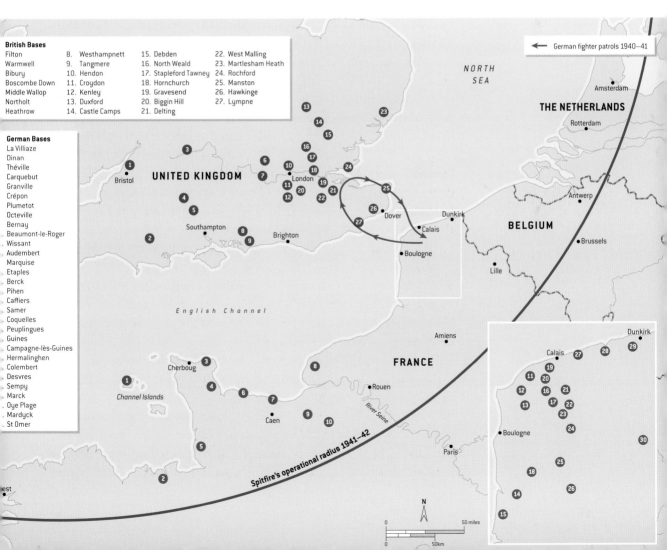

British Bases
Filton
Warmwell
Bibury
Boscombe Down
Middle Wallop
Northolt
Heathrow

8. Westhampnett
9. Tangmere
10. Hendon
11. Croydon
12. Kenley
13. Duxford
14. Castle Camps

15. Debden
16. North Weald
17. Stapleford Tawney
18. Hornchurch
19. Gravesend
20. Biggin Hill
21. Delting

22. West Malling
23. Martlesham Heath
24. Rochford
25. Manston
26. Hawkinge
27. Lympne

German Bases
La Villiaze
Dinan
Théville
Carquebut
Granville
Crépon
Plumetot
Octeville
Bernay
Beaumont-le-Roger
Wissant
Audembert
Marquise
Etaples
Berck
Pihen
Caffiers
Samer
Coquelles
Peuplingues
Guines
Campagne-lès-Guines
Hermalinghen
Colembert
Desvres
Sempy
Marck
Oye Plage
Mardyck
St Omer

German fighter patrols 1940–41

NORTH SEA

THE NETHERLANDS

Amsterdam

Rotterdam

Antwerp

BELGIUM

Brussels

UNITED KINGDOM

Bristol

London

Lille

Dover

Dunkirk

Calais

Boulogne

Southampton

Brighton

English Channel

Amiens

Cherboug

Channel Islands

Caen

Rouen

FRANCE

River Seine

Paris

Spitfire's operational radius 1941–42

est

N

0   50 miles
0   50km

Dunkirk

Calais

Boulogne

aircraft on the ground, staff cars, enemy troops and the like. They were usually arranged on a voluntary basis and a few pilots seemed to prefer this type of individual, low-level work to the clean, exhilarating teamwork of the dogfight. But the great majority of fighter pilots thought privately that the dividends yielded by the numerous 'Rhubarb' operations fell far short of the cost in valuable aircraft and trained pilots.

I loathed those 'Rhubarbs' with a deep, dark hatred. Apart from the flak, the hazards of making a let-down over unknown territory and with no accurate knowledge of the cloud base seemed too great a risk for the damage we inflicted. During the following three months, hundreds of pilots were lost on either small or mass 'Rhubarbs' and, when I later held an appointment of some authority at No. 11 Group, my strong views on this subject were given a sympathetic hearing and 'Rhubarbs' were discontinued over France, except on very special occasions.

A Bf 109F of JG 2 has its MG 17 and MG 151/20 guns replenished. The latter was belt-fed from an ammunition box located in the front part of the upper surface of the port side wing only. (EN Archive)

For the Jagdwaffe, the start of the Fighter Command offensive in early January 1941 came at a time when many of its units in France and Belgium had been stood down for rest and recuperation following months of intensive operations that had inflicted a heavy toll on them. Although a small number of *Jabo* missions continued to be flown against targets in southern England, the onset of winter had given the units a chance to send *Gruppen* back to Germany to re-equip with either late-build 'Emils' or the latest Bf 109Fs. Decisions on which *Jagdgeschwader* would be the first to receive the still scarce F-1s were made at a meeting of the *Oberkommando der Luftwaffe* Operations Staff in early November 1940. Approximately 12 aircraft would be delivered to one *Staffel* each of JG 2, JG 27 and JG 51. JG 27 was later replaced by JG 26, however, so that the fighter could be introduced into combat with units led by the best-known commanders at the time – Major Helmut Wick (killed in action before JG 2 received Bf 109Fs), Oberstleutnant Adolf Galland and Major Werner Mölders.

Although as many as eight *Jagdgeschwader* (admittedly not all at full strength) opposed the RAF offensive during the first six months of 1941, following the invasion of the Soviet Union in June, only JG 2 and JG 26 remained on the Channel Front to counter the raids. JG 2 was given responsibility for an area from Cherbourg northeast to the River Seine estuary, while JG 26 continued the defensive line from the Seine to the coast of Holland. These two units would be Fighter Command's principal opponents for the rest of the war. At best, these *Jagdgeschwader* typically had around 250 fighters at their disposal, although fluctuating serviceability rates often reduced this figure. Fielding highly skilled aviators who had seen more than a year of combat, and now receiving the definitive Bf 109F-4, JG 2 and JG 26 would find no shortage of opponents as Fighter Command's ranks continued to swell with more and more Spitfires – Mk IIs and, increasingly, Mk Vs – during the course of 1941.

THE MEN

Some of the most experienced and successful fighter pilots to serve with the RAF and the Luftwaffe would slug it out on the Channel Front during the period of intense action examined in this chapter. Many were veterans of combat in the early stages of World War II, having survived the *Blitzkrieg* in Poland and the Low Countries as well as the fierce fighting of the Battle of Britain. Some of the leading aces of the conflict's first years enjoyed great success flying the Bf 109F or the Spitfire II/V in 1940–42. Many of them were pre-war aviators who had benefitted from well-established training regimes that involved vastly experienced instructors.

But by September 1940, as the Battle of Britain was reaching its climax, both the RAF and the Luftwaffe found themselves increasingly short of pilots. For Fighter Command in particular this meant corners had to be cut in training to bolster front-line numbers. And once the campaign was over, many aviators – both British and, to a lesser extent, German – were now suffering from combat-fatigue and were duly removed from the front line and sent to training units as instructors. Their quality varied greatly. Some pilots were well suited to the job but others resented their removal from combat. Among the latter was Flg Off Hugh Dundas, who was posted away from No. 616 Sqn to No. 59 Operational Training Unit (OTU) in the autumn of 1941:

> In retrospect I can see clearly how unenviable and difficult was the task of Air Cdre F J Vincent, who commanded No. 81 Group, with responsibility for all Fighter Command operational training units.

Although an effective fighter pilot who was awarded the DFC and DSO and ended the conflict as both an ace and a wing leader, Yorkshireman Hugh 'Cocky' Dundas was not a success as a flight instructor. Indeed, he lasted just three weeks in the job with No. 59 OTU after completing a two-year tour with No. 616 Sqn. Dundas was duly sent back to Fighter Command. (© IWM, CH 4545)

His job was supremely important. He had to ensure that a steady flow of competent pilots was continually available to the squadrons. To provide the necessary training Vincent had a collection of instructors of whom some were so operationally fatigued that they had no enthusiasm for the job, while others preferred the comparative safety of instructing to the hazards of squadron life, and were therefore unlikely to imbue their pupils with a proper sense of dash and aggression. Perhaps it was partly in order to counter that situation that Vincent imposed a regime of strict discipline throughout his command. The easy-going habits of dress and behaviour common on all fighter stations were severely discouraged by his unit commanders and Vincent made regular tours of inspection to see for himself that proper standards were being maintained. The imposition of discipline came easy to him, for he had received his early service training in the Royal Marines.

I am afraid that I did nothing to ease the situation for the station commander at Crosby-on-Eden [home of No. 59 OTU]. I lasted just three weeks as an instructor. So far as I was ever able to discover, this established a record for brevity which remained unbeaten in Fighter Command throughout the war.

Despite the unsuitability of some instructors, it was not long before RAF fighter squadrons were having to cope with a massive influx of new and untried pilots – many of whom only spoke English as a second language. Although eager to emulate the feats of their predecessors, they had had insufficient time to attain operational status and gain the fighter pilot's mind-set during their brief spell with an OTU. New pilots were often little more than cannon fodder, and grave losses resulted.

With fewer aircraft on the Channel Front, the Jagdwaffe's requirement for pilots was significantly less than Fighter Command's. Nevertheless, the high attrition rate suffered by the *Jagdgeschwader* during the Battle of Britain, when they lost roughly a quarter of their number, meant that they too were in need of replacement pilots by early 1941.

RAF pilot training

Having managed to make good the losses of the Battle of Britain, the RAF would never be short of fighter pilots again. Indeed, the 'Few' quickly became the 'Many' as young men poured out of the growing number of OTUs created within Training Command. At the start of the Channel Front offensive, Fighter Command had 71 squadrons, compared with 44 Hurricane and Spitfire units on 1 July 1940. With an increasing number of aircraft, particularly Spitfire IIs and Vs, reaching the front line, more pilots would be needed to man the new units being hastily formed. By the end of 1940 many of the aviators sent to squadrons in Nos. 10, 11 and 12 Groups were from abroad. Belgian, French, Polish, Czech, Canadian, American, Australian, New Zealand and Rhodesian pilots were liberally distributed throughout the front-line force. Indeed, units staffed exclusively by these nationalities were also being formed.

Thanks to these foreign volunteers, and the thousands of recruits from the UK inspired by the RAF's exploits in the summer of 1940, Fighter Command would always have enough pilots to fill its ranks. The dashing image of the World War I ace had actually struck a chord with the British public during the interwar period and this fascination with aviation was fuelled by the national press. When war broke out and the National Service Act came into force, the prospect of compulsory military service pushed many young and talented men towards the more glamorous and somewhat 'safer' RAF. Unfortunately, the fictional image of the ace jarred with the reality of front-line combat, particularly on the Channel Front during 1941–42.

This aircraft was assigned to No. 57 OTU in July 1941. One of the last Spitfire IAs built for the RAF, AR213 is seen here marked up as a 'bounce' aircraft, complete with red and white horizontal stripes on its nose. Today, it is kept in airworthy condition at Duxford by Spitfire The One Ltd. (Wojtek Matusiak)

New recruits would encounter the Tiger Moth during short flying courses at an Elementary Flying School, and later during a prolonged training programme at an Elementary Flying Training School. (Philip Jarrett)

For the young volunteer eager to jump into a Spitfire or Hurricane, the training process would come as a shock. Preparing young men to fly these powerful machines required a great deal of time and expert instruction. After volunteering for aircrew service many applicants were surprised to find themselves going home to await their call-up letter. When it arrived, new recruits reported to an Air Crew Reception Centre (ACRC), where they spent between two and ten weeks. Given the classification of 'aircraftsman second class' upon arrival at the ACRC, the aspiring fighter pilots learned the basics of service life. After that the ACRC new recruits were sent to an Initial Training Wing (ITW) where, building on the lessons learned at ACRC, recruits honed their skills with more detailed instruction on meteorology, the principles of flight and drill.

In late 1941 an extra step was introduced to ITW to save time and resources. Short flying courses at an Elementary Flying School (EFS) were arranged to give new students a limited number of hours of dual instruction on de Havilland Tiger Moths or Miles Magisters. After about 12 hours of flying, students needed to show the necessary skills required to go 'solo'. Those unable to do so were reassigned, thereby saving the RAF valuable time and human resources in the later stages of training. Having shown aptitude for flight and been promoted to the rank of leading aircraftsman, successful trainees were now ready for more advanced flying training.

At the Elementary Flying Training School (EFTS) they began a prolonged flying programme on either the Tiger Moth or the Magister. Students were taught the relatively simple but vital skills of straight and level flight, medium turns, climbing, diving and stall recovery. Once these skills had been mastered the student pilot could begin flying circuits, which involved taking off, climbing to a safe height and then flying straight and level downwind parallel to the runway. They then turned and lined the aircraft up for landing, before carrying out a full stop landing. Having mastered these skills, student pilots then flew their first solos. Further instruction included spinning, formation flying and navigation. After successfully logging some 50 hours of flight time, half of which was solo, new pilots moved on. Many students failed EFTS and a large number were listed as KIFA – Killed in Flying Accidents.

The next stage involved an increase in horsepower. Moving on to Service Flying Training (SFT), students were introduced to the North American Harvard or the Miles Master. Both featured dual controls and

After mastering a Tiger Moth or Magister, students progressed to Service Flying Training (SFT). Here they would be introduced to the North American Harvard or the Miles Master. These are Master IIIs of No. 5 FTS, flying from Ternhill, in Shropshire. Training Command was of the opinion that if a pilot could handle the Harvard or Master he would be able to fly a front-line fighter like the Spitfire. (Philip Jarrett)

were far more powerful, with 550hp and 870hp engines, respectively. These aircraft were far more demanding too. The first half of the course involved repeating flights made during EFTS. After a short period, student pilots were expected to fly solo, followed by further dual instruction and night flying. Those capable of handling the Harvard or the Master were then judged able to fly a front-line fighter. To reach that point they had to complete a further 120 hours, including 20 hours of night flying during three-and-a-half months of training. Finally, with 200 hours in their logbooks, the cadets were awarded their wings.

The final step before being assigned to a fighter squadron was the OTU. For those of the pre-war era and veterans of the first few months of World War II, front-line training was undertaken at squadron level. That meant new pilots were posted to operational units with very little time on their assigned fighter and no tactical training of any sort. While this worked well before the war, combat attrition soon provoked a major change. Because there were no two-seat Spitfires in which to give pilots their first flights, young trainees could only learn about the fighter by familiarising themselves with the controls and then going up for a solo flight. In some

SPITFIRE VB: IN THE COCKPIT

1. Boost control cut-out
2. Brake triple pressure gauge
3. Elevator tabs position indicator
4. Undercarriage position indicator
5. Oxygen regulator
6. Flaps control
7. Blind flying instrument panel
8. Lifting ring for sunscreen
9. Reflector gunsight switch
10. Sunscreen
11. Gun and cannon three-position push button
12. Camera-gun push button (for activation)
13. Barr and Stroud GM 2 reflector gunsight
14. Voltmeter
15. Ventilator control
16. Tachometer
17. Fuel pressure warning lamp
18. Boost pressure gauge
19. Oil pressure gauge
20. Oil temperature gauge
21. Radiator temperature gauge
22. Fuel contents gauge and push button
23. Remote contactor and contactor switch
24. Slow-running cut-out
25. Engine priming pump
26. Engine starting push button
27. Booster coil push button
28. Fuel cock control
29. Rudder pedals
30. Radiator flap control lever
31. Two-position door catch
32. Cockpit floodlight
33. Camera indicator supply plug
34. Navigation lights switch
35. Control friction adjusters
36. Propeller speed control lever
37. Radio control plug storage
38. Elevator trimming tab hand-wheel
39. Camera-gun switch
40. Map case
41. Pressure head heater switch
42. Rudder trimming tab hand-wheel
43. Oil dilution push button
44. Stowage for reflector gunsight lamps
45. Signalling switchbox
46. R.3002 Identification Friend or Foe (IFF) master push buttons
47. Harness release control
48. R.3002 IFF master switch
49. CO_2 cylinder for emergency lowering of undercarriage
50. Oxygen supply cock
51. Windscreen de-icing pump
52. Windscreen de-icing needle valve
53. Undercarriage emergency lowering control
54. Windscreen de-icing cock
55. External fuel tank jettison lever
56. Undercarriage control unit lever
57. Rudder pedal adjusting star-wheels
58. Ignition switches
59. Signal discharger control
60. T.R. 1196 or T.R. 1304 transmitter and receiver controls
61. Fuel tank pressurising cock control
62. Air intake control
63. Throttle control
64. Seat
65. Oxygen hose
66. Airspeed indicator
67. Artificial horizon
68. Rate-of-climb indicator
69. Altimeter
70. Turn-and-slip indicator

(Artwork by Jim Laurier, © Osprey Publishing)

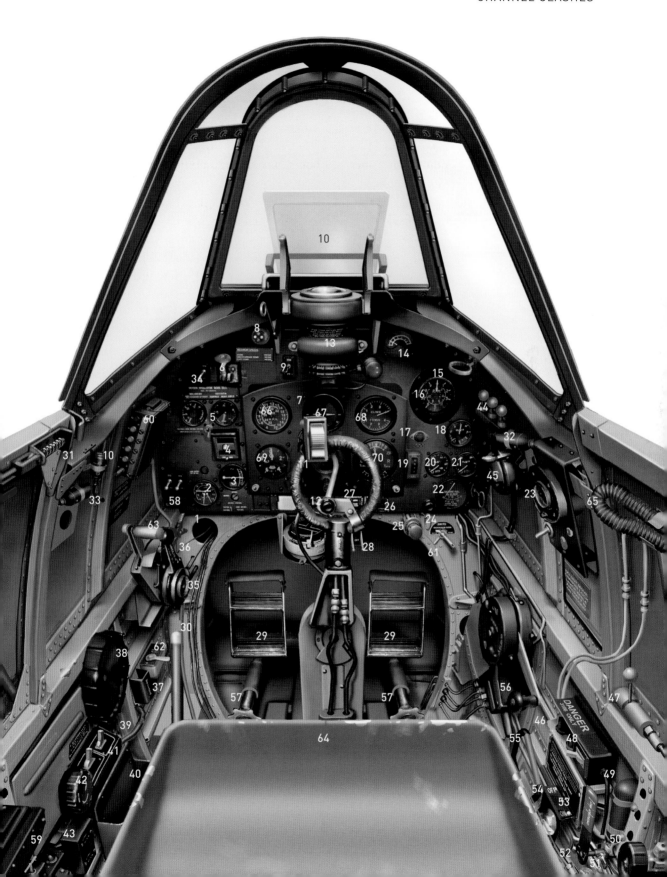

Sqn Ldr 'Jamie' Rankin inspecting the Spitfire he once flew, c.1950. (Photo by Chris Ware/Keystone Features/ Getty Images)

With ten Bf 109Fs and seven Bf 109Es claimed as destroyed, 'Jamie' Rankin was one of the most successful Spitfire V pilots of the Channel Front campaign. Rankin was born in Portobello, Edinburgh, on 7 May 1913. He joined the RAF in 1935 and received a commission. On completing his flying training with No. 2 Flying Training School he joined Fury II-equipped No. 25 Sqn. Following a spell with the Fleet Air Arm's 825 Naval Air Squadron, flying Fairey IIIFs from HMS *Glorious*, Rankin became an instructor with No. 5 OTU. In early 1941 he was promoted to squadron leader and attached to No. 64 Sqn to gain operational experience flying Spitfire IIAs. He claimed a shared victory and two probables during his brief time with the unit.

In February of that year Rankin took command of No. 92 Sqn just as it was re-equipping with the first Spitfire Vs to reach Fighter Command. His score mounted rapidly as he led the unit on fighter sweeps and bomber escort missions over northern France. In June Rankin received the Distinguished Flying

Cross (DFC) after he had claimed nine victories (all bar one of them being over Bf 109s). In September he was promoted to wing commander and became Biggin Hill Wing Leader. Sgt Walter 'Johnnie' Johnston of No. 92 Sqn served with Rankin during 1941–42 and he recalled his leadership qualities in Peter Caygill's volume *Spitfire Mark V in Action*:

> When 'Jamie' took over as Wing Leader things did change a little bit. Malan [Wg Cdr Adolf 'Sailor' Malan, Rankin's predecessor and a high-scoring ace] was a very hard taskmaster. He expected that everybody who he picked to put into a job could do it, and if they couldn't, he got rid of them. He was an excellent tactician, but he was quite ruthless and had a bit of a reputation for losing his No. 2s. Quite often he would take evasive action without any warning and the No. 2 was left high and dry, miles behind, which was why some of us used to find ourselves stuck on our own at times.
>
> 'Jamie' was different. He had been a good CO, but he freely admitted that he was learning, the same as everybody else, because 92 was his first operational trip after time as an instructor. As far as gunnery was concerned he was damn good, but the thing that impressed me most was his flying, which was absolutely immaculate. If you were supposed to be going into a turn of 110 degrees, you did 110, not 105 or 115, but 110 exactly, so personally, I found life easier with him as Wing Leader.

Between December 1941 and April 1942 Rankin held a staff post at HQ Fighter Command, before returning to Biggin Hill for a second tour leading the wing. In 1943 he commanded No. 15 Fighter Wing in the newly formed 2nd Tactical Air Force and when that unit was disbanded he assumed command of No. 125 Wing, which he led during the Normandy invasion. Promoted to air commodore by war's end, Rankin reverted to group captain rank post-war. Having been Air Attache in Dublin in 1948 and OC RAF Duxford in 1954, he eventually retired from the RAF in 1958. 'Jamie' Rankin passed away in 1975. During his service on the Channel Front he had claimed 17 and five shared aircraft destroyed, three and two shared probably destroyed, 16 and three shared damaged and one destroyed on the water.

cases during the desperate days of the Battle of Britain when Fighter Command was short of pilots, trainees missed out on instruction on Harvards and Masters and went straight on to the Spitfire or Hurricane. This did not happen after the late summer of 1940, however.

Two OTUs had been established by March 1940, and they were equipped with a mixture of Hurricanes and Spitfires. Here, young aviators learned to fly the aircraft they would operate in combat so that by 1941 fighter pilots could expect to start squadron service with a minimum of 270 hours of flight time.

By mid-1941 one of the war's most successful training operations was in full swing. Hundreds of aircrew were being trained in Canada, Australia, South Africa, New Zealand and Rhodesia as part of the British Commonwealth Air Training Plan. The BCATP was truly remarkable and would be responsible for training nearly half the aircrew who served in the RAF, RCAF, RAAF, RNZAF and SAAF.

Luftwaffe pilot training

Before the official creation of the Luftwaffe, all air activity in Germany had been geared towards training because of the ban on military flying under the terms of the 1919 Treaty of Versailles. Those quasi-military aviation organizations formed in Germany during the late 1920s and early 1930s functioned under the cover of civilian activities. Although this stalled the development of both combat aircraft and tactics, the focus on flying training provided the newly created Luftwaffe with plenty of military-trained aircrew. Men came from Lufthansa, gliding clubs and, until 1936, the army. However, the army was also expanding rapidly, and senior officers forbade the Luftwaffe from recruiting from within the Wehrmacht. Conscripts and volunteers would make up the numbers from then on.

In Germany, pilot recruitment and training was strongly influenced by Prussian military tradition. Initially, all future officers and NCOs could expect to undertake six months of labour service, organized in a paramilitary fashion with the *Reichsarbeitdienst*. Those who were particularly air-minded chose service with the Party-controlled *Nationalsozialistisches Fliegerkorps* instead and flew gliders. But with the Luftwaffe desperately short of personnel, labour service was reduced to just three months.

Induction into the Luftwaffe then followed, after which all recruits spent between six and 12 months undertaking basic infantry training at a *Flieger-Ersatzabteilung*. Once deemed to be an effective infantryman, all recruits were reviewed for possible advancement as pilots. Likely candidates were sent to a *Flug-Anwärterkompanie* (aircrew candidate company) for evaluation in a series of tests in basic aviation theory.

Veteran *Jagdflieger* flying Bf 109Fs in 1941–42 would have taken the full Luftwaffe training course. However, from late 1940 onwards, with the growing demand for pilots following the outbreak of World War II, training and recruiting staff rationalized and compressed the initial stages of aircrew selection. This enabled trainees to start the most appropriate training regime without delay. The *Flieger-Ersatzabteilung* was now replaced by a series of *Flieger-Ausbildungsregiments*, where recruits would receive basic military training and preliminary aviation instruction. Potential pilots were then sent for the standard selection process within a *Flug-Anwärterkompanie*, where the rest of their basic training, conducted over a period of three to four months, was completed alongside the aircrew evaluation tests.

On assignment to a *Flug-Anwärterkompanie*, the *Flugzeugführer-Anwärter* (pilot candidate) received instruction in basic flight theory and rudimentary aeronautics in aircraft such as the Bü 131, Ar 66C, He 72 Kadett, Go 145 and Fw 44 Stieglitz biplane trainers. Assessed for advancement throughout this phase, those candidates displaying the required aptitude were then sent to *Flugzeugführerschule A/B* as soon as a space became available – typically two months after arrival at the *Flug-Anwärterkompanie*. Here, flight training proper would be undertaken.

At these schools students underwent four principal levels of instruction, each requiring qualification for its own licence, before advancement to the next stage. These licences, earned over a period of six to nine months, gave

Bf 109F-4: IN THE COCKPIT

1. Revi C12D reflector gunsight
2. Gunsight pad
3. Ammunition counters
4. Armament switch
5. Repeater compass
6. Artificial horizon/turn-and-bank indicator
7. Manifold pressure gauge
8. Clock
9. Canopy jettison lever
10. Main light switch
11. Instrument panel lights
12. Ignition switch
13. Start plug cleansing switch
14. Altimeter
15. Airspeed indicator
16. Tachometer
17. Propeller pitch position indicator
18. Fuel warning lamp
19. Combined coolant exit and oil intake temperature indicator
20. Starter switch
21. Fuel gauge
22. Undercarriage position indicator
23. Undercarriage retraction switch
24. Undercarriage extension switch
25. Undercarriage emergency release lever
26. Oil and fuel contents gauge
27. Throttle
28. Propeller pitch control
29. Dust filter handgrip
30. Bomb release button
31. Gun firing trigger
32. Control column with KG 12A grip
33. Drop tank flow control tube
34. Rudder pedals
35. Radiator cut-off handle
36. Ventilation control lever
37. Oil cooler flap control
38. Fuel cock lever
39. MG 151/20 cannon breech cover
40. Radiator shutter control lever
41. FuG 16ZY radio control panel
42. Drop tank pipe
43. Oxygen supply indicator
44. Oxygen pressure gauge
45. Radio controls
46. Oxygen supply
47. Fuel injection primer pump
48. Tailplane incidence indicator
49. Undercarriage emergency lowering hand-wheel
50. Tailplane trim adjustment wheel
51. Seat
52. Radio tuner panel

(Artwork by Jim Laurier, © Osprey Publishing)

the schools their name. The *A1-Schien* introduced students to basic practical flying in dual-controlled training aircraft, instructors teaching recruits how to take off and land, recover from stalls and attain their solo flight rating. Before the war and up to early 1941, each instructor was assigned four trainees, a number which rose as the conflict progressed.

At the *A2-Schien*, cadets were required to learn the theory of flight, including aerodynamics, meteorology, flying procedures and aviation law, as well as the practical application of aeronautical engineering, elementary navigation, wireless procedure and Morse code. In the air, they gained more flying experience on larger single-engined two-seat aircraft.

The next level of training, known as the *B1-Schien*, saw pilots progress to high-performance single- and twin-engined machines typically fitted with a retractable undercarriage. Pilots selected to fly fighters were assigned to train on older types of combat aircraft such as early Bf 109s. Precision landings, night flying and landings, and cross-country flying were all tested in this phase. Student pilots also had to complete at least 50 flights in a B1 category aircraft. On graduation from the *B1-Schien*, having accumulated 100 to 150 hours of flight time over the previous 14 to 17 months, students then undertook training aimed at acquiring the final *B2-Schien*. In late 1940 the *Flugzeugführerschule A/B* was streamlined to take into account wartime demand for pilots. From the outset far greater emphasis was now being placed on practical flying skills. The A2 licence was dropped, with that phase being amalgamated into the remaining grades.

Cadets practise formation flying in Arado Ar 96B-2 trainers. Used for advanced, night and instrument flying training, the Ar 96 was a single-engine, low-wing monoplane of all-metal construction. All three student pilots are flying solo, which would indicate that they are nearing the end of their training. (EN Archive)

The A-licence generally took three months to complete, with pilots flying more advanced types during the B phase. An elementary K1 *Kunstflug* (stunt-flying) aerobatics course was also included in the latter phase to provide pilots with a good understanding of rudimentary evasive manoeuvres like barrel rolls, loops and formation splits. This phase also allowed instructors to identify potential fighter pilots, who then received more flying time than their fellow students.

On completion of the B2 phase cadets were finally granted their *Luftwaffeflugzeugführerschein* (air force pilots' licence), accompanied by the highly prized *Flugzeugführerabzeichen* (pilot's badge) – their 'wings'. After an average of ten to 13 months at *Flugzeugführerschule A/B*, they were now fully qualified as pilots.

It was at this point that they were categorized for service on single- or multi-engined aircraft, with each being assigned to a specialist flying school. Here, they underwent intensive training for their allotted aircraft type. Potential fighter pilots were sent directly to *Jagdfliegervorschulen* or *Waffenschule* for three to four months for 50 hours of flying on semi-obsolescent types. For Bf 109F pilots this usually meant Ar 68 and He 51 biplanes, Bf 109B/C/D/Es and Ar 96s. By the time they were eventually posted to front-line units, pilots could expect to have logged 200 hours of flying time. On reaching the *Jagdgeschwader*, a tyro fighter pilot initially served with its *Schulstaffeln* to gain further experience. By then, officer candidates had also attended *Luftkriegschule* to learn tactics, air force law and military discipline, before assignment to a *Jagdfliegervorschulen*.

The realities of war led the Luftwaffe to further modify the final stages of its training syllabus for fighter pilots in early 1940. Individual *Schulstaffeln* were replaced by the single *Ergänzungsjagdgruppe* (Operational Fighter

This veteran Bf 109B was flown by student pilots undertaking their B1/2-Schien training at *Jagdfliegervorschulen* or *Waffenschule* in 1940–41. Over a three- to four-month period aviators accumulated 50 hours of flying on semi-obsolescent types. (EN Archive)

Oberst Werner Mölders in 1941. (Bundesarchiv, Bild 146-1971-116-29, Fotograf: o. Ang)

The leading German ace of the Spanish Civil War, Werner Mölders was instrumental in the development of the new fighter tactics so effectively employed by the Luftwaffe in World War II. Born on 18 March 1913 in Gelsenkirchen, he was the third of four children. Like his father, who had been killed in action in March 1915, Mölders joined the infantry, in April 1931, before transferring to the fledgling Luftwaffe in early 1934. Despite initially suffering from chronic airsickness, he successfully completed the early stages of his flying training and was posted to a *Jagdfliegervorschulen*.

Mölders was sent to I./JG 162 in July 1935, became leader of the training squadron within II./JG 134 in April of the following year, and was promoted to *Staffelkäpitan* of 1./JG 334 in March 1937. In early 1938 he volunteered for service with the *Legion Condor*, which had been formed by the Luftwaffe to assist the Nationalists in their civil war with the Republicans in Spain. Mölders arrived in April 1938 and was assigned to the 3rd squadron of *Jagdgruppe* 88, which was then equipped with Heinkel He 51 biplanes. He replaced Oberleutnant Adolf Galland as CO of 3./JG 88 in late

May 1938 upon the latter's return to Germany, the unit having by then received Bf 109B-2s.

While in Spain, Mölders and other German airmen developed the formation known as the 'finger-four', which improved the all-round field of vision and combat flexibility of the standard Luftwaffe *Schwarm*. Encouraging pilot initiative through enhanced mutual protection, the 'finger-four' comprized two elements (*Rotten*) whose positions mirrored the fingertips of an outstretched hand. Between 15 July and 3 November 1938 Mölders used these tactics to great effect, downing 15 enemy aircraft – although he was credited with only 14 victories – to become the leading ace of the *Legion Condor*.

Returning to Germany in December 1938, he served concurrently with both I./JG 133 and the *Reichsluftfahrtministerium*, devising new fighter tactics with the latter organization based on his experiences in Spain. In March 1939 he was made *Staffelkapitän* of 1./JG 133. This *Jagdgeschwader* later became JG 53 and Mölders claimed his first victory with the unit on 20 September 1939 when he downed a French Hawk H-75A. Mölders had taken his tally to 38 victories (and received the Knight's Cross) by the time he was himself shot down and captured during the Battle of France on 5 June 1940. Released after the French capitulation, he was posted to JG 51 as its *Kommodore* the following month and remained in the vanguard of the action with the *Geschwader* throughout the Battle of Britain. During the latter stages of the conflict Mölders gave the Bf 109F its combat debut, claiming the first of at least 22 victories in the 'Friedrich' on 11 October 1940.

In the early summer of 1941, having taken his score to 76, Mölders led JG 51 east in preparation for the invasion of the USSR. Like most Jagdwaffe pilots involved in the massive Eastern Front offensive codenamed Operation *Barbarossa*, he enjoyed astonishing success in his Bf 109F. Indeed, between 22 June and 15 July, Mölders's tally rose to 108 victories. By then he had added the Oak Leaves, Swords and Diamonds to his Knight's Cross. Posted away from the front line to become Inspector General of Fighters, he was killed in a flying accident on 22 November 1941 while travelling to the funeral of his superior officer, World War I ace Generaloberst Ernst Udet.

Training Group) *Merseburg* for instruction in tactics and further familiarization with front-line types. It was hoped that its creation would free *Jagdgeschwader* to operate more efficiently in the front line. In reality, *Ergänzungsjagdgruppe Merseburg* was found to be too large to operate effectively and too remote from the front line to allow pupils to be briefed on current combat techniques, as the *Jagdgeschwader* were complaining that the replacement pilots they were receiving had little chance of achieving success on the Channel Front. In an effort to rectify this, the Luftwaffe decided to disband the *Ergänzungsjagdgruppe* in October 1940 and enlarge and reassign its *Staffeln* to each operational *Jagdgeschwader* once again.

The increase in demand for pilots, combined with the high attrition rate during the summer of 1940, eventually resulted in the *Ergänzungsstaffel* being enlarged to *Gruppe* strength and given the designation IV. *Gruppe* within the *Jagdgeschwader* to which it was attached. Each new *Gruppe* comprised a *Stab*, a 1. *Einsatzstaffel* (Operational Training Squadron) and a slightly larger 2. *Schulstaffel* (Training Squadron), which had more aircraft and personnel. The latter were transferred in from the parent *Geschwader*, although each *Ergänzungsgruppe* was controlled directly by the *General der Jagdflieger* to ensure that uniform standards were maintained. The expansion of these units began during the early spring of 1941.

It was the *Schulstaffel*'s job to train new pilots in operational tactics and techniques, with instructors being *Jagdflieger* drawn from the front line.

A line-up of Bf 109Es and Fs of IV./*Ergänzungsgruppe* JG 3 at Monchy-Breton during the late spring of 1941. By then the *Jagdgeschwader* had enough F-2s on strength to pass a few to its *Stab*, 1. *Einsatzstaffel* and 2. *Schulstaffel*, although the bulk of the aircraft flown by the tyro fighter pilots were war-weary 'Emils'. (EN Archive)

During their time with the *Schulstaffel*, pilots gained familiarity with the fighters then in service with the *Jagdgeschwader*. Most training units had to make do with combat-weary Bf 109Es for much of 1941 as there were few F-models available to *Schulstaffeln*. Instructors concentrated on teaching the tactics used by standard Jagdwaffe fighter formations, namely the *Rotte* and the *Schwarm*. They were practised in the air over and over again. Low-level flying and aerial gunnery were also taught. Trainee pilots would eventually graduate to the *Einsatzstaffel*, where they would gain combat experience in quieter parts of the Channel Front.

The conversion course was meant to last eight to 12 weeks, but the demand for pilots in the front line often meant that trainees were frequently rushed into service after a few weeks with the *Schulstaffel* and the *Einsatzstaffel*. And although instructors with recent combat experience could directly pass their knowledge to new pilots in a timely fashion thanks to the creation of the *Ergänzungsgruppen*, these same individuals were also urgently needed in the *Jagdgeschwader* too. Eventually, front-line commitments carried the day to the detriment of the student pilots.

Although the *Ergänzungsgruppen* experiment had initially worked well enough initially, it was found that the methods and quality of training within the various *Staffeln* and *Gruppen* varied due to a growing lack of qualified instructors. This meant that the conversion course for students was getting progressively shorter. In the summer of 1942, just as the last Bf 109Fs were being replaced on the Channel Front, the *Ergänzungsgruppen* attached to specific units were disbanded and three *Ergänzungsjagdgruppen* were formed in their place. These Fighter Pools were situated in the three main operational areas, with replacement pilots for the Channel Front coming from *Ergänzungsjagdgruppen Süd* (south) at Cazeaux, in France. Although this new arrangement reduced the number of instructors required, it also curtailed the operational training of new pilots just when such experience was becoming vitally important for replacement front-line aviators.

INTO COMBAT

Spitfire II/Vs and Bf 109Fs were engaged in aerial combat from the autumn of 1940 to the late summer of 1942. Yet for almost 12 months after the F-model had made its front-line debut, its slow delivery meant that German fighter units in the West continued to employ late-build Bf 109E-7/8s. Similarly, the last of the Spitfire IIs on the Channel Front had been replaced by the end of 1941, leaving the Spitfire V as Fighter

Command's principal type until the first Mk IXs started appearing in July 1942. By then, the only 'Friedrichs' still in service with JG 2 and JG 26 were the relative handful of Bf 109F-4/B *Jabos*, most of the fighter *Gruppen* from both units having switched to the superior Fw 190A.

The early F-models were powered by the same DB 601N engine as the Bf 109E-7/8 to give them a similar performance, although the refined aerodynamics of the 'Friedrich' meant the new fighter was superior at higher altitudes. Major Werner Mölders, *Kommodore* of JG 51, proved this during October 1940 when the *Jagdgeschwader's Stabsschwarm* was issued with three early-build Bf 109F-1s. JG 51 was the most active German fighter unit on the Channel Front at the time, with Mölders its most successful pilot. Indeed, in October he claimed 12 of the *Stab*'s 13 victories – over nine Hurricanes and three Spitfires, achieved while escorting high-flying JG 51 *Jabos* or during fighter-only 'Freie Jagd' sweeps. Although most of Mölders's claims that month involved Hurricane Is and Spitfire Is, he also downed two Spitfire IIAs and badly damaged a third during a brief encounter on the morning of 25 October. This was almost certainly the first time the Bf 109F had fought the latest version of the Vickers Supermarine fighter.

No. 603 Sqn was the RAF's most successful Battle of Britain unit in terms of enemy aircraft destroyed, and on the 25th it had scrambled 12 of its recently delivered Spitfire IIAs from Hornchurch after high-flying German aircraft were detected approaching London. It was the first raid of the day and comprized three waves of aircraft arriving in a steady stream between 0845 and 1030 hrs. Of an estimated 140 Luftwaffe aircraft

The first Bf 109Fs to reach the Channel Front were three F-1s issued to *Stab*. JG 51 in October 1940. Displaying 54 victory bars on its rudder and still bearing traces of its original four-letter delivery code (SG+GW) on the fuselage – but with no command markings yet applied – Wk-Nr 5628 was assigned to Major Werner Mölders. (John Weal) detected over southeast England, ten to 12 were Do 17 bombers in the first wave, while the rest were Bf 109s. Most were engaged over Kent, although some reached London, where they dropped their bombs.

As the No. 603 Sqn aircraft desperately climbed through thick cloud to get above the approaching German formations, they made full use of the extra 18lb of boost introduced with the Merlin XIII engine. But their pilots were alarmed to hear over their radios that the fighter controller vectoring the unit towards the enemy had been informed by radar plotters that there were already Bf 109s in their immediate vicinity. Moments later they received a second warning: enemy fighters were almost on top of them. As the 12 Spitfires finally broke through the overcast into clear blue skies at 25,000ft, they were bounced by a gaggle of Bf 109E/Fs from *Stab. JG 51*. They had been heading northwest at 30,000ft, taking advantage of their superior high-altitude performance. Leading the formation was Major Mölders, looking for his 63rd victory. No. 603 Sqn immediately broke formation. Some pilots were simply fighting to survive while others pursued the rapidly disappearing Bf 109s. The aim of the Luftwaffe's leading ace had been good during JG 51's solitary pass. Mölders targeted the last 'vic' of three Spitfire IIAs, flown by Plt Offs Peter Olver, John Soden and Ludwik Martel. Olver and Soden were both forced to bail out of their mortally damaged Spitfires over the Sussex–Kent border, having just become Mölders' 63rd and 64th victims. Martel's P7350 had sustained damage to its left wing when a cannon shell passed through it. The Polish officer also heard banging noises behind him and then felt a sharp pain in the left side of his body and leg.

Diving back into cloud to shake off his unseen assailant, Martel then checked his wounds. There was little blood but his leather flying jacket had been torn and he realized he had been hit in the left leg by shrapnel when the cannon shell exploded. Now he would have to nurse his badly damaged Spitfire back through the thick cloud cover. Martel struggled to concentrate on his cockpit instruments as he descended. 'I lost consciousness,' he recalled many years later, 'and when I came to I realised I was below the cloud upside down. There was a large hole in the left wing and my engine was not working.' Righting his aircraft just above the ground, Martel force-landed in a grassy field near Hastings, in East Sussex. He reported:

When I looked out of the cockpit I saw a windmill. I had not seen one since arriving in England, and I knew that there were plenty of them in Holland. I now began to wonder if, while I was unconscious, I had flown across the North Sea. I feared that I would be taken prisoner by German soldiers, but none came. Soon, a Home Guard patrol arrived – old grandpas, or so they seemed to me – but I was unable to communicate with them. Although I now knew that I was safely in England, the Home Guard thought that I was a German! Finally, an officer appeared and I was correctly identified as a pilot in the RAF. My wounds were dressed and I was taken to a hospital. I must have been suffering from a fever by then for I threatened to shoot a German flyer who had been admitted at the same time as me.

After ten days' recuperation, Martel returned to operations with No. 603 Sqn on 6 November. P7350 was also repaired and sent back into the front line.

It would appear that No. 603 Sqn was also the first Spitfire IIA unit to down a Bf 109F when, shortly after noon on 11 November, its pilots claimed three Messerschmitt fighters destroyed and one probable (together with a Ju 87 probable) without loss ten miles north of Margate. Twelve of the unit's aircraft were flying a convoy protection patrol over the Thames estuary at an altitude of 20,000ft when they spotted Ju 87s and an escort of Bf 109s approaching from the northwest. The ensuing one-sided action was described by Major Fritz von Forrell in his 1941 volume *Mölders und seine Männer* (*Mölders and his Men*):

R6923/QJ-S was built as a rare cannon-armed Mk IB and delivered to No. 19 Sqn in July 1940. The fighter was relegated to No. 7 OTU when persistent jamming of its two 20mm weapons saw all Mk IBs swapped by No. 19 Sqn for standard Spitfire IIAs. Converted into a Spitfire VB in April 1941, the aircraft was then issued to No. 92 Sqn and regularly flown by ace Flg Off Alan Wright. (Philip Jarrett)

11 November proved one of the blackest days in Oberstleutnant Mölders's career. For weeks, owing to a bad case of flu, he had had to stay out of the cockpit of his Messerschmitt. Finally, he felt fit enough to direct his fighters from the ground control room. In the meantime, the best of his boys, Oberleutnant Georg Claus [who had 11 victories to his name, including a trio of Hurricanes claimed in a Bf 109F three days earlier], took command of the first *Staffel*. Despite adverse weather conditions in November, the *Geschwader* flew many tough escort missions for the benefit of bomber units. Claus excelled in his new post, proving that, even without his tutor around [he had often flown as Mölders's wingman], he was a capable *Kapitän* and an excellent fighter pilot.

On that fateful day the *Geschwader* again took to the air to shepherd the dive-bombers to their target at the mouth of the Thames river. Banks of thick cloud hung low over the Channel and intermittent rain squalls limited the already poor visibility even more. Finally, the bomber formation located its target, a coastal convoy. A burst of excited R/T betrayed a fight breaking out in the air. Someone declared a victory, then someone else feverishly shouted a warning. The intense radio traffic suggested that the skirmish was particularly heavy. Then ... what happened? One of the pilots reported he was hit. Moments later another report followed – a ditching in the Channel!

Mölders anxiously left the ground control room and walked out towards the landing ground. The first of the returning machines, rocking its wings, came into sight. This was Oberleutnant Friedrich Eberle, who was announcing his victory over a Spitfire [two Hurricanes from No. 17 Sqn were in fact downed, but no Spitfires] in the usual Luftwaffe manner. As soon as he clambered out of the cockpit he reported with a shaken voice that Oberleutnant Claus had ditched in the Thames estuary because of a coolant leak from his shot-up radiator. Mölders listened no longer. He rushed to a telephone. For the first time Mölders's men saw their Kommodore, known for his nerves of steel, look apprehensive. With his hand trembling, he gripped the receiver, instructing the air-sea rescue service. He immediately ordered the groundcrew to ready an aircraft for him – and, accompanied by Oberleutnant Eberle, took to the air for the first time in two weeks to search for the man who was closer to him than any other pilot in his *Geschwader*.

The two Messerschmitts skimmed the land beneath them, going flat out towards the murky waters of the English Channel. They flashed past the Cape of Margate and approached the Thames estuary. Mölders seemed unconcerned about six Spitfires still circling above the convoy. He kept on looking around, scanning ever-larger areas of empty sea. He stayed over the spot until his Bf 109 had no more fuel to remain, straining his excellent eyesight in the hope of picking up a trace of the missing man against the dark surface of the water. Finally, with a heavy heart, he returned to base. This loss was a personally disheartening blow to him. They were friends and comrades in combat, for good and for bad. So many times they had fought side by side, protecting each other.

No trace of Claus's body was ever found.

Production delays with the 'Friedrich' slowed conversion to the new fighter during the first half of 1941. This, in turn, meant that Bf 109Fs clashed with Spitfire IIs and, from February onwards, Vs, albeit infrequently until the summer of that year. *Jagdgeschwader* would send individual *Gruppe* back to Germany to re-equip with the Bf 109F-1/2, starting with *Stab.* and I./JG 51 in February, followed by III. and IV./JG 51. Like all units 'converting' to the 'Friedrich' at this time, these units returned to France predominantly equipped with Bf 109E-7/8s. In March a small number of F-models were issued to *Stab.* and I./JG 3, *Stab.* and III./JG 26 and *Stab.*, I., II. and III./JG 53.

By then the first Spitfire VBs had reached No. 92 Sqn at Manston, these aircraft in fact being re-engined Spitfire IBs fitted with the new Merlin 45. As with the Bf 109F, production of the new Mk V was initially a slow affair, leaving the Spitfire I/IIA and Hurricane I/II units that predominated in Fighter Command to undertake the early offensive missions over France. The first 'Circus', flown on 10 January 1941, had seen six Blenheim IVs target an airfield and an ammunition dump a few miles inland from Calais. Six Spitfire and three Hurricane units were tasked with escorting the bombers, which they successfully shielded from sporadic attacks by Bf 109s. The latter were E-models from I./JG 3 and 2(J)./LG 2. It would appear that the first RAF fighters engaged by Bf 109Fs (of I./JG 51) during 'Circus' operations were probably Hurricane Is or IIs, which were initially involved as bomber escorts.

With partially re-equipped Jagdgeschwader returning to the Channel Front throughout March, the number of F-models in France began to rise. After spending a few days re-acclimatising to operations in the front line, 'Channel work' began in earnest. But conditions had changed since the previous autumn. Now there were few escort missions for bombers heading for England. 'Freie Jagd' sweeps over Kent and Sussex were also rare.

Instead, most missions now took the form of defensive patrols off the French coast as well as interceptions of the incoming RAF fighters and bombers that were attacking targets in occupied France with increasing frequency.

IV./JG 51 enjoyed one of its best days with the Bf 109F on 5 March when its pilots intercepted 12 Spitfire IIAs of No. 610 Sqn that were supposed to be providing high cover for six Blenheim IVs targeting Boulogne in 'Circus No. 7'. Four Spitfires were downed in short order, resulting in the deaths of two pilots and two more being captured. These losses alarmed AVM Leigh-Mallory, who described the action in the following report:

Fighter Sweep to Boulogne 5 March 1941
Three Spitfire squadrons (610, 616 and 145) were ordered to leave the ground at 1230 hours and rendezvous over Hastings at 1300 hrs. 610 Squadron (leader, F/L Norris DFC) led the formation and was told to fly at 25,000ft, with 616 at 26,000 and 145 at 30,000. The formation circled Hastings at the right time and at the proper heights but failed to find the bomber formation or its escort fighters. After circling for about 20 minutes, leader asked Controller for instructions and said he was unable to contact 'friends'. Controller took 'friends' to mean other two squadrons i.e.: 616 and 145, whereas, of course, the leader meant the bomber formation.

At about 1330 hrs (by which time the formation had been in the air for an hour), Control vectored its three squadrons on 100 degrees which took them out to sea towards Boulogne. About mid-Channel, leader was told by Controller that bandits were approaching from southeast in his vicinity. Immediately afterwards leader sighted 4 Me109s (yellow noses) which attacked from about 500ft higher, apparently with great determination. A dogfight ensued and the whole squadron (610) broke up and eventually eight pilots returned to their base singly, landing between 1410 and 1430 hrs. Neither the leader nor anyone else know what happened to the 4 missing pilots, who were inexperienced, and the only information I was able to obtain was that one of the pilots saw six other 109s approach from the south after the dogfight had been going on for some time.

In the meantime, the two higher squadrons (616 and 145) had lost touch with the leading squadron (610) and 616 did not see any enemy aircraft, and eventually returned to base. 145 ran short of oxygen and returned to its base at 1340 hrs without having anything to report.

Conclusion – this whole operation seems to have been unfortunate and it was incredible that four 109s with only 500ft advantage in height should have been able to break up completely a squadron of 12 Spitfire IIs and presumably bring down four of them, and that no information can be obtained as to what happened.

Very short notice of this operation was given by Group and in fact 610 Squadron only received orders at 1215 hrs to leave the ground at 1230 hrs. This was the first notification the Squadron had had that there was to be a

Aces abound in this shot of No. 92 Sqn at Manston on 6 February 1941. The pilots with five or more victories are Sgt R. E. Havercroft (fourth from left), next to him Flt Lt C. B. F. Kingcome, then Sqn Ldr J. A. Kent (holding the scoreboard), Flt Lt J. W. Villa, Plt Off C. H. Saunders, Flg Offs R. H. Holland and A. R. Wright and Sgt D. E. Kingaby. (© IWM, CH 2538)

sweep, and actually at that time Red Section was in the air on an operational flight. It just had time to land and refuel and took off at 1230 hrs with the rest of the squadron.

Recommendations – if possible, considerably more notice should be given of a large operation of this sort so that squadron leaders can get together and discuss details. In this particular case the S/Ldr of 610 did not know there was going to be a sweep and as a result the Wing was led by a flight commander.

No operational orders have been issued as to what should be done in the event of the fighter formations missing the bomber formation.

Squadrons are keeping too far apart – in this case 5,000ft between the top and bottom squadrons – with the result that they lost each other. Squadrons should not be more than 1,000ft apart or at any rate close enough to keep in touch.

If possible, squadrons detailed for sweep or large scale operations should not be given operational jobs for at least an hour before the sweep commences. Pilots in 610 Squadron had breakfast at 0830 hrs and were not able to obtain their next meal until 1830 hrs, when they were given 30 minutes notice until 1900 hrs. They expect this kind of thing when there is a 'blitz' on, but it seems rather unnecessary during the present quiet times.

Including time from takeoff to 28,000ft, pilots run short of oxygen in about one hour and consequently have often to return from patrol. Would it not be advisable for Spitfires to carry two bottles of oxygen? Super long-range PRU Spitfires now carry three bottles.

The average number of experienced war pilots in squadrons I have visited lately is five and I don't think squadrons are being allowed nearly enough training from their experienced pilots. Squadrons ought to go up and carry out surprise attacks on each other, and especially practise regaining formation after being split up. I think perhaps fighter pilots are so busy keeping formation that they are not able to keep a good enough lookout.

Despite having to adopt a more defensive posture, the Jagdwaffe was still keen to dominate the Channel and the southeast corner of England whenever possible. As the weather improved in March and April 1941, the returning *Jagdgeschwader* would undertake 'Freie Jagd' patrols. Typically, a handful of Bf 109s made landfall at Dungeness, circled north to Sheerness and then turned southeast to leave England via the North Downs. These missions, together with the interception of 'Circuses' as they appeared more frequently over France, allowed future high-scoring aces to claim their first victories with the F-model. Oberfeldwebel Josef Wurmheller of II./JG 53 and Hauptmann Hermann-Friedrich Joppien of I./JG 51 enjoyed

BF 109: THROUGH THE GUNSIGHT

All Bf 109s were fitted with different versions of the Reflexvisier (dubbed Revi in front-line service) reflector gunsight. The Revi C12D fitted to the Bf 109F differed from its predecessor, the C12C, in having its orange-coloured reticule calibrated for fixed gunnery as well as bombing. All C12 gunsights lacked computing aids of any kind. They did, however, have a built-in dimmer to regulate reticule intensity. The glass onto which the reticule was projected was manufactured as 'sun dark', which also helped to reduce glare. Some pilots – most famously Adolf Galland – had various types of telescopic sight fitted alongside the C12D as an out-in-the-field modification, striving to harmonize them with the standard reflector gunsight. They would not collimate, however, which meant that their only use was to allow pilots to identify objects that were usually beyond clear visual range with the naked eye. The Bf 109F boasted an ergonomically designed KG 12A grip, which allowed for the simultaneous firing of both the cowling machine guns and the engine-mounted cannon. The grip was also fitted with a radio actuation button. (Artwork by Jim Laurier, © Osprey Publishing) early success. So too did Oberstleutnant Adolf Galland, *Kommodore* of JG 26. On 15 April, during his first day of operational flying in an F-model, he claimed two Spitfire IIAs destroyed and one probable. All his victims were from No. 266 Sqn. He would be credited with a total of 36 victories in the Bf 109F by year-end, taking his tally to 94 overall. Galland described the action in his autobiography, *The First and the Last*:

15 April was Osterkamp's birthday [World War I ace Theo Osterkamp was the Luftflotte 2 *Jagdfliegerführer* at Le Touquet] and he invited me to come over. As a present, I packed a huge basket of lobsters with the necessary bottles of champagne into my Me [Bf] 109F and took off, with Oberfeldwebel [Hans-Jürgen] Westphal as my wingman. It was too tempting not to make a little detour on the way and to pay a visit to England. Soon, I spotted a single Spitfire. After a wild chase fate decided in my favour. My tough opponent crashed in flames in a little village west of Dover.

A few moments later we saw a flight of Spitfires climbing ahead of us. One of them lagged behind the formation. I approached him unnoticed and shot him to smithereens from a very short distance. We flew right on, close to the formation, where I shot down a third Spitfire, which I nearly rammed. I was unable to observe the crash. Westphal was now in a good firing position but suddenly his guns jammed. Now it was time to bolt as the Spitfires waded in on us. Throttle full open in a power dive down to the Channel! We were heavily attacked. Westphal was noticeably faster than I. Something was wrong with my crate.

As I came in to land at Le Touquet the ground staff waved frantically and fired red light signals. At last I understood their gestures: I had nearly made an involuntary crash landing. When I worked the mechanism to let down the undercarriage it did not go down but retracted instead. It must have been down the whole time. I must have touched the button with my knee during the action over England. I remembered that I had had to do some readjusting with the trim tabs and that the flying properties of the aeroplane had definitely changed. Lobster and champagne bottles were safe. Hunter's luck! Together with the report of the Spitfires, I handed the birthday present to Osterkamp.

The Spitfire V was now on the verge of front-line service over France following a series of mechanical problems and political intervention from the Prime Minister himself. Churchill had minuted ACM Portal, on 28 February, 'It would be a mistake to exhibit the Merlin 45 to the enemy till there are at least half a dozen squadrons capable of using them. Certainly, they should not be used over the other side without further

Oberstleutnant Mölders' arch-rival in the race to be the Luftwaffe's ranking ace during the early Channel Front period was Oberstleutnant Adolf Galland, *Kommodore* of JG 26. Galland is seen here wearing an RAF Bomber Command issue Irvin sheepskin flying suit over his service dress. Although very bulky for the Bf 109's cramped cockpit, such suits were highly coveted amongst *Jagdflieger* during the winter months on the Channel Front. (EN Archive)

instruction.' Although Portal agreed to the Prime Minister's request, he eventually managed to persuade Churchill to rescind his order by explaining that 'there is nothing in the Merlin 45 which the Germans could themselves make use of with advantage in the near future. There is nothing new for the pilots to learn in the way of tactics and handling of the aircraft, such as might justify the holding back of an entirely new type of fighter until we are ready to spring an effective surprise on the enemy.' He also noted that it would take several months to re-equip six squadrons with the new fighter.

It would appear that the first encounter between the Bf 109F and the Spitfire V finally occurred on 11 April when four fighters from No. 92 Sqn were scrambled to attack an He 59 seaplane that was under tow towards Boulogne harbour. It was quickly sunk by the strafing Spitfires, but then they were bounced by a number of 'Friedrichs' from III./JG 51. Sgt T. G. Gaskell was shot down and killed by future 55-victory ace Leutnant Hermann Staiger. No. 92 Sqn opened its account with the Mk V when Bf 109s were downed off the Kent coast on 24 and 26 April, the latter machine being Unteroffizier Werner Zimmer's F-2 from 4./JG 53, which was destroyed by ace Plt Off Ronnie Fokes. Zimmer was killed.

The Mk V had become operational at almost the same time as the Bf 109F-2. The German fighter's maximum speed of 373mph at 19,700ft and service ceiling of 36,100ft were remarkably similar to those of the Spitfire VB. However, the Bf 109F could climb higher than the British fighter, as No. 92 Sqn's Walter 'Johnnie' Johnston discovered during a sweep in the summer of 1941:

We used to get up to 25/26,000ft quite regularly, but 30,000ft and above was really stretching it. On those occasions it was bitterly cold. On one trip we were up high and all of us were really hanging on our props. I was flying No 3 behind James Rankin and we were at the point where, if we tried to fire our cannon, we would have stalled. Then I looked up to starboard and, completely unannounced, a 109 came up alongside us. He was slightly above and he knew damned fine that he was as safe as houses. He looked over and gave me a wave and then pulled up and climbed merrily away, and I thought 'My God, what would I give for that?'

As well as boasting superb performance at high altitude, the Bf 109F-2 was also the superior aircraft low down. It was 27mph faster than the Spitfire V at 10,000ft and had a better rate of climb. Indeed, it was reported that a good pilot could perform four complete rolls while climbing before having to level off. Like the E-model before it, the 'Friedrich' was also quicker both in a dive and a zoom climb. The direct fuel-injection system fitted to its engine enabled pilots to join and break off combat at will. While the standard evasive half-roll and steep dive was still employed by Bf 109F pilots – as it had been when they were flying the 'Emil' – such a manoeuvre usually resulted in the engagement being broken off or the resulting loss of height placing the *Jagdflieger* at a tactical disadvantage. The 'Friedrich's' improved performance, however, gave its pilots the confidence to disengage from the Spitfire by climbing away and re-engaging from a tactically advantageous position. This was particularly marked at altitudes above 2,500ft.

The Merlin's float-type carburettor, by contrast, ceased to deliver fuel during sustained manoeuvres involving negative G, causing the engine to cut out. Bf 109 pilots had soon learned that when being chased by a British fighter, a bunt followed by a high-speed dive was usually enough to shake off any adversary. This continued to be the case with the Mk V until modifications were made to later aircraft. But the Spitfire V could still out-turn any German fighter, as had been demonstrated by the Mk I/II. Bf 109F pilots usually stuck to the 'one pass and away' rule that had been observed in 1940. Yet, according to JG 26 historian Donald Caldwell,

Some early Bf 109Fs suffered structural failure when subjected to high-G manoeuvring, resulting in a number of pilots being killed. Perhaps the most prominent victim of the 'Friedrich's' fragility was 40-victory ace Hauptmann Wilhelm Balthasar, *Geschwaderkommodore* of JG 2. Seen here in an earlier F-2, he was killed when the wing of his Bf 109F-4 broke off during a dogfight with Belgian ace Flg Off Victor Ortmans of No. 609 Sqn near Aire on 3 July 1941. Ortmans claimed to have damaged a Bf 109 during this engagement, so Balthasar's demise may, in fact, have been caused by enemy fire. (EN Archive)

author of *The JG 26 War Diary* (Vol. 1), some more experienced *Jagdflieger* felt confident enough in their new 'Friedrichs' to challenge the Spitfire in the horizontal plane too:

> Flg Off Franciszek Surma of No. 308 Sqn [participating in 'Circus No. 100A' on 20 September 1941] had a long, inconclusive dogfight over the Channel with an experienced German pilot. His opponent was almost certainly from JG 2, but these comments from his combat report are pertinent: 'From my experience on this Circus I have formed the opinion that the Me 109F is superior to the Spitfire V in both speed and climbing power. The German pilots' tactics have changed as they did not attack from high above, but mostly on the same level.' This was a prescient observation. The superiority of the Spitfire in turning combat was drummed into the German pilots from flight school, especially by instructors who had been withdrawn from the Western Front for a rest. The pilots of the *Kanalgeschwader* now had enough confidence in the Bf 109F to take on the Spitfires on the latter's own terms.

Although now capable of matching the Spitfire in respect to its manoeuvrability, the Bf 109F was at a disadvantage in terms of firepower. The Spitfire I/II had been outgunned by the Bf 109E from the start of the war, but the cannon-armed Mk VB packed a more destructive punch than the F-model. Its two 20mm Oerlikon cannon and four 0.303 in. machine guns gave it a greater weight of fire than the single 15mm or 20mm cannon and two 7.92mm machine guns in the 'Friedrich'. The reduced weaponry of the F-model came in for such criticism from front-line pilots that Messerschmitt made it a priority to rectify this with the follow-on Bf 109G. This variant entered service on the Channel Front in the summer of 1942.

In the spring of 1941, the Spitfire V and Bf 109F were more or less equally matched in their encounters over France as the RAF's daylight offensive increased in scope. The Jagdwaffe units, however, would be at a distinct tactical advantage. Not only were they able to pick and choose when they engaged in combat, they were also fighting over friendly territory.

By early June Nos. 91, 74 and 609 Sqns had received Mk Vs, with the latter two units joining No. 92 Sqn within the Biggin Hill Wing. Although this new mark of Spitfire gave Fighter Command a boost as the tempo of the offensive against targets in France increased, losses suffered by No. 11 Group began to mount as more *Jagdgeschwader* equipped with late-model 'Emils' and new 'Friedrichs' returned to the Channel Front. The Luftwaffe had been quick to build up an air defence system to oppose these raids, with Freya FuMG 39G and Würzburg early warning radar sets in the

Pas-de-Calais combining with the German radio Listening Service to give fighter units timely notice of impending attacks. The *Jagdgeschwader* adopted an alarm-start system similar to that employed by Fighter Command the previous summer, scrambling aircraft against approaching formations as weather and time permitted. Although the RAF chose the time, course and strength of their raids, the advantage rested with the Luftwaffe. Its fighter pilots usually enjoyed the all-important advantage of height and surprise when launching their attacks. And just as Fighter Command had formed No. 421 Flight in the autumn of 1940 to check on the strength and composition of impending raids, the Jagdwaffe resorted to a similar tactic as RAF fighter sweeps increased in frequency. Two or three 'spotters' would be sent aloft, and if they reported bomber formations in strength, large numbers of Bf 109s would be scrambled. If there were no bombers, the *Jagdgeschwader* would remain on the ground due to the numerical strength of Fighter Command.

The imbalance between the two sides in terms of fighter strength would increase dramatically from late May 1941 as the Luftwaffe started redeploying for the planned invasion of the Soviet Union on 22 June. Conversely, the RAF stepped up its campaign by launching its Non-Stop Offensive on 16 June. This was aimed at inflicting further losses on the now depleted Jagdwaffe to the point where the RAF hoped it would take control of the skies over France. Although dubbed the 'Nonsense Offensive' by Nazi propagandists, Fighter Command was buoyed by the level of opposition provoked by the raid. By now only JG 2 and JG 26 remained in the West. Between them they were able to field around 250 fighters, although no more than 150 were serviceable at any one time. Even so, they were more than able to inflict growing losses on the RAF formations, taking a particularly heavy toll of Fighter Command units. Historian Donald Caldwell explained how more British aircraft were sent into combat from the early summer of 1941, and the tactics that were so effectively employed by the *Jagdgeschwader* to counter the Non-Stop Offensive, in *The JG 26 War Diary* (Vol. 1):

> The ability of JG 26 to penetrate the escort would lead to larger and larger British formations. A 'Circus' ultimately required up to 20 squadrons of fighters, some 240 aircraft, to protect a dozen or so Blenheims. The fighters were deployed as follows. First across the target were three Target Support Wings, each of three Spitfire squadrons. One paralleled the path of the bombers, overtaking them en route. The other two approached from different directions, crossing in the vicinity of the target. They then split up into flights of four, which had finally replaced sections of three in most

(but not all) Fighter Command squadrons, and patrolled the target area until their fuel state forced them to return. The Escort Wing contained four squadrons of Spitfires or Hurricanes. Their functions can be inferred from their titles – Close Escort, Medium Escort, High Escort and Low Escort squadron. The obsolescent Hurricanes were replaced by Spitfires over the course of 1941. Above the Escort Wing was the Escort Cover Wing of three squadrons, while coming along behind to mop up were the Forward Support Wing and the Rear Support Wing, each of two squadrons. The deployment of this armada required great skill by the British ground controllers and airborne wing commanders. Timing was critical because of the British fighters' short endurance, which limited them to targets no further inland than Lille. Cloudless conditions were essential at the assembly point over southern England, thus 'Circuses' were rarely attempted other than in the spring and summer months.

The German defenders did not attempt to confront these massive formations directly. JG 26 entered combat in *Staffel* or *Gruppe* strength, rather than as a *Geschwader*. The German battle plan never changed: their fighters were to get off the ground quickly, gain height and make use of sun and cloud to attack any part of the enemy 'beehive' that appeared vulnerable. General Osterkamp and his two *Kommodoren*, Galland and Hauptmann Wilhelm Balthasar of JG 2, understood that their role was to inflict maximum damage on the RAF while preserving their own limited forces. It was not required or expected that the bombers be attacked by every German intercept formation. Only the most skilled formation leaders, such as Galland himself, could judge the proper moment at which the escort could be penetrated at minimum risk in order to reach the bombers. The British fighters were even less of a threat to the Germans than the bombers. For German morale and propaganda purposes it was essential that every reasonable opportunity be taken to inflict harm on the RAF, but fairly strict guidelines had to be met. According to Fighter Command's combat reports, Luftwaffe fighter formations large and small 'avoided combat' on most RAF missions, to the frustration (or relief) of the Allied pilots – but the well-disciplined German pilots were just following orders.

As Donald Caldwell noted, Adolf Galland was the master tactician on the Channel Front in 1941. When JG 26 was ordered aloft, he would take his time to position his fighters, waiting patiently for moments of confusion in the large and often unwieldy RAF formations. A year earlier, Fighter Command had endeavoured to shoot down bombers at almost any cost. The tactics employed by the Jagdwaffe in 1941, however, greatly reduced the risk of losses among its *Jagdgeschwader*. Galland would always try to position his fighters higher and to the rear of their often unsuspecting prey, their presence being hidden by the sun behind them. Once in position, he would lead a slashing attack through the fighter screen to the bombers, firing as they closed on the Blenheims and Stirlings. The pilots would then continue down to outrun any pursuers thanks to the Bf 109's superior performance in a dive. Galland also employed another method of attack that could be far riskier to his men. He would order the majority of his fighters to remain above the escorts and attract their attention while he led a *Rotte* or *Schwarm* from his *Stab* to attack from below. This tactic worked best in a cloudy sky because it allowed the hunting Messerschmitts to close on their prey unobserved.

Proof of just how proficient JG 2 and JG 26 had become with the Bf 109F came with the claims made by the two units between 22 June and 31 December 1941. No fewer than 838 victories were credited to the *Jagdflieger*, for the loss of 100 pilots killed or missing, one captured and 48 wounded. These units had had 168 fighters destroyed, 110 of them in combat. In the same period 1,036 RAF aircraft were destroyed and 464 heavily damaged during the Channel Front offensive. Conversely, the pilots of Fighter Command claimed to have shot down 731 German aircraft. This glaring disparity between claims and losses was a repeat of Fighter Command's inflated tallies of the summer of 1940.

Clearly, the Luftwaffe had won the battle over occupied France in 1941. It would continue to do so the following year as the Spitfire VB struggled to protect the growing number of medium and heavy bombers committed to the Channel Front campaign from attack by the Fw 190 and the small number of high-altitude Bf 109G-1s that entered service in the summer of 1942. Nevertheless, the RAF's numerical superiority in 1941 would only increase as the war went on, denying the Germans a tactical victory in countering the British Non-Stop Offensive. During 1941 Spitfire production far exceeded losses, allowing a massive expansion in the number of units operating the type so that by the end of the year 46 squadrons were flying Spitfires, mostly Mk Vs.

In an attempt to reduce the casualties being inflicted on their units, a number of wing leaders

In March 1941 the first wing leaders were appointed. At Biggin Hill, Wg Cdr A. G. 'Sailor' Malan was promoted to the position following his success as CO of No. 74 Sqn from early August 1940. One of Fighter Command's leading tacticians, he was also an accomplished ace credited with 27 and seven shared victories, including nine Bf 109Fs. (© IWM, CH 12661)

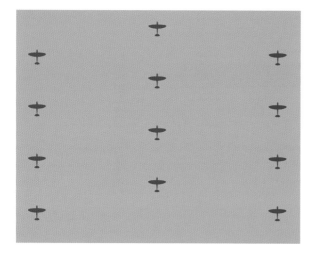

The loose line astern formation widely adopted by Fighter Command from late 1940 in place of the pre-war battle formation had been championed by Sqn Ldr 'Sailor' Malan when he was CO of No. 74 Sqn. This formation allowed pilots to provide each other with better mutual support if engaged by the enemy. There was also improved coverage of blind spots to the rear and better cohesion if forced to turn in combat, and the formation was much easier to fly than rigid battle formation.

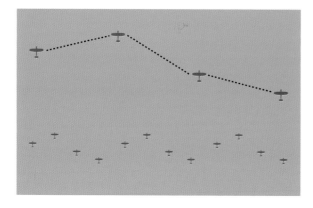

German fighter units opposing the RAF's Channel Front operations used tactical formations devised by Werner Mölders following his experiences in the Spanish Civil War. The basic fighting unit was the two-aircraft *Rotte*, two of which were combined to form a *Schwarm*. The leader of each pair, and his wingman, flew far enough apart to allow them to remain in formation with the minimum of effort, while concentrating on searching the sky around them. Typically, *Staffeln* flew with *Schwarme* in loose line abreast formation covering about a mile of sky.

began to abandon the traditional battle formation flown by Fighter Command for many years. Several units had, in fact, taken it upon themselves to modify their formations when going into combat during the Battle of Britain. Spitfire-equipped No. 74 Sqn was at the forefront of these changes. At the time its CO, Sqn Ldr 'Sailor' Malan, was effectively the Werner Mölders of Fighter Command, being one of the best tacticians in the RAF. He had claimed nine Bf 109Es destroyed during 1940 and would add at least 13 more during 1941, so his theories on fighter formations had been formulated through bitter combat experience.

During the final stages of the Battle of Britain, Malan began dividing his 12-aircraft formations into three sections of four, rather than the traditional four sections of three in an unwieldy 'vic'. Now, if a formation of Spitfires broke up after being bounced, its four-aircraft sections would split into two fighting pairs and operate in a similar way to the German *Rotte*. With the three section leaders flying in a widely spaced 'V', and the rest of their sections in line astern behind them, Malan's formation now possessed mutual support, coverage of blind spots to the rear and cohesion if forced to turn in combat. The loose line astern formation was much easier to fly than a tight battle formation, thus freeing pilots to look for the enemy rather than watching what their section leader was doing. Malan's new formation was soon officially implemented throughout Fighter Command, as was the German 'finger-four' *Schwarm*. This had been championed by Douglas Bader who, like Malan, was both an ace and, from March 1941, one of the first wing leaders.

No. 616 Sqn's Plt Off 'Johnnie' Johnson was one of the pilots within the Tangmere Wing led by Bader, and he was impressed by the ace's leadership qualities:

When we began to reach out and take on the Luftwaffe over the Pas-de-Calais, Douglas's greatest qualities came to the fore – leadership, the ability to inspire and his great desire to get out and at them. It was quite extraordinary. The qualities of moral courage, the ability to command, and the fact that he spoke the same language as these chaps – I was still a pilot officer and Douglas was a wing commander. We were all rather like his pupils. Like master and apprentice. He always went to great lengths to have a post-mortem afterwards and explain things to us. Everyone loved him.

During the second half of 1941 Fighter Command's Spitfire squadrons suffered badly at the hands of the Jagdwaffe and its Bf 109Fs – virtually all remaining 'Emils' had been replaced by F-2s and F-4s by mid-summer. This rather large 'trophy' resided in 9./JG 2's dispersal area at St Pol during this period. (John Weal)

Tactically, because the enemy abreast formation was better than the three-vic astern pattern, Fighter Command lagged behind the German Fighter Arm. It was not until this spring [1941] that Douglas Bader copied the *Schwarm*, which he called the 'finger-four' because the relative positions of the fighters are similar to a plan view of one's outstretched fingertips. Bader's pilots were immediately impressed with their 'finger-fours', for, unlike the line astern pattern, all pilots were always covered, and all stood an equal chance of survival. Soon all fighter squadrons followed Bader's lead.

Yet according to Johnson's squadronmate, Flg Off Hugh Dundas, there was some resistance to the 'finger-four'. 'A number of other wings adopted this idea, although there were exceptions. The Biggin Hill Wing, for instance, led by "Sailor" Malan, continued to fly with their aircraft in line astern. Malan was never converted and there were many arguments over the years between those who supported his tactics and those who adopted "finger-four". For myself, I was a militant champion of the new method and stuck to it unwaveringly until the end of the war.' The line astern formation seemed to remain longest with wings in Nos. 10 and 12 Groups, which did not see quite as much action as units in No. 11 Group. Sgt Sid Watson of No. 234 Sqn, which was part of No. 10 Group's Ibsley Wing on the south coast, was still flying in line astern formation as late as 1943. He was adamant that such tactics contributed to the high attrition rate suffered

Wg Cdr Douglas Bader, leading the Tangmere Wing in his distinctively marked Spitfire IIA P7966, hits a Bf 109F with a well-aimed burst of machine gun fire west-southwest of Lille during 'Circus No. 29' on 2 July 1941. He also hit a second aircraft, but only claimed it as damaged. This victory was his 18th success and it was one of 16 credited to Spitfire units that day for the loss of eight fighters and five pilots. (Artwork by Gareth Hector, © Osprey Publishing)

by Spitfire units in 1941–42. On his first mission, which he had to abort with engine problems, his flight lost four aircraft and their pilots (one killed and three captured). He reported:

> Because of the formation that was flown by the RAF – i.e. three sections of four in line astern – it was almost impossible to keep a good look out because all one's time was spent trying to play follow the leader. This silly formation stayed with us until 1943, when Wg Cdr 'Laddie' Lucas took over. He inaugurated the 'finger-four' approach (as used by the Germans) and it was a great improvement. Even then there were still some that resisted, if that can be believed!

By the end of 1941 Fighter Command was stronger than ever despite the heavy losses suffered during the second half of the year. The infrastructure was now in place for continued expansion, both in terms of aircraft production and pilot training. Those individuals fortunate enough to have survived months of combat were by now battle-hardened, and ready to impart their experience and expertise to new pilots leaving the OTUs and being sent to front-line units. Yet despite the advent of the new tactics, the arrival of Spitfire VBs and a steady increase in the number of Fighter Command squadrons, a growing number of Channel Front veterans were becoming increasingly disillusioned with the seemingly endless cycle of operations over France, together with the growing casualty list.

Many of these pilots had survived the Battle of Britain, yet they had no hesitation in stating that flying 'Circuses' and 'Rhubarbs' was far more nerve-racking. They particularly detested crawling along at less than 200mph as they escorted the Blenheims and Stirlings over France, being rocked around by exploding flak and nervously waiting for enemy fighters to bounce them. Once engaged, to stand any chance of survival, let alone defeat an aggressive and often elusive enemy, a Spitfire pilot would have to wring every ounce of performance from his machine. This could physically drain him in just minutes, as future high-scoring ace Plt Off Neville Duke of No. 92 Sqn recalled:

> Despite a lot of adrenalin flowing, there was considerable physical effort involved in handling the controls during high-G manoeuvres while at the same time straining to hold off black-out. Pre-engagement, there had to be a constant scanning to the rear, which was pretty wearing on the neck. Chafing was relieved by wearing a parachute silk scarf. Of course it was very cold at altitude, with no heating in the Spitfire. Numb hands were a particular problem, in spite of wearing silk inner gloves and outer gauntlets. Fur-lined boots were the norm. Misting or icing up was also a major difficulty. Ice occurred mainly on the inside of the front bulletproof screen.

Squadronmate Sgt Walter 'Johnnie' Johnston recalled how he coped with violent manoeuvring when trying to engage enemy fighters:

Bf 109F-2 Wk-Nr 9552 was assigned to 9./JG 2's *Staffelkapitän*, Oberleutnant Siegfried Schnell, the leading ace on the Channel Front in terms of Spitfire II/Vs destroyed. His immaculate fighter is seen here shortly after he had scored his 57th victory on 4 June 1942. (EN Archive)

In a steep turn you were pulling an awful lot of G but you became adept at seeing a little bit of grey come across your eyes and you knew that you were about on the verge of blacking out. Then you either kept it where it was or eased off a little bit. You could hear all right, but you just couldn't see properly. I think everyone blacked out a number of times; hauling it around, you actually went before the aircraft shuddered, but with experience you were able to keep it just on the verge.

Pilots flying close escort for RAF medium and heavy bombers were now getting a taste of what the *Jagdflieger* had experienced during the late stages of the Battle of Britain. No one liked these missions. High-scoring ace Sqn Ldr Brendan 'Paddy' Finucane described them simply as 'murder'. Although the more common 'Rhubarbs' did not generate the same levels of trepidation among their participants, they were still unpopular due to the increasing levels of flak they generated. Biggin Hill wing leader Wg Cdr Al Deere described them as 'useless and hated'. He noted that at best they 'served only as a means of letting off steam in that they enabled pilots to fire their guns in anger, more often than not against some unidentified target'.

Sqn Ldr Dennis Armitage, CO of the newly formed No. 129 Sqn at Tangmere in the early autumn of 1941, stated that the offensive 'wasn't like fighting a battle on your home ground. It seemed to us very pointless. It was a political, psychological exercise so that the French could see British aircraft overhead. I didn't enjoy it. I didn't enter into the spirit of it in the same way as I had the Battle of Britain.' His aircraft was one of 13 Spitfire VBs, together with a solitary Hurricane, shot down by Bf 109s from JG 26 on 21 September 1941. On that day the Germans claimed 19 for the loss of one 'Friedrich' and its pilot. Armitage was trying to keep his formation together as it flew bomber escort duty for 'Circus 101' when his fighter was hit by an incendiary round. He was forced to bail out into captivity.

Heavy losses continued through to year-end, despite the last 'Circus' (No. 110) having been flown on 8 November, when 17 Spitfires were lost to JG 2 and JG 26. By then JG 26 had been flying Fw 190As alongside its Bf 109Fs for several months and it would complete its full conversion to the fighter in the new year. JG 2 remained exclusively equipped with 'Friedrichs', however, and both units formed *Jabo Staffels* with Bf 109F-4/Bs in January 1942. They would attack English coastal targets and convoys throughout the year, running the gauntlet of flak batteries and also No. 91 Sqn (formerly No. 421 Flight) and its Spitfire VBs.

In March the RAF daylight offensive resumed with the advent of better weather. It was hoped that there would be more success and reduced losses due to the increased number of Spitfire squadrons now available and the faster and more capable Douglas Boston bombers supplied via lend-lease replacing the Blenheim IVs. Fighter Command was, however, still feeling the effects of 1941's heavy losses and the posting to the Mediterranean and the Far East of many of its experienced pilots. To make matters worse, the Jagdwaffe was now at its most effective both in terms of tactics and aircraft operated. The Fw 190 was in widespread service and those *Gruppen* still flying the 'Friedrich' were equipped with the Bf 109F-4 II, the ultimate F-model to reach the front line. The pilots of these aircraft had gained valuable experience at little cost to themselves during the aerial battles of 1941, enabling even average pilots to significantly improve their combat skills. As a result, RAF losses were again considerable. During April 1942 four Spitfires were being shot down for every German fighter destroyed. Fighter Command's situation had not improved by the end of June, by which time it had lost 265 aircraft for the destruction of 58 fighters since 8 March. Apart from its *Jabo Staffel* (10(J)/JG 26), JG 26 had by then been fully equipped with Fw 190As. In late July the unit also established 11(*Höhen*)/JG 26 to operate a small number of Bf 109G-1s that had been introduced to provide high-altitude interception of Allied bombers like the USAAF B-17 Flying Fortresses, which would appear over France the following month, and also cover the altitude-limited Fw 190s. JG 2 would follow a similar path, although its final F-4s – serving with I.*Gruppe* – would not be fully replaced by Fw 190s until the end of June. The *Jagdgeschwader* also had a *Jabo Staffel* (10(J)./JG 2) and high-altitude unit 11(*Höhen*)./JG 2 equipped with Bf 109s into 1943.

It is difficult to say with any certainty when a Bf 109F last fought a Spitfire V on the Channel Front. JG 2 suffered its final combat Bf 109F losses on 5 June, when three F-4s were downed by Spitfire VBs from Nos. 72 and 133 Sqns. Part of the Biggin Hill Wing, these units had caught elements of JG 2 climbing away from JG 26's base at Abbeville and heading for Le Havre. The pilots involved claimed three Messerschmitts destroyed and two probables. It would appear that the last JG 26 'Friedrich' to be downed by a Spitfire fell four days later, when a lone Bf 109F-4/B *Jabo* was intercepted by a No. 131 Sqn Mk VB while searching for shipping off Selsey Bill at dusk. From then on, aside from the occasional encounter with a Bf 109G-1, Spitfire units would be exclusively fighting the Fw 190A well into 1943.

Despite his natural ebullience, Hauptmann Hans 'Assi' Hahn was an outstanding fighter pilot and tactician. Under his leadership, III./JG 2 became one of the most successful of the Channel Front *Jagdgruppen*. Hahn would be credited with 26 Spitfires while flying the Bf 109F with III./JG 2. (EN Archive)

Two of Oberst Adolf Galland's three specially modified Bf 109Fs were on display during his change-of-command ceremony on 5 December 1941, which was unexpectedly attended by Hermann Göring. The Reichsmarschall is seen here at top right paying tribute to Galland's leadership and to the success of his *Geschwader*. Galland claimed 13 victories with his trio of 'specials'. (EN Archive)

ANALYSIS

Following Fighter Command's success in the Battle of Britain, the popular conception among the Allies at the time was that the Hurricane and, in particular, the Spitfire were vastly superior to the Bf 109E. The fallacy behind this belief was glaringly exposed during the Channel Front offensive of 1941–42, although misleading statistics on the number of Luftwaffe fighters shot down during this period masked that fact during the war. Close study of German losses reveals that Fighter Command's over-claiming had started in May 1940 when RAF pilots claimed to have shot down three times as many aircraft over Dunkirk as they had actually destroyed. Despite bellicose national newspaper headlines during the Battle of Britain, RAF fighter losses had, in fact, been substantially higher than Bf 109 losses.

The bulk of the victories claimed by the Jagdwaffe in 1941–42 were credited to JG 2 and JG 26, which were the sole fighter units remaining on the Channel Front from early June 1941. By any measure, their record for this period is an impressive one. The confirmed claims for all *Jagdgeschwader* in the West in 1941 totalled about 950 aircraft, with the bulk of victories credited to JG 2 and JG 26. For the second half of the year these two units rarely had more than 150 serviceable fighters at their disposal at any one time. Yet according to Fighter Command, it lost 849 fighters that year, thus proving that the *Jagdfliegers'* claims were reasonably accurate. British claims, conversely, were optimistic to say the least. Fighter pilots received confirmation for 775 victories during 1941, while Jagdwaffe records reveal that actual losses from all causes during the year totalled 236. Only 103 of

Major Walter Oesau, *Kommodore* of JG 2, poses with three of the unit's high-scoring aces. From left to right: Leutnant Egon Mayer, *Staffelkapitän* of 7./JG 2; Oesau; Oberleutnant Rudolf Pflanz (*Geschwader* Technical Officer); and Oberleutnant Erich Leie (*Geschwader* Adjutant). Mayer, Pflanz and Leie had all been awarded the Knight's Cross on 1 August 1941 for passing the 20-victory mark. Between them these four pilots claimed an astonishing 117 Spitfire II/Vs shot down in 1941–42. (EN Archive)

these aircraft were destroyed in combat, reflecting the fact that the Bf 109 was notoriously difficult to handle during take-off and landing, particularly on the austere airfields of northern France.

The RAF first got an inkling that its pilots were not perhaps downing as many aircraft as they were claiming during the interrogation of Hauptmann Rolf Pingel, *Kommandeur* of I./JG 26, who was captured after force-landing his Bf 109F-2 near Deal, Kent, on 10 July 1941. A 27-victory ace (who had scored six of his kills in Spain), Pingel told his interrogators that he was pleased the RAF was now operating over France as many German aviators had been lost when they bailed out over England or the Channel. Now, if they were forced to take to their parachutes, they were coming down in friendly territory. He also stated that more than 100 RAF aircraft had been downed over France since the beginning of the year, with German losses totalling between one-fifth and one-third of this number. His own I./JG 26 had claimed close to 50 victories for the loss of just eight pilots. When Pingel was told that Fighter Command had claimed 125 Bf 109s downed in the previous six months, he replied that such losses would have wiped out half the available fighter strength in France. Furthermore, the Jagdwaffe would have been hard pressed to make good such attrition. This explained why JG 2 and JG 26 were still able to oppose the bombing raids in strength – something that had mystified the RAF.

Following the German invasion of the Soviet Union on 22 June 1941, the British had been encouraged by their new communist allies to step up the RAF's offensive over France in an attempt to force the Luftwaffe to transfer fighters from the Eastern Front to combat the RAF's daylight raids.

Overleaf

On 8 November 1941 the RAF mounted its last 'Circus' (No. 110) of the year, and Fighter Command suffered heavy losses in its defence of Blenheim IV bombers at the heart of the operation. No fewer than 15 Spitfire VBs and one Mk IIA were lost to enemy fighters. Among the victors was Hauptmann Josef 'Pips' Priller, *Staffelkapitän* of 1./JG 26, who claimed his 57th and 58th successes when he engaged Spitfires northeast of Calais. Piloting one of them was the high scoring ace Flt Lt Keith 'Bluey' Truscott. Both pilots bailed out over the Channel and were rescued east of Ramsgate. German losses consisted of two Fw 190s destroyed and one pilot killed and three more aircraft damaged. (Artwork by Gareth Hector, © Osprey Publishing)

Hauptmann Rolf Pingel, *Kommandeur* of I./JG 26, provided a series of revelations to his interrogators after he crash-landed his Bf 109F-2 near Deal on 10 July 1941. The 27-victory ace was almost certainly brought down by return fire from the Stirling bomber he had chased back across the Channel. (John Weal)

Pingel's statements during his interrogation clearly showed that the Allies had failed to achieve this, and also that he considered the supposedly weak German opposition in France to be a great temptation for the RAF to maintain its high tempo of operations and so lose more pilots.

Despite Pingel's revelations, Fighter Command kept up its Non-Stop Offensive throughout July, flying 525 sorties (including 400 on 'Circus' operations) and claiming 185 enemy aircraft destroyed. The cost was 97 pilots killed, captured or missing. Another 98 were lost the following month.

The topic of over-claiming was examined by historian Norman Franks in his book *Fighter Command's Air War 1941*:

RAF fighter pilots could claim an enemy aircraft destroyed, probably destroyed or damaged. If confirmed as destroyed it had to have been witnessed by an independent person and seen to crash, crash in flames, break up in the air, or the pilot take to his parachute. If it merely fell or spun away out of sight trailing smoke or flame but was not actually seen to crash, blow up or its pilot bail out, then it was a probable. Even if the victorious pilot reported it had crashed but had no witnesses to the event, the squadron intelligence officer could only give credit for a probable, although it became obvious that certain pilots – those with a track record for shooting down enemy machines – were often given credit.

The German pilots had similar categories of victory credits, especially the confirmation by another pilot or ground observer. However, neither side, obviously, kept to these rules, as witnessed by the number of claims and credits against actual losses. It was generally a case of the head seeing what the eye did not. If a pilot was convinced that his opponent had been destroyed, even if he had to admit to himself he had not actually seen it, he might easily report it destroyed because he could not believe it could have survived the damage he had inflicted.

The problem of speed also contributed to over-confidence in claiming a victory. A pilot could have fired at an opponent and then taken his eyes from it to check his own safety, before looking back and seeing what he assumed to be the aircraft he had just attacked crash. The speed of combat meant that a pilot very quickly exited the immediate combat zone. It was this more than anything else, especially in a fight where there were several aircraft of both sides involved, that one falling aircraft could become the 'victory' of several pilots. And if an aircraft was seen to fall into the sea or crash several thousand feet below, it was easy to say that it was a German aircraft when, in fact, it might well have been a British one.

Fighter Command's propensity for over-claiming decreased somewhat in 1942, while the Jagdwaffe's force levels remained much the same as they had done the previous year. The RAF continued with its daylight offensive, allowing JG 2 and JG 26 to claim 972 victories during the course of the year. Fighter Command's losses totalled 915 aircraft. The RAF, however, claimed 560 German fighters destroyed on the Channel Front, but only 272 aircraft were actually lost to all causes, not just combat.

LEADING Bf 109F SPITFIRE II/V KILLERS			
	Victories	Final Score	Unit(s)
Oblt Siegfried Schnell	40	83	4. and 9./JG 2
Oblt Rudolf Pflanz	38	52	Stab. and I./JG 2
Oblt Egon Mayer	37	102	7./JG 2
Hptm Josef Priller	36	100	1./JG 26
Hptm Johann Schmid	32	40	Stab. and 8./JG 26
Obslt Adolf Galland	28	100	Stab. JG 26
Oblt Erich Leie	28	121	Stab. JG 2
Hptm Hans Hahn	26	105	III./JG 2
Ltn Erich Rudorffer	18	219	2. and 6./JG 2
OFw Josef Wurmheller	17	103	5./JG 53 and I. and II./JG 2

LEADING SPITFIRE II/V Bf 109F KILLERS			
	Victories	Final Score	Unit(s)
Wg Cdr 'Paddy' Finucane	13 (+2sh)	26 (+6sh)	Nos. 452 and 602 Sqns
Wg Cdr 'Jamie' Rankin	12	17 (+5sh)	No. 92 Sqn and Biggin Hill Wing
Wg Cdr 'Sailor' Malan	9	27 (+7sh)	No. 74 Sqn and Biggin Hill Wing
Sqn Ldr 'Bluey' Truscott	9	14	No. 452 Sqn
Wg Cdr 'Micky' Robinson	8	16	No. 609 Sqn and Biggin Hill Wing
Wg Cdr Douglas Bader	6	20 (+4sh)	Tangmere Wing
Sqn Ldr Jean-Francis Demozay	6	18	No. 91 Sqn
Flg Off Don Kingaby	5	21 (+2sh)	No. 92 Sqn
Flg Off Adolf Pietrasiak	5	7 (+4sh)	Nos. 92 and 308 Sqns
Flg Off 'Johnnie' Johnson	4 (+2sh)	34 (+7sh)	Nos. 616 and 610 Sqns

AFTERMATH

Although all Bf 109Fs had disappeared from front-line units on the Channel Front by the autumn of 1942, the Spitfire VB would soldier on with Fighter Command well into 1944. Indeed, the better performing Spitfire IX had started to roll off the production line in mid-1942, yet the venerable Mk V still dominated Fighter Command's order of battle in the summer of 1943. By then the less than effective 'Circus' operations were a thing of the past, having been replaced by 'Ramrod' missions – an attack by a large force of bombers or fighter-bombers expressly tasked with destroying targets. The specific role of escorting fighters on such missions was to protect the bombers from the Jagdwaffe. No fewer than 18 of the 32 Spitfire squadrons which supported 'Ramrod S.36' on 6 September 1943 were flying Mk Vs.

The fighter was outclassed at high altitude – the domain of the Bf 109G, increasing numbers of which were appearing in the West by the summer of 1943 – but the low-altitude-optimized Spitfire LF V remained a formidable opponent below 6,000ft. With its 'M' series Merlin engine equipped with a cropped supercharger impeller, it was as fast as an Fw 190A at this altitude and faster than a Bf 109G.

As previously noted, a small number of pressurized Bf 109G-1s had been issued to both JG 2 and JG 26 in July 1942 just as the last of the 'Friedrichs' were being replaced by Fw 190As. The arrival of the high-altitude Messerschmitts coincided with the escalation of daylight raids by B-17 and B-24 heavy bombers of the US Eighth Air Force. The Luftwaffe high command was not slow to realize that the USAAF would pose a

Perhaps caught at the wrong moment, an unusually sombre Oberleutnant Josef Priller, *Staffelkapitän* of 1./JG 26, peers from the cockpit of his Bf 109F-4 as a groundcrewman helps him prepare for his next sortie from St Omer-Clairmarais sometime in the autumn of 1941. Like all of Priller's fighters, this 'Friedrich' carries his personal insignia below the cockpit: an ace-of-hearts bearing his wife's name, Jutta. Priller would claim 36 Spitfire II/Vs destroyed with the Bf 109F in 1941. (John Weal)

serious threat once its strength had built up at bases in eastern England and sufficient high-flying escort fighters (albeit then still lacking in range for deep-penetration missions) had been shipped in from the USA. Although the well-armed Fw 190s then in service on the Channel Front were ideal anti-bomber platforms, the fighter's performance degraded sharply at high altitude. What was needed was a purpose-built interceptor to engage the bombers en route to their targets. Just such a fighter was about to enter service – the Bf 109G-4.

Before 1942 was out, both JG 2 and JG 26 were operating a mix of Fw 190As and Bf 109G-4s. Eventually, II/JG 2 and III/JG 26 would totally re-equip with the 'Gustav', the Messerschmitt fighter remaining with these *Gruppen* until the final months of the war when they converted to the Fw 190D-9.

Throughout 1943 and the early months of 1944, while still expected to challenge the RAF's sweeps into the airspace over northwest Europe, the Bf 109G pilots of II./JG 2 and III./JG 26 would find themselves increasingly opposing the USAAF 'heavies' and their P-38 Lightning, P-47 Thunderbolt and P-51 Mustang escorts. In effect, these two *Gruppen* formed the first line of defence in what was developing into the Battle of the Reich.

How many mechanics does it take to push a 'Gustav'? Eight, if this photograph is anything to go by. 5./JG 2's Bf 109G-6 'Black 12' would be lost in action on 20 October 1943. Both JG 2 and JG 26 were operating a mix of Fw 190As and Bf 109G-4s by the end of 1942. Eventually, II./JG 2 and III./JG 26 would totally re-equip with the 'Gustav', and later the Fw 190D-9. (John Weal)

PART II

BY EDWARD M. YOUNG

HELL IN THE PACIFIC

F4F Wildcat vs A6M Zero-sen

Rarely in the annals of air combat has a fighter made such a sudden and dramatic impact as the Mitsubishi Zero-sen in the first few months of the Pacific War. Arriving seemingly out of nowhere, the Type 0 Carrier Fighter (A6M2 Reisen, or Zero-sen in English) of the Imperial Japanese Navy Air Force swept all before it as the armed forces of Imperial Japan rampaged through Southeast Asia and the Pacific. To the astonishment of their pilots, the fighters of the American, British and Dutch air and naval forces – Curtiss P-40s and Hawk 75s, Brewster Buffaloes and Hawker Hurricanes – were roughly handled and pushed aside in the overwhelming tide of Japanese conquest.

The Zero-sen fighters of the IJNAF's carrier- and land-based *kokutai* (air groups) rapidly established air superiority wherever they encountered Allied fighters, appearing to be almost invincible. Fast, well armed, highly manoeuvrable, with exceptional range and climbing ability, and flown by skilled and experienced pilots, the Zero-sen's appearance and performance came as a distinct shock. Indeed, its dominance during the first year of the Pacific War would become legendary. Over time the Zero-sen would become as iconic an aeroplane for the Japanese as the Spitfire was for the British. The extent of the West's rude awakening was due in no small measure to the disparity between the Western view of Japan and Japanese technological abilities, and the Zero-sen's superlative performance. Prior to the outbreak of the war, Western views of Japan's aviation industry were dismissive and wrapped in racial stereotypes. It was widely believed that Japanese aeroplanes were decidedly inferior to their Western counterparts, as were Japanese aircrews. Few observers gave the Japanese any credit for originality or independent invention.

An article in the March 1941 edition of British aviation magazine *The Aeroplane* stated that, 'The Japanese are, by nature, imitators and lack originality. Japanese aviation has, therefore, a long way to go before it will be able to compete successfully with, or even combat, the "decadent European and American democracies".' An American aviation writer commented in a similar vein that the Japanese 'have not yet gotten much beyond merely imitating what others have done. At that they are the World's finest, but imitativeness is little help in aeronautics'. And yet, in its March 1939 Information Bulletin on the conflict then raging in China, the US Navy's Office of Intelligence had warned against this very complacency.

Crewmen wait for the signal to remove the chocks from Type 0 Model 21s on the deck of a carrier in early 1942. (Edward M. Young Collection)

'No possible benefits can be derived,' the report read, 'from underestimating their war-making powers on the land, on the sea or in the air.' Yet the Western powers badly underestimated Japan's capabilities, to their cost.

The Japanese surprise attack on Pearl Harbor on 7 December 1941 made it inevitable that there would be battles between the aircraft carrier forces of the IJNAF and the US Navy. This was a battle that both sides had expected, planned for and trained for. In the carrier battles that took place during 1942, the premier carrier fighters of the two navies, the Japanese Type 0 Carrier Fighter and the US Navy's Grumman F4F Wildcat, came into confrontation. This confrontation continued as land-based Zero-sen units and US Marine Corps and Navy Wildcats joined in furious air battles over Guadalcanal.

The duel between the Zero-sen and the Wildcat is a classic example of the challenge a pilot faces when dealing with an adversary flying a more capable aircraft. The Zero-sen was, in many respects, superior to the Wildcat. The Japanese fighter had a better rate-of-climb, was faster and was far more manoeuvrable. It could out-climb, out-turn and be on the tail of a Wildcat in a heartbeat. The encounters between the Zero-sen and the Wildcat at the battles of the Coral Sea and Midway demonstrated the Japanese fighter's superiority in no uncertain terms.

The US Navy and Marine Corps pilots flying the Wildcat during 1942 had to develop tactics that exploited the few advantages (more rugged construction and superior armament) the Grumman fighter had over the Zero-sen, while negating the Mitsubishi's advantage in manoeuverability. Fortunately for America, these tactics did emerge in time. Building on the lessons Lt Cdr James Flatley distilled from his experiences during the Battle of the Coral Sea, US Navy and Marine Corps Wildcat pilots learned

An F4F-4 Wildcat taxis in after returning from a mission over Guadalcanal in late 1942. The stalwart F4F was the principal fighter of the US Navy and the US Marine Corps throughout the first year of the Pacific War. (NARA)

to adopt hit-and-run attacks against the Zero-sen. They also avoided low-speed manoeuvering combat, where the Japanese fighter excelled. Finally, US Navy and Marine Corps pilots took advantage of the Zero-sen's greatest weaknesses – its lack of protection for fuel and pilot, which meant that the aeroplane was unable to absorb damage.

Lt Cdr John 'Jimmy' Thach developed a defensive weaving manoeuvre that enabled two pilots or two sections to provide mutual support to each other when under attack. Successfully tested at Midway, this manoeuvre came to be called the 'Thach Weave' and was used against the Zero-sen throughout the war. This combination of defensive and offensive tactics enabled US Navy and Marine Corps Wildcat pilots to inflict heavy losses on the IJNAF's Zero-sen units during the grueling battle of attrition over Guadalcanal.

When the IJNAF attacked Pearl Harbor the United States was not prepared for war. The US Congress had passed the Two-Ocean Navy Act in July 1940, approving the construction of 18 new aircraft carriers and authorizing 15,000 aircraft for the US Navy and the Marine Corps, but it would take time for the carriers and aeroplanes to be built and to train the men to man them. Newer and more powerful fighter aeroplanes were under development – the Vought XF4U Corsair and the Grumman XF6F, for example – but these, too, were by no means ready when America was attacked. The US Navy and the Marine Corps went to war with the Grumman F4F Wildcat, the best carrier fighter available at the time.

Bronzed and gaunt Marine TSgt R. W. Greenwood was plane captain for this F4F-4 Wildcat on Guadalcanal. Flown by multiple pilots, the aeroplane miraculously survived to claim 19 victories over Japanese aircraft. (NARA)

Groundcrew from a land-based fighter *kokutai* wave off a pilot of a Zero Model 21 in early 1942. (Edward M. Young Collection)

Naval Aviators flying the Wildcat, and their compatriots in the US Army Air Forces, had to hold the line against the Japanese onslaught until America's vast industrial capacity could produce the newer and better weapons needed to defeat Japan. Knowing that it faced a much stronger enemy, Japan's strategy was to fight America to exhaustion and hopefully inflict a decisive defeat as quickly as possible. Grumman's Wildcat fighter helped derail the Japanese plan.

THE MACHINES
Grumman F4F Wildcat

In the mid-1930s, the US Navy began the transition from the biplane to the monoplane. The streamlined, all-metal, stressed skin monoplane with enclosed cockpit, flaps and retractable landing gear, with engines of increasing horsepower, pointed to a future where performance would considerably surpass the biplane.

During 1934, the US Navy's Bureau of Aeronautics awarded contracts for prototypes of a new all-metal monoplane torpedo-bomber, the Douglas XTBD-1, and for new monoplane dive-bombers, with contracts for the Brewster XSBA-1, Northrop XBT-1 and Vought XSB2U-1. A year later, in August 1935, the Bureau sent out a request for a competitive design of a new single-seat fighter. The Bureau informed the manufacturers that it wanted to continue development of high-performance fighters, and requested that the designs submitted have the maximum performance possible. This meant a top speed exceeding 250mph within restrictions of size and weight, and a stalling speed of not more than 65mph. The Bureau appears not to have

An F4F-3 from VF-6 prepares to take off from USS *Enterprise* (CV-6) in early 1942. Note the 100lb bomb beneath the fighter's starboard wing. (NARA)

specified a preference for a monoplane or a biplane, and stated that folding wings were 'not necessary or desirable'. The request for higher maximum speeds reflected the Bureau's concern at the time that the speed margin between the latest monoplane bombers and biplane fighters was declining. The US Navy's then-current fighters, the Curtiss BF2C-1 and the Grumman F2F-1, had a less than 20mph speed advantage over the US Army Air Corps' Martin B-10 bomber, and the newer Grumman F3F-1, ordered that summer, was no better. That same August the Seversky SEV-1, precursor of the Seversky P-35, achieved a top speed of 284mph in tests for the USAAC at Wright Field – well in excess of the BF2C and the F3F. Hedging its bets after reviewing preliminary design submissions, the Bureau of Aeronautics purchased an experimental monoplane from the Brewster Aeronautical Corporation and a more conservative biplane from the Grumman Aircraft Corporation in November 1935.

Founded in 1929 by Leroy Grumman, the Grumman Aircraft Corporation had won a contract in 1931 for its first US Navy carrier fighter, the two-seat FF-1 biplane. The single-seat F2F-1 followed in 1934, the portly fighter replacing the older Boeing F4B aboard US Navy carriers and establishing Grumman as the leading manufacturer of American carrier fighters. Flight tests on the similar but improved Grumman F3F-1 had begun during 1935, providing a starting point for the US Navy's design request issued in August. On 2 March 1936, Grumman was awarded a contract for its proposal, the XF4F-1. The company had submitted a design for a biplane fighter – basically a refinement of its F3F-1, but with a more powerful 800hp Pratt & Whitney or Wright engine, giving an estimated top speed of 264mph. The aircraft was armed with single 0.30in. and 0.50in. machine guns in the nose.

Two developments soon made the success of this proposal doubtful. Grumman's engineers had calculated that equipping its F3F-1 with the 950hp Wright XR-1820 Cyclone engine would push its top speed to over 255mph – close to the estimate for the XF4F-1. Then in June 1936 the US Navy awarded a contract to Brewster for the XF2A-1 monoplane fighter. Grumman duly abandoned the XF4F-1, with the US Navy's concurrence, and submitted a completely new design for a monoplane fighter designated the XF4F-2. Following a review of detailed design drawings, wind tunnel tests on a scale model and inspection of a mock-up, Grumman received a contract on 28 July 1936 for this new aeroplane.

The XF4F-2 retained the XF4F-1's retractable landing gear and cockpit location, the latter giving the pilot good visibility over the nose for both landing and gunnery. Grumman placed the new monoplane wing at mid-fuselage. The US Navy wanted the newly developed Pratt & Whitney XR-1830-66 engine fitted in one of its experimental fighters, so Grumman obliged accordingly. The XR-1830 was a 14-cylinder, two-row engine with single-stage supercharger, offering 1,050hp on take-off and 900hp at 9,000ft, with the possibility of even more power with further development. Grumman engineers estimated that this engine would give the XF4F-2 a top speed of 290mph.

Interestingly, in light of its future battles with the cannon-armed Mitsubishi A6M Type 0 Carrier Fighter, the US Navy requested the capability of mounting two 20mm cannon in the wings of the XF4F-2 in addition to two 0.50in. machine guns in the nose, synchronized to fire

A Grumman F3F-3 from VF-5. Grumman engineers found that when fitted with the more powerful 950hp Wright XR-1820 Cyclone radial engine, the F3F-3's top speed would be close to that of the biplane XF4F-1 – its intended replacement! (NARA)

through the propeller. However, the initial armament fitted to the prototype consisted of only the two 0.50in. machine guns in the nose, with the provision for two more 0.50in. weapons mounted in the wings. At the insistence of front-line units in the Fleet, which at the time wanted fighters that were also capable of dive-bombing, the XF4F-2 featured mountings for two 100lb bombs under the wings.

The XF4F-2 made its first flight on 2 September 1937 at Grumman's plant at Bethpage, Long Island. It was subsequently sent to Naval Air Station (NAS) Anacostia, on the outskirts of Washington, DC, where the fighter commenced official US Navy trials alongside the Brewster XF2A-1 and the Seversky NF-1 (a navalized equivalent to the USAAC's P-35). The testing programme lasted into April 1938 and included a thorough evaluation of the flight characteristics and armament of each of the three aeroplanes.

Problems with the Pratt & Whitney engine hampered testing of the XF4F-2, causing one serious accident when the engine cut out shortly after take-off from the Naval Aircraft Factory in Philadelphia, where the aeroplane had been conducting catapult tests and simulated carrier landings. Despite having a higher speed than the XF2A-1, the US Navy decided in June 1938 to place a contract with Brewster for 54 production versions of the XF2A-1.

The US Navy, however, was sufficiently impressed with the potential of Grumman's entry to continue its development. In October 1938 Grumman received a contract for a revised XF4F-3. The new fighter incorporated the heavier, but more powerful Pratt & Whitney XR-1830-76 engine, with a two-stage, two-speed supercharger providing 1,200hp for take-off, 1,050hp at 11,000ft and 1,000hp at 19,000ft.

The revised Grumman XF4F-2. With the US Navy's concurrence, Grumman abandoned the biplane XF4F-1 design for a revised monoplane fighter. The XF4F-2 had an armament of two 0.50in. machine guns in the nose, with the provision for two more in the wings. (NARA)

Grumman increased the wingspan from 34ft to 38ft and added square tips to the wing, the horizontal stablizers and the vertical tail. The larger wing brought the XF4F-3's wing loading with the heavier engine back to within acceptable limits.

The XF4F-3 made its first flight on 12 February 1939 and then began six months of intensive flight tests at Bethpage and Anacostia. With the newer engine and supercharger, the XF4F-3 achieved a maximum speed of 333.5mph during the US Navy tests. In July, the US Navy's Bureau of Inspection and Survey, which had completed flight tests on the XF4F-3, recommended that the Grumman fighter be accepted as a service type, despite a conclusion that the fighter was longitudinally and laterally inadequate in landing. Accordingly, the following month, after nearly two years of effort, the US Navy awarded Grumman a contract for 54 F4F-3 fighters.

In late 1939 the XF4F-3 went to the National Advisory Committee for Aeronautics' full-scale wind tunnel at Langley, Virginia, where tests led to several aerodynamic refinements to improve the stability issues. The area of the vertical tail was increased and moved slightly back, increasing the length of the XF4F-3 by 19 inches, while the tailplanes were raised 20 inches to the base of the tail fin. An extended turtledeck was also added between the tail fin and the cockpit, giving a smoother contour.

The first production F4F-3 made its maiden flight in February 1940. The first two aircraft had an armament of two 0.30in. machine guns in the nose and a single 0.50in. machine gun in each wing, but all subsequent F4F-3s had the nose-mounted weapons removed in favour of two additional 0.50in. machine guns in each wing. Armour plating was also fitted, but at this time the F4F-3 did not have self-sealing fuel tanks.

The first deliveries of production F4F-3s were not to the US Navy but to the Royal Navy's Fleet Air Arm, which had taken over a French order for 100 Wright Cyclone-powered aircraft after the fall of France in June 1940. Placed into service as the Martlet I, these aeroplanes achieved the Grumman fighter's first aerial victory when a Luftwaffe Ju 88 bomber was shot down on Christmas Day 1940. The first production F4F-3 for the US Navy, BuNo 1845, arrived at Anacostia on 20 August 1940. Deliveries to front-line squadrons began during December 1940 when VF-4, assigned to the air group embarked in USS *Ranger* (CV-4), and VF-7, aboard USS *Wasp* (CV-7), received their first aeroplanes.

The F4F soon demonstrated a clear superiority over the F2A, becoming the US Navy's choice for its fighter squadrons. Following the fall of France, the US Congress approved a substantial increase in appropriations for US Navy aircraft carriers and aeroplanes through the Two-Ocean Navy Act. Grumman received production orders for more F4Fs, ending the year with contracts covering the construction of 578 examples.

Concerned with persistent difficulties with the R-1830-76's two-stage supercharger, the US Navy had an F4F-3 fitted with a single-stage, two-speed supercharged Pratt & Whitney R-1830-90 engine in the autumn of 1940. Although the re-engined fighter (designated the XF4F-6) handled in the same way, it now had a lower maximum speed of 319mph. As a precaution against delays with the two-stage supercharged engine, the US Navy ordered 95 R-1830-90-powered fighters, re-designated F4F-3As. Thirty were assigned to a Greek order, but they were diverted to the Fleet Air Arm as Martlet IIIs following the capture of Greece by Axis forces in the spring of 1941. The remaining 65 were allocated to US Navy and US Marine Corps fighter squadrons. As more F4F-3s and the F4F-3As became available during 1941, they went to US Navy and US Marine Corps fighter squadrons on both the east and west coasts. Some squadrons operated a mix of both aircraft.

On 1 October 1941 the US Navy announced that it was giving names to many of its warplanes. The Grumman F4F duly becoming the 'Wildcat', the first in a long line of Grumman feline names. At the time of the attack on Pearl Harbor, eight US Navy squadrons (VF-3, VF-5, VF-6, VF-8, VF-41, VF-42, VF-71 and VF-72) and three US Marine Corps squadrons

Opposite
During his time on Guadalcanal, VMF-223's Capt Marion Carl flew two Wildcats that bore the side number black '13'. He scored 12 victories flying his first '13', BuNo 02100, depicted here. Remarkably, Carl was at the controls of this aircraft on 9 September 1942 when, on his 13th mission, a Zero-sen shot him down just after he had claimed his 13th victory! Bailing out at 22,000ft, Carl landed in the sea off Guadalcanal, from where he was rescued by a local. (Artwork by Jim Laurier, © Osprey Publishing)

F4F-4 WILDCAT

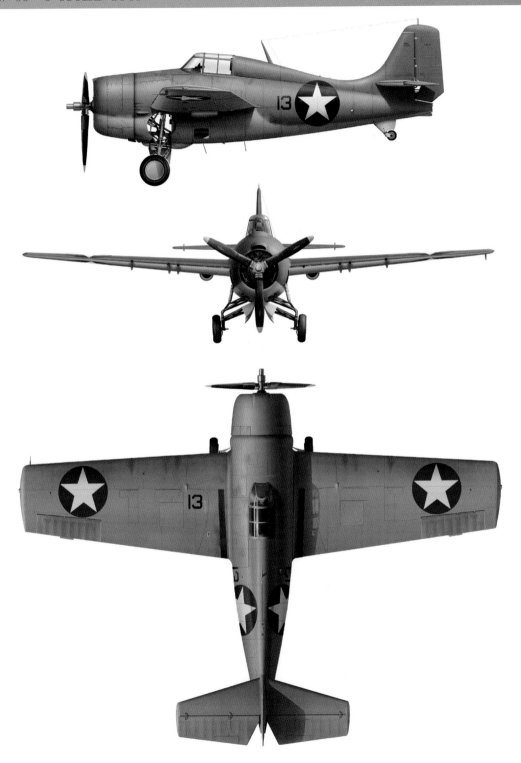

(VMF-111, VMF-121 and VMF-211) were equipped with the Wildcat, with Grumman having delivered 183 F4F-3s and 65 F4F-3As.

The Grumman-built Wildcat variant that saw the most combat service, the F4F-4, was developed following the US Navy's interest in acquiring a folding-wing version of the fighter so that it could embark more aircraft on a carrier. In March 1940 the company developed a folding-wing mechanism and installed it in an F4F-3. Legend has it that Grumman engineers worked out the concept using a rubber eraser and paper clips. The folding-wing section, attached to two stubs connected to the fuselage, allowed the outer wings to be pivoted back against the fuselage, thus reducing the span from 38ft to a little over 14ft. The aeroplane made its first flight as the XF4F-4 on 14 April 1941. At first the folding-wing mechanism was hydraulic, but to save weight the hydraulic system was removed and the wings folded manually. The US Navy added an additional 0.50in. machine gun in each of the XF4F-4's wings.

The first F4F-4s appear to have been assigned to VF-71 on board *Wasp* in February 1942, followed by VF-8 on board USS *Hornet* (CV-8), both carriers then serving with the Atlantic Fleet. By the end of May 1942, most of the US Navy's fighter squadrons, and two Marine Corps squadrons, had converted to the F4F-4. During the course of that year Grumman would deliver 1,164 F4F-4s to the US Navy and the US Marine Corps.

Mitsubishi A6M Type 0 Carrier Fighter (Zero-sen)

On 5 October 1937, the IJN's Koku Hombu (Aviation Bureau) sent its 'Planning Requirements for the Prototype 12-shi Carrier-based Fighter' to the Mitsubishi Kokuki K. K. (Mitsubishi Aircraft Company Ltd) and the Nakajima Hikoki K. K. (Nakajima Aeroplane Company Ltd). This document listed the final design requirements for a fighter aeroplane to replace the Mitsubishi A5M Type 96 Carrier Fighter then on active service in China.

Five months earlier, the Koku Hombu had issued its preliminary requirement for a new carrier fighter, and had begun discussions with the two aircraft companies. Jiro Horikoshi, who had designed the A5M, participated in these conferences, and in the following months started working on some ideas for a new fighter. His A5M had been a quantum leap over its predecessor, the Nakajima A4N1 biplane fighter. An all-metal, semi-monocoque low-wing monoplane fighter with fixed landing gear, the A5M was faster and had a longer range than the A4N1, but was still highly manoeuvrable. At the time of its entry into service, the A5M was the first monoplane carrier fighter in service in any navy, and was without a doubt the finest carrier fighter in the world. The IJNAF was now asking Mitsubishi and Nakajima to make another quantum leap in fighter design.

In the months between May and October 1937, the IJNAF had entered combat over China in what became known as the Sino-Japanese 'Incident'. As the Koku Hombu worked to refine its requirements for a new carrier fighter, the bureau benefited from combat reports coming in from units on the China front. Perhaps the most influential of these concerned heavy losses sustained by the IJNAF's Mitsubishi G3M Type 96 Attack Bombers during unescorted bombing missions. Entering combat in mid-September, the Type 96 Carrier Fighter and its skilled pilots quickly established air superiority over the Chinese fighters they encountered, allowing the bombers to attack targets with impunity.

Although enjoying great success over China when engaging enemy fighters, A5M pilots found it difficult to knock down Chinese bombers with the Type 96's two 7.7mm machine guns. Recommendations began coming in to the Koku Hombu calling for a fighter with greater range, heavier armament and even better performance in speed and altitude. These coincided with the IJNAF's own evolving view of the role of the carrier fighter from simple air defence over the fleet to acting as escort to a carrier strike force, clearing the skies of enemy fighters for the accompanying dive- and torpedo-bombers.

The requirements laid down in the planning document the Koku Hombu circulated in October called for an aeroplane with a performance equal to or better than any other fighter in the world. The IJNAF wanted a machine that had the range to escort its bombers all the way to their targets, with a combat performance superior to any enemy fighters it might encounter. But the IJNAF still needed a fighter that could defend the fleet against air attack with an armament powerful enough to defeat enemy bomber and attack aircraft. Specifically, the Planning Requirement called for the following:

The A6M Type 0 Carrier Fighter's large wing, low wing loading and long ailerons gave the Zero-sen exceptional manoeuvrability at low speeds, making carrier landings no more difficult than in the Type 96 fighter. (Edward M. Young Collection)

- A maximum speed in excess of 310mph
- Ability to climb to 9,800ft in 3 minutes, 30 seconds
- A range of 1,010 miles with a normal fuel load and 1,685 miles with an auxiliary drop tank
- Manoeuvrability equal to or better than the A5M Type 96 Fighter
- A wingspan of no more than 39ft 4in. (12 metres)
- Armament of two 20mm cannon in the wings and two 7.7mm machine guns in the nose
- Ability to take off in less than 230ft into a 30mph wind (essentially from a carrier deck)
- A landing speed of less than 67mph

Jori Horikoshi immediately realized that the IJNAF's individual requirements were incompatible with each other. To meet the range requirement, an escort fighter would have to carry a considerable amount of fuel in addition to the weight of the 20mm cannon, implying the need for a large, heavy aircraft with a large powerful engine, while an interceptor fighter needed to have an exceptional rate-of-climb and superlative manoeuvrability – performance only a lighter-weight aeroplane could achieve. As a Japanese aeronautical engineer described the challenge some years later, the Imperial Japanese Navy was asking for the aeronautical equivalent of an athlete with the endurance of a marathon runner, the speed of a sprinter, the powerful punch of a heavyweight boxer and the quick footwork of a welterweight. The Nakajima Company soon bowed out, leaving Jiro Horikoshi and his design team with the unenviable task of trying to make the impossible possible.

Horikoshi lacked a suitable engine for his new design. The weight, power, shape, fuel consumption and dimensions of the engine determined the shape of the fuselage and how much drag it created, as well as the fighter's weight, wing area and probable performance. Japanese aviation engine development lagged behind that of America and Europe, for in the 1930s Japan was still an industrializing nation. The machine tool and automotive industries – foundations for the production of aircraft engines – were small and comparatively less well developed. In its planning

Opposite

This A6M2 Zero-sen Model 21 belonged to the 3rd Kokutai, one of the IJNAF's leading land-based fighter units. During the fighting over Guadalcanal, this particular aircraft had been flown by two of the 3rd Kokutai's aces, namely Lt Takahide Aioi, who had claimed four victories fighting in China in the Type 96 Carrier Fighter, and PO2/c Yoshiro Hashiguchi, another China veteran. They were ultimately credited with around ten victories each.
(Artwork by Jim Laurier, © Osprey Publishing)

A6M2 ZERO-SEN MODEL 21

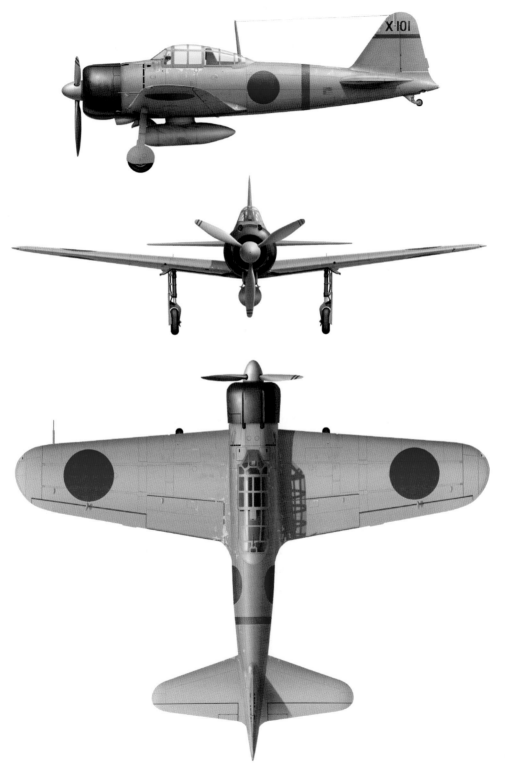

requirements the Koku Hombu had specified two engines for the new carrier fighter design, the Mitsubishi 'Zuisei' (Holy Star) and the Mitsubishi 'Kinsei' (Golden Star), both 14-cylinder, two-row radial engines. Horikoshi preferred the Kinsei-46 engine for his design, as its 1,070hp rating was superior to the Zuisei-13's rating of 870hp, but the Kinsei was heavier and had a larger diameter and higher fuel consumption than the Zuisei. This would have required a larger and heavier airframe to accommodate both the engine and more fuel. Using the Zuisei-13 instead, Horikoshi and his team calculated that they could build a fighter weighing around 5,000lb – some 1,600lb less than an aircraft equipped with a Kinsei-46.

Therein lay the source of the Zero-sen's superlative performance, but also its inherent flaw – vulnerability to combat damage. To fulfill the IJNAF's exacting requirements with an engine of around 900hp, Horikoshi and his team had to design as light an aeroplane as possible, yet still make it strong enough to stand up to the rigours of carrier operations. It also had to be capable of carrying sufficient fuel and armament to allow the aeroplane to function effectively as a fighter.

Weight reduction became the priority for the new aircraft, prevailing over concerns about ease of manufacturing or maintenance. Breaking with the traditional approach to structural strength, Horikoshi realized that not every part in the aeroplane had to conform to the IJNAF's standard safety factor of 1.8 times the expected maximum load. Wherever possible, the design team used a safety factor slightly below the 1.8 standard. To eliminate the heavy fittings normally used to attach the wing to the fuselage, the wing was designed as a single element running from the root to the tip, integral with the fuselage centre section.

Fortuitously, the Sumitomo Metal Company had just developed a new strong zinc-aluminum alloy, known as Extra Super Duralumin, which meant thinner sheets could be used for the fighter's skinning. Every single component of the new fighter was carefully evaluated for further weight reduction. Armament for the pilot and self-sealing fuel tanks were not considered due to weight restrictions, although the Zero-sen was not unique in this respect, as few of the world's fighter aircraft incorporated these protections at the time. The result was an aeroplane that was light in weight for its size, but not flimsy. Examining captured Zero-sens later in the war, American engineers were impressed that its strength compared favourably to American aeroplanes.

To provide the necessary manoeuvrability, Horikoshi designed a relatively large wing with a low wing loading, although this reduced the fighter's diving and level speeds. The larger wing allowed for the installation of the 20mm cannon and extra fuel tanks for added range. Horikoshi added a slight downward twist of the wing at the tip to delay the onset of wingtip stall, thereby improving lateral control and manoeuvrability. Each wing was also fitted with a long aileron. The fighter's excellent lateral stability made it easier to land on carrier decks. IJNAF pilots were to find the Zero-sen no more difficult to land than the earlier Type 96 fighter.

To make the fighter a better gun platform, the design team lengthened the fuselage and increased the area of the vertical and horizontal tail. The use of flush riveting and careful attention to aerodynamic refinement reduced drag, thereby improving speed and range. A streamlined drop tank (one of the first employed on a fighter) helped boost the range to meet the IJNAF's requirement, while wide retractable landing gear facilitated carrier landings. The new fighter incorporated a fully enclosed cockpit, with a streamlined canopy providing excellent vision all around.

The first flight of the Prototype 12-shi Carrier Fighter took place on 1 April 1939 from the airfield at Kagamigahara, 30 miles away from the Mitsubishi Aircraft Company factory in Nagoya. After making several ground runs to test the brakes, Mitsubishi's chief test pilot Kasuzo Shima took the aeroplane aloft on a short flight, travelling 1,500ft down the runway at 30ft before returning to report that all control surfaces operated effectively. The brakes fitted to the fighter were inadequate, however. With the first flight accomplished, Mitsubishi began an intensive flight programme to test the new fighter's stability and control.

On 1 May 1939, the Koku Hombu advised Horikoshi that the IJNAF intended to replace the Mitsubishi Zuisei-13 engine with the Nakajima 'Sakae' (Prosperity). The Sakae-12 was also a 14-cylinder radial engine offering 950hp, and it was only slightly larger in diameter than the Zuisei-13. First installed on the third prototype, the Sakae would power almost every model of the Zero-sen fighter until the final months of the war. At the same time the IJNAF designated the first and second prototypes of the 12-shi fighter the A6M1 and the Sakae-powered model the A6M2.

After completing tests with Mitsubishi, the first prototype was turned over to the IJNAF in September 1939, the second prototype following a month later. Flight tests had confirmed that in most respects the A6M1 fighter had met the IJNAF's specifications except for maximum speed. With the change to the Sakae engine, the A6M2 achieved a maximum speed of 331mph, exceeding the initial requirement. By any measure this outstanding fighter was a remarkable achievement for Jiro Horikoshi and his design team.

On 31 July 1940, the IJNAF formally accepted the Mitsubishi A6M2 as the Type 0 Carrier Fighter Model 11 (shortened to Reisen, or Zero-sen Fighter, in Japanese). The Type 0 designation was based on the year of introduction into service – 2600 (1940 AD) – according to the Japanese Imperial calendar.

Even before formal acceptance, the IJNAF Navy sent a small batch of 15 Zero-sens to China for operational testing with the 12th Kokutai, based at Hankow. When the first examples arrived at the airfield, cheers went up among the pilots and groundcrews as these exciting new fighters landed. The Type 96 pilots were in awe of the Zero-sen at first, with its enclosed cockpit, retractable landing gear and the impression it gave of speed and power. The few experienced pilots chosen to fly the A6M soon found it to be exceptional, easily outperforming the Type 96 fighter.

The Zero-sen formation flew its first mission on 19 August 1940, but the aeroplane did not engage Chinese fighters in combat until 13 September. Escorting Type 96 bombers to Chungking, the Zero-sen pilots returned to the city after the bombers had departed to find 30 Polikarpov I-15bis and I-16 fighters circling over the target area. In a ferocious ten-minute air battle the Japanese pilots claimed 27 Chinese fighters shot down.

By the end of 1940 pilots flying the Zero-sen had claimed 59 fighters shot down and an additional 101 destroyed on the ground, all for the loss of just three planes to anti-aircraft fire. The legend of the Zero-sen's invincibility originated with this performance in China.

To make the fighter an easier fit on the elevators of the IJN's aircraft carriers, Mitsubishi fitted folding wingtips beginning with the 65th production aircraft. This led to a change in designation, this and subsequent

A6M2 Type 0 Model 21 fighters running up on the deck of *Shokaku*, waiting for the carrier to turn into the wind so that they can take off for the attack on Pearl Harbor on 7 December 7, 1941. (NARA)

aircraft being designated the Type 0 Carrier Fighter Model 21. A more intractable problem was the emergence of aileron flutter, which caused the deaths of two pilots in accidents. The IJNAF had installed balancing tabs on the ailerons in an attempt to improve responsiveness at higher speeds, but this apparently contributed to the problem. Working intensively, Mitsubishi found a solution to the problem by thickening the outer wing skin, increasing the torsional strength of the wing and adding small external balances to it. Fortunately for the IJNAF, these fixes were in place before the start of the Pacific War.

The Zero-sen fighter demonstrated superlative performance at low to medium speeds and low to medium altitudes. The very elements that gave the aeroplane its superb low-speed manoeuvrability – its large wing with low wing loading and long ailerons – caused the Zero-sen to lose manoeuvrability as speeds increased. At speeds above 180mph aileron response became sluggish and at speeds above 230mph the controls stiffened considerably and aileron control became poor. While the Zero-sen had a high operational ceiling, engine power fell off at higher altitudes, and the aeroplane's light weight and thin skinning limited its diving speeds. Pilot reports from China recommended improving high-speed aileron control and altitude performance.

In mid-1941, Mitsubishi began testing a prototype of a new Zero-sen model, designated the A6M3, equipped with a more powerful Sakae 21 engine of 1,130hp. At the suggestion of test pilots, Mitsubishi eliminated the folding wing feature, shortening the wingspan by three feet, and installed blunt wingtips. This also reduced the length of the ailerons by about a foot, improving the rate of roll at higher speeds for a small loss in overall manoeuvrability. Although the gain in maximum speed was a disappointment (the A6M3 was only some 6–8mph faster than the A6M2), the new model entered production in early 1942 as the Type 0 Carrier Fighter Model 32 to indicate both a change in engine and a change in overall configuration.

By the time the IJNAF went to war on 7 December 1941, the A6M had replaced the older A5M in almost all of its fighter units. During 1941 the Mitsubishi Aircraft Company delivered 409 Zero-sens to the IJNAF. In an ironic turn, given its earlier withdrawal from the competition, the Nakajima Aircraft Company was also ordered to begin production of the Type 0 Fighter – the firm delivered its first aircraft to the IJNAF in November 1941.

On the first day of the Pacific War, the six aircraft carriers of the 1st Koku Kantai (1st Air Fleet) had more than 100 A6M2 fighters on strength, while the land-based 11th Koku Kantai deployed around 120 A6M2s in the 21st, 22nd and 23rd Koku Sentai (Air Flotillas), principally in the 3rd and Tainan Kokutai. The several hundred Zero-sen pilots available had been through a rigorous selection process, resulting in them being both highly trained and supremely confident in their ability. They were also acutely aware of the quality of their Zero-sen fighters. Many began the war with combat experience in China. They were, in all likelihood, the finest group of carrier fighter pilots in any navy in 1941.

TYPE HISTORY
The F4F Wildcat

XF4F-2

The XF4F-2 was an all-metal mid-wing monoplane with an Alclad stressed-skin covering over metal bulkheads and stringers. The wings featured a single main spar, with the outer panels attached to a centre section bolted to the fuselage. Flaps beneath the wings were pneumatically operated. The XF4F-2 retained the barrel-shaped fuselage, enclosed cockpit and rounded wingtips, vertical and horizontal stabilizers of the earlier F2F and F3F fighters, but it had a slightly wider span and longer fuselage. Ailerons, elevators and rudder were fabric covered.

The Grumman fighter featured what was for the time a heavy armament – two 0.50in. machine guns in the upper cowling of the fuselage and two more mounted in the wings. Alternatively, the wing guns could be replaced with mounts for a single 100lb bomb under each wing. Two Plexiglas windows were fitted into the fuselage beneath the wing to give some downward visibility. The landing gear was similar to the F2F/F3F, with main wheels retracting into the fuselage under the wings. The gear could be raised or lowered with 30 turns of a hand crank in the cockpit. The powerplant was the Pratt & Whitney XR-1830-66, a two-row, 14-cylinder, air-cooled radial engine with a single-stage, single-speed supercharger giving 1,050hp for take-off and 900hp at 12,000ft.

XF4F-3

The revised XF4F-3 featured an increase in wingspan from 34ft to 38ft and a lengthened fuselage, while retaining the overall shape of the XF4F-2. The wingtips, horizontal stabilizers and vertical fin and rudder took on the squared-off, rectangular form that became characteristic of Grumman's wartime aircraft. Flight and wind tunnel tests resulted in an increase in the area of the vertical fin, the addition of a dorsal fillet between the vertical fin and the top of the fuselage and a raised horizontal stabilizer.

For a brief period F4F-3 Wildcats wore the colourful pre-war markings that identified individual aircraft carriers. This F4F-3 from VF-42, with a red tail indicating its assignment to USS *Yorktown* (CV-5) and yellow wings, taxis out behind another F4F-3 from VF-7 painted in the duller light gray Neutrality camouflage scheme. (Peter M. Bowers Collection, Museum of Flight)

Armament changed to two cowl-mounted 0.30in. machine guns and two 0.50in. weapons in the wings. A more powerful Pratt & Whitney XR-1830-76 engine with a two-stage, two-speed supercharger replaced the earlier XR-1830-66, giving 1,200hp on take-off and 1,000hp at 19,000ft. With this engine the XF4F-3 attained a maximum speed of 334mph at 20,500ft, with a gross weight of 6,099lb.

F4F-3

The first two examples built of the first production model of the F4F fighter had the same armament as the XF4F-3, but all subsequent aircraft featured an armament of four 0.50in. machine guns in the wings with 430 rounds per gun. By the end of the 1930s the US Navy had realized that the 0.30in. weapon was outdated following the advent of all-metal aircraft and the introduction of armour and self-sealing fuel tanks. Fighters needed greater punch, so the US Navy abandoned the 0.30in. weapon in favour of a battery of 0.50in. machine guns. While the latter did not have the destructive power of the 20mm cannon, it did have a higher rate of fire and a higher muzzle velocity, giving it a longer range.

Early production aircraft had a telescopic sight protruding through the front windscreen, but this was later replaced with a N2AN reflector gunsight as these became available. Like the XF4F-3, the production aircraft had non-folding wings. The F4F-3 was equipped with the Pratt & Whitney R-1830-76 engine or the similar R-1830-86. When the F4F-3s were delivered to US Navy and US Marine Corps squadrons they did not have self-sealing fuel tanks and featured only limited armour plate protection for the pilot.

The Wildcat was a rugged aeroplane, able to stand up to repeated carrier landings, which British Naval observers likened to 'controlled crashes'. Gross weight was normally 7,065lb. The F4F-3 had a service ceiling of 37,000ft and a nominal range of 860 miles. By the end of 1941, Grumman had delivered 185 F4F-3s to the US Navy and the US Marine Corps.

XF4F-6/F4F-3a

Concerned about nagging problems with the Pratt & Whitney R-1830-76 engine, and the potential delays these could cause in their delivery, the US Navy ordered Grumman to test one F4F-3 fitted with the Pratt & Whitney R-1830-90 engine, with a single-stage, two-speed supercharger. Designated the XF4F-6, its flying characteristics were essentially the same as the F4F-3, but the XF4F-6 proved to be around 10mph slower at altitude. The US Navy gave Grumman a contract for 95 of these aircraft, re-designated F4F-3As. The Greek government was allocated 30 aircraft from this contract, and these machines found their way to the Fleet Air Arm as Martlet IIs following Greece's capture by German and Italian forces. The remaining 65 served with US Navy and US Marine Corps squadrons.

F4F-4

The F4F-4 was a major redesign of the F4F-3 to accommodate folding wings and greater armament. The F4F-4 was the main Wildcat model to see combat during 1942, with Grumman completing production of 1,169 aircraft by the end of the year. These were all allocated to US Navy and US Marine Corps fighter squadrons. The adoption of a folding wing, reducing the span of the Wildcat from 38ft to 14ft on a carrier flightdeck, proved invaluable when the need to equip vessels with more fighter aircraft became evident following the battles of the Coral Sea and Midway.

The F4F-4 featured an additional 0.50in. machine gun outboard of the two wing guns, with 240 rounds per gun. While increasing the Wildcat's firepower, this change resulted in a reduction in the total amount of

The great advantage of the F4F-4 Wildcat was its folding wings, which meant that US Navy fleet carriers could carry more fighters. This in turn allowed fighter squadrons to boost their complement of Wildcats from 18 to 36 aircraft. Two F4F-4s could fit on the elevator of an aircraft carrier that could previously take only one F4F-3. (NARA)

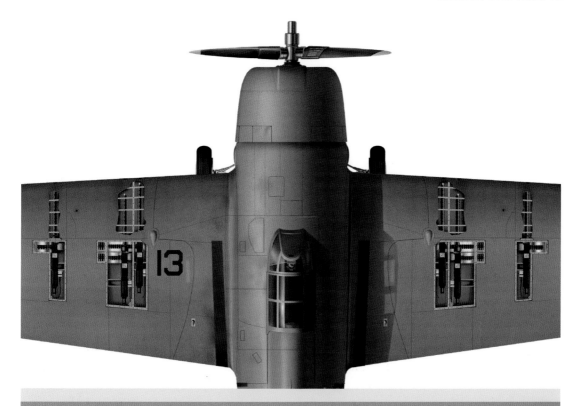

F4F-4 WILDCAT MACHINE GUNS

The F4F-4 model of the Wildcat featured three Browning M-2 0.50in. machine guns in each wing (one more than in the preceding F4F-3), with the third gun placed outboard of the inner two weapons. The M-2 had a rate of fire of 750–850 rounds per minute, which meant that a two-second burst from all six machine guns sent about 80 rounds towards a Zero-sen. Adding the two extra machine guns forced a reduction in rounds per weapon from 450 in the F4F-3 to 240 in the F4F-4 – a retrograde step in the eyes of many pilots, who thought four 0.50in. machine guns adequate against the vulnerable Zero-sen, and preferred having more ammunition available. Some, like Capt Joe Foss, used only four of their six machine guns in an effort to make their ammunition last longer. (Artwork by Jim Laurier, © Osprey Publishing)

ammunition carried – a negative change in the view of many pilots, who after experiencing combat with Japanese aircraft thought that the four 0.50in. machine guns of the F4F-3 were perfectly adequate for dealing with the less ruggedly constructed Zero-sen.

Reports from combat in Europe and the first few months of the war in the Pacific saw the hurried addition of self-sealing fuel tanks and around 150lb of armour for the oil tank and behind the pilot's seat, with a 27lb bullet-resistant windscreen replacing the earlier standard glass windshield. All the additions added around 900lb to the Wildcat's gross weight, with no increase in engine power. As a result, maximum speed dropped from 331mph in the F4F-3 to 318mph in the F4F-4 and rate-of-climb from 2,300ft per minute to 2,190ft per minute. The heavier F4F-4 was also less manoeuvrable than the F4F-3 – another negative step in the eyes of many Wildcat pilots.

The A6M Zero-sen

A6M1

The first two prototypes of the Zero-sen were initially referred to as 12-shi Carrier Fighters, but they eventually became A6M1s. The prototypes were powered by the Mitsubishi Zuisei-13 engine with a rating of 875hp.

The A6M1 set the basic configuration of the Zero-sen. Its fuselage was built in two sections, with the forward part being attached to the wing structure – the top of the wing served as the cockpit floor. While building the wing and forward fuselage as one integral section saved weight, it made construction more time-consuming and repair and maintenance more difficult. If part of the wing received major damage, the entire wing had to be replaced. The forward fuselage section ended at the aft end of the cockpit canopy and the trailing edge of the wing, the rear fuselage section beginning at this point. Both forward and rear sections were built using stressed-skin, semi-monocoque construction. The wings contained two 51.5-US gal fuel tanks, with an additional 38-US gal tank placed ahead of the cockpit. The main landing gear, tail wheel and arrestor hook were all fully retractable.

The pilot entered the aeroplane from the left side of the fuselage via three retractable steps and two handgrips, all carefully fitted for aerodynamic smoothness. Jiro Horikoshi and his team placed the cockpit high on the fuselage to give excellent all-around vision in combat. The cockpit itself was compact. The pilot's seat was adjustable up and down, but not forward – instead, the rudder pedals could be moved forward or backward. The arrangement of the instruments and controls followed conventional practice, with the exception of the gun controls. On the Zero-sen the gun selector and the firing button were placed on the throttle control, not on the control stick as in most other fighters.

The armament of the Zero-sen represented a sharp break with tradition. Definition of the requirements for the proposed 12-shi Carrier Fighter took place at a time when many of the world's air forces were reconsidering the efficacy of the standard armament of two-rifle calibre machine guns – a hangover from World War I. Alternatives then under development were multiple batteries of rifle-calibre machine guns or weapons of a larger size. Recognizing the need for more powerful armament to deal with larger and stronger all-metal aeroplanes, the Imperial Japanese Navy's research programme led to the decision to bypass the standard 7.7mm machine gun and adapt the 20mm cannon for fitment to the new fighter.

The IJNAF duly purchased a licence to build the Oerlikon FF aircraft cannon in Japan. This became the Type 99-1 cannon, which traded a low muzzle velocity and rate-of-fire for light weight. This made it ideal for the planned new carrier fighter. The prototype and production models of the Zero-sen contained a short-barrel Type 99-1 cannon in each wing, equipped with a drum magazine containing 60 rounds of 20mm ammunition. Two 7.7mm machine guns were placed on the top of the fuselage to fire through the propeller, each gun having a magazine containing 500 rounds of ammunition. A selector switch on the throttle enabled the pilot to fire the machine guns or the cannon separately, or all four weapons together.

Although clearly less powerful than the 20mm cannon, the 7.7mm machine guns were still considered to be valuable for close-in fighting, where a Zero-sen pilot could use his aeroplane's superior manoeuvrability to close with his opponent to deliver a telling strike against the pilot or the fuel tanks of the enemy aeroplane. The greater explosive power of the 20mm cannon would enable the Zero-sen to deal effectively with larger aircraft threatening the fleet. This seemingly powerful armament proved to be less effective in combat than the IJNAF had hoped, however.

A6M2 Model 11

Adoption of the more powerful Nakajima Sakae-12 engine for the production versions of the A6M led to a change in designation to A6M2. With the Sakae engine, the maximum speed increased to 331mph. The A6M2 incorporated several minor modifications. Moving the vertical tail further aft added 11 inches to the length of the fuselage, while the span of the horizontal tail surfaces was increased by four inches and

Type 0 Model 21s belonging to the Yamada Unit of the 22nd Koku Sentai at Kota Bharu, in Malaya, in early 1942. The Yamada Unit consisted of one *chutai* drawn from the 3rd Kokutai and one from the Tainan Kokutai. (P00618_001, Australian War Memorial)

raised 7.4 inches above the fuselage centreline. The air scoop for the Sakae engine's carburetor was relocated to the bottom of the engine cowling – a distinctive feature of the A6M2.

After the IJNAF's formal acceptance of the A6M2, the new fighter became the Type 0 Carrier Fighter Model 11, shortened to Reisen. The first digit in the model number indicated changes in the airframe and the second digit changes in the engine. Mitsubishi built 64 Model 11 fighters.

The Model 11 was the first version to see combat when 15 aircraft were sent to the 12th Kokutai for operational testing. Additional Model 11s were sent to China to augment the IJNAF's fighter force, operating from land bases.

A6M2 Model 21

Carrier trials apparently indicated that even though the Zero-sen was within the specified wingspan, the aeroplane was a tight fit on the standard aircraft carrier elevator.

To remove the chance of accidental damage to the wings, Mitsubishi designed a simple mechanism to fold the outer 20 inches of the wing vertically, reducing the wingspan to just under 36ft. The IJNAF rejected the idea of incorporating a greater degree of wing folding due to the weight penalty it would have imposed. The modified wing configuration led to a change in model number, the revised aeroplane becoming the Model 21. The Type 0 Model 21 replaced the A5M Type 96 Carrier Fighter within IJNAF carrier- and land-based air groups as production at Mitsubishi and Nakajima built up. Ironically, the Nakajima Company would ultimately build more Zero-sens than Mitsubishi.

A significant difference between the carrier- and land-based versions of the Model 21 was the provision of a radio. The quality of Japanese airborne radio technology at the beginning of the Pacific War was barely adequate for air-to-air and air-to-ground communications, lacking both clarity in communication and range. For carrier fighters radio was clearly a necessity, even if poor quality, but in some land-based Zero-sen units the pilots removed the radios, viewing the equipment as so much useless weight.

A6M3 Model 32

As IJNAF pilots gained experience with the Zero-sen in combat over China and through continued testing, complaints and recommendations began to come in to the Koku Hombu and to Mitsubishi. The most vocal complaint concerned the fighter's poor lateral control at high speeds. As air speed increased above 180mph, aileron response deteriorated rapidly, and above 230mph the Zero-sen became difficult to roll. Additionally, pilots wanted better performance at altitude and more ammunition for the Type 99-1 cannon.

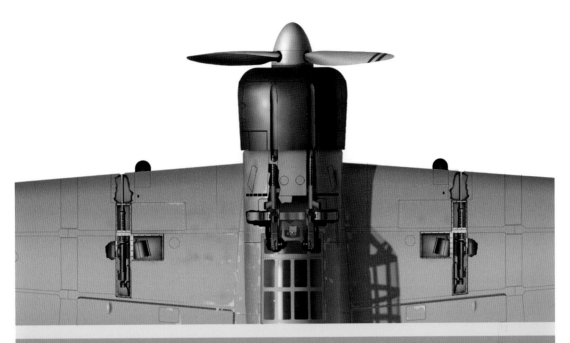

A6M2 ZERO-SEN MODEL 21 COWLING/WING GUNS

The A6M2 Zero-sen Model 21 had two 7.7mm Type 97 machine guns mounted in the upper fuselage decking synchronized to fire through the propeller. Each machine gun was fed belted ammunition held in a fuselage-mounted box containing 500 rounds. The Type 97 had a decent rate-of-fire, but the 7.7mm rounds were less effective against the Wildcat, which could absorb a considerable amount of damage. The Model 21 had two Type 99-1 20mm cannon in the wings. Based on the Oerlikon FF, this was an exceptionally light weapon, but had a low rate-of-fire and a low muzzle velocity. Ammunition was also a problem – each weapon had a drum housing just 60 rounds, which gave less than ten seconds' worth of firing time at a rate of around 540 rounds per minute. The Zero Model 32 increased the load to 100 rounds. (Artwork by Jim Laurier, © Osprey Publishing)

In response, in mid-1941 Mitsubishi fitted two standard A6M2 aeroplanes with the improved Sakae-21 engine, which featured a two-stage, two-speed supercharger and a higher rating of 1,130hp. Slightly longer and heavier than the Sakae-12, the Sakae-21 required a new engine cowling, with openings in the front for the two 7.7mm machine guns, and a revised carburetor air scoop. After initial test flights, pilots recommended eliminating the wing-folding mechanism and fairing over the wingtips. In shortening the wing by around three feet, the Mitsubishi engineers also shortened the ailerons. This combination improved aileron control, roll rates and the fighter's performance in a dive at higher speeds for a relatively small loss in overall manoeuvrability and rate-of-climb.

The ammunition feed system for the Type 99-1 cannon was changed from a drum magazine to a belt feed and the number of rounds increased to 100.

The Type 0 Model 32, which entered service during 1942, attempted to address the need for better performance at altitude and control at high speed. Note its clipped wingtips – the most visible distinguishing feature of the Model 32. (Peter M. Bowers Collection, Museum of Flight)

With both a revised fuselage and a new engine, the A6M3 was designated the Type 0 Carrier Fighter Model 32. Disappointingly, the Zero-sen Model 32 proved to be only marginally faster than the Zero-sen Model 21, due in part to the added weight of the new engine and more ammunition. More critically, although the capacity of the two wing fuel tanks was increased slightly, a reduction in the size of the fuselage fuel tank reduced the overall fuel capacity. As the Sakae-21 had higher fuel consumption than the Sakae-12, this reduced the Zero-sen Model 32's range.

Entering production in early 1942, the Zero-sen Model 32 went into action over New Guinea and the Solomon Islands later in the year.

F4F-4 WILDCAT AND A6M2 TYPE 0 CARRIER FIGHTER MODEL 21 COMPARISON SPECIFICATIONS		
	F4F Wildcat	A6M2 Type 0 Model 21
Powerplant	1,200hp Pratt & Whitney R-1830-86	950hp Nakajima Sakae-12
Dimensions		
Span	38ft	39ft 4.7in.
Length	28ft 9in.	28ft 8in.
Height	11ft 1in.	10ft
Wing area	260sq. ft	241.5sq. ft
Weights		
Empty	5,766lb	3,704lb
Loaded	7,964lb	5,313lb
Performance		
Max speed	318mph at 19,400ft	331mph at 14,930ft
Range	830 miles	1,160 miles
Climb	to 10,000ft in 5 min 40 sec	to 19,685ft in 7 min 27 sec
Service ceiling	33,700ft	32,810ft
Armament	6 x 0.50in. M-2 Browning machine guns	2 x 7.7mm Type 97 machine guns and 2 x 20mm Type 99-1 cannon

THE STRATEGIC SITUATION

Japan went to war on 7 December 1941 to oust the Western colonial powers from Southeast Asia and gain control of the region's resources – food for the Japanese people, raw materials for Japan's war industries and, above all, oil for the IJN. In a carefully planned and brilliantly executed campaign, the Imperial Japanese Army and Navy effectively conquered all of Southeast Asia in a little over five months. By the end of April 1942, Japan's conquests stretched from the Kurile Islands in the north, across the Central Pacific, with footholds in the Bismarck Archipelago and New Guinea, through the Netherlands East Indies to the Andaman Islands in the Bay of Bengal and to the border between India and Burma. This was an achievement that astonished the Western powers.

The IJNAF's Zero-sen was in the vanguard of the assault. Using the fighter's exceptional range, the 3rd and Tainan Kokutai flew from their bases in Taiwan to engage American aeroplanes over Luzon, in the Philippines – a distance of more than 500 miles. Zero-sens detached from these units assisted in the invasion of Malaya and participated in air attacks on Singapore and during the occupation of Sumatra, while their parent units advanced through the Netherlands East Indies, leapfrogging from captured airfield to captured airfield. Following the attack on Pearl Harbor, the carrier-based Zero-sen units assisted in the capture of Rabaul, on New Britain, and Lae, in New Guinea, and flew strikes against targets in Java,

Re-arming an F4F-3 on board *Enterprise* during February–March 1942. (NARA)

before attacking Darwin, on Australia's northern coast, and participating in the raid on British naval bases in Ceylon in early April 1942.

In the air battles over Southeast Asia, American, British and Dutch fighter aeroplanes and fighter pilots proved to be no contest for the experienced IJNAF Zero-sen pilots and their exceptional fighter. Flying inferior aircraft, lacking combat experience and using tactics that played to the Zero-sen's strengths, many young Allied fighter pilots paid with their lives when they tried to dogfight with a Japanese machine. The Zero-sen's superlative manoeuvrability and the skills of its pilots shocked many. Seeming to have come from nowhere, the Zero-sen quickly gained a reputation as a nearly invincible 'wonder plane', at least in the opinion of the Western press.

The Japanese attack on Pearl Harbor caught the US Navy preparing for war, but by no means ready. On 20 July 1940, President Franklin Roosevelt signed a $4 billion Two-Ocean Navy appropriations bill authorizing a 70 per cent increase in authorized tonnage, including the construction of 18 aircraft carriers, and a build-up to 15,000 aircraft by 1946. The US Navy had begun to expand its pilot force in 1939, but by 1941 the enlarged training programme was still ramping up. On the eve of war the US Navy had 4,112 officer and enlisted pilots while the US Marine Corps had 505. The US Navy's pilots were spread among seven fleet aircraft carriers, one small escort carrier and five patrol wings, in addition to other shore establishments, while the US Marine Corps pilots were allocated to two Marine aircraft wings (MAWs).

On 7 December 1941, the US Navy had approximately 157 F4F-3/3A Wildcats distributed among eight fighter squadrons, training units and aircraft pools in the Atlantic and Pacific Fleets, and 57 F4F-3/3As in three Marine Corps fighter squadrons in the 1st and 2nd MAWs.

The overwhelming speed and sweep of the Japanese advance created multiple strategic challenges for the US military. War Plan Orange, the pre-war joint Army–Navy plan for a potential conflict with Japan, had envisioned an offensive through the Central Pacific to capture the Caroline and Marshall Islands en route to Japan. The Japanese seizure of the Netherlands East Indies and positions in the Bismarck Archipelago and New Guinea now threatened Australia and New Zealand. The South Pacific had not figured in American pre-war planning, but it now became vital to defend Australia and to secure the shipping routes from the USA.

Although agreeing to a strategy of 'Germany First', President Roosevelt and the American Joint Chiefs committed US forces to the defence of Australia and New Zealand in the early months of the war, and agreed to send reinforcements of troops, aircraft and ships to the South Pacific.

However, lacking adequate ships, men and aircraft, there was little the US Navy could do to mount a determined resistance to the Japanese onslaught during the early months of 1942. Instead, during February and March, the Pacific Fleet's aircraft carriers conducted a series of lightning raids in the Central and Southwest Pacific, striking Japanese targets in the Marshall and Gilbert Islands, on Wake and Marcus Islands, at Lae and Salamaua, in New Guinea, and at Rabaul, on New Britain.

Japan's strategy was to create a defensive barrier around its newly conquered territories to repel the inevitable American and British counter-offensives. Japan had no hope of defeating the United States in a protracted war of attrition. Instead, the Japanese leadership believed that by employing its superior military skill and spirit along interior lines of defence, Japan could fight US forces to exhaustion and break America's will.

As Australia was the likely base for an American counter-offensive, strengthening the Japanese position in the South Pacific seemed imperative. In January the Japanese seized Rabaul, on the island of New Britain, to prevent its use as an Allied base for operations against the main Japanese stronghold at Truk. The IJN wanted to create a defence in depth around Rabaul by seizing Lae, Salamaua and Port Moresby, in eastern New Guinea, and Tulagi, in the Solomon Islands. From these bases Japanese aeroplanes could attack Australia.

The IJN also made plans for further advances beyond the Solomons to New Caledonia and Samoa to disrupt the line of communications between Australia and the United States. However, Adm Isoroku Yamamoto, commander of the IJN's Combined Fleet, argued instead for the vital

New F4F-4 Wildcats on the deck of *Enterprise* shortly before the Battle of Midway. By the end of May, all the fighter squadrons on *Enterprise*, *Yorktown* and *Hornet* had been re-equipped with the F4F-4. (NARA)

necessity of completing the destruction of the US Navy's Pacific Fleet, especially its aircraft carriers. Rather than concentrating their forces against one objective, however, the Japanese chose to pursue both. By mid-April the Kaigun (Navy of the Greater Japanese Empire) had committed itself to Operation MO – the invasion of Port Moresby and the island of Tulagi, in the Solomons, in early May as a preliminary step to further operations in the South Pacific – and, in early June, Operation MI. The latter targeted Midway and the Aleutian Islands in an effort to further expand the defensive barrier in the Central Pacific and confront the American carriers.

Once US Naval Intelligence became aware of Japanese intentions in the South Pacific, Adm Ernest King, Chief of Naval Operations and Commander-in-Chief US Fleet, and Adm Chester Nimitz, Commander-in-Chief Pacific Fleet and Pacific Ocean Areas, decided to contest the Japanese advance on Port Moresby, thus setting the stage for what became the Battle of the Coral Sea. On 7–8 May 1942, in the first naval battle in history where the opposing ships never sighted each other, the US Navy sank the light carrier *Shoho* and damaged the *Shokaku*, but lost the USS *Lexington* (CV-2). Although the Battle of the Coral Sea was a tactical victory for the Japanese, it ultimately proved to be a strategic loss. The island of Tulagi, in the Solomons, was indeed captured, but without carrier protection for the invasion force, the planned capture of Port Moresby had to be abandoned by the Japanese. The battle also deprived Adm Yamamoto of two of his most powerful carriers, the *Shokaku* and the *Zuikaku*, a month before the advance on Midway.

As is well known, the Battle of Midway marked the end of Japanese plans for expansion in the Central Pacific and Yamamoto's hopes for a decisive battle against the remaining American carriers. The loss of the four Japanese fleet carriers *Akagi*, *Kaga*, *Soryu* and *Hiryu* (the core of the Combined Fleet's striking power) on 4 June 1942 was a severe blow. The US Navy had suffered as well, losing USS *Yorktown* (CV-5) – the second fleet carrier sunk in the space of one month – and 80 carrier aircraft.

The battles of the Coral Sea and Midway had seen the first confrontations between the F4F Wildcat and the Zero-sen. In air combat the Japanese fighter had proven to be faster, far more manoeuvrable and in possession of a better rate-of-climb than the Wildcat, but the US aircraft's stronger construction, armour protection, self-sealing fuel tanks and more effective armament enabled its pilots to begin to take the measure of the Zero-sen. At Coral Sea and Midway, US Navy pilots quickly began developing tactics to counter the Zero-sen's advantages.

In the aftermath of Midway both sides, for different reasons, renewed their focus on the South Pacific. The Japanese losses at Midway forced a

US Marine Corps fighter squadron VMF-212 was one of the small number of units sent out to defend the islands in the Pacific along the route from the USA to Australia. VMF-212's aggressive leader, Maj Harold Bauer, stands just to the right of the squadron sign. (NARA)

cancellation of the plans to advance against New Caledonia and Samoa, but increased the importance of seizing Port Moresby and strengthening their position in the Solomon Islands in order to exert control over the Coral Sea. The Japanese Army and Navy agreed on an overland advance against Port Moresby, capturing Buna and its airfield on 21 July to serve as a jumping-off point.

As air support for the operation, the IJNAF had the 5th Koku Kushu Butai (the 5th Air Attack Force, with the administrative title of the 25th Air Flotilla), consisting of the Tainan Kokutai (Type 0 Model 21s), the 4th Kokutai (Type 1 Medium Bombers) and the newly activated 2nd Kokutai (Type 0 Model 32 Fighters and Type 99 Carrier Bombers). These units were operating out of Rabaul and Lae, in New Guinea. At the same time, the IJNAF decided to build an air base on the island of Guadalcanal to extend the reach of Japanese air power. After preliminary surveys, two construction battalions arrived on Guadalcanal in early July to begin work on an airfield.

For some months Adm King had been urging an offensive against the Solomon Islands to protect the US–Australia line of communications and to serve as a base for an assault on Rabaul. In late June the Joint Chiefs agreed to King's plan to seize the Japanese base at Tulagi and the nearby Santa Cruz Islands. When intelligence reports reached them that the Japanese had started construction of an airfield on Guadalcanal, King immediately switched the objective from the Santa Cruz Islands to Guadalcanal, with a target date of 1 August 1942 for the invasion. In the event, the 1st Marine Division landed on Tulagi and Guadalcanal on 7 August. Thus began a six-month campaign for control of the island that turned into a grinding battle of attrition involving five major naval surface actions, two carrier battles (the Battle of the Eastern Solomons and the Battle of Santa Cruz), three major Japanese land offensives and a sustained air campaign against US Marine Corps, US Navy, and USAAF aeroplanes based on Guadalcanal.

The battle for Guadalcanal was the first test of Japan's strategy of fighting American forces to the point of exhaustion. While the Japanese came perilously close to success on several occasions, in the end they failed.

THE MEN

The battles between the Grumman Wildcat and the Mitsubishi Zero-sen during 1942 brought together the best of the IJNAF's and the US Navy's pre-war aviators – what historian John Lundstrom has called the US Navy's 'First Team', and their US Marine Corps counterparts. In both navies these were men of considerable flying experience and, in the case of many of the Japanese pilots, combat service in China. A number were professional officers, graduates of their respective naval academies, but many more had come to flying by other recruitment paths. Their training had been rigorous and they had had to meet high standards of performance to gain their wings. They were well versed in fighter tactics, confident in their abilities and their aircraft. Later in that first year of the war younger, less-experienced pilots who had been rushed through more abbreviated training programmes joined the surviving pre-war pilots in the maelstrom of combat over the South Pacific.

IJNAF pilot training

A fundamental difference between IJNAF and US Navy pilot training in the years leading up to World War II centred on contrasting philosophies with respect to military manpower. US armed forces traditionally relied on a core of trained professionals who maintained a small military force in peacetime, backed up by a reserve force, and who in war would lead greatly expanded armed forces mobilized from the civilian population. The IJN, in contrast, adopted a philosophy of 'quality over quantity' in both peace and war, creating a limited cadre of exceptionally well-trained and experienced officers and men equipped with superior weapons.

This philosophy was in tune with the IJN's obsession with the 'Decisive Battle' concept – the view that one supreme engagement would decide the

The Yokosuka K5Y Type 93 Intermediate Trainer, nicknamed 'akatombo' (red dragonfly) because of its training colours, was familiar to all IJNAF pilots. (Edward M. Young Collection)

outcome of any war. The IJN planned for a short, victorious war, not a war of attrition. As a result of this philosophy, up until shortly before the outbreak of the Pacific War the IJNAF lacked the infrastructure for mass pilot and aircrew training. Its existing pilot training scheme was selective in the extreme, producing a very small number of exceptional pilots who represented only a fraction of those considered eligible.

The IJNAF drew its pilots from three sources. A small number of officer pilots came from the IJN Academy at Eta Jima, and they were duly trained in their own separate classes for eight months to a year. The vast majority of IJNAF pilots – up to around 90 per cent – were non-commissioned officers and enlisted men. Many came from within the ranks of the IJN through a highly selective and competitive examination process. The IJNAF also recruited young men directly from the civilian world through the so-called Yokaren (Flight Reserve) programmes. The initial programme set up in the early 1930s recruited boys aged 15 to 17, who were given three years of education and flight training. In 1937 the IJNAF began a new programme to recruit young men who had completed three and a half years of their middle school education, thereby reducing the time spent before they commenced flight training to 18 months. This subsequently became the largest source of aviation cadets.

During their pre-flight training the students were regularly subjected to strict regimentation, frequent corporal punishment and demanding physical activities. In 1940 the training programmes for enlisted men were revised and flight training standardized.

Prior to 1940, the flying training programme lasted seven to nine months and covered primary and intermediary instruction. In the primary phase, trainees began instruction on the Yokosuka K2Y1/2 Primary

Trainer, before moving on to the Yokosuka K5Y1/2 Type 93 Intermediate Trainer. Practice included the usual basic flying skills, aerobatics, formation flying, instrument flying and cross-country navigational exercises. After accumulating around 100 flying hours, and completing comprehensive examinations on their flying skills, trainees were assigned to a specialized aircraft type (such as fighters, dive-bombers, torpedo-bombers and multi-engined bombers) and began their advanced training programme, lasting around three months. Neophyte fighter pilots joined the Saeki, Omura or Oita Kokutai for training in older operational aircraft, flying the Nakajima A2N Type 90 and A4N Type 95 Carrier Fighters, before moving on to the Mitsubishi A5M Type 96 Carrier Fighter when the Type 0 replaced it in front-line units.

During their advanced training, students received another 100–150 flying hours, when they were introduced to combat tactics and basic combat manoeuvres, aerial gunnery, more formation flying and aerobatics in heavier and more powerful operational aircraft. Upon completion of their entire training programme enlisted pilots would have accumulated around 250–300 flying hours and officer pilot trainees around 400 hours. After 1940, as the IJNAF began to expand its training programme, the length of the latter was reduced to ten months to increase the output of trained pilots.

After joining a tactical unit, the newly graduated pilots continued their training. Up until the outbreak of the Pacific War the IJNAF's tactical

A6M2 ZERO-SEN: IN THE COCKPIT

1. IJNAF Type 98 Reflector Gunsight
2. Artificial horizon
3. Turn-and-bank indicator
4. Compass
5. IJNAF Type 97 7.7mm machine guns
6. Rate-of-climb indicator
7. Fuel pressure gauge
8. Tachometer
9. Cylinder head temperature gauge
10. Oil temperature gauge
11. Intake manifold pressure gauge
12. Oil cooler shutter control handle
13. Ignition plug charger switch
14. Brake pedals
15. Oxygen control
16. Oxygen pressure gauge
17. Oxygen quantity gauge
18. Control column
19. Wing fuel tank quantity gauge

20. Fuselage fuel tank quantity gauge
21. Switchboard
22. Fuel injection pump
23. Engine main switch
24. Radio direction indicator
25. Altimeter
26. Exhaust temperature gauge
27. Clock
28. Airspeed indicator
29. Interior lights
30. Radio homing control unit
31. Type 3 Mk 1 Radio Control panel
32. Arrestor hook retraction handle
33. Arrestor hook/flap down angle indicator
34. Radio homing equipment control lever
35. Cowl gills control handle
36. Cockpit ventilation air intake
37. Seat adjustment lever

38. Seat
39. Elevator trim tab control handle
40. Machine gun safety lever
41. Throttle lever
42. Machine gun selector switch
43. Propeller pitch adjustment lever
44. Mixture control lever
45. Drop tank release lever
46. Bomb release levers
47. Switchboard
48. Flap control
49. Landing gear lever
50. Wing tanks fuel gauge
51. Fuselage/wing tank switching cock
52. Wing tanks selector lever
53. Emergency gear down lever
54. High altitude automatic mixture control

(Artwork by Jim Laurier, © Osprey Publishing)

units served the same function as operational training units. This was not necessarily a burden, as new pilots were often assigned to new units forming in Japan. The new pilots undertook an intensive training programme to refine the combat skills they had begun to learn during their advanced training course. Working with their more experienced colleagues, they practised combat tactics, combat formations, gunnery and, for the carefully selected few, carrier operations. Only the very best pilots were selected for the carrier air groups – these were the IJNAF's elite, the 'best of the best'.

During the war in China, newer pilots could be gradually broken into combat and carefully shepherded by the veterans in the air group. In his memoir *Samurai!*, future high-scoring ace Saburo Sakai recalled how he was assigned to flying close air support missions for the Japanese Army for several weeks before he was allowed to join the veterans on combat air patrols.

The IJNAF's pilot training system was successful in producing a relatively small number of superbly trained and exceptionally skilled flyers. In December 1941, the IJN went to war with approximately 3,500 pilots, of which some 600 were assigned to the carrier air groups. They had an average of between 600 and 800 flying hours, and many benefited from having seen combat in China. But there was no real reserve of pilots, and as nearly every unit became heavily involved in combat duties, there was little time to perform the operational training role for newly assigned pilots.

IJNAF student pilots prepare for a lesson in the A5M4-K advanced fighter trainer. The Mitsubishi A5M4-K was a two-seat version of the Type 96 Carrier Fighter that supplemented older operational types during basic combat training. (Edward M. Young Collection)

During 1941 the IJNAF developed a plan to train upwards of 15,000 pilots a year, but with the outbreak of the war this plan fell by the wayside. The training system was subsequently expanded to produce around 2,000 pilots a year, but events would prove that this was not enough. As Mitsuo Fuchida and Masatake Okumiya (both formerly IJN officers) wrote in their history of the Battle of Midway, the IJN high command 'failed to realize that aerial warfare is a battle of attrition, and that a strictly limited number of even the most skillful pilots could not possibly win out over an unlimited number of able pilots'.

US Navy and US Marine Corps pilot training

The US Navy and the US Marine Corps recruited their pilots from two sources – the US Naval Academy and the Volunteer Naval Reserve class V-5 Naval Aviation Cadet programme for civilian and enlisted candidates. Prior to 1939, Naval Aviation Cadets who had come in through the V-5 programme undertook 18 months of training and served for three years on active duty as Naval Aviators with the rank of Aviation Cadet, after which they were eligible for promotion to Lieutenant in the US Navy Reserve. In June 1939 Congress amended the programme to allow for Aviation Cadets to receive immediate commissions as Ensigns or Second Lieutenants after 12 months of training.

Non-US Navy candidates for the V-5 programme went to one of 13 Naval Reserve Bases around the country for initial evaluation. These so-called elimination bases evaluated prospective candidates and their potential for completing pilot training. Candidates received physical training, and were taught basic military skills and Navy customs, but most importantly received ten hours of flight training leading to a solo flight. Having successfully passed these tests, the prospective candidates went on to NAS Pensacola, Florida, for flight training. Naval Academy graduates went directly to Pensacola after completing a period of service at sea.

Up to October 1939, with a relatively small number of aeroplanes and pilots authorized for the US Navy's aviation branch, the goal of the US Navy's aviation training was to give its prospective pilots instruction on how to fly all types of naval aircraft. After completing 33 weeks of ground school, the trainees spent a year working their way through Pensacola's five training squadrons.

Students began with nine weeks in Squadron One flying primary seaplanes (the float-equipped version of the N3N biplane trainer), learning basic flying procedures, before progressing to Squadron Two and 18 weeks of flying primary land aeroplanes. Here, they would master aerobatics, formation flying, night flying and cross-country navigation. In their nine

Three US Marine Corps F4F Wildcats flying over Quantico in May 1941. Up until July of that year, US Navy and US Marine Corps fighter squadrons, like their IJNAF counterparts, conducted much of the operational training for newly graduated fighter pilots, refining and honing the skills they had learned in advanced training through hours of practice. (NARA)

weeks in Squadron Three, the trainees flew more powerful, but second-line, operational aeroplanes like the Vought O3U and SBU and the new SNJ trainer, developing the skills they had mastered in Squadron Two and beginning to work on instrument flying. The trainees spent another nine weeks in Squadron Four, learning how to fly operational seaplanes and flying boats, before completing their training in Squadron Five. Here, they flew operational carrier aeroplanes and were instructed in aerial gunnery and combat tactics, dive- and torpedo-bombing and carrier landings.

By the end of a full year's training, students would have accumulated around 300 hours of flying time. After earning his wings of gold, a newly minted pilot would be qualified to be assigned to any US Navy carrier, observation or land-based squadron. With the shorter syllabus introduced after October 1939, trainees received around 200 hours of flying time.

F4F-4: IN THE COCKPIT

1. Clock
2. Cylinder head temperature gauge
3. Rudder pedal adjustment levers
4. Propeller control
5. Ignition switch
6. Propeller selector switch
7. Emergency electrical fuel pump switch
8. Check-off switch
9. Carburetor air control
10. Altimeter
11. Directional gyro
12. Padded electrical Mk 8 gunsight
13. Airspeed indicator
14. Turn-and-bank indicator
15. Rate-of-climb indicator
16. Gyro horizon
17. Manifold pressure gauge
18. Tachometer

19. Outside air temperature gauge
20. Fuel quantity gauge
21. Primer pump
22. Cowl flaps hand crank
23. Engine temperature gauge
24. Compass
25. Oil dilution switch
26. Radio signal light
27. Electric wiring diagram
28. Fuel tank selector valve
29. Rudder tab control
30. Aileron tab control
31. Throttle control
32. Recognition lights switches
33. Mixture control
34. Elevator tab control
35. Arrestor hook control
36. Starter switch
37. Tailwheel castor lock

38. Friction adjusting knob
39. Gunsight light rheostat
40. Electrical distribution panel and switch box
41. Fuse panel (spare fuses and bulbs under door)
42. Gun charging handle
43. Landing gear handcrank
44. Electric circuit breaker reset buttons
45. Control column
46. Pilot seat
47. Pilot seat belts
48. Cockpit lighting
49. Rudder pedals
50. Fire extinguisher switch

(Artwork by Jim Laurier, © Osprey Publishing)

Following President Franklin D. Roosevelt's declaration of a limited national emergency after the outbreak of the war in Europe in September 1939, the US Navy restructured its training syllabus in October to facilitate an immediate expansion of pilot training. From now on trainees would specialize in carrier, patrol/observation or utility aircraft. The ground school was cut to 18 weeks, and the flying training programme reduced from a year to six months. Instead of going through all five training squadrons, trainees began with primary land aeroplanes in Squadron One to acquire basic flying skills, before moving on to basic service types in Squadron Two, where they were introduced to formation flying and instrument flying. After completing the Squadron Two syllabus, the trainees split off. Those assigned to carrier aircraft learned the basics of aerial combat, aerial gunnery and dive- and torpedo-bombing, before being assigned to active duty squadrons. Other trainees went on to multi-engined patrol aeroplanes or scouting and observation types, the latter operating from battleships and cruisers.

This new training framework enabled the US Navy to respond to the increase in authorized aeroplane strength to 15,000 machines under the Two-Ocean Navy Act. Planning for a long war, the US Navy began ramping up its training programme. During 1941 the monthly quota of pilot trainees was increased from 800 to 2,500 a month.

Much like the IJNAF, the US Navy's squadrons had served as their own operational training units. In order to free squadrons from this responsibility, the US Navy authorized the formation of Advanced Carrier Training groups in July 1941 to provide additional training in operating the latest combat types, advanced aerial gunnery and advanced fighter tactics. New pilots received 75 to 150 hours of additional flight training at the ACTGs. In addition, to speed up the output of trained Naval Aviators, the requirement to have pilots capable of flying all three types of carrier aircraft was abolished. Students were now selected for fighters, dive-bombers or torpedo-bombers only, and trained on the type of aircraft they would fly when assigned to a carrier squadron.

Where the US Navy differed from other air services was its emphasis on aerial gunnery, particularly deflection shooting. The mission of the fighter pilot was the destruction of enemy aircraft, so the US

The US Navy put heavy emphasis on air-to-air gunnery, and devoted many hours to training Naval Aviators in deflection shooting. This cover from a 1942 US Navy training manual summarizes the official approach taken to aerial gunnery. (Edward M. Young Collection)

Navy's objective was to train its fighter pilots in a routine designed to be simple and effortless, and have them practise this routine 'until its performance becomes as automatic and instinctive as breathing in your sleep'.

There were two key elements in the US Navy's approach – where to aim and when to fire. Fighter pilots were trained to aim at 'a definite spot in space that will become full of enemy airplane when your bullets reach there' based on the speed and flightpath of their intended target and the speed and line of travel of their bullets. Having calculated the proper lead, or deflection, pilots were instructed to open fire 1,000ft from the target, but continue firing as they closed in to the best range of 200–300ft. Pilots were trained to fire with one-quarter, one-half, three-quarter and full deflection.

Once the principles of lead and range were absorbed, pilots received training on specific approaches to a target – from the side, from overhead, from head on and from the stern – and were taught to adapt their approach both to the type of aircraft they were attacking and the tactical situation at the time. After the theory came practice, practice and more practice until gunnery approaches became second nature. As a later gunnery manual advised new fighter pilots, these approaches were the basis for the laws of combat tactics, and the penalty for disobeying these laws was death.

INTO COMBAT
IJNAF fighter tactics

The basic combat unit in the IJNAF was the three-plane *shotai*, which was a variation of the three-plane V-formation consisting of a leader and two wingmen that was common to most of the world's air forces in the interwar period. While perfectly adequate for flying to and from a target, IJNAF fighter pilots found that in combat a tight V-formation was too rigid and less than effective. They duly developed a looser V-formation, with the wingmen flying further back and at different altitudes, instead of being tied closely to the leader.

In this revised combat formation, one wingman would fly 200m (660ft) behind the leader and the second wingman around 300m (985ft) behind, with one stepped up 200m in altitude and the second some 300m higher. In this formation the wingmen were not glued to the leader and concentrating on avoiding collisions. Instead, they could spend time scanning the sky for enemy aircraft. The *shotai* leader initiated the attack on an enemy aircraft or formation, and could deploy his wingmen in line astern or line abreast as the tactical situation required for sequential passes against the target.

While excelling at individual combat, during the first year of the Pacific War the Zero-sen pilots more often employed hit-and-run tactics against an enemy aeroplane, with each pilot in the *shotai* diving down to make an individual firing pass, pulling out underneath the enemy aircraft and climbing swiftly back up to altitude to regain the initiative. Alternatively, the leader could have one of the wingmen remain above the target as top cover.

Defensively, the *shotai* provided mutual support. If attacked, the leader could pull up in a climbing turn, using the Zero-sen's fast climbing ability, while the wingmen came in against the attacking enemy fighter from different angles. If a Zero-sen pilot could draw an enemy fighter into a dogfight, a favourite tactic was the *hineri-komi* – a twisting manoeuvre the IJNAF pilot would execute at the top of a loop to come down on his opponent's tail, employing the Zero-sen's phenomenal manoeuvrability at low speeds.

To be effective in the turmoil of air combat the pilots within the *shotai* required superlative flying skills, exceptional coordination and an almost intuitive understanding and anticipation of the actions, or reactions, of the other members of the formation. This was especially true for the land-based Zero-sen fighter units, who often removed the radios from their aircraft. Perfecting this coordination came from hour after hour of relentless practice. The Zero-sen units that went to war in December 1941 benefited from having experienced pilots who had trained together for months.

The combination of pilot experience, the flexibility of the *shotai* formation and the performance of the Zero-sen proved too much for

The three-aeroplane *shotai* was the IJNAF's basic combat unit, consisting of a leader and two wingmen. When employed by the Japanese, it was more flexible than the standard V-formation common to many of the world's air forces at that time. (Edward M. Young Collection)

PO2/c Yoshiro Hashiguchi. (Courtesy of Yasuho Izawa)

Yoshiro Hashiguchi is representative of the many enlisted pilots who comprized the core of the IJNAF's air groups during World War II. These men were trained in a hard school. Many were exceptional pilots, and fought tenaciously as the odds against them steadily worsened as the war progressed.

Hashiguchi was born in 1918 in Fukuoka City on the island of Kyushu, in southern Japan. He joined the IJN in 1937 and entered flying training through the Flight Reserve Enlisted Trainee programme for non-commissioned officers. Hashiguchi graduated in September 1938 as a member of the 42nd Class. He was one of 16 trainees selected to specialize in flying fighter aircraft. After completing his training Hashiguchi served with the Saeki, Oita and Omura Kokutai in Japan, flying the A5M Type 96 Carrier Fighter. In June 1939 Hashiguchi was posted to the 12th Kokutai based at Hankow, in China, where he flew Type 96 fighters until being wounded in October when Chinese Air Force bombers attacked his airfield. After recovering from his wounds, Hashiguchi returned to Japan in January 1940 to join the Suzuka Kokutai as an instructor pilot.

In November 1941 Hashiguchi was assigned to the newly reorganized 3rd Kokutai. Established in April 1941 as a Type 1 Attack Bomber unit, the 3rd Kokutai was re-formed as a fighter unit in September and equipped with the A6M2 Type 0 Model 21 fighter. As part of the 11th Koku Kantai, the 3rd participated in the invasion of the Philippines and the Netherlands East Indies. Fighting against Dutch Brewster Buffaloes and Curtiss Hawk 75s and American P-40s, Hashiguchi achieved several victories, but was wounded again while strafing a radio station. He returned to combat in April 1942 when the 3rd Kokutai was operating against Darwin. In September the unit was transferred to Rabaul, and for the next two months Hashiguchi flew missions against US Marine Corps and US Navy Wildcats on Guadalcanal. On 18 October 1942 he was involved in an intense battle with F4Fs that ended with Hashiguchi and two other pilots in the *shotai* that he was leading claiming five fighters shot down. The 3rd Kokutai was finally withdrawn from Rabaul in November, returning to the Netherlands East Indies.

Hashiguchi was sent back to Japan in June 1943, where he again instructed, before becoming a carrier fighter pilot with the 601st Kokutai aboard *Shōkaku* as the senior NCO pilot. Having survived the bloodbath of the First Battle of the Philippine Sea in June 1944, he transferred to the 653rd Kokutai embarked in the light carrier *Chiyoda*.

Hashiguchi was posted missing in action during the Battle of Cape Egano off the Philippines on 25 October 1944 when his carrier was sunk with all hands. During nearly three years of combat he had accumulated at least ten, and possibly a few more, victories. He was not one of the IJNAF's leading aces, but he and the many other NCO pilots he flew with were the backbone of the IJN's fliers.

Their victories were hard won through months of intensive, grueling air combat, and they fought on until almost all of them were killed. Of the 16 fighter pilots in the 42nd Class, Hashiguchi and 12 others were killed in action, and two more died in flying accidents.

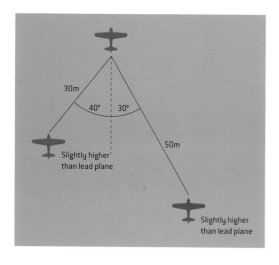

30m

40° 30°

50m

Slightly higher
than lead plane

Slightly higher
than lead plane

The IJNAF's basic fighter formation consisted of three Zero-sens flying in a V-formation. With combat experience, Japanese pilots modified the basic V into a looser formation, with the wingmen staggered above and behind the leader to give the formation more tactical flexibility and a better lookout for enemy aeroplanes.

Allied fighter units encountered over the Philippines, Malaya and the Netherlands East Indies in early 1942. However, as attrition began to take its toll, newer replacement pilots came in who did not have the same levels of experience. With the Zero-sen units heavily involved in combat, there was less time to devote to training missions, where pilots could perfect their coordinated *shotai* tactics. Without radio communication, coordination of the formation with less well-trained pilots became more difficult. Although these formation tactics proved less adaptable to the realities of air combat over the South Pacific, the IJNAF took an inordinate amount of time to institute changes.

The IJNAF's fighter escort tactics were also a product of experience in China. The standard escort procedure that had been developed in the late 1930s was for the fighters to provide bombers with what was termed 'direct cover'. The fighters normally flew above and behind the bomber formation they were escorting. While this gave the fighters maximum flexibility to manoeuvre, in the air battles over Guadalcanal this tactic often meant the escorts were poorly placed to counter enemy fighters attacking the bomber formation. The inability of the bombers to communicate with their fighter escort, due to the lack of radios in the Zero-sens, compounded the problem. On some occasions the escorts would not be aware that their charges were under attack until they saw a burning Type 1 bomber falling from the sky.

US Navy and US Marine Corps Fighter Tactics

During the interwar period US Navy and the US Marine Corps fighter squadrons also used the V-formation of three aircraft as the basic tactical unit. With fighters flying at higher speeds and with larger turning circles, such a tactical unit became less effective as a combat formation as it prevented sharp radical turns and forced the two wingmen to spend too much time looking inward to avoid colliding with their leader rather than outward searching for enemy fighters.

Soon after the war in Europe began, the US Navy began experimenting with a two-plane formation that saw the leader designated as the attacker and the wingman protecting him from attack. Spacing between the two aircraft increased to around 150ft to allow for more freedom of movement, easier turns and to enable better lookout for enemy aeroplanes. The US

Capt Joseph Foss. (NARA)

Capt Joseph 'Joe' Foss was the top-scoring Wildcat pilot against the Zero-sen. Born in Sioux Falls, South Dakota, on 17 April 1915, he learned to fly while attending college, enlisting in the US Marine Corps in 1940 after graduation from the University of South Dakota. Foss did his flight training at NAS Pensacola, winning his wings and a commission as a Second Lieutenant in March 1941. To his intense frustration Foss was assigned as a Primary Instructor at Pensacola, after which he was posted to a reconnaissance squadron. He eventually talked his way into the Advanced Carrier Training Group, and after completing the course was promoted to Captain and made executive officer of VMF-121 in August 1942. By this time Foss had accumulated around 1,000 flying hours, which served him well in combat.

VMF-121 arrived on Guadalcanal on 9 October 1942. Four days later, on his fifth combat mission, Foss shot down his first Zero-sen, and then had a narrow escape when three more A6Ms badly shot up his Wildcat, forcing him to make a deadstick landing. Over the next six weeks Foss claimed 23 victories, including 16 Zero-sens.

He learned not to open fire until he was as close as possible to his target – so close that one of his pilots supposedly accused him of leaving powder burns on the IJNAF fighters that he shot down. If they could, Foss and the other pilots tried to use high-speed hit-and-run tactics to avoid the Zero-sen's superior manoeuvrability, although many times they fought from a less than advantageous position. To conserve ammunition Foss often used only four of his six machine guns – more than enough to explode a Zero-sen at close range.

Foss claimed four Zero-sens shot down on 23 October 1942, returning to Guadalcanal once again in a shot-up Wildcat. Two days later he went one better when he claimed two Zero-sens during a morning mission and three more during the afternoon. He claimed his last victories – three more Zero-sens – on 15 January 1943 after VMF-121 had returned from leave in Australia. These last claims made Foss the first American pilot in World War II to equal Capt Eddie Rickenbacker's World War I record of 26 victories, and gave him a total of 19 Zero-sens shot down – the highest score of any US Marine Corps or US Navy Wildcat pilot against the Mitsubishi fighter. For his achievements during the Guadalcanal campaign Capt Foss was awarded the Congressional Medal of Honor on 18 May 1943.

Promoted to Major, Foss subsequently returned to combat as CO of VMF-115, but enjoyed no more aerial success. He went on to have a distinguished post-war career, serving several terms as Governor of his home state. Foss passed away on 1 January 2003.

Navy designated two squadrons, VF-2 and VF-5, to experiment with the new formation. Reports from American observers in England reinforced the concept of the two-aeroplane section as the superior tactical formation. It took until mid-1941, however, for the US Navy to adopt the two-aeroplane element. Fighter squadrons, which at the time had a complement of 18 aircraft, were divided into three divisions of six machines in three two-aeroplane sections, with the most senior pilot flying as the division leader. The sections would fly around 300ft apart in line astern or in an echelon formation behind the division leader. Approaching a formation of enemy aircraft, the division leader would assess the situation and determine the type of attack to be executed, ordering the three sections to engage the enemy in succession or separately as necessary. A section leader could employ one of the standard gunnery approaches, knowing that his wingman would be following behind guarding his tail. With more distance between aircraft, division and section leaders abandoned the hand signals of the open-cockpit era for radio and quick rocking of wings to alert others to an impending manoeuvre.

Introduction of the folding-wing F4F-4 in early 1942 enabled an increase in the number of aircraft in the carrier fighter squadrons from 18 to 27, but the units retained the six-aeroplane division. When combat losses or other missions limited the number of aircraft available, a squadron might send off a division of six fighters accompanied by a division of four, but always in sections of two machines.

There was one tactical innovation developed before the outbreak of war with Japan that was to prove invaluable in countering the Zero-sen fighter. In the spring of 1941, then Lt John Thach, commander of VF-3, came across an intelligence report on a new Japanese fighter aircraft with performance superior to the F4F-3s to which VF-3 was about to convert. The report stated that the fighter had a superior rate-of-climb, higher speed and the ability to out-turn any opponent. As Thach recalled in a post-war interview, 'when I realized that this airplane, if this intelligence report were correct, had us beat in all three categories, it was pretty discouraging.'

Some of his pilots refused to believe the report and thought it was a gross exaggeration, but Thach argued that even if it was only half true, the Japanese fighter would still be superior to the Wildcat. Thach believed he had to do something about this. Looking at the Wildcat, and the gunnery training his pilots had received, Thach believed they had one advantage. 'We had good guns, and could shoot and hit even if we only had a fleeting second or two to take aim. Therefore, we had to do something to entice the opponent into giving us that one all important opportunity – it was the only chance we had.'

Lt Cdr John Thach, who as CO of VF-3 during the Battle of Midway successfully employed the weaving tactic he had developed to counter the Zero-sen's superior manoeuvrability. (NARA)

Working at night at his kitchen table, using matches to represent aeroplanes, Thach experimented with different formations, trying out his ideas the next day using real ones. The key was to create that one opportunity to get in a killing burst of fire against an enemy opponent.

It was standard practice at the time to turn into an attacking enemy. Thach realized that if he placed two sections at a tactical distance from each other – that is, the distance equal to the diameter of their tightest turning circle – he could create the opportunity he was looking for by having both sections turn towards each other if one was attacked. If enemy aircraft made a stern attack on the section flying on the right, this section would quickly turn towards the section flying on the left, which would turn into the enemy attack and gain a head-on firing position. This also had the benefit of throwing off the enemy's attack, and presenting him with a more difficult full deflection shot. For the tactic to work, Thach used a division of four aircraft in two sections, instead of six aircraft.

One of the advantages of the tactic was that it did not need radio communication between the two sections. Thach worked out a system whereby the section on the right looked out over the section on the left, and vice versa. If the right-hand section saw enemy aircraft coming in to attack the section on the left, it would immediately turn in on the left-hand section, which, seeing their colleagues initiating a turn, would immediately begin its turn to the right. The scissoring tactic could be used repeatedly to fend off enemy attacks.

Lt Cdr John Thach developed this defensive tactic to counter the Zero-sen's superior manoeuvrability. When an IJNAF fighter (1) attacked a division of two elements (2) from the rear, the elements would turn sharply towards each other (4), giving the second element a head-on shot at the attacking Zero-sen (3). Dubbed the 'Thach Weave', (5) this became the standard defensive tactic for Naval Aviators fighting against the Zero-sen.

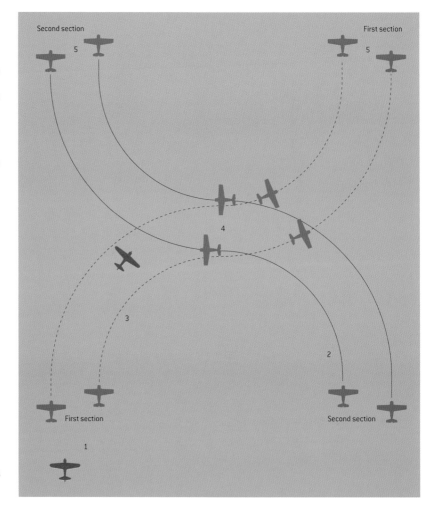

Lt Cdr John Thach's defensive weave manoeuvre was based on a division of two elements flying in what he called the 'Beam Defense Position', in line abreast at a distance equal to the Wildcat's turning radius. The Beam Defense Position and the Thach Weave could be used either by elements within a division of four aircraft, or by single aeroplanes in an element of two.

To test the tactic, Thach and three other pilots flew their fighters with their throttles retarded against other Wildcats flying at full throttle. It worked, time and again. The 'Beam Defense Position', as Thach named it, gave him and his pilots 'something to work on, to keep us from being demoralized'. At Midway, Thach got his chance to try out his tactic in the only school that really mattered.

The F4F-3 was the first model of the Wildcat to see combat with the Zero-sen fighter, during the Battle of the Coral Sea on 7–8 May 1942. (Peter M. Bowers Collection, Museum of Flight)

Coral Sea and Midway

The first clash between the Wildcat and the Zero-sen took place on 7 May 1942 over the Coral Sea. That morning strike groups from *Lexington* and *Yorktown* (Task Force 17) attacked the IJN's light carrier *Shoho*, whose aircraft were covering the Port Moresby invasion force. Lt Cdr James 'Jimmy' Flatley led eight F4F-3s from VF-42 as escort for *Yorktown*'s VT-5 TBD Devastator torpedo-bombers. *Shoho* had sent up a combat air patrol of Type 96 and Type 0 fighters to defend the carrier.

As the Japanese pilots went after the torpedo-bombers, Flatley's division fell on them. Although the Wildcat pilots were astonished at the manoeuvrability of the fighters flown by their IJNAF opponents, Flatley managed to shoot down a Type 96 fighter and two of his pilots traded fire with a Zero-sen. Having climbed above the melee, Ens Walter Hass saw a Japanese fighter – one of three Zero-sens from *Shoho* – break away and head towards him. With the advantage of altitude, Hass dived on the unsuspecting fighter, getting in a solid burst that sent the Japanese aeroplane crashing into the sea below. Hass had just become the first US Navy or US Marine Corps pilot to shoot down a Zero-sen.

The next day search planes from Task Force 17 and the Japanese Striking Force (*Shokaku* and *Zuikaku*) located their rival carrier forces and sent off strike groups to attack. *Yorktown*'s strike group went out first, with a division from VF-42 escorting the torpedo-bombers from VT-5 once again. *Lextington*'s strike group followed, with an escort of nine Wildcats from VF-2. Combat air patrols from *Shokaku* and *Zuikaku* intercepted the American formations, and in the fighting that followed the Wildcat pilots claimed three Zero-sens shot down for the loss of three fighters. Following the attacks on the Striking Force, *Shokaku*'s Zero-sen pilots claimed five Wildcats destroyed, while their counterparts aboard *Zuikaku* claimed no fewer than 13 F4F-3s shot down.

Shokaku and *Zuikaku* sent out a combined force of 33 Type 99 carrier bombers, 18 Type 97 attack planes and an escort of 18 Zero-sen fighters to

One of the US Navy's great fighter leaders of World War II, Lt Cdr James 'Jimmy' Flatley. After the Battle of the Coral Sea he began working out tactics to counter the Zero-sen. (NARA)

attack Task Force 17. VF-2 and VF-42 sent up 20 Wildcats on combat air patrol who engaged the IJNAF fighters in a series of fierce engagements at low and medium altitude, losing two Wildcat pilots killed in action and one fighter that had to ditch. Sections sometimes broke up in the heat of the action, and this resulted in Wildcat pilots repeatedly finding Zero-sens on their tails just as they positioned themselves to attack another Japanese fighter. This was an effective demonstration of the *shotai* tactics of mutual support. When faced with such a situation Wildcat pilots resorted to high-speed dives and cloud to escape their pursuers.

Lt Cdr Flatley led his division in a hit-and-run attack against nine Zero-sens, claiming one shot down before the division broke up into individual combats. Flatley took on three fighters on his own in a hit-and-run attack, attempting to pull up into a firing position on one Zero-sen before diving away to escape. Flatley's wingman, Lt(jg) Richard Crommelin, claimed two fighters shot down, but it appears that none was actually lost in this fight.

US Navy Wildcat pilots came away from their first confrontations with the Zero-sen confident that they could take on the Japanese fighter and win, despite its obvious superiority over the F4F-3. As Lt Cdr Flatley stated in his after-action report, 'The F4F-3 airplane properly handled can beat the enemy carrier-based fighters encountered so far. This includes type "Zero".' Recognizing that the Zero-sen was far more manoeuvrable than the Wildcat, Flatley recommended tactics that could counter the fighter's advantage:

The most effective attack against a more manoeuvrable fighter is to obtain altitude advantage, dive in, attack and pull up using speed gained in a dive to maintain altitude advantage. The old dogfight of chasing tails is not satisfactory and must not be employed when opposing Jap VF [fighter] planes.

Flatley distilled his experiences into eight points he termed 'Hints To Navy VF Pilots':

1. Gain plenty of altitude before contact with enemy VF. You can lose altitude fast but you can't gain it fast enough when up against enemy VF.

2. Use hit-and-run attacks, diving in and pulling out and up. If your target maneuvers out of your sight during your approach pull out and let one of the following airplanes get him. If you attempt to twist and turn you will end up at his level or below, and will be unable to gain the advantage.

3. If you get in a tough spot dive away, maneuver violently, find a cloud.

4. Stay together. The Japs' air discipline is excellent, and if you get separated you will have at least three of them on you at once.

5. You have the better airplane if you handle it properly. In spite of their advantage in maneuverability, you can and should shoot them down with few losses to yourselves. The reason for this is your greater firepower and more skillful gunnery.

6. Don't get excited and rush in. Take your time and make the first attack effective.

7. Watch out for ruses. The Japs have a method of creating smoke from their exhaust which doesn't mean a thing [this was apparently simply exhaust from acceleration]. Set them on fire before you take your guns off them.

8. Never hesitate to dive in. The hail of bullets around their cockpit will divert and confuse them, and will definitely cause them to break-off what they are doing and take avoiding action.

Upon returning home Flatley assumed command of VF-10 and prepared a short manual for his squadron titled 'Combat Doctrine', encapsulating all his thinking on fighter tactics against enemy aircraft. Copies apparently circulated to other US Navy and US Marine Corps fighter squadrons on the west coast. One pilot who pored over Flatley's manual on his way to the Southwest Pacific was the newly appointed Executive Officer of VMF-121, Capt Joseph Foss.

Less than a month after the Battle of the Coral Sea, Marine Corps Wildcat pilots on Midway and US Navy pilots aboard USS *Enterprise* (CV-6), *Hornet* and *Yorktown* prepared to repel a major Japanese attack as the four aircraft carriers of the IJN's Combined Fleet neared the island.

In April the US Navy carrier fighter squadrons based in Hawaii had begun to convert to the F4F-4. The Coral Sea battle had shown the need for more fighters on carriers. Fortunately, the F4F-4's folding wings enabled the carrier fighter squadrons to increase their complement to 27 aeroplanes. The three US Navy fighter squadrons that saw action during

the Midway battle – VF-3 aboard *Yorktown*, VF-6 aboard *Enterprise* and VF-8 aboard *Hornet* – all had F4F-4 Wildcats. Towards the end of May, VMF-221 (the sole US Marine Corps fighter squadron on Midway) received seven F4F-3 Wildcats to augment its 21 F2A-3s.

During the Japanese attack on Midway on the morning of 4 June 1942, future ace Capt Marion Carl shot down his first Zero-sen while flying a Wildcat. A short while later the American aircraft carriers sent off their strike groups to hit their Japanese counterparts. On board *Yorktown*, Lt Cdr John Thach made preparations to escort the TBD torpedo-bombers of VT-3. At the last minute, the eight VF-3 Wildcats he intended to take were cut to six. Thach instructed Machinist Tom Cheek to fly with his wingman, Ens Daniel Sheedy, as close escort to the TBDs, while Thach flew several thousand feet above with his division of four Wildcats as high escort. Thach had not had time to brief the two pilots (transferred in from VF-42) flying in his second section in his Beam Defense tactics.

Heading off, Cheek and Sheedy took station 1,000ft above the TBDs, while Thach and his division flew 3,000ft above. At 1003 hrs one of the TBD crews spotted the Japanese carriers to the northwest and turned towards them. As the TBD formation and its six Wildcat escorts closed on the Japanese ships, a combat air patrol of some 40 Zero-sens fell on them.

Cheek watched as a fighter made a head-on run against the TBDs, then climbed up and around for another pass. 'I was momentarily spellbound watching the fighter's clean, seemingly effortless maneuvers,' he recalled.

Within seconds it was in a position to make a run on the last airplane on the formation's right flank. Nosing down slightly, the pilot continued his curving approach, 500ft above and slightly to my right, as though I had not yet been seen. I moved my engine controls into combat power range and pushed the throttle to the forward stop. Easing back on the control stick until the F4F was hanging on the prop, I brought the gunsight pip to an almost full deflection lead on the Zero's nose.

The six 0.50in. wing guns rumbled. I held the trigger down just long enough to see the red stream of tracers converge on the Zero's engine and start to drift back into the fuselage. The fighter's nose bucked momentarily, dropped back and then the airplane came diving down in my direction. At the moment my guns were still firing and the tracers were curving up and into their target, I was literally hanging in the air. The muzzle blast and recoil of the six 'fifties' was all that was needed to push my overloaded, underpowered, F4F over the edge into a control-sloppy stall. As I let my fighter's nose drop and started a recovery by rolling to the left, the Zero swept past on my right with black smoke and flames spewing from the engine, a river of fire trailing back along its belly.

Lt Cdr John 'Jimmy' Thach, second from right, with his pilots from VF-3, shortly before the Midway battle. Machinist Tom Cheek, on the left claimed a Zero-sen destroyed at Midway. (Courtesy Linda Cheek Hall and Elizabeth Cheek-Jones)

The Zero-sens also fell on Thach's division flying above the TBDs, quickly hitting the F4F of the second section leader, Lt(jg) Brainard Macomber, knocking out his radio. They also shot down his wingman, Ens Edgar Bassett. Thrown on the defensive, Thach led his men in a series of manoeuvres aimed at fending off the constant attacks by the Zero-sens. He also got a good burst off at an enemy fighter from close range as it pulled out of its attack.

Unable to raise Macomber on the radio, Thach ordered his wingman, Ens Robert 'Ram' Dibb, whom he had trained in the Beam Defense, to pull away and act as a section leader. With Macomber sticking close on his wing and Dibb flying several hundred yards away, Thach started weaving, keeping a sharp lookout for Zero-sens. Soon enough one came in on Dibb, who radioed Thach that he had a fighter on his tail. Thach told Dibb to turn left into him, as they had practised. Thach turned into Dibb for a head-on run against the Zero-sen attacking him. Coming under the fighter, Thach opened fire as the Zero-sen pulled up to pass over him. The Japanese fighter burst into flames as it went by. Thach's Beam Defense had worked exactly as he had intended. Under repeated attack, he and Dibb continued using the tactic, weaving and turning into the attacking Zero-sens as they came in on the Wildcats' tails. Thach shot down a third fighter, then stopped counting – Dibb claimed one as well.

VF-3 was the only Wildcat unit to engage the Zero-sens during the attack on the Japanese carriers, Thach and his fellow pilots claiming six fighters shot down and two more damaged. All but Bassett returned, with their Wildcats badly shot up. Later that day pilots from VF-3 tangled with Zero-sens during two attacks on *Yorktown*, claiming five shot down for the loss of four Wildcats. In many ways, however, the most important fighter battle of 4 June was Thach's successful debut of his Beam Defense during what the historian John Lundstrom has called 'one of the classic encounters of the Pacific air war'.

Despite the success of his new defensive tactic, Thach came out of the Midway fighting highly critical of the F4F-4. In his after-action report he said, 'It is indeed surprising that any of our pilots returned alive. Any success our fighter pilots may have had against the Japanese Zero fighter is not due to the performance of the airplane we fly but is the result of the comparatively poor marksmanship of the Japanese, stupid mistakes made by a few of their pilots and superior marksmanship and team work of some of our pilots. The F4F airplane is pitifully inferior in climb, maneuverability and speed.'

Guadalcanal

From the first landings on Guadalcanal on 7 August 1942 until the destruction of the last major Japanese convoy on the night of 14/15 November that ended the threat to the Island, US Marine Corps and US

Navy Wildcat squadrons battled Zero-sen fighters. These aircraft were from the IJNAF's land- and carrier-based fighter units under the command of the Kichi Kushu Butai (Base Air Force, administratively the 11th Koku Kantai (Air Fleet)) with its two component units, the 5th Koku Kushu Butai (Air Attack Force) and the 6th Koku Kushu Butai.

The mission of the Wildcat squadrons was to protect the vital airfields on Guadalcanal from the Japanese bombers attempting to destroy Henderson Field and the subsequently built Fighter 1 strip. Based at the former, the island's small force of SBD Dauntless dive-bombers and TBF Avenger torpedo-bombers of the 1st MAW, along with a handful of USAAF P-39 and P-400 Airacobras, were soon to be dubbed the 'Cactus Air Force' after the code name for Guadalcanal. These aircraft regularly went out to attack enemy convoys bringing in supplies for the Japanese Army as it strived to take back the airfields from the Americans. The IJNAF urgently needed to establish air superiority over Guadalcanal to end the American air attacks on the convoys. With adequate men and supplies, the Japanese Army could then defeat US forces on the ground, retake the island and, it was hoped, exhaust the American will to continue fighting.

Establishing air superiority over the island was by no means a simple task. Guadalcanal lay 560 miles from Rabaul, the IJNAF's main base. For the Zero-sen pilots, this represented an exhausting six-hour flight to and from Guadalcanal – longer than the flight from Taiwan to Clark Field, in the Philippines, at the start of the war.

In order to make the flight to the island and then return to Rabaul, the Zero-sens had to be equipped with and retain their drop tanks. Even with the additional fuel, Japanese fighter pilots had only 15 minutes of flying time over Guadalcanal. And if damaged in combat, their only alternative was the long flight back to Rabaul.

A Type 0 Model 21 returns to one of the airfields on Rabaul from a mission over Guadalcanal. (Edward M. Young Collection)

The IJNAF had been surprisingly lackadaisical about building additional airfields at Rabaul, or in-between Rabaul and the islands along the Solomon chain to the south. From early August until early October, when the Japanese completed an airstrip at Buin, on the southeast coast of Bougainville, there were no airfields between Rabaul and Guadalcanal apart from a rough emergency field on Buka Island, northeast of Bougainville. This lack of facilities meant that the IJNAF could not deploy all the air units it had available, nor could it use the shorter-range Type 0 Model 32 fighters as escorts for the Type 1 bombers for a full two months.

Not unlike their RAF counterparts during the Battle of Britain, the Wildcat squadrons on Guadalcanal had two advantages that proved critical during the air battles – an early warning system and proximity to their airfields. Before the war the Royal Australian Navy had established a network of observers along the Solomon Island chain equipped with radios. The Coastwatchers, as they were called, gave vital early warning of Japanese formations heading south to Guadalcanal. Alerted to an incoming raid, US Marine Corps radar stations on the island could pick up the Japanese formations when they were 125–140 miles away from the island. This gave the Wildcat squadrons the critical time they needed to get their slow-climbing fighters to higher altitude, above the Japanese bomber formations and in a position to intercept. As Lt Cdr Flatley had found, against the more manoeuvrable Zero-sen altitude was critical.

In the air battles that followed an interception, the Wildcat pilots would often break away from combat with the Zero-sens with their aeroplanes mangled and engines damaged. On numerous occasions Marine and Naval Aviators brought their aircraft back for a safe landing, while their Japanese opponents struggled, and often failed, to return safely to Rabaul.

The air battles began the day of the landings, US Navy Wildcats from VF-5 (USS *Saratoga* (CV-3)), VF-6 (*Enterprise*) and VF-71 (*Wasp*) covering troops as they came ashore on Tulagi and Guadalcanal on 7 August. In the first contest between US Navy carrier fighters and a land-based IJNAF fighter group, the Wildcats received a mauling from the experienced aces of the Tainan Kokutai flying out of Rabaul – nine of 18 Wildcats were shot down in fierce fighting.

On 20 August the first US Marine Corps fighter squadron arrived at Henderson Field when VMF-223 (from Marine Air Group (MAG) 23), with 19 F4F-4 Wildcats, flew in from USS *Long Island* (ACV-1).

Under the command of Maj John L. Smith, VMF-223 was staffed by a mix of experienced pilots, including Capt Marion Carl, and newly fledged fighter pilots fresh from training. VMF-224, under Maj Robert Galer, arrived as reinforcements on 30 August. Shortly after, following damage to

Saratoga, Lt Cdr Leroy Simpler brought VF-5 ashore to Henderson Field for a spell of operations. With replacement pilots drawn from other US Marine Corps squadrons in the South Pacific, these three units bore the brunt of the air fighting until mid-October.

The day after their arrival, the pilots of VMF-223 had their first run-in with Zero-sens when Smith and his division engaged six Japanese fighters while on patrol. He claimed one shot down when his attacker pulled up directly in front of him, but the Zero-sens shot up all four Wildcats, forcing one pilot to make the first of many Wildcat deadstick landings at Henderson Field. The encounter gave Smith and his pilots confidence in the F4F's rugged construction.

On 24 August, during the Battle of the Eastern Solomons, VMF-223 intercepted a strike force of Type 97 Carrier Attack aeroplanes with a Zero-sen escort from the light carrier *Ryujo* that had been sent to attack Guadalcanal. The American pilots claimed 11 bombers and five Zero-sens destroyed for the loss of three Wildcats (in fact the IJNAF had lost three bombers and one Zero-sen, and claimed 15 Wildcats shot down in return). Carl claimed three bombers and one Zero-sen, making him the first US Marine Corps ace. In the carrier battle fought that same day US Navy aeroplanes sank *Ryujo* and Wildcat pilots from VF-5 and VF-6 claimed 15 Zero-sens shot down. Ens Francis Register of VF-6, who would subsequently become the only US Navy pilot to claim five Zero-sens destroyed during 1942, downed two of the fighters to open his score against the A6M.

Forty-eight hours later the 5th Koku Kushu Butai launched the first of many bombing raids against Guadalcanal, sending out 16 Type 1 Attack Bombers ('Betty') from the 4th Kokutai with an escort of Zero-sen fighters from the Tainan Kokutai. As the bombers came over Henderson Field in an impressive V-formation, Smith led three divisions in to intercept them – the VMF-223 pilots duly claimed eight bombers and five Zero-sens destroyed. In reality three Japanese fighters had been lost that day, one of which was flown by Lt(jg) Junichi Sasai, the top-scoring Tainan Kokutai pilot at Rabaul. Carl had claimed a Zero-sen destroyed in a high-side run and then had a second A6M jump him as he came in to land at Henderson. In a head-on run, Carl held his fire until the Zero-sen pulled up in front of him, at which point the fighter exploded.

Four days later, on 30 August, *Shokaku* and *Zuikaku* sent out a fighter sweep to Guadalcanal. Smith was flying at 15,000ft with seven other Wildcats and seven P-400s from the 67th Fighter Squadron when they saw Zero-sens below them. Coming in out of the sun, the Wildcats claimed eight IJNAF fighters on their first pass, before using their speed to climb

Overleaf
On 4 June 1942 Lt Cdr John Thach, commanding VF-3, embarked in *Yorktown*, took off with five other F4F-4s as escort to VT-3's TBD Devastators on their way to attack the Japanese carrier force. The formation ran into the Zero-sen combat air patrol, which shot down one Wildcat. Thach decided to try out the Beam Defense tactic he had worked out before the war began. Sending Ens Robert 'Ram' Dibb out to his right, and with Lt Brainard Macomber clinging closely onto his wing, Thach waited for his opportunity. He recalled, 'I got a shot at one or two of them and burned them. One of them had made a pass at my wingman, pulled out to the right and then came back. We were weaving continuously, and I got a head-on shot at him.' Thach's manoeuvre worked as well as he had hoped. Dubbed the 'Thach Weave' by Lt Cdr James Flatley, it became the standard defensive counter employed by all US Navy and US Marine Corps fighter pilots when dealing with the Zero-sen's superior manoeuvrability. (Artwork by Gareth Hector, © Osprey Publishing)

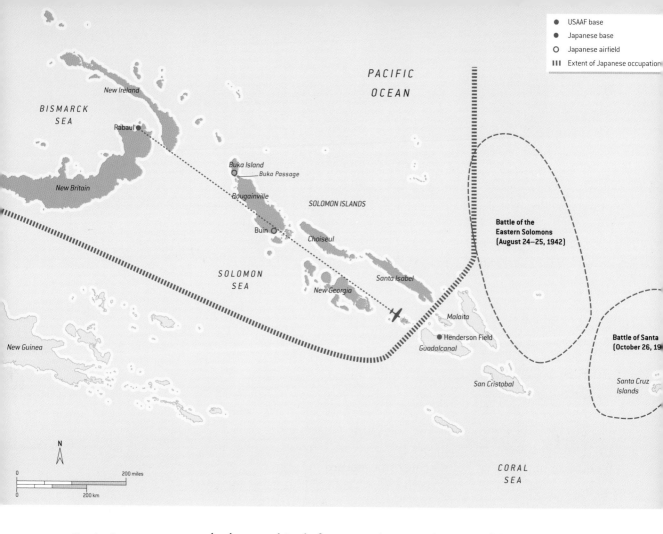

Map labels:

PACIFIC
OCEAN

BISMARCK
SEA

New Ireland

Rabaul

New Britain

Buka Island
Buka Passage

Bougainville

SOLOMON ISLANDS

Buin

Choiseul

SOLOMON
SEA

Santa Isabel

New Georgia

Battle of the
Eastern Solomons
(August 24–25, 1942)

New Guinea

Malaita

Henderson Field
Guadalcanal

Battle of Santa
(October 26, 19

San Cristobal

Santa Cruz
Islands

CORAL
SEA

N

0   200 miles
0   200 km

Legend:
● USAAF base
● Japanese base
○ Japanese airfield
III Extent of Japanese occupation

For the first two months of the Guadalcanal battle, the IJNAF Zero-sen pilots had to fly the 1,120-mile round trip from their base at Rabaul to Guadalcanal. Australian Coastwatchers regularly provided radio warnings of impending raids to the 'Cactus Air Force', enabling the Wildcat pilots to gain altitude in time to intercept Japanese formations.

back up to altitude for a second run. In the space of three minutes the US Marine Corps pilots claimed 14 Zero-sens shot down for no loss. Smith was credited with four victories and Carl three, this being their best day against the Mitsubishi fighter. The Japanese appear to have lost nine A6Ms, all flown by veteran carrier pilots.

Over the next two weeks, until bad weather over Rabaul brought a hiatus, the Japanese carried out eight raids on Guadalcanal. The units at Rabaul were all below their authorized strength, so the raids tended to consist of 18 or 27 Type 1 bombers, with an escort of 12 to 14 Zero-sens flying behind and above the bomber formation. John Smith quickly developed intercept tactics that all subsequent US Marine Corps and US Navy Wildcat squadrons fighting on Guadalcanal adopted. When they had adequate warning, Smith would lead his divisions up to an altitude some 4,000–5,000ft above the Japanese bomber formation, pulling ahead and off to one side of the enemy aeroplanes. The Wildcats would then take the opposite course, flying towards the bombers and then rolling in on a high-side run to avoid the Type 1's 20mm tail gun. If they could, the Wildcat pilots launched their attack from right to left in sections, pulling up in a climbing turn to the left after their first pass to take stock. If there were no Zero-sens around, they would carry out another attack on the bombers.

When the escorts did attempt to intercept them, the Wildcat pilots would try for a quick high-side pass and a deflection shot before diving away, using their speed and rapid manoeuvring to escape the Zero-sens if they could.

Manoeuvring combat, in which the IJNAF fighter excelled, was to be avoided. Both US Marine Corps and US Navy pilots found that when the Zero-sens bounced them they would often overshoot and recover ahead of the Wildcat, leaving themselves open for a devastating burst of 0.50in. fire.

Flying behind the bomber formations, the Zero-sen pilots had difficulty countering the American hit-and-run tactics. When they did catch the Wildcats, they were astonished at the Grumman fighter's ability to absorb punishing fire, compared with their lighter Zero-sens.

It seemed to some that the 7.7mm rounds would barely penetrate the wings of a Wildcat. In his memoir, Saburo Sakai recorded his amazement when, in his one combat with a Wildcat, he fired more than 200 rounds of 7.7mm ammunition into his opponent. The Zero-sen ace noted that 'the Wildcat continued flying as if nothing had happened'.

The 20mm cannon was also proving less than ideal in combat with a wildly manoeuvring Wildcat because of its low rate-of-fire. This meant that getting a sufficient number of shells into an F4F to bring it down was

Capt Marion Carl, from VMF-223, claimed a total of 16.5 kills over Guadalcanal during 1942. Eight of his victories were Zero-sens. (NARA)

Lt(jg) Junichi Sasai was the top-scoring Tainan Kokutai pilot at Rabaul at the time of his death in combat with VMF-223 on 26 August 1942. Having first seen action during the invasion of the Philippines in December 1941, he had claimed 54 victories prior to being killed. A veteran of 76 missions with the Tainan Kokutai, Sasai was officially credited with 27 kills. (Michael John Claringbould)

a challenge for all but the best marksmen. As one US Marine Corps officer put it, with some exaggeration, 'a Zero can't take two seconds' fire from a Grumman, and a Grumman can sometimes take as high as 15 minutes fire from a Zero.'

The American pilots impressed and surprised at least some of their opponents with their tactics and their aggressiveness. Long after the war had ended, one Zero-sen pilot who fought over Guadalcanal recalled that 'behind the thick glass [of their canopies] the enemy pilots were surprisingly young, dignified-looking. And although they were young, they were highly skilled and well trained. They escaped us quickly'. But this was not always the case. On 9 September the US Marine Corps lost three Wildcats to the Zero-sens. Four days later three more US Marine Corps F4Fs were downed, as were two US Navy examples.

After a two-week weather-related lull, the Japanese resumed their attacks with a change in escort tactics. A reinforced 5th Koku Kushu Butai increased the number of escorting Zero-sens and divided the fighters into two forces – the direct escort force covering the bombers from behind and an air control force sweeping ahead of the bomber formation to disrupt the enemy fighters as they climbed to intercept. On 27 September the new tactic was tried out for the first time, but it failed. The air control force saw no American fighters and headed back to Rabaul. The bombers saw the Wildcats rising up to meet them, but as the Zero-sens had no radios, they had no way of contacting their escort. Two bombers were lost over Guadalcanal and one on the way back to base. The next day things were even worse. Wildcats from VMF-223, VMF-224 and VF-5 shot down five Type 1 bombers, two more crash landed and one was scrapped – a 30 per cent loss rate for the mission. Increasing the size of the escort had failed to protect the bombers, so the 5th Koku Kushu Butai decided on a new tactic – using the bombers as a feint to draw up the Wildcats for a Zero-sen fighter sweep.

The first attempt at this tactic, on 29 September, brought mixed success, but on 2 October the Zero-sen pilots scored their most decisive victory over US Marine Corps and US Navy Wildcats in a near perfect ambush. Maj Smith scrambled with 13 Wildcats from VMF-223 and VMF-224. Climbing out of the clouds at 25,000ft, he was shocked to see 17 Zero-sens diving down on his division. The IJNAF fighters shot up Smith's Wildcat, forcing him to crash land a few miles from the airfield. Fellow ace Maj Robert Galer was shot down, for the second time, and three other US Marine Corps and one VF-5 pilot were missing.

Having recognized the change in tactics, Marine and Naval Aviators turned the tables on their Zero-sen attackers the very next day. Heading towards Guadalcanal, 27 IJNAF fighter pilots found extensive cloud cover, so they split the formation up into three separate *chutai* (squadrons). Having been alerted to the approaching enemy aeroplanes, 29 Wildcats from VMF-223, VMF-224 and VF-5 took off and climbed higher than usual. Flying at 33,000ft, Capt Marion Carl, with four other Wildcat pilots, looked down to see Zero-sens flying well below him in a broad V-formation. Diving down, Carl came in on the last fighter on the right, opening fire from 100 yards and seeing the Zero-sen burst into flames. Within a few minutes Carl's division had shot down five fighters.

Legendary ace CPO Saburo Sakai engaged the Wildcat only once, on 7 August 1942. Participating in the first long-range mission flown by Zero-sens to Guadalcanal, he shot down the F4F-4 flown by future ace Lt J. J. Southerland of VF-5. Minutes later he downed a lone SBD from VS-71, only to then be severely wounded by return fire from eight Dauntlesses from VB-6 that he had attempted to intercept – Sakai had mistaken them for Wildcats. Despite having suffered terrible head wounds that left him almost totally blind (he eventually lost the sight in his right eye), Sakai somehow managed to fly back to Rabaul. (Michael John Claringbould)

Lt Col Joseph Bauer, CO of VMF-212 and an experienced and aggressive fighter pilot, was flying with Carl's division that day, and he claimed four Zero-sens shot down. Carl's division claimed nine fighters in total (for once this figure was close to the number of Zero-sens actually lost) at a cost of one Wildcat – one of the best scores achieved by either side during the entire campaign.

On 9 October 1942, VMF-121 from MAG-14 arrived on Guadalcanal, followed shortly thereafter by Bauer's VMF-212, to replace the battered VMF-223 and VMF-224, the exhausted survivors of which departed three days later. VMF-121's executive officer, Capt Joseph Foss, began his astonishing run against the Zero-sen on 13 October. On the voyage across the Pacific, Foss and his squadronmates had studied Lt Cdr Flatley's manual on fighter tactics. Foss clearly took its lessons to heart. Over the next 12 days he would claim 15 Zero-sens shot down to become the leading scorer against the Mitsubishi fighter in 1942.

Foss's first victory was almost his last. Going after a group of Zero-sens escorting 'Betty' bombers, Foss failed to spot a fighter behind him. However, his opponent made the mistake of overshooting the inattentive Foss, who quickly fired at the Zero-sen and claimed it destroyed. Moments later the remaining IJNAF fighters in the attacking *shotai* badly damaged

An F4F-4 damaged on Guadalcanal in one of the many Japanese air raids on the island. Aircraft such as this became a valuable source of spare parts for those still operational. (NARA)

Foss's Wildcat when they followed him all the way back to Fighter 1, where he made a barely controlled landing. Learning quickly from experience, he downed another Zero-sen the next day. In his autobiography Foss recalled that 'experience put the finishing touches on my fighter training. I quickly learned that the best results came when I flew close to a Zero before opening fire. I always tried to surprise the enemy by coming up on his tail, but if I ended up playing a game of chicken with him, I would wait until the Zero pulled up to avoid a collision and then I'd send a short burst into the base of his wing.'

Lt Col Joe Bauer was appointed head of Cactus Fighter Command on 17 October. The aggressive Bauer told his pilots to challenge the Zero-sens in head-on runs, relying on the Wildcat's armament to knock them down. 'When you see Zeros,' Bauer said, 'dogfight 'em!' The Kichi Koku Butai gave the Marine and Naval Aviators plenty of opportunity to do so,

Type 0 Model 21 fighters preparing to take off for a mission to Guadalcanal. The Japanese also suffered operational losses from poor field conditions and inadequate maintenance. (Edward M. Young Collection)

launching a seven-day campaign timed to coincide with a ground offensive that was intended to overcome the US Marine Corps and US Army defenders once and for all.

Taking Bauer's admonition to heart, Joe Foss claimed two Zero-sens at the very beginning of the offensive on 18 October, adding two more two days later, four on 23 October and a remarkable five in two missions 48 hours later. Between 18 and 23 October, the US Marine Corps and US Navy Wildcat pilots actually shot down 12 Zero-sens (although they claimed 50) for the loss of seven F4Fs. On 25 October – the last day of the offensive – the Japanese sent out wave after wave of fighters and bombers against Guadalcanal, losing 11 Zero-sens to the 1st MAW, which had two Wildcats destroyed in return. This steady attrition was robbing the IJNAF's fighter *kokutai* of many of their best pilots.

The next day saw the final carrier clash of 1942, the Battle of Santa Cruz, which resulted in a tactical defeat for the US Navy with the loss of *Hornet* and damage to *Enterprise*. Fighter losses were about even. In attacks on the Japanese carriers and defence of their own task force, 13 Wildcats were shot down and another ten ditched or crashed, while the Japanese carriers had 15 Zero-sens shot down and another nine lost to ditching or other crashes.

Lt Cdr Flatley, commanding VF-10 aboard *Enterprise*, had learned Thach's Beam Defense tactic from Lt Butch O'Hare over the summer, and

On 8 May 1942, two sections of F4F-3 Wildcats from VF-2, flying off USS *Lexington*, were escorting VT-2's TBD Devastators on their way to attack the Japanese carriers *Shokaku* and *Zuikaku* when four Type 0 fighters from *Zuikaku* jumped them. The Zero-sen pilots used slashing hit-and-run attacks to quickly shoot down Ens Dale Peterson and Ens Richard Rowell. Division leader Lt Noel Gaylor found safety in a cloud formation, before firing at a Zero-sen, claiming a probable. (Artwork by Gareth Hector, © Osprey Publishing)

A Type 0 Model 21 fighter accelerates down the flightdeck of an IJN carrier during the Battle of Santa Cruz, which was fought during 25–27 October 1942. (P02887_001, Australian War Memorial)

he duly trained his pilots in the technique. Escorting VT-10's torpedo-bombers in an attack on the Japanese carriers, several of Flatley's pilots utilized the Beam Defense when they came under attack. Leading a division in defence of Task Force 16 that afternoon, Flatley employed the Beam Defense against attacking Zero-sens and became a convert. He dubbed the manoeuvre the 'Thach Weave' and did much to promote it. The Thach Weave became the standard US Marine Corps and US Navy defensive and escort tactic against the Zero-sen for the rest of the Pacific War.

After a comparative lull, the Japanese made one final push to retake Guadalcanal in mid-November 1942, assembling a convoy of 12 transports with formidable naval escort. Both sides had reinforced their air units, the Kichi Koku Butai gaining the 1st Koku Kushu Butai (with one Type 1 bomber group and three Zero-sen groups) to replace the battered 5th Koku Kushu Butai, which returned to Japan. The 1st MAW added more Wildcats from VMF-121, VMF-212 and VMO-251, while the USAAF flew in more P-39s and new P-38 Lightnings.

On 11 November the Japanese sent out two raids. The Wildcats failed to find Type 99 Carrier Bombers in the clouds around the island, but the Zero-sen escort jumped a flight of six F4Fs, shooting down four pilots for the loss of two fighters. Later that morning the Wildcats shot down four Type 1 bombers. The next day the 6th Koku Kushu Butai sortied 16 Type 1 bombers armed with torpedoes, with an escort of 30 Zero-sens, to attack American transports off Guadalcanal. The intercepting Wildcats and P-39s destroyed 11 of the bombers, and the remaining five were written off due to battle damage. On 13–14 November there were intensive air battles over the convoy the IJN was trying to get to Guadalcanal. US

WILDCAT: THROUGH THE GUNSIGHT

The first F4F-3 Wildcats were fitted with a telescopic gunsight extending through the windscreen. Although more accurate than the older ring and bead sights of the 1930s, the telescopic sight sharply restricted the pilot's field of vision at a critical point in air combat. During 1941 the US Navy introduced illuminated reflector gunsights, initially borrowing the USAAC's N2 sight while working on its own design. When the latter proved problematic, the US Navy obtained copies of the RAF's Barr & Stroud Mk II Reflector Sight and arranged for production in the USA as the Illuminated Sight Mk 8. Much more effective for deflection shooting, the Mk 8 was fitted to the F4F-4 after the Battle of Midway.

Gunnery training for fighter pilots drummed in the two most critical questions – where to aim, and when to fire. Naval Aviators were taught how to calculate the correct lead, or deflection, using the Mk 8 sight until it became automatic, and to open fire when no more than 1,000ft away from their target. The Wildcat's guns were set to converge at 1,000ft and closer. Many found that against the Zero-sen it paid to get in even closer, and to fire when only a few hundred feet away.

Most importantly, pilots had to learn to calculate the proper deflection, and determine the range almost instantly. Capt Marion Carl later wrote: 'I was blessed with the ability to look at another airplane and instantly know what it could do relative to my speed and position. I rarely made conscious decisions in a combat – mostly, I acted on instinct.' (Artwork by Jim Laurier, © Osprey Publishing)

Deck crews unfold the wings of an F4F-4 from VF-10 on board *Enterprise* during the Battle of Santa Cruz. (NARA)

Marine Corps Wildcat pilots claimed 21 Zero-sens shot down, while Flatley's VF-10, flown in to Guadalcanal, was credited with eight A6Ms destroyed on the 14th.

The destruction of the convoy and the loss of IJN warships attempting to protect the merchant vessels in the Battle of Guadalcanal ended the Japanese effort to retake the island.

The last confrontation between the Wildcat and the Zero-sen in 1942 took place just before Christmas over Munda Point, on the island of New Georgia, where the Japanese were belatedly building an airfield closer to Guadalcanal. On 23 December, Maj Donald Yost of VMF-121, escorting US Marine Corps SBDs that had been sent to bomb the new airfield, claimed two Zero-sens shot down. He enjoyed even more success on a similar mission the next day when he intercepted six A6Ms and claimed four destroyed.

Years later Yost recalled how he missed the Zero-sens on his first pass on 24 December, but spotted a weak point in their tactics as they flew by him. For some reason, as each fighter went past him, its pilot recovered by doing a slow roll. Yost said, 'I anticipated where he would be in his roll. I was shooting at him before he got on his back. When he got there, he was a ball of fire.' Aside from his four Zero-sens destroyed, Yost's wingman, Lt Kenneth Kirk Jr from VMO-251, claimed three.

The one-sided result from this final aerial engagement of the year was a measure of how far US Marine Corps and US Navy pilots had progressed in their battles with the Zero-sen, and evidence of the beginning of the inexorable decline in the quality of the IJNAF.

ANALYSIS

In the carrier battles at Coral Sea and Midway, and in the nearly three months of intensive air combat around Guadalcanal that followed, US Marine Corps and US Navy Wildcat pilots flying an aeroplane that was in many ways inferior to the Zero-sen did well in air combat against their adversary, and held their own against the best IJNAF fighter pilots. In the ferocity of combat both sides over-claimed the number of planes they had shot down (the Japanese to a far greater extent than the Americans) – by no means an uncommon occurrence during World War II. The actual loss figures show that the Wildcat pilots did surprisingly well. John Lundstrom found that at Coral Sea and Midway the US Navy's Wildcat squadrons actually shot down 14 Zero-sens for the loss of ten F4Fs. During the most intensive period of action in the skies over Guadalcanal, from 7 August to 15 November 1942, research by Lundstrom, James Sawruk and Richard Frank indicates that the fighter units of the Kichi Koku Butai lost 72 Zero-sens in aerial combat while the 1st MAW had 70 Wildcats destroyed. Finally, the Japanese carrier air groups lost 43 Zero-sens in aerial combat, the majority of these almost certainly falling to carrier-based Wildcat squadrons, who in turn lost 31 Wildcats. This gives a total of 129 Zero-sens lost from May to November 1942 against the loss of 111 Wildcats.

What is more significant is what lies behind these numbers. From one perspective, the US Navy's carrier force fought the IJN's Combined Fleet to a draw – both sides lost four fleet carriers during 1942. But this was in reality a victory for the United States, as it sharply reduced Japanese offensive power and inflicted losses that the US Navy, supported by a far greater industrial capacity, could more easily replace.

In the carrier battles of the Coral Sea, Midway, the Eastern Solomons and Santa Cruz, the IJNAF suffered irreplaceable losses among its elite pilots. During the air battles over Guadalcanal no fewer than 95 Type 1 bombers were destroyed and most of their crews killed – many of the best Zero-sen pilots perished trying to defend these aircraft. The famous Tainan Kokutai, for example, lost 32 pilots fighting over Guadalcanal. These men, too, particularly the *chutai* and *shotai* leaders, were irreplaceable.

Capt Joseph Foss, the highest scoring Wildcat pilot against the Zero-sen, with the other members of his VMF-121 flight. They are, from left to right, Roger Habermann, Danny Doyle, Foss, Bill Marontate and Roy Ruddell. Doyle and Ruddell were both killed in combat. (National Museum of Naval Aviation)

The US Marine Corps and US Navy Wildcat pilots on Guadalcanal, who did the bulk of the air fighting in defence of the island, prevented the Japanese from establishing air superiority. Had they failed, Guadalcanal might well have been retaken. While the fighting on the island continued until the Japanese evacuation in February 1943, it was the Japanese who were exhausted, not the Americans.

Three factors contributed to the Wildcat's success against the Zero-sen – its structural strength and protection for fuel and pilot, better armament and gunnery and tactics. When reading accounts of the air battles in the Pacific War from this period, one encounters time and again stories of Wildcats coming back with shredded tails, wings full of holes, shattered cockpits and instrument panels, and engines damaged, but still returning to a carrier deck or one of the airfields on Guadalcanal. Lacking armour protection for the pilot and self-sealing fuel tanks, the Zero-sen simply could not stand up to such punishment. Where Wildcat pilots survived, Zero-sen pilots, more often than not, died. It is interesting to note that all three of the top US Marine Corps aces against the Zero-sen at Guadalcanal – Marion Carl, Joe Foss and John Smith – were shot down but survived to fight again.

While many Naval Aviators criticized the reduction in ammunition that came with the increase to six 0.50in. machine guns in the F4F-4, a burst of fire, especially at close range, was devastating against the Zero-sen's unprotected fuel tanks. While the A6M's 20mm cartridge was heavier and individually more destructive than a 0.50in. shell, the weight of fire of a two-second burst from the Zero-sen's two 20mm cannon was actually less than a two-second burst from the six faster-firing 0.50in. machine guns installed in the wings of the Wildcat.

The US Navy's emphasis on deflection shooting was critical to the success of many Wildcat pilots. Trying to get on the tail of a Zero-sen risked getting involved in a slower-speed turning fight where the Japanese machine held the advantage. US Marine Corps and US Navy Wildcat pilots learned to take snap shots from all angles. Having guns of the same calibre also gave them an advantage in deflection shooting over their Japanese counterparts. The Zero-sen's mixed armament of 7.7mm machine guns and 20mm cannon, with different muzzle velocities and rates of fire, made deflection shooting more complicated.

Tactics were also critical to the Wildcat's success. Men such as James 'Jimmy' Flatley, John Thach and John Smith (all experienced fighter pilots) developed tactics to negate the Zero-sen's phenomenal manoeuvrability and enable the Wildcat pilots to use their superior armament and training in deflection shooting to get in a killing blow. The hit-and-run attack, a quick burst and then a high-speed twisting dive away from the target proved effective, as did the Thach Weave as a defensive tactic. With the Zero-sen being unable to match the F4F in a dive, and suffering reduced aileron response at higher speeds, IJNAF pilots found these tactics difficult to counter.

The tactics the Wildcat pilots developed during 1942, and the lessons they learned, became standard for Naval Aviators for the rest of the Pacific War.

VMF-121's Capt Joe Foss emerged as the highest-scoring US Marine Corps or US Navy pilot against the Zero-sen during the Guadalcanal campaign with 16 victory claims – he added three more A6Ms to his total on 15 January 1943 for his final kills of the Pacific War. Maj John Smith and Capt Marion Carl, both from VMF-223, were credited with eight victories against the Zero-sen over Guadalcanal.

Of the 12 US Marine Corps and US Navy Wildcat pilots who claimed five or more Zero-sen victories during 1942, half had completed their flying training before June 1941 and half after that date. That the former should have done well in air combat is less of a surprise given their greater flying experience, and the fact that most were leading squadrons or divisions in combat. That several younger pilots only a few months out of training claimed almost as many victories is a tribute not only to their flying ability, but to the US Navy's training programme and good tactics.

Regrettably, although a number of IJNAF aces fought during the Guadalcanal campaign, Japanese records do not note their individual victories.

LEADING A6M TYPE 0 KILLERS IN 1942			
Ace	Unit(s)	Zero-sen Claims	Total Claims
Capt Joseph Foss	VMF-121	16	26
Maj John Smith	VMF-223	8	19
Capt Marion Carl	VMF-223	8	18.5
Maj Robert Galer	VMF-224	6	13
Lt Col Harold Bauer	VMF-212	6	11
Lt Jack Conger	VMF-223/212	6	10
Maj Donald Yost	VMF-121	6	8
2Lt Cecil Doyle	VMF-121	5	5
2Lt Kenneth Frazer	VMF-223	5	12.5
Lt James Percy	VMF-112	5	6
Capt Francis Pierce	VMF-121	5	6
Ens Francis Register	VF-6/5	5	7
Capt Loren Everton	VMF-212	4	10
Mar Gun Henry Hamilton	VMF-223/212	4	7
2Lt Roger Haberman	VMF-121	3.5	6.5
2Lt Joseph Narr	VMF-121	3	7
2Lt William Freeman	VMF-121	3	6
2Lt Kenneth Pond	VMF-223	3	6
Lt Cdr John Thach	VF-3	3	6
Lt(jg) Scott McCusky	VF-42/3	3	13.5

AFTERMATH

On 12 February 1943, the first F4U-1 Corsairs arrived on Guadalcanal with VMF-124. As the months went by, the Corsair progressively replaced the Wildcat in US Marine Corps' land-based fighter squadrons in the South Pacific. By August all eight such units were flying the Corsair. The US Navy's Wildcat squadrons continued battling the Zero-sens over the Solomons until the end of the summer of 1943. By then the superior Grumman F6F Hellcat had begun to replace the Wildcat aboard the Pacific Fleet's new *Essex*-class fleet carriers and *Independence*-class light carriers. As the US Navy's principal carrier fighter for the remainder of the Pacific War, the Hellcat would establish a dominance over the Zero-sen using the tactics the Wildcat pilots had pioneered during 1942.

The F4F gained a new lease of life as a fighter flying from the many small escort carriers built to provide close air support to the amphibious landings in the Pacific. The Eastern Aircraft Division built 4,437 FM-2 Wildcats for the US Navy. With a more powerful engine, lighter weight,

and with armament reduced to four 0.50in. machine guns, the FM-2 offered drastically improved performance over the F4F-4. During the invasions of the Philippines and Okinawa, FM-2s established a kill ratio of 32-to-1, admittedly against older types of Japanese aircraft and less well-trained pilots. This figure was remarkable nonetheless.

The Zero-sen was destined to soldier on until the very end of the Pacific War. With the introduction of the Corsair and the Hellcat, as well as the second generation of USAAF fighters (P-38, P-47 and P-51), the Zero-sen lost its ascendancy and never regained it. Modest improvements incorporated into the A6M5 Type 0 Carrier Fighter Model 52 gave increases in maximum and diving speeds and improved armament, but at a cost to manoeuvrability, and still left the Zero-sen well short of its American adversaries in terms of performance.

As the training of IJNAF fighter pilots declined steadily as the conflict progressed, few could get the best out of their aeroplanes. Towards the end of the Pacific War Zero-sen pilots were going into combat with 200 flying hours or less – perhaps a quarter of what their opponents had. However, in the hands of the few remaining veterans, the Zero-sen could still be a deadly adversary. Indeed, Corsair and Hellcat pilots could never completely ignore the admonition 'Never dogfight with a Zero'.

The Zero-sen's intended replacement, the Mitsubishi A7M Reppu, encountered innumerable delays in its development and never entered production. Two fighters that might have helped address the balance, the Mitsubishi J2M Raiden and the Kawanishi N1K2-J Shiden Kai, were built in too few numbers. The IJNAF had no choice but to continue with the Zero-sen as its main fighter, Mitsubishi and Nakajima completing construction of 10,449 examples before war's end. Many were destroyed as *kamikaze*, with poorly trained pilots heading off to die attacking the American fleet off Okinawa.

A captured Mitsubishi A6M5 Type 0 Carrier Fighter Model 52 is put through its paces near war's end. With no real replacement, the Zero-sen soldiered on until the very end of the fighting in the Pacific. (NARA)

165

PART III

BY DMITRIY KHAZANOV AND ALEKSANDER MEDVED

AIR WAR IN THE EAST

La-5/7 vs Fw 190

Soviet aeronautical engineers and pilots from the Red Army Air Force (*Voenno-Vozdushniye Sily Krasnoy Armii*, abbreviated to VVS-KA) were able to familiarize themselves with German military aircraft long before the invasion of the USSR in June 1941. Some had been captured in Spain during the Civil War and sent back to the Soviet Union, while others were bought from the Germans following the signing of the infamous non-aggression pact between the two countries in August 1939.

Having studied the Luftwaffe's principal fighter, the Messerschmitt Bf 109E, and compared its flight data with

Opposite

On 22 March 1945, as the Red Army battled its way to Berlin, the ranking Soviet ace Major Ivan Kozhedub of 176th GIAP engaged a formation of eight Fw 190s near the Seelow Heights. Despite the uneven odds, Kozhedub and his wingman, Dmitriy Nechaev, managed to turn defence into attack, singling out an Fw 190 when the formation split up, and then making the most of the La-7s excellent manoeuvrability to turn and attack again. Kozhedub scored his 60th victory during the dogfight. (Artwork by Gareth Hector, © Osprey Publishing)

167

the then new MiG-3, Yak-1 and LaGG-3, both the leadership of the VVS-KA and senior aircraft designers came to the conclusion in early 1941 that Soviet fighters had at last attained parity with their western European equivalents.

However, in the immediate aftermath of the launching of Operation *Barbarossa* on 22 June 1941, it quickly became apparent that the E-model's replacement, the Bf 109F, was clearly superior to all Russian fighters then in front-line service. For example, the 'Friedrich' was faster than all three new Soviet fighters up to an altitude of 16,500ft – fighting rarely occurred at higher altitudes on the Eastern Front.

The Bf 109F's resulting mastery of the skies greatly assisted the Wehrmacht in its advance into the USSR. Indeed, German troops had progressed so far east by the autumn and winter of 1942 that the Soviet aviation industry had to endure a painful, but necessary, evacuation to the country's eastern regions. Such a move further hindered the development of a homegrown fighter with the performance to rival the Bf 109F at just the time when front-line units in the VVS-KA were crying out for such a machine. Fortunately, the harsh Soviet winters of 1941 and 1942 did what Russian forces could not, stopping the German advance short of Moscow and allowing the Red Army to launch a series of counter-offensives in the south of the country.

Despite some success on the ground, VVS-KA units were still struggling to field a fighter that could match the Bf 109F. However, leading fighter designer Semyon Alekseyevich Lavochkin and his team of engineers had

An Fw 190 in flight. The first examples of the aircraft arrived on the Eastern Front with I./JG 51 on 6 September 1942. (From archives of D. Khazanov and A. Medved)

Pilots from 159th IAP conduct a preflight briefing in front of an La-5, complete with a rousing inscription, on the Leningrad front in the spring of 1943. Note the absence of the distinctive 'F' marking on the fighter's engine cowling, which means that the aircraft was powered by an early version of the M-82 engine. (From archives of D. Khazanov and A. Medved)

commenced work the previous year on a radial-engined version of his LaGG-3, the latter machine's 1,240hp Klimov M-105PF inline engine being replaced by an air-cooled Shvetsov M-82 radial of 1,700hp. Initially christened the LaG-5, the prototype proved to be some 37mph faster than the LaGG-3 in early flight testing, and it also boasted a superior rate of climb and better horizontal manoeuvrability, although its agility in the vertical plane was somewhat diminished. The new fighter was hastily rushed into production in Molotov (now Perm).

By the time the first examples reached front-line units in August 1942, the LaG-5 had been redesignated the Lavochkin La-5. That same month saw the service debut of the re-engined Bf 109G-2, which was fitted with a more powerful Daimler-Benz DB 605. Perhaps more importantly, on 6 September I./JG 51 arrived on the Eastern Front with the first examples of an all-new fighter type that would rival the La-5 for aerial supremacy – the Focke-Wulf Fw 190A. Like its Soviet rival, the Focke-Wulf was powered by an air-cooled radial engine of much the same horsepower in the form of the BMW 801. The new fighter was both fast and highly manoeuvrable, and was at its best at medium to low altitudes.

In an effort to retain parity with the Bf 109G and Fw 190A, Lavochkin improved the reliability and performance of the Shvetsov engine, initially with the introduction of the M-82F, which gave the resulting La-5F better performance at lower altitudes thanks to its unlimited boost. Just as this variant entered service in late 1942, Lavochkin commenced flight testing the definitive M-82FN-engined La-5FN. With direct fuel injection, the new motor was 10 per cent more powerful than the standard M-82. And with

A fantastic view inside an assembly hall at Focke-Wulf's Bremen plant. The Fw 190 was a well-designed aeroplane, with good access to most of its major systems and equipment. Focke-Wulf provided excellent access to the aircraft's BMW 801 engine, incorporating large cowling panels into the design which, if necessary, could be removed altogether for maintenance. (From archives of D. Khazanov and A. Medved)

most of the early structural and mechanical defects that plagued the La-5 now eradicated, the La-5FN could rival – and in some instances better – the performance of the Bf 109G-6 and Fw 190A-5 by the summer of 1943.

Although the Focke-Wulf would remain a significant threat to the VVS-KA into early 1944, by then Soviet pilots had come to realize that most of the fighter units equipped with the Fw 190 had been posted back to Germany to defend its cities against daylight bomber raids being mounted by the USAAF's Eighth and Fifteenth Air Forces. Indeed, by the spring of 1944 most Fw 190-equipped *Gruppen* on the Eastern Front were *Schlacht* (ground attack) units. These machines were not flown by *Experten* who had amassed vast experience engaging Soviet fighters, but by ex-Ju 87 and Hs 129 pilots with only limited knowledge of aerial combat. The Focke-Wulf gradually became a less dangerous foe for Soviet fighter pilots as a result, although the Bf 109G/K remained a threat for the rest of the war.

The VVS-KA enjoyed even greater supremacy in the air from the autumn of 1944 following the introduction of the La-7. Flight testing of the new Lavochkin fighter at the VVS NII KA (Red Army Air Force Scientific Research Institute) showed that its performance was superior to any version of the Bf 109 or Fw 190 fielded by the Luftwaffe at the altitudes at which combat occurred on the Eastern Front. Indeed, it could be claimed that the La-7 was the best Soviet fighter in series production in May 1945.

THE MACHINES
Lavochkin La-5 and La-7

On 29 July 1939 a small team of designers under the leadership of Vladimir Gorbunov received instructions via a decree from the Soviet government to design and manufacture a fast, all-wooden fighter that was to be designated the I-301. Two days later, Gorbunov and his engineering colleagues Semyon Lavochkin and Mikhail Gudkov were sent by order of the People's Commissariat for the Aviation Industry (NKAP) to small aircraft plant No. 301, which had been specially established as an experimental and production base for the group. This site had previously housed a factory making furniture for the Palace of the Soviets.

Gorbunov was placed in overall charge of the fighter project, Lavochkin was responsible for the aircraft's design and durability and Gudkov oversaw the supply of raw materials and manufacturing. The new design bureau was christened LaGG, the name being derived from the initials of its principal engineers. Shortly after the company had been formed, the NKAP leadership replaced Gorbunov with Lavochkin, officially making him the Chief Designer of the I-301.

On 30 March 1940, test pilot Aleksey Nikashin took to the skies for the first time in the new machine. Unlike rival designs from MiG and Yakovlev, which featured conventional mixed construction, LaGG's fighter was built from a special plywood known as *delta-drevsina*, which had been impregnated with phenols derived from birch tars. The latter allowed the plywood to be moulded into various aerodynamic shapes, and although heavier than conventional wood, it was also stronger and fire resistant. This material had been specifically chosen by LaGG due to its ease of manufacture and reliance on a natural resource that the Soviet Union had a limitless supply of – trees. By contrast, the USSR could only secure duralumin in modest quantities in 1940, thus slowing production of rival designs from Yakovlev and MiG. Once built, the streamlined I-301 received a coat of deep cherry red varnish that earned it the nickname 'the piano' because of its colour. Powered by a Klimov M-105P engine, the unarmed prototype achieved a top speed of 376mph in level during one of its early test flights. This impressive performance was systematically eroded in the coming months as the VVS-KA asked for various modifications to the aircraft that made it increasingly heavy. On 2 October 1940 LaGG was told that the fighter's range had to be doubled to 621 miles, so additional fuel tanks were fitted in the wings between the spars. The I-301's nose-mounted armament of a single MP-6 23mm cannon and two Berezin UB 12.7mm machine guns was also installed, as was other basic operational equipment such as seat armour and radio receivers.

An airframe checklist is consulted by a foreman and an assembly line worker in Factory No. 21 at Gorkiy in late 1944 as near complete La-7s are prepared for roll-out following construction. Factories No. 99 in Ulan-Ude and No. 391 in Moscow also built La-7s. (From archives of D. Khazanov and A. Medved)

By 1 December 1940, when the I-301 was renamed the LaGG-1 (from then on fighters in Soviet service were designated with odd numbers and aircraft of other purpose even numbers), the fighter's top speed had dropped to 357mph and its rate of climb had also been reduced. Not a single LaGG-1 was built, however, as all plants had been prepared for construction of the improved LaGG-3 – the Soviet government had ordered that 805 examples were to be delivered to front-line units by 1 July 1941. Five aircraft plants were chosen to fulfill this request, namely No. 21 at Gorkiy (today's Nizhniy Novgorod), No. 23 in Leningrad (now St Petersburg), No. 31 in Taganrog, No. 153 in Novosibirsk and No. 463 in Tallinn. Chief Designer Lavochkin was sent to Gorkiy to oversee production while Vladimir Gorbunov travelled to Taganrog.

The first production LaGG-3s were completed in December 1940 at Plant No. 23, and once examples started to reach operational units several months later they began to suffer from engine overheating, radiator and hydraulic system leakages and the breaking of connecting rods due to heavy ailerons and elevators. The general build quality of the aircraft also left much to be desired, with rags left in pipelines, tools forgotten in the airframe, nuts and bolts left loose and parts fitted carelessly. Finally, the cockpit transparency, made of a nitro-cellulose compound, also drew heavy criticism for its poor visibility and rapid yellowing when exposed to sunlight.

Things only got worse for LaGG-3 units following the German invasion of the Soviet Union on 22 June 1941, for the fighter's now-poor performance was cruelly exposed. With its top speed reduced to 332mph at best, plagued by poor handling characteristics, sluggish controls and an inadequate rate of turn, the 322 LaGG-3s that had reached the front line by June were 'easy meat' for the swarms of Bf 109E/Fs that hunted down VVS-KA fighters during Operation *Barbarossa*. These problems were further exacerbated by poor leadership in Soviet fighter regiments, outdated tactics and a general lack of familiarity with new types such as the LaGG-3. Surviving pilots in the front line whispered among themselves that the type designation LaGG stood for '*Lakirovannyi, Garantirovannyi Grob*', which translates into 'Guaranteed, Lacquered Coffin'.

Early combat reports detailing its poor showing provoked stinging criticism from Premier Joseph Stalin himself, and the leadership of VVS-KA bluntly stated that the LaGG-3 was seriously inferior to the Yak-1 fighter in terms of its speed, manoeuvrability and ease of flying. Nevertheless, the LaGG-3 remained in production because unlike the Yak-1, it was easy to build due to an abundance of raw materials.

Stung by official criticism of his aircraft, Lavochkin was hastily looking for ways to save his 'baby' by the autumn of 1941. Meanwhile, more than 400 new 1,700hp M-82 radial engines designed by Arkadiy Shvetsov had accumulated at Engine Factory No. 19 in Perm. Examples of this powerplant had by then been flight tested in the MiG-3 and Yak-7 (both normally fitted with inline engines), although neither type had shown a great improvement in speed when paired with the M-82.

Now, with the NKAP seeking to solve the problems surrounding the supply of Klimov engines, it requested that the LaGG-3 be paired up with an alternate powerplant in the form of the readily available M-82

A quartet of La-5FNs have their M-82FN engines run up on a snow-covered airfield during the early months of 1944. All four machines have the distinctive FN diamond marking on their tight-fitting engine cowlings. (From archives of D. Khazanov and A. Medved)

(designated the ASh-82 by the VVS-KA from the spring of 1944), despite the latter being almost one-and-a-half times heavier than the fighter's M-105P. Lavochkin calculated that installation of the Shvetsov in the LaGG-3 was only possible after the fighter's slender airframe had been drastically reworked. Indeed, the diameter of the M-82 was 18in. greater than the maximum cross-section of the LaGG-3's fuselage. And as previously mentioned, it was 551lb heavier and significantly shorter than the M-105P, which in turn meant that the fighter's centre of gravity would be shifted dangerously forwards.

Despite these problems, an engineering team from Plant No. 21 led by Semyon Alexeyev set about modifying a production LaGG-3 fuselage to accept an M-82. The task proved to be an extremely complicated one, but after many weeks they had created a radial-engined fighter. Because the M-82's mid-section was much wider than the fuselage of the LaGG-3, a plywood skirting was bonded to both sides of the fuselage's load-carrying skin. The engine mounts were reworked to take the new engine and ShVAK 20mm synchronized cannon fitted above the M-82. Finally, engine cooling was achieved by the installation of two variable cooling flaps on the fuselage sides, the M-82's cooling-air baffles (surfaces which regulated the flow of cooling air for the engine's cylinders) being slightly modified so as to provide uniform thermal conditions for the upper and lower cylinders.

The new fighter, designated the LaGG-3 M-82, was rolled out of the Gorkiy plant in February 1942, and by early March it was ready for its first flight. The latter event was undertaken by Plant No. 21 test pilot G. A. Mishchenko, who told an anxious Lavochkin upon his return that 'The aircraft is good, pleasant to control and responsive, but the cylinder heads become hot. Measures should be taken to correct this'. Further test flights confirmed this problem, the M-82 overheating even when the outside air temperature was below zero. The oil cooler was subsequently replaced with a more efficient design, the supercharger air intake was repositioned in the upper section of the cowling and the baffles were improved. On a more positive note, early testing had also shown the LaGG-3 M-82's speed to be 372mph in level flight at medium to low altitudes – some 37mph faster than a production-standard LaGG-3.

Opposite

This La-7 was flown by Maj Vladimir Lavrinenkov, Regimental Commander of 9th GIAP, during the final months of the war. Maj Lavrinenkov used '17' as his personal number throughout the war (he was born on 17 May 1919), whilst the lightning bolt marking on either side of the fuselage was similar to the symbol applied by the French-manned *Normandie-Niemen* Regiment to its Yaks. Both units served in the same division. By May 1945 Lavrinenkov had claimed 36 individual and 11 shared kills. (Artwork by Andrey Yurgenson, © Osprey Publishing)

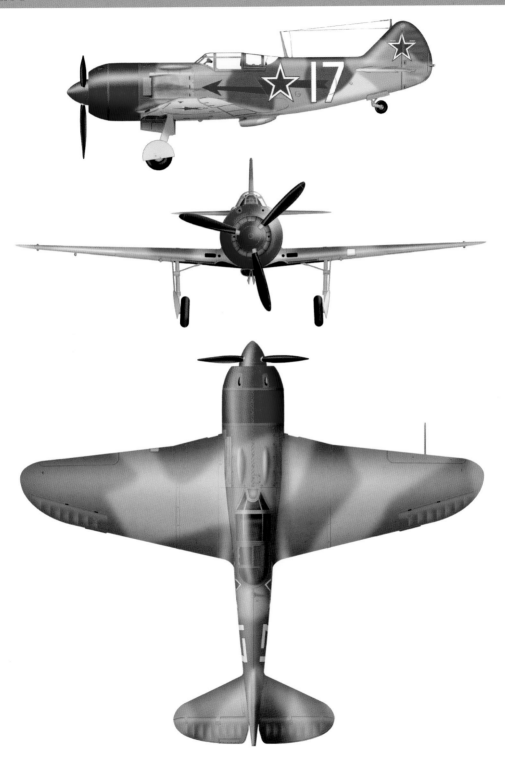

By mid-April 1942 the most serious problems afflicting the new aircraft had been solved, and it was handed over to the VVS NII KA for testing. Further evaluation was undertaken in May, when the LaGG-3 M-82 outperformed not only indigenous fighter types but also captured enemy aircraft. At the conclusion of the test period VVS NII KA Chief Engineer Gen A. K. Repin noted, 'The first experiment in using an M-82 engine in a LaGG fighter aircraft has produced satisfactory results – flight and technical personnel give the LaGG-5 a positive evaluation'. The VVS NII KA recommended that the fighter be put into series production at Plant No. 21, and this was officially approved by the State Committee for Defence on 19 May 1942.

Although the tests had proven the soundness of the design, they had also highlighted some problems. The fighter was even more difficult to fly than the notoriously poor-handling LaGG-3. This was particularly the case when changing direction in a banked turn, the pilot needing great physical strength to cope with the stick forces required to perform such a manoeuvre. It also took 25 seconds to complete a banked turn – too long for a single-engined fighter. This was primarily because the fighter was overweight. Engine oil splashing on the windscreen and 'supercooling', which saw the M-82 stall due to power loss, were also regular afflictions.

Nevertheless, production LaG-5s (as the aircraft was now designated – this was shortened to La-5 in September 1942) started to leave Factory No. 21 from July, with the first examples to reach the front line being issued to 49th Red Banner IAP.

In the autumn of 1942 the VVS first documented the appearance at the front of new German fighters in the form of the Bf 109G-2 and

For much of the war all Lavochkin fighters were armed with a pair of 20mm ShVAK cannon synchronised to fire through the propeller – two ammunition cans contained a total of 400 rounds for the ShVAKs. In the final months of the conflict a number of new-build La-7s had their ShVAKs replaced by three Berezina UB-20 cannon. (From archives of D. Khazanov and A. Medved)

Fw 190A-3. Both aircraft had a maximum speed of more than 380mph in level flight, while the La-5 could only accelerate up to 362mph at an altitude of 20,000ft. In an effort to achieve parity with the new breed of Luftwaffe fighters, Shvetsov introduced the M-82F *forsirovannyi* ('boosted') engine in December 1942. Improvements to its durability meant that pilots could now build up supercharger boost pressure without suffering the mechanical woes that often afflicted the engine – previously, using boost for more than five minutes was forbidden, as it tended to burn through the exhaust pipes. Improving the engine's performance by 160hp, the new powerplant made the Lavochkin fighter more effective up to 10,000ft. The 'boosted' engine was installed in the La-5F at Gorkiy from January 1943.

Initially, unmodified La-5 airframes were fitted with the new engines. However, Lavochkin had also been working on aerodynamic improvements to his fighter, giving the pilot a better view from the cockpit. The La-5's poor handling characteristics in certain flight regimes were also addressed, and the aircraft underwent a strict weight reduction programme, which included decreasing the fighter's fuel capacity from five to three internal tanks. The end result was the definitive La-5F, which had lowered rear fuselage decking, sealed cowling joints, reshaped oil cooler ducts and myriad other detail changes. Armament consisted of two ShVAK 20mm cannon. These changes gave the aircraft a top speed of 364mph at 12,000ft, which made it faster than the Fw 190A-4 at this altitude.

Just as the new variant was entering production, Shvetsov commenced testing the M-82FN at his Perm factory, this engine featuring direct fuel injection into the cylinders. Although 66lb heavier than the M-82F, the new engine produced 1,850hp – 150hp more than its predecessor. Lavochkin also improved the La-5 to take advantage of the new powerplant, introducing fuselage pressurization, a retractable tail wheel and larger tail surfaces to reduce stick forces when manoeuvring.

The La-5FN first saw combat with 32nd GIAP of 1st GIAK (Guards Fighter Aviation Corps) on the Bryansk Front in July and August 1943. Participating in the bitter aerial engagements over the Kursk Bulge, the unit completed 25 combat missions and claimed 33 aircraft destroyed (including 21 Fw 190As) for the loss of six La-5FNs – it is likely that these successes were seriously exaggerated. Nevertheless, the Luftwaffe quickly realized that the latest incarnation of the Lavochkin fighter was to be avoided at medium to low altitudes.

With La-5FN production finally getting into full swing by late 1943 following restricted availability of M-82FN engines, Lavochkin set about further refining his by now outstanding fighter. Dubbed the '1944 standard'

An early-build La-7 from an unidentified unit rests between sorties in late 1944. The fighter's key recognition feature was its clean cowling, devoid of the La-5FN's extended supercharger intake trunk fairing and engine oil cooler intake. (From archives of D. Khazanov and A. Medved)

aircraft, the new aircraft had metal rather than wooden wing spars, improved internal and external sealing of the powerplant to the airframe and three 20mm UB-20 cannon. The fighter's oil cooler was also relocated from the bottom of the engine cowling to the underside of the rear fuselage and the supercharger air intake moved from atop the cowling to the wing centre section leading edges. Flown for the first time on 1 February 1944, the '1944 standard' aircraft was 121lb lighter than the La-5FN. This meant that a top speed of 425mph could be attained at 20,200ft (making it 50mph faster than the Fw 190A-8 at this altitude), despite the aircraft using a standard 1,850hp M-82FN engine.

Although possessing promising performance, the new aircraft also suffered a series of problems during further testing that slowed its introduction into service. The principal fault centred on the UB-20 cannon, as in certain flight profiles spent cartridges from the weapons hit the fighter's tail fin when ejected. It was decided that the aircraft, designated the La-7, would keep the La-5FN's weaponry.

Production of the aircraft commenced at Gorkiy in the spring of 1944, followed by Plant No. 381 in Moscow. Service testing by 63rd GIAP started in mid-September, with 30 aircraft being assigned to the regiment. It had flown the La-5 since late 1942, so both pilots and groundcrew quickly converted to the new fighter. These early machines suffered from poor engine reliability, and four La-7s were lost through powerplant failure. This was caused by the ingestion of sand and dust into the cylinders through the La-7's relocated air intake. The armament was also causing problems, as the reworking of the cowling area made the guns less accessible for reloading. The hitting power of the weapons was also criticized, as a single burst of fire was proving insufficient to down an Fw 190 even from close range. However, the most serious problem was the spate of in-flight wing failures that resulted in six crashes and the deaths of four pilots in late October 1944. The La-7 was grounded until the fault (reduced density of the metal used to build the spars) was found.

These technical issues were eventually overcome, and by the end of the war more than 5,750 La-7s had been built. The last of these were fitted with three synchronized Berezina UB-20 cannon, production of this variant having finally commenced in January 1945.

Focke-Wulf Fw 190

Arguably, the Focke-Wulf Fw 190 evolved into wartime Germany's most effective fighter, offering the Luftwaffe the benefit of manoeuvrability combined with stability as a formidable gun platform and the flexibility to perform as an air superiority fighter, a heavily armed and armoured interceptor and as an ordnance-carrying ground-attack aircraft. Yet the development of the Fw 190 was often protracted and tortuous. Following a specification by the *Technisches Amt* (Technical Office) of the *Reichsluftfahrtministerium* (RLM) in 1937 to Focke-Wulf Flugzeugbau GmbH for a fighter with a performance that would be superior to that of the still new and largely untested Bf 109, Dipl.-Ing. Kurt Tank, the firm's Technical Director, and his design team at Bremen dutifully turned to the drawing board. Tank described his approach to the development of the fighter as follows:

> The 'aircraft-soldier' should be simple and undemanding, capable of operating from rough, front-line airfields, easy for flight/technical staff to familiarise themselves with, able to 'hold its ground' and return to its home base after sustaining considerable battle damage and carry powerful weaponry. Therefore, ideologically, the Fw 190 is not a 'racing stallion' but a simple, strong and sturdy 'cavalier's horse'.

Yet before the first project drawings of the 'cavalier's horse' were issued there were voices of discontent – not from Messerschmitt or other manufacturers, but from within the RLM itself. There were those who considered the Bf 109 to be of such advanced design that it would be impossible to develop and construct another fighter of comparable performance and quality. In any case, claimed the dissenters, any future war involving German arms would not last long enough to justify the time and expense of its development, or to find the aircraft sufficient employment. Furthermore, Focke-Wulf 's response was to think in terms of a rugged aircraft built first and foremost for *interception*, and therefore able to absorb considerable punishment in action, not specifically for *offence* or *attack*. This philosophy won little support in the corridors of the RLM, however.

German air doctrine at this stage envisaged a short war – weeks or months at the most, with an enemy defeated by swift movement and overwhelming force – and debate coursed through the RLM about the Focke-Wulf proposal. Many believed that there would be no requirement for an aircraft whose *raison d'être* was essentially that of *defence*, let alone one which incorporated apparently highly dubious, heavy and expensive radial engine technology in preference to a more aerodynamically favourable inline, liquid-cooled engine.

However, Tank, a decorated war veteran, and Focke-Wulf 's resolute and exceptionally gifted designer, remained undaunted, and within some quarters of the *Technisches Amt* he found support. Because an air-cooled radial was capable of withstanding more combat stress (a single bullet hole could sever a coolant line and rapidly cause a liquid-cooled inline engine to seize up through overheating), and because Tank's design would not impinge upon production of the liquid-cooled DB 601 – the powerplant of the Bf 109 – the RLM eventually relented and permitted Focke-Wulf to proceed with the design.

In the summer of 1938 the RLM issued a contract for construction of three prototypes of the 'Fw 190', a single-seat fighter to be powered by the 18-cylinder, 1,550hp BMW 139 radial engine. Maintaining the tradition

A BMW 801D-2 fitted in an Fw 190A. The whole powerplant arrangement was neat and closely cowled, being one of the finest examples of radial engine installation in a World War II fighter. This aircraft has 'tropical' filters fitted to its open-fronted supercharger air intakes (the large pipe-like structure beneath the open side cowling panel). (From archives of D. Khazanov and A. Medved)

of naming its machines after birds, Focke-Wulf came to know the Fw 190 as the *Würger* (Shrike). Drawings of the V1 dating from the autumn of 1938 show proposals to install an armament of two 7.9mm MG 17 and two 13mm MG 131 machine guns, all wing-mounted.

Focke-Wulf took its time and made strenuous efforts to ensure that structure and build were second to none, and that the design would demand the minimum of maintenance in operational conditions. Early on it was realized that the BMW 139 was suffering from teething problems, and this would prove to be the main fault in an otherwise exemplary prototype by the time the unarmed Fw 190 V1 flew for the first time on 1 June 1939. Focke-Wulf 's chief test pilot, Hans Sander, was nearly suffocated by exhaust fumes from an overheating engine that reached a temperature of more than 130°F (54°C) during the flight.

BMW quickly offered a replacement in the form of the BMW 801, which was another radial engine of the same diameter, but longer and heavier by 350lb. This necessitated moving the cockpit further back and strengthening the airframe, which helped alleviate the problem. However, Luftwaffe engineers noted that the whole project would hinge on the performance of the 1,600hp BMW 801. Problems still occurred with the new powerplant too, and in the case of the armed V6, the engine temperature soared to the extent that the ammunition in the cowl machine guns became dangerously hot during test flying.

Focke-Wulf was fortunate in that no less a figure than Reichsmarschall Hermann Göring happened to be present when the BMW 801C-0-equipped fifth prototype flew with a reworked fuselage from Bremen in April 1940. It quickly became evident that the alterations to the design adversely affected wing loading, and thus manoeuvrability, but Göring apparently viewed the new aircraft with enthusiasm. Indeed, his endorsement provided the catalyst for the further production of a series of six Fw 190A-0s, and these were delivered to the test unit *Erprobungsstaffel* 190, under Oberleutnant Otto Behrens, at Rechlin in late February 1941.

Difficulties were initially encountered with these machines. Occasionally the propeller mechanism proved troublesome, but it was the BMW 801C that caused the most headaches. Between the arrival of the Fw 190A-0s and the early summer, Behrens, a trained motor mechanic, and his engineers and pilots (most of the latter seconded from II./JG 26) undertook intensive trouble-shooting in an effort to improve engine reliability – powerplants were routinely failing after just 20 flying hours, the BMWs erupting in flames. Finally, by August 1941, things were deemed safe enough to allow the first Fw 190A-1 production machines, each armed with four Rheinmetall-Borsig MG 17s (two in the cowling and two in the

Seemingly oblivious to the roar of the BMW 801D-2 ticking over just feet away from them, two suitably insulated groundcrew turn their thoughts to Bavaria in July. The pilot, meanwhile, has gone 'head down' in the cockpit in order to check that the engine oil temperature is rising correctly in his Fw 190A-4 prior to undertaking I./JG 54's first sortie of the day from Krasnogvardeisk in early 1943. (From archives of D. Khazanov and A. Medved)

wing roots) and a pair of 20mm Oerlikon MG FF cannon in the outer wings, to be handed over to 6./JG 26 in Belgium.

Unfortunately, despite the best efforts of *Erprobungsstaffel* 190, problems persisted – nine Fw 190s crashed in August and September, and according to Behrens's reports, the finger of blame was pointed at BMW, whose engines continued to be plagued by overheating and compressor damage. There were also further delays in the delivery of the much-anticipated 801D, these again being caused by mechanical failures.

Towards the end of 1941 deliveries of the Fw 190A-2 to Major Gerhard Schöpfel's *Stab.*/JG 26 at Audembert and Major Johannes Seifert's I./JG 26 at St Omer commenced, this time in greater numbers than the A-1, since Focke-Wulf was supplemented in its output from Bremen by sub-contractors Ago in Oschersleben and Arado at Warnemünde.

The A-2 benefited from an improved 1,600hp BMW 801C-2 that was cooled by extra ventilation slots at the rear of the engine. The aircraft also featured an uprated weapons array that included two 20mm Mauser MG 151 cannon built into the wing roots, with interrupter gear incorporated to allow synchronized fire through the propeller arc. The aircraft was fitted with a Revi C/12D reflector gunsight, FuG 7 transmitter/receivers and FuG 25 IFF (identification friend/foe) equipment. The production lines delivered 425 Fw 190A-2s between August 1941 and July 1942.

Earlier that year, in April 1942, the first examples of the Fw 190A-3 had been delivered to JG 26, with Ago and Arado having been engaged in production since late in the previous year. The A-3 was fitted with the new 1,700hp BMW 801D-2 engine, its uprated power achieved by increasing the compression ratio in the cylinders and refining the two-speed supercharger. The variant was also equipped with a pair of MG 17s and two MG 151s, and it also featured a modified tail fin to accommodate an aerial antenna, as well as a redesigned cowling. Production of the A-3 continued into 1943, by which time 509 had been built. The A-3 was graced with the ability to adapt easily to the role of a fighter-bomber using a series of *Umbau* (modifications) – as the A-3/U1 (by means of installation of an ETC 500 bomb rack), U3 (ETC 250 fuselage rack and SC 50 underwing racks) and U7 sub-variants.

The Fw 190A-4 was developed into a fully 'convertible fighter/fighter-bomber', with low-level capability provided by a Methanol-Water (MW) 50 power boost system when flying below 16,500ft. Capitalising on the A-3's adaptability, the Fw 190A-4, although carrying the same fixed armament as its predecessor, introduced an even more wide-ranging and sophisticated family of sub-variants. The A-4/U1, armed with only two MG 151s, was fitted with a pair of ETC 501 bomb racks for carrying two SC 250 bombs, while the A-4/U3 emerged in October 1942 as a true 'assault' aircraft. It boasted a 6mm armoured ring ahead of the cowling and 5mm steel armour plates beneath the cowling and cockpit that were designed to protect the pilot, fuel tanks and engine on ground-attack missions. The A-4/U8 was a long-range fighter-bomber fitted with a 66-gal drop tank and four SC 50 bombs on wing racks, together with full armament. Benefiting from an MW 50 power boost system, the A-4 also carried a FuG 16Z VHF transceiver.

Bombs gone from their ventral racks, a pair of Fw 190Fs –possibly from II./SG 77 – return to base somewhere in the southern Russian steppe in the spring of 1944. (From archives of D. Khazanov and A. Medved)

From April 1943 the Fw 190A-4 was superseded by the A-5. With the exception of a lengthened fuselage (by 6in.) and strengthened housing for the BMW 801D-2 engine, the A-5, of which 723 were built up to the summer of 1943, was essentially unaltered, but offered an even more inventive selection of sub-variants, reflecting the versatility of the fighter. Provision was made for cannon, drop tanks, fuselage/wing-mounted bombs and 21cm underwing air-to-air mortars for operations against US heavy bombers.

The fighter-bomber and attack aircraft variants that would feature so prominently on the Eastern Front were based on the Fw 190A-5. Indeed, in July 1943 an Fw 190A-5/U3 attack aircraft was captured by the Soviets and handed over to the VVS NII KA for evaluation. Its specialists established that apart from the usual armour protection weighing 242lb, A-5/U3 aircraft also carried 16 additional armour plates totalling 441lb. Attack versions of the Fw 190A had started to arrive on the Eastern Front with Luftwaffe *Schlachtgruppen* from March 1943, and these were routinely engaged by La-5/7 pilots through to the end of the war. Based on the Fw 190A-5/U8, the G-1 was equipped with racks under the fuselage to carry bombs up to a weight of 4,000lb. Strengthened landing gear was introduced to allow the Fw 190G to cope with the extra weight. The G-2 and G-3 differed only in the type of wing racks they used for their external stores, and they started to reach front-line units in the late summer of 1943. The final variant was the G-8, produced from the autumn of 1943 through to the spring of 1944. Powered by an uprated 1,800hp BMW 801D-2 engine and incorporating upgrades introduced in the Fw 190A-8, this version, fitted with a nitrous oxide injection system, was designated the Fw 190G-8/R4.

Entering service after the G-1, the Fw 190F-1 was based on the A-4. Its outboard wing cannon were removed and 793lb of armour plating fitted to protect the engine and cockpit from groundfire. This variant was further modified to carry a centreline ETC 501 bomb rack. The follow-on F-2 was related to the Fw 190A-5 but it introduced a bubble canopy, while the F-3, which corresponded to the Fw 190A-6, could carry a 66-gal drop tank or 550lb bomb on its centreline. F-3/R1 and R2 sub-variants had additional wing racks or MK 103 30mm cannon options. The F-8 was based on the

Opposite
Fw 190A-6 'Yellow 5' was assigned to Oberleutnant Otto Kittel of 3./JG 54 when the unit was based at Riga-Skulte in August 1944. In keeping with Eastern Front anonymity, there is nothing to distinguish this perfectly standard A-6 as being the mount of JG 54's most successful pilot. The vast bulk of Kittel's final total of 267 confirmed victories were scored with the Focke-Wulf, making him arguably the greatest Fw 190 ace of the Russian Front. (Artwork by Andrey Yurgenson, © Osprey Publishing)

Fw 190A-6

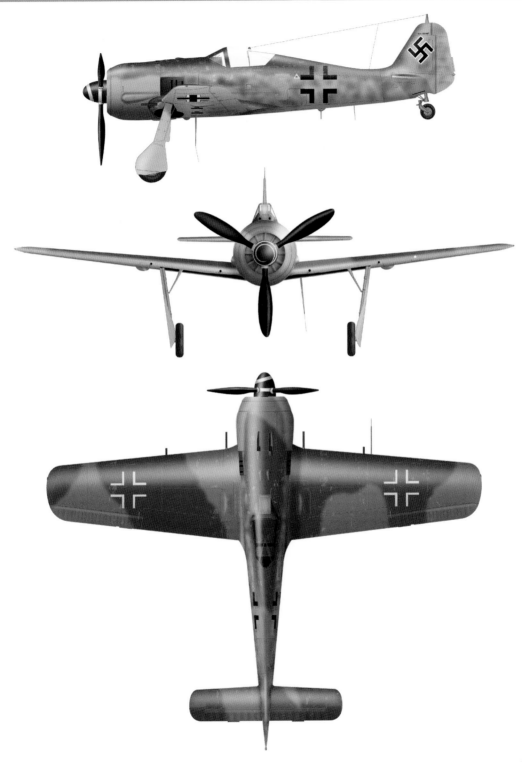

Fw 190A-8, with two engine-mounted MG 131 machine guns and ETC 50 bomb racks. The F-8/U2 and U3 had a TSA bombsight for anti-shipping strikes with, respectively, the BT 700 or BT 1400 bombs. The final Fw 190F variant was the F-9, which was similar to the F-8 but powered by the BMW 801 TS/TH.

The factor of weight provided the genesis for the first variant in a series that saw Focke-Wulf redesign certain elements in the Fw 190, such as internal wing structure, in order to allow for greater capability and adaptation in ordnance load. Units in the field had found that the MG FF outer wing cannon did not provide sufficient firepower, and simply added weight on the A-5. Thus emerged the Fw 190A-6.

Originally conceived as a fighter for the Eastern Front, the A-6 was designed to accept an array of *Rustsätze* (field conversion kits) that could be added quickly to, or removed from, an airframe for mission flexibility. The A-6 went into production in May 1943, and up to February 1944 1,192 machines had been built by Arado at Warnemünde, Ago at Oschersleben and Fieseler at Kassel. The aircraft was fitted with a 1,700hp BMW 801D-2. The standard fuel load – and thus range – was enhanced by the installation of a centreline ETC 501 bomb rack, to which could be hung a 66-gal drop tank. Standard armament consisted of two fuselage-mounted 7.92mm MG 17 machine guns (replaced with MG 131s in the A-7) and four electrically fired 20mm Mauser MG 151/20 cannon. The tracer ammunition of the former weapon allowed Luftwaffe pilots to sharpen their aim when using the latter.

The heavier armed, and armoured, versions of the Fw 190A-6, A-7 and A-8 were used almost exclusively by Defence of the Reich units in the West (although IV./JG 3 used its anti-bomber Fw 190A-8/R8s in strafing attacks on Soviet troops as the latter advanced on Berlin), and are therefore not detailed in this chapter.

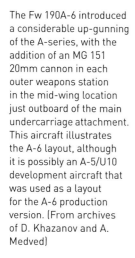

The Fw 190A-6 introduced a considerable up-gunning of the A-series, with the addition of an MG 151 20mm cannon in each outer weapons station in the mid-wing location just outboard of the main undercarriage attachment. This aircraft illustrates the A-6 layout, although it is possibly an A-5/U10 development aircraft that was used as a layout for the A-6 production version. (From archives of D. Khazanov and A. Medved)

The Fw 190A-8 was by far the most numerous and most potent of all the BMW-engined Focke-Wulf fighter variants. Indeed, more than 2,500 examples were produced between Focke-Wulf at Cottbus and Aslau, Ago at Oschersleben, Fieseler at Kassel, Weserflug at Tempelhof and Norddeutsche Dornier at Wismar.

Also powered by a BMW 801D-2, it could attain a maximum speed of 404mph at 18,000ft, reaching 410mph with GM 1 nitrous oxygen boost. Fuel was held in two self-sealing tanks (of 51 and 64 gallons respectively) beneath the cockpit, but another 25 gallons could be carried in the area normally assigned to the GM 1 fuel tank or the MW 50 methanol-water boost. Range was 646 miles at 23,000ft, extending to 920 miles when carrying a 66-gal drop tank.

The last all-new variant of the Focke-Wulf fighter to engage La-5/7s in the final months of the war was the Fw 190D-9. Developed in 1942 as a replacement for the aborted Fw 190B/C high-altitude fighter, the *Langnasen-Dora* (Longnose-Dora) made use of the inverted inline Junkers Jumo 213 engine, combined with an MW 50 booster, to achieve an impressive rate of climb and top speed – crucial ingredients for a Defence of the Reich fighter. Service entry came in August 1944, with the first fighters to reach the Jagdwaffe being used as Me 262 airfield defenders. Although most D-9s served in the West, a small number from JGs 3, 4, 6 and 51 saw sporadic action in the ill-fated defence of Berlin in the last months of the war, and claims were made by some of the higher scoring aces against the best Soviet fighters of the day.

TYPE HISTORY
The La-5/7
LaGG-3 M-82

This experimental aircraft was made when a standard production LaGG-3 had its water-cooled Klimov M-105P engine replaced with a Shvetsov M-82A radial by an engineering team from Plant No. 21 in Gorkiy in February 1942. The air-cooled powerplant weighed 1,895lb and produced 1,700hp at low level, 1,540hp at an altitude of 6,725ft and 1,330hp at 17,700ft. By contrast, the output of the M-105P did not exceed 1,100hp at any altitude. The diameter of the M-82 was 18in. greater than the cross-section of the M-105P, and this meant that the LaGG-3's forward fuselage had to be reworked in order to accommodate the engine. The aircraft was to have been armed with four ShVAK 20mm cannon, but problems with engine cooling meant that two of them had to be removed so that two

The LaGG-3 M-82 experimental aircraft is seen with its cowlings open to reveal the snug-fitting Shvetsov M-82 radial engine. This one-off machine was created by an engineering team from Plant No. 21 in Gorkiy in February 1942, the standard production LaGG-3 having its water-cooled Klimov M-105P engine replaced with the Shvetsov radial. (From archives of D. Khazanov and A. Medved)

variable cooling flaps could be added to the fuselage sides. First flown in March 1942, the aircraft was subsequently destroyed in a crash on 12 July 1942 following engine failure.

LaG-5

This variant was produced from the end of July to 8 September 1942 at Gorkiy's Factory No. 21. The first 200 aircraft had a forward fuselage section made of double-thickness bakelite ply (layers of birch strip bonded with bakelite film) skinning, which could be shaped to provide smooth contours from the circular engine cowling forward of the cockpit through to the oval framing of the rear fuselage and tail section. New technology in the manufacturing process introduced with the LaG-5 meant that the fighter's weight was reduced by 188lb in comparison with the LaGG-3 M-82. In contrast to the prototype, the wings of production aircraft featured leading edge slats on the outer sections. The fuel system consisted of five tanks, four of them in the wings. Some aircraft were manufactured with a single ShVAK cannon and a Berezin UBS 12.7mm machine gun.

La-5

The LaG-5 became the La-5 following order number 683 from NKAP dated 8 September 1942. Virtually identical to its predecessor, the fighter was built at Plant No. 21 from September 1942 through to the end of that year, by which time 1,107 La-5s had been constructed – a further 22 were completed by Factory No. 31 in Tbilisi. The fighter had a maximum speed of 355mph at an altitude of 6,500ft and 362mph at 18,500ft. Complaints from former LaGG-3 pilots that the LaG-5's heavier weight and insufficient control surface size and balance made it more demanding to fly led to an increase in the size of the elevator and the tail fin in production La-5s, although the horizontal tailplane area remained the same. Flat armoured glass 57mm thick was added to the windscreen, and external store shackles were also introduced.

La-5F

NKAP order number 778, dated 16 September 1942, instructed aircraft engine Factory No. 19 in Molotov to commence production of the M-82F *forsirovannyi* ('boosted') engine. Its improved supercharger boost only worked up to an altitude of 10,000ft, its output at an altitude of 2,600ft having been increased to 1,760hp. Aircraft fitted with this engine had their cowling flaps inscribed with a small letter 'F' in a circle (later changed to a diamond shape). The supercharger intake trunk fairing atop the engine cowling was increased in size so as to channel more air to the M-82F. Additionally, every second La-5F was fitted with an RSI-4 radio set.

More significantly, in an effort to improve visibility, the fighter's rear fuselage decking behind the cockpit was lowered and the canopy lengthened, with a transparent rear section fitted with armoured glass. These aircraft were given the identifier 'Type 39' at Factory No. 21, with the modification first being seen on the ninth batch of La-5Fs built in November 1942. Factory No. 21 was joined in production of the La-5F by Factory No. 99 in Ulan-Ude and Factory No. 381 in Nizhniy Tagil from January 1943.

La-5FN

Bench testing of the M-82FN engine with fuel injection at Shvetsov's Perm factory was completed by late June 1942. The M-82 had shown a propensity for overheating due to the La-5's close-fitting cowlings, so the FN version was re-engineered with enlarged cylinder ribbing to improve cooling in-flight. Internally, its pistons and rods were also reinforced and every cylinder was fitted with an individual exhaust pipe. Finally, the engine featured direct fuel injection into the cylinder heads in place of the carburettors fitted to the M-82 and M-82F. The engine's output increased to 1,850hp at low level, 1,670hp at 5,000ft and 1,460hp at 15,000ft.

The prototype La-5FN was first tested in December 1942, this aircraft being a highback 'Type 37' La-5. In March 1943 a second prototype La-5FN was built utilizing the latest 'Type 39' airframe, and this was handed over for state testing at the end of that month. Featuring metal wing spars and a flight weight of just 7,000lb, the second prototype

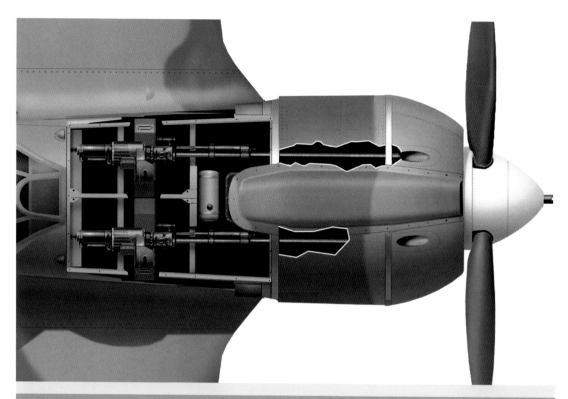

La-5FN CANNON

All versions of the La-5, and most La-7s, were armed with two synchronised ShVAK 20mm cannon, each weapon having its own ammunition tank containing 200 rounds per gun. The Lavochkin fighter was originally to have been armed with four synchronised ShVAKs, but problems with engine cooling meant that two of the weapons had to be removed so that two variable cooling flaps could be added to the fuselage sides. Some early-build LaG-5s were also manufactured with a single ShVAK cannon and one large-calibre Berezin UBS 12.7mm machine gun. Whilst Soviet pilots rarely complained about the reliability of their weaponry, the two synchronised ShVAK cannon occasionally proved insufficient to knock down the well-armoured Fw 190. (Artwork by Jim Laurier, © Osprey Publishing)

exhibited outstanding performance characteristics – a maximum speed of 372mph at low level using boost, 391mph at 10,500ft and 405mph at 20,500ft. Lavochkin made various improvements to the airframe to take advantage of the new powerplant, introducing fuselage pressurization, a retractable tail wheel and larger tail surfaces to improve handling and reduce stick forces when manoeuvring. The radio mast was angled against the airflow and the air intake for the gear-driven supercharger was enlarged atop the engine cowling. The letters 'FN' within a diamond shape were inscribed on the sides of the engine nacelles.

The cyrillic letters 'FN' within a diamond stencilled onto the engine nacelle denote that this aircraft is an La-5FN. Another feature unique to this variant was the replacement of the La-5Fs distinctive small exhaust vent with a larger, flatter panel. (From archives of D. Khazanov and A. Medved)

In spite of its improved performance, the La-5FN was not put into immediate mass production because of a shortage of M-82FNs. Indeed, the Gorkiy plant had to wait until the autumn of 1943 before it had sufficient engines available to switch to La-5FN production. Other plants started building La-5FNs in early 1944.

La-7

Initially dubbed the '1944 standard' La-5FN, this aircraft featured a number of significant differences from its immediate predecessor. The fighter had metal wing spars in place of wooden examples, improved internal and external sealing of the powerplant to the airframe and three 20mm UB-20 cannon. Its oil cooler was also relocated (from the bottom of the engine cowling to the underside of the rear fuselage) and the supercharger air intake moved from atop the cowling to the wing centre section leading edges. The aircraft's take-off weight had also been reduced by 121lb, and its aerodynamics improved. As a result, the prototype displayed outstanding performance characteristics, with a maximum speed of 373mph being achieved at low level, 419mph at 10,500ft and 425mph at 20,000ft.

Soon designated the La-7, production examples (classified as 'Type 45s' by Lavochkin) started to emerge from Gorkiy's Plant No. 21 in the spring of 1944, with Plant No. 381 in Moscow and Plant No. 99 in Ulan-Ude coming on line in April and September 1944, respectively. Aircraft were initially built with two ShVAK cannon rather than the planned trio of more modern UB-20s, due to problems with the latter weapon. The La-7 remained in production until late 1945.

Officially captioned as 'an La-7 of an unidentified Guards regiment on the Baltic Front, 1944', this aircraft may have been the personal mount of Vasiliy Zaitsev (36 individual and 19 shared kills), deputy commander of 11th GIAD. Most of his fighters featured a white nose marking identical to the one seen here. (From archives of D. Khazanov and A. Medved)

The Fw 190

Fw 190 V1 and V2

The Fw 190 prototype was rolled out in May 1939 and flew for the first time from Bremen airfield on 1 June. The aircraft was powered by a fan-cooled 1,550hp BMW 139 radial fitted with a special ducted spinner to reduce drag, but the engine overheated rapidly nevertheless, and eventually the ducted spinner was removed and replaced by a new tightly fitting NACA cowling. The Fw 190 V2 second prototype was also fitted with a large ducted spinner and powered by a BMW 139 engine. The latter was subsequently replaced by the longer and heavier BMW 801, which necessitated structural changes to the aircraft and the relocation of the cockpit. These prototypes were armed with two 13mm MG 131 machine guns in the wings and two 7.92mm MG 17 weapons in the upper forward fuselage. The third and fourth prototypes were abandoned.

Fw 190 V5/V5G

Once powered by the newly developed 1,660hp BMW 801C-0 engine, the V2 was modified to take a wing of increased span. To compensate for the greater engine weight, the cockpit was moved further aft. With the introduction of the V5g ('g' standing for *gross* or large), the V5 short-span version (which had a wing area of 161.46 sq ft) was redesignated the Fw 190 V5k ('k' standing for *klein* or small). The V5k had a wing area of 196.98 sq ft.

Fw 190A-0

The pre-production batch, nine of these aircraft were fitted with the small wing, while the remainder had the larger-span version. 100 production Fw 190As were ordered, the first five of which bore the alternative designations V7 to V11.

Several Fw 190A-0 pre-production aircraft are seen here at Bremen. All the A-0s were manufactured at Focke-Wulf's Bremen plant. The nearest aircraft, Wk-Nr. 0010, was fitted with a BMW 801C-1 engine, unlike the C-0 model installed in most, if not all, preceding A-0 airframes. Its engine cowling is clearly marked to signify the slightly different powerplant. (From archives of D. Khazanov and A. Medved)

Fw 190A-1

This initial production model was essentially similar to the V5g, being powered by a 1,660hp BMW 801C-1 radial, and having the long-span wing, 7.92mm MG 17 machine guns and FuG 7a radio equipment. In August 1941 the first Fw 190A-1s were delivered to *Stab./JG 26*.

Fw 190A-2

The Fw 190 V14 first prototype had two 7.9mm MG 17 machine guns above the engine cowling and two 20mm MG FF cannon in the wing roots. The production Fw 190A-2, which was powered by the BMW 801C-2 engine, often carried an additional pair of MG 17 machine guns in the outboard wing panels.

Fw 190A-3

This was the first major production variant to be powered by the 1,700hp BMW 801D-2. It had the MG FF cannon moved to the outer wing panels, and their original location used instead for two of the much faster-firing 20mm MG 151/20 weapons. The canopy could be jettisoned with the aid of explosive bolts and the pilot was protected by 12.7mm and 19mm armour plate. The first examples were introduced into service in autumn 1941.

The Fw 190A-3 was delivered during the late summer of 1942 with FuG 16Z radio and a fin-mounted radio mast atop the fin. The BMW 801D-2 had provision for MW 50 water-methanol fuel injection to boost output to 2,100hp for short periods, and thus raise the maximum speed to 416mph at 21,000ft.

Fw 190A-4/R6

The MW 50 was removed for this model. The Fw 190A-4/R6 was capable of carrying a pair of underwing Werfergranate WGr. 21 210mm rocket launchers for the unguided WGr. 21 Dodel missile. Fixed armament was reduced to two MG 151/20s.

Fw 190A-4/U5

This model was able to carry a 66-gal drop tank beneath each wing and a 1,102lb bomb under the fuselage.

Fw 190A-5

Introduced in early 1943, this version was similar to the A-4 but had a revised engine mounting that enabled the BMW 801D-2 to be fitted 6in. further forward in an attempt to cure a tendency for the engine to overheat. Many sub-variants were produced, including the U3 equipped with underwing and centreline bomb racks, the camera-toting U4 and fighter-bomber optimized U6, U8 and U11.

Fw 190A-6

The Fw 190A-6 was developed from the experimental Fw 190A-5/U10 in June 1943. A redesigned, lighter wing could take four MG 151/20s while retaining the two MG 17s mounted above the engine. FuG 16ZE and FuG 25 radio equipment was also carried.

Fw 190A-6/R1

Developed following successful trials with the Fw 190A-5/U12, this aircraft had six MG 151/20 cannon.

The neat installation of the two Rheinmetall-Borsig MG 17 7.9mm machine guns in the upper forward fuselage weapons station of all production A-model Fw 190s up to and including the A-6. (From archives of D. Khazanov and A. Medved)

Fw 190A-5 WING GUNS

The Fw 190A-5 packed a powerful punch when compared to its relatively lightly armed Soviet opponents. Oerlikon MG FF 20mm cannon (and their single 140-round ammunition boxes) were fitted in the outer weapons stations in the mid-wing area. The MG FFs proved to be less than reliable in service, and they were often removed in an effort to save weight. The MG FFs were replaced by Mauser MG 151 20mm cannon from the Fw 190A-6 onwards, these weapons having initially been fitted in the wing-root bays of the A-5 only. The two ammunition boxes for the wing-root cannon were housed within the fuselage behind the main spar, each magazine holding 250 rounds. (Artwork by Jim Laurier, © Osprey Publishing)

Fw 190A-6/R3

This version was armed with two 30mm MK 103 cannon in underwing gondolas.

Fw 190A-6/R6

The final A-6 variant, this aircraft could carry a 210mm Werfergranate WGr. 21 rocket tube beneath each wing.

Fw 190A-7

Introduced in December 1943, and basically similar to the Fw 190A-6, the first prototype was the Fw 190A-5/U9, which had two MG 151/20 cannon in the wings and two 13mm MG 131 machine guns above the engine cowling. The second prototype (Fw 190 V35) was similar, but had

FW 190A-5 COWLING GUNS

A pair of Rheinmetall-Borsig MG 17 7.9mm machine guns were installed in the upper forward fuselage weapons station in all production A-model Fw 190s up to and including the A-6. These guns were often disparagingly known as 'door knockers' due to their inability to penetrate the armour fitted to Soviet aircraft, in particular the Il-2. The MG 17s were fed ammunition from two fuselage-mounted boxes that each contained up to 475 rounds per gun. (Artwork by Jim Laurier, © Osprey Publishing)

four MG 151/20s in the wings and a strengthened undercarriage. It was later re-engined with a 2,000hp BMW 801F. The *Rüstsatz* produced for the A-7 was similar to that for the A-6, with much emphasis being placed on the A-7/R6 with WGr. 21 rocket tubes.

Fw 190A-8/R7

This variant was fitted with an armoured cockpit for use by anti-bomber *Sturmgruppen*.

Fw 190A-8/R11

The Fw 190A-8/R11 was an all-weather fighter with a heated canopy and PKS 12 radio navigation equipment.

Fw 190F-1

A dedicated ground attack version of the A-4, this aircraft had its outboard wing cannon removed and 793lb of armour plating fitted to protect the

Despite suffering terrible losses, the VVS-KA had become more adept at staging surprise hit and run raids on Luftwaffe airfields by early 1943, and take-offs and landings became times of great peril for Fw 190 pilots. Amongst the first things taught to new arrivals in the East was how to take off from any position on the field, either from a standing start or taxiing, and how to land quickly and safely from a low-level formation. Here, Leutnant Walter Nowotny does just that, skimming in low over a huge snow bank at Krasnogvardeisk. (From archives of D. Khazanov and A. Medved)

engine and cockpit from groundfire. The F-1 could also carry a centreline ETC 501 bomb rack.

Fw 190F-2/3

The F-2 was related to the A-5, but it introduced a bubble canopy, while the F-3, which corresponded to the A-6, could carry a 66-gal drop tank or 550lb bomb on its centreline. F-3/R1 and R2 had wing racks or MK 103 30mm cannon options.

Fw 190F-8/9

The F-8 was based on the A-8, with two engine-mounted MG 131s and ETC 50 bomb racks. The F-8/U2 and U3 had a TSA bombsight for anti-shipping strikes with, respectively, BT 700 or BT 1400 bombs. The final Fw 190F variant was the F-9, which was similar to the F-8 but powered by the BMW 801 TS/TH engine.

Fw 190G-1

Based on the Fw 190A-5/U8, the G-1 was equipped with bomb racks under the fuselage to carry bombs up to a weight of 3,970lb. Strengthened landing gear was introduced to allow the Fw 190G to cope with the extra weight.

Fw 190G-2/3

The G-2 and G-3 differed only in the type of wing racks used for their external stores, the former employing Messerschmitt-built racks and the latter Focke-Wulf equipment.

The smart, newly built Fw 190D-9 Wk-Nr. 210051 with a straight-topped cockpit cover from the first production batch of D-9 airframes. The completely changed nose contours of the Junkers Jumo 213-powered 'Dora-9' compared to the BMW 801-engined Fw 190 models, plus the lengthened rear fuselage, are evident in this view. (From archives of D. Khazanov and A. Medved)

Fw 190G-8

The final variant was the G-8, powered by an uprated 1,800hp BMW 801D-2 and incorporating upgrades introduced in the Fw 190A-8. This version, fitted with a nitrous oxide injection system, was designated the Fw 190G-8/R4.

Fw 190D-9

The last all-new variant of the Focke-Wulf fighter to engage La-5/7s in the final months of the war was the Fw 190D-9. Developed in 1942 as a replacement for the aborted Fw 190B/C high-altitude fighters, the *Langnasen-Dora* made use of the exceptional 2,000hp inverted inline Junkers Jumo 213 engine, combined with an MW 50 water-methanol booster, to achieve an impressive rate of climb and top speed. Only 700 had been built by the end of the war, and very few were encountered on the Eastern Front in the final months of the conflict.

La-5FN AND Fw 190A-4 COMPARISON SPECIFICATIONS		
	La-5FN	Fw 190A-4
Powerplant	1,850hp ASh-82FN	1,700hp BMW 801D-2
Dimensions		
Span	32ft 1.78in.	34ft 5.5in.
Length	28ft 2.75in.	28ft 10.5in.
Height	8ft 4in.	12ft 11.5in.
Wing area	188.37 sq ft	196.98 sq ft
Weights		
Empty	6,173lb	6,393lb
Loaded	7,407lb	8,770lb
Performance		
Max speed	403mph at 20,670ft	418mph at 21,000ft (with override boost)
Range	360 miles	497 miles
Rate of climb to 16,500ft	4.7 min	5.83 min
Service ceiling	31,170ft	34,775ft
Armament	2 x 20mm ShVAK	2 x 7.9mm MG 17 2 x 20mm MG 151/20 2 x 20mm FF

La-7 AND Fw 190D-9 COMPARISON SPECIFICATIONS		
	La-7	Fw 190D-9
Powerplant	1,850hp ASh-82FN	2,000hp Junkers Jumo 213
Dimensions		
Span	32ft 1.75in.	34ft 5in.
Length	29ft 2.5in.	33ft 5in.
Height	8ft 6.25in.	11ft 0.25in.
Wing area	189.35 sq ft	197 sq ft
Weights		
Empty	5,842lb	7,694lb
Loaded	7,496lb	10,670lb
Performance		
Max speed	423mph at 20,000ft	426mph at 21,650ft
Range	413 miles	520 miles
Rate of climb to 16,500ft	5.1 min	4.9 min
Service ceiling	37,000ft	39,370ft
Armament	2 or 3 x 20mm ShVAK or UB-20	2 x 13mm MG 131 2 x 20mm MG 151/20

THE STRATEGIC SITUATION

By early September 1942 the first examples of the LaG-5 (the new aircraft had not yet been redesignated the La-5) had been combat tested by six fighter regiments of the Soviet VVS. Five of these units had been involved in the successful defence of Stalingrad as part of 287th IAD, while the sixth regiment, 49th IAP on the Western Front, had given the LaG-5 its combat debut the previous month. Their opponents for aerial supremacy at this time were the Bf 109F/G – these were the only German fighters then operating in the central and southern sectors of the Eastern Front.

During the second half of 1942, the VVS-KA had started to form all-new Fighter Air Corps within the Central Command Reserve, their regiments being equipped with the very latest fighters, bombers and attack aircraft available to the Soviets. 1st IAK, led by Gen E. M. Beletskiy, was ready for combat in the autumn, its 235th IAD being solely equipped with La-5s – its sister division, 274th IAD, flew Yak-7Bs, however. It was duly sent to the Kalinin Front, where the corps came under the control of 3rd *Vozdushnaya Armiya* (Air Army). No fewer than 78 La-5s (of which 68 were serviceable) were now committed to combat on the Kalinin Front – the largest concentration of Lavochkin fighters in VVS-KA at that time. A further 180 La-5s were in the process of being readied for front-line units, these machines being used to convert pilots onto the new fighter.

Early September had also seen the arrival of the first Fw 190A-3s in-theatre, and by coincidence these aircraft – assigned to I./JG 51 – had been sent to Lyuban, also on the Kalinin Front. Led by Hauptmann Heinrich Krafft, the *Gruppe* performed sweeps southeast of Leningrad. III./JG 51 (with II./JG 51's 6. *Staffel* attached, as its parent *Gruppe* had been rushed to North Africa following the Allied *Torch* landings) converted to the Fw 190 in December and returned to the Kalinin Front.

By then 235th IAD had been transferred out of 1st IAK, its place being taken by 210th IAD. Only one of its regiments (169th IAP, led by Maj I. P. Ivanov) was equipped with La-5s, 32 examples having been delivered to the unit directly from the factory in Gorkiy. According to figures published by division headquarters, 210th IAD had made 32 combat sorties and destroyed 53 aircraft – including six Fw 190As – by the end of December. Its own losses were 13 La-5s and two Yak-1s.

During this same period the Luftwaffe lost 12 Fw 190s from I./JG 51 to various causes. Most were downed by ground fire, with *Gruppenkommandeur* Hauptmann Krafft (a highly decorated ace with 78 victories to his name) falling victim to Soviet flak on 14 December. Despite the Focke-Wulf pilots' well-founded belief in the survivability of their new aircraft and its rugged BMW radial – especially when compared with the liquid-cooled Daimler Benz engine in the Bf 109 – by the end of 1942 the squadron had lost 12 Fw 190As in combat and a further 26 in operational accidents. La-5 losses were around double this number in December 1942, although there were, of course, far more of them serving in front-line units at this point.

More Fw 190As were sent east in early 1943 as I. and III./JG 51 tried to provide support for the defenders of Velikiye Luki – the scene of one of

With its multiplicity of electrical systems, the Fw 190 embodied the very latest in German technology, but some things on the Eastern Front were best done the old way. And in Russia the panje pony, whether pulling a cart in summer or a sledge in winter, was an integral and indispensable part of life for Luftwaffe units such as I./JG 54 at Krasnogvardeisk in early 1943. (From archives of D. Khazanov and A. Medved)

three Soviet breakthroughs in German lines in November 1942. The *Gruppen* were also doing their best to shore up the Central Sector of the front line as it came under repeated attack from seven Soviet armies supported by VVS-KA regiments. They got some support from late January 1943 when individual *Staffeln* from I. and II./JG 54 completed their conversion from the Bf 109F to the Fw 190A-4 and returned to snow-covered runways at Siverskaya and Krasnogvardeisk on the Leningrad front. Led by Hauptmann Hans Philipp, I. *Gruppe* in particular soon made its mark with the Fw 190 thanks to Feldwebel Otto Kittel and Leutnant Walter Nowotny. The two men would claim 525 victories between them, more than 70 of which were La-5/7s. In mid-February, 43 Fw 190A-5s landed at Ryelbitzi airfield, west of Lake Ilmen on the Kalinin Front. These machines were assigned to I./JG 26, the *Gruppe* being led by Major Johannes Seifert. Making its debut on the Eastern Front, I./JG 26 had been swapped with III./JG 54, which had been sent to Lille-Vendeville, in northern France, to operate on the Channel Front. In March IV./JG 51 replaced the last of its Bf 109Fs with Fw 190s, thus completing the re-equipment of fighter *Gruppen* on the Eastern Front. Those units still flying Bf 109Gs would continue to do so through to the end of the war. There were also a small number of Fw 190As serving with I. and IV./JG 5 in Norway, but these saw very little combat against the VVS-KA.

By the early spring Major Hubertus Hitschhold's I./SchlG 1 had also arrived at Kharkov, in the Southern Sector, with the first Fw 190F fighter-bombers to be seen in the East. Many more *Schlachtstaffeln* would receive Focke-Wulfs during the course of the year, and by early 1944 *Schlacht* Fw 190Fs outnumbered Fw 190As in-theatre.

Meanwhile, the number of fighter regiments equipped with La-5s had also grown rapidly by April 1943. According to a VVS Central Headquarters report, the People's Commissariat for the Aviation Industry handed over 1,129 Lavochkin fighters in 1942. These numbers continued to increase in 1943, with 645 La-5Fs reaching front-line units in May alone. At the end of that month 13 air regiments were transferred into the VGK (Supreme High Command) fighter Reserve Air Corps and Air Armies, having completed their conversion onto the La-5. Each regiment had a complement of 32 fighters. In June the industry handed over a further 373 La-5Fs and, significantly, 36 uprated La-5FNs. The conversion of a further five air regiments onto the Lavochkin fighter was also under way at this time, thus allowing the VVS-KA to continue its strengthening of new air forces for the summer campaigns that were to come.

On the major fighting fronts of the Northern, Central and, to a much lesser extent, Southern Sectors, the full weight of the Fw 190 fighter presence in the USSR continued to be felt – if 'full weight' is the proper term to describe a force the numbers of which never once topped the 200 mark along a front 1,200 miles in length. In fact, the weeks prior to the Kursk offensive were to see Fw 190 serviceability totals in Russia reach their all-time peak – 189 in May and 196 in June 1943.

On 5 July the long-awaited Operation *Zitadelle*, Hitler's last huge gamble to break the deadlock and turn the tide in the East once and for all, finally commenced. All but one of the five Fw 190 *Jagdgruppen* in the East were directly involved in *Zitadelle*. Leaving just Hauptmann Heinrich Jung's II./JG 54 with its mixed bag of 50 Fw 190s and Bf 109s under *Luftflotte* 1 to guard the sectors further to the north, I./JG 54, together with I., III. and IV./JG 51 (140 Fw 190s in all, 88 serviceable) gathered along the northern flank of the salient as the fighter component of *Luftflotte* 6, the Air Fleet tasked with supporting Generaloberst Walter Model's 9th Army. Moreover, Fw 190Fs from I. and III./SchlG 1 were active on the southern front of the Kursk bulge.

The main aim of *Zitadelle* was to forestall the next Soviet offensive and, if possible, disrupt – or at least delay – the enemy's plans for further advances. In the six months since the successful defence of Stalingrad, the Soviets had recaptured vast areas of lost territory, particularly in the southern and central sectors, where the Red Army had stormed back across the Don and Donets rivers. But the rate of advance was not uniform, and around Kursk, close to the boundary of the two sectors, a salient had developed that thrust like a clenched fist 100 miles into the German front line.

The aim of *Zitadelle* was to eliminate this salient, together with Red Army formations massed in and around it, by launching coordinated attacks against both its northern and southern flanks. The resulting clash of armour (2,700 panzers versus 3,600 Soviet tanks) has gone down in military history as the world's greatest tank battle. It was also the last time that the Luftwaffe would appear en masse against the Red Army. All other areas of the line were stripped to the bone until 70 per cent of the Luftwaffe strength in the East – more than 2,100 aircraft – was concentrated on either side of the Kursk salient, those to the north controlled by *Luftflotte* 6 and those in the south by *Luftflotte* 4.

Hitler placed great faith in new heavy tanks and aircraft (including Fw 190 fighter and fighter-bomber variants) that were making their combat debuts in large numbers during *Zitadelle*. In a message to the troops, he announced that victory at Kursk would stun the world, and that the future of the war, and its outcome, depended on it.

Soviet troops defending the Central and Voronezh Fronts heavily outnumbered their German counterparts, while in the air, 2nd, 16th and 17th Air Armies shared 2,900 aircraft between them.

The most important campaign of 1943 began at dawn on 5 July when the Germans put no fewer than 700 tanks into battle, with the support of principal forces from *Luftflotten* 4 and 6. The first morning of the offensive was occupied in providing bomber and Ju 87 escort, and it was not until the afternoon that the first serious clashes with Soviet fighters took place. Having exchanged their Fw 190A-3s for newer A-4s and A-5s just prior to *Zitadelle*, the pilots of JG 51 managed to wrest local air superiority from the Russians for the first few days of the assault. Typically, the fighter *Gruppen* would send formations of 30–40 aircraft aloft in order to keep the VVS-KA Il-2s and Pe-2s away from German armour as the latter advanced towards Kursk.

The Fw 190 pilots were also kept busy escorting Ju 88s and He 111s as they targeted specific Soviet divisions in key areas along the front line. These strikes often proved deadly, with entire divisions being all but wiped out at the height of the German attack in the early days of the offensive. However, the sheer depth of the Soviet defensive positions eventually slowed down the Wehrmacht's advance, and German units also started to accrue serious losses. A similar thing happened in the air.

On 5 July, 16th Air Army (VA) under Gen S. I. Rudenko lost 98 aircraft primarily in aerial battles with Fw 190s. 286th IAD, which had three regiments equipped with La-5s, lost 33 Lavochkin fighters between 5 and 9 July. These disastrous losses could be blamed on poor training, for many of the newer pilots in the division had not flown the La-5 in combat before, as well as the failure of more experienced regimental commanders to correctly direct their fighter assets in the air from the ground. Senior officers in 16th VA also failed to change the tactics employed by their fighter regiments in response to the enemy's targeting of Soviet bombers in considerable strength.

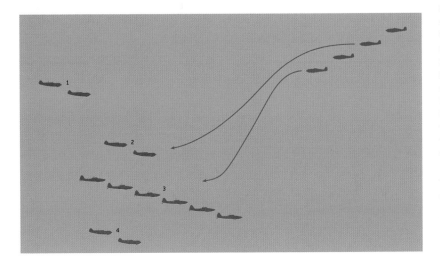

In a typical Eastern Front engagement, a formation of four Fw 190s attempts to engage six Il-2s (3), escorted by a similar number of La-5s, from above. The trailing pair of Fw 190s would target Formations 1 and 2, thus leaving the remaining two fighters to attack the Il-2s before they too were intercepted by La-5 Formation 4. If the Soviet fighters repelled the attacks, the German pilots would endeavour to escape by using the superior speed of their Fw 190s in a dive.

The Battle of Kursk lasted for a full 50 days, and losses on both sides were huge. More than 3,500 VVS-KA aircraft were lost on all fronts in July and August 1943, 500 of which were La-5s. During the same period the Luftwaffe lost 2,419 aircraft on the Eastern Front, 432 of them Fw 190s (both A- and F-models).

As the Wehrmacht had found on the ground, the Jagdwaffe's *Zitadelle* attrition steadily began to climb as the battle continued. JG 51 was to lose five pilots during the first five days of the offensive, but on 10 July events took a more ominous and alarming turn. Aerial opposition was hardening, with Russian bomber attacks on the increase and their fighters beginning, for the first time, to mount their own version of the 'Freie Jagd' sweep over German-held territory.

On the ground, the Soviet counter-offensive was launched north of Orel, smashing into 9th Army's rear. The strength of resistance was now being reflected in JG 51's losses. By 17 July, when the German assault was broken off, ten more pilots had gone down. Present in only single *Gruppe* strength, JG 54's Kursk casualties were commensurately lighter. But on the second day of the action I./JG 54 also suffered the loss of its *Gruppenkommandeur*. At least five more pilots were lost at Kursk. But it was in the immediate aftermath of *Zitadelle* that the most grievous losses of all were sustained, among them a number of highly experienced formation leaders, and aces. Still concentrated along the northern flank of the dwindling salient, JG 51's three *Gruppen* also continued to suffer attrition in the days and weeks that followed the abandonment of the offensive. Lying in the very path of the Soviet counter-attack, their losses were not just restricted to pilots – an increasing number of groundcrew were being killed by Russian bomber and Il-2 raids on airfields in and around Orel. But for the Jagdwaffe the real repercussions of the failure at Kursk were far wider reaching than individual unit losses, as swingeing as these had been. Although the initial Soviet counter-thrust had been halted at great cost just short of Orel, the respite was short-lived. No fewer than 61 Soviet armies lay coiled behind their front line, and in August Stalin unleashed them in a series of smashing blows. To the north of Kursk the offensive was renewed not just against Orel, but now also against Yelnya, Smolensk and Velizh. To the south Kharkov and Poltava were threatened, while further south still, Stalino and the entire Ukraine as well. Only the 12 armies opposite the Northern Sector still remained relatively dormant. And this time the Soviet offensives would not be halted, not by the Germans, not by the weather. Maintaining their pressure throughout the winter, they would continue until the spring of 1944.

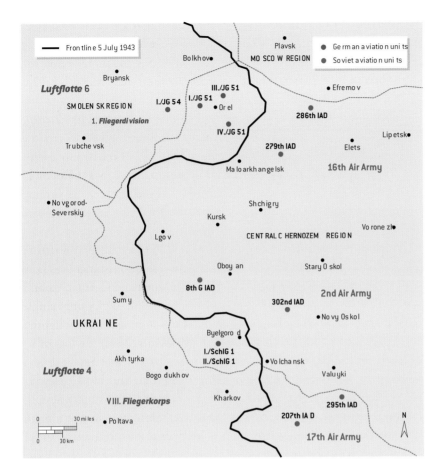

Front line 5 July 1943

● German aviation units
● Soviet aviation units

Luftflotte 6

Plavsk
Bolkhov●
MOSCOW REGION

Bryansk
SMOLENSK REGION
1. Fliegerdivision

III./JG 51
I./JG 54   I./JG 51
● Or el
IV./JG 51

● Efremov

286th IAD

279th IAD

Lipetsk●
Elets

Trubchevsk

Maloarkhangelsk

16th Air Army

● Novgorod-
Severskiy

Shchigry

Kursk

Lgov

CENTRAL CHERNOZEM REGION

Vorone zh●

Oboyan

Stary Oskol

8th G IAD

302nd IAD

2nd Air Army

Sumy

● Novy Oskol

UKRAINE

Byelgorod
I./SchlG 1
II./SchlG 1

● Volchansk

Akhtyrka

Bogodukhov

Valuyki

Luftflotte 4

Kharkov

295th IAD

VIII. Fliegerkorps

0   30 miles
● Poltava

0   30 km

207th IAD

N

17th Air Army

This map shows the disposition of VVS-KA and Luftwaffe fighter units in the central region on the day the Battle of Kursk (known as Operation *Zitadelle* to the Germans) commenced. Since the successful defence of Stalingrad, the Soviets had recaptured vast areas of territory, particularly in the southern and central sectors. But the rate of the advance was not uniform, and around Kursk a large salient had developed, which thrust for some 100 miles deep into the German front line. *Zitadelle* was intended to eliminate this salient, together with Red Army formations massed within and around it.

This entire eight-month period was one of unparalleled movement for the Fw 190 *Gruppen* of JGs 51 and 54 as an increasingly hard-pressed General Staff shuffled them around on their operations maps like so many chessmen from one new breach along the endangered 700-mile front to the next. For not only were the Russians growing stronger by the day, the Jagdwaffe's Eastern Front strength was being eroded.

The seven *Jagdgeschwader* that had accompanied the launch of *Barbarossa* two summers earlier had since been reduced to four by the demands of the Mediterranean fronts. Now it was the defence of the Reich that needed shoring up. And the result? The departure of another *Jagdgeschwader*, leaving just three – in theory, one neatly allocated to each of the sectors, North, Central and South – to stand in the way of the greatest advance in military history.

Nor was it simply in numbers that the defence of Germany took precedence. The reality of US heavy bombers parading their might deeper into Reich airspace had focused the collective Berlin mind wonderfully. And the supply of

Lavochkin fighters bearing the inscription 'Valerii Chkalov ... skadrilya' served with several VVS-KA regiments, the construction of these machines having been financed by a specially established fund that generated sufficient money to purchase enough La-5/5Fs to equip no fewer than six squadrons. These La-5Fs were assigned to 159th IAP on the Karelian Front in the late summer of 1943. (From archives of D. Khazanov and A. Medved)

new Fw 190s to the far flung, low priority, reaches of Russia – never good at the best of times – became precarious. The first *Gruppe* to suffer, IV./JG 51, had already perforce reverted to the Bf 109G-6. Others followed.

It was the Fw 190's misfortune to arrive on the Eastern Front at the very moment that the balance of power began to shift slowly, but irrevocably, into the hands of the Soviets. After its reversal at Stalingrad and failure in the Battle of Kursk, the Wehrmacht would be subjected to a succession of counter-offensives – some large, some small – that would force it out of Russia, right across the states of eastern Europe and back into the very heart of Berlin itself. The Fw-190-equipped *Schlachtgruppen* would fight alongside the ground troops every foot of the way. Despite all efforts, and significant sacrifice, the sum total of their endeavours was simply to protect the process of withdrawal. The best that can be said, perhaps, is that on many occasions it was only the direct intervention of the *Schlachtflieger* in their Fw 190s that prevented the retreat becoming a rout.

In early November the Red Army committed its forces to a decisive offensive aimed at liberating Kiev. According to figures from the VVS-KA, some 2,276 combat aircraft assigned to four air armies (2nd, 5th, 17th and 8th) were available to support this endeavour. Of this number, 1,253 were fighters, 400 of them La-5s. Opposing the Soviet air forces was *Luftflotte* 4, which, according to VVS-KA intelligence, had 950 aircraft at its disposal, 125 of them fighters. According to German sources, II./JG 54 (34 aircraft) and the *Schlachtgruppen* II./SG 77 (16 aircraft) and I./SG 10 (64 aircraft) flew Fw 190s in the southern sector on 1 November 1943. Further south, Fw 190F-equipped II./SG 2 would see action against La-5s of 4th VA in the Crimea.

Soviet forces liberated Kiev on 6 November, but intense land and aerial battles continued until 23 December. Now firmly in the ascendancy on the Eastern Front, the Red Army fought a series of successful offensives in the first half of 1944, in full possession of the strategic initiative. The first of these came in mid-January when the Northern Sector of the front suddenly exploded into life when the Red Army captured Mga and then lifted the almost 900-day siege of Leningrad. I. and II./JG 54 were hurriedly recalled from the Central and Southern Sectors, respectively. Returning to their old stomping grounds, it quickly became clear that this new northern tide of the Russian advance would prove as impossible to stem as that currently surging across the Ukraine far to the south. In fact, JG 54 soon found itself retracing its steps back through the Baltic States almost as rapidly as its predecessors had advanced across them in 1941.

By February I. *Gruppe* had taken up residence at Wesenberg, in Estonia. It was joined the following month by II./JG 54, which occupied Dorpat and Petschur west of Lakes Peipus and Pleskau. Fortunately, it was a time of minimal losses for the *Gruppen*. On 23 June 1944 the Soviets unleashed their massive Central Front offensive that would cut off the coastal regions of the Baltic States to the north from the main bodies of the German armies as they were pushed back towards the Reich. This offensive was supported by six air armies and long-range aviation and air defence fighter units that, combined, fielded 8,000+ aircraft. In response, German Army Group Centre had just the 920 aircraft of *Luftflotten* 4 and 6 to protect it.

The Red Army also attacked Finnish forces still occupying the Karelian Isthmus north of Leningrad at this time. In the face of this threat, I./JG 54 vacated Estonia for neighbouring Latvia. II. *Gruppe* also went to Finland

Here, groundcrew check the engine and tune the radio of 'White 20' while part of *Gefechtsverband* Kuhlmey's main striking force – Ju 87Ds of I./SG 3 – fly overhead in a ragged formation. (From archives of D. Khazanov and A. Medved)

On 23 June 1944 the Red Army unleashed its massive Central Front summer offensive that would cut off the coastal regions of the Baltic states to the north from the main bodies of the German armies as they were pushed back towards the borders of the Reich. This offensive was supported by six air armies and long-range aviation and air defence fighter units which, combined, fielded more than 8,000 aircraft. In response, German Army Group Centre had just the 920 combat aircraft of *Luftflotten* 4 and 6 to protect it.

as the fighter component of *Gefechtsverband* (Battle Group) Kuhlmey – a mixed-bag formation of Stukas and ground-attack Fw 190s sent to aid the hard-pressed Finns. During their month's sojourn at Immola in northern Karelia II./JG 54 claimed 66 Soviet aircraft destroyed. A surprise arrival on the Russian Front that same June was a rejuvenated and reinforced IV./JG 54. After earlier retiring through Romania, this Bf 109 *Gruppe* had withdrawn to Germany to re-equip with Fw 190A-8s and be brought up to full current Defence of the Reich establishment of four *Staffeln* each of 16 aircraft. In one of the first instances of precedence being given to the Eastern Front over home defence requirements, IV./JG 54 was suddenly despatched to the Soviet–Polish border region on 30 June to provide air cover for the retreating ground troops. It would suffer grievously in the ensuing two months before retiring back to the Reich early in September.

By then the two long-serving Fw 190 *Gruppen*, I. and II./JG 54, had retired deeper into isolated Latvia, occupying bases on the Courland peninsula.

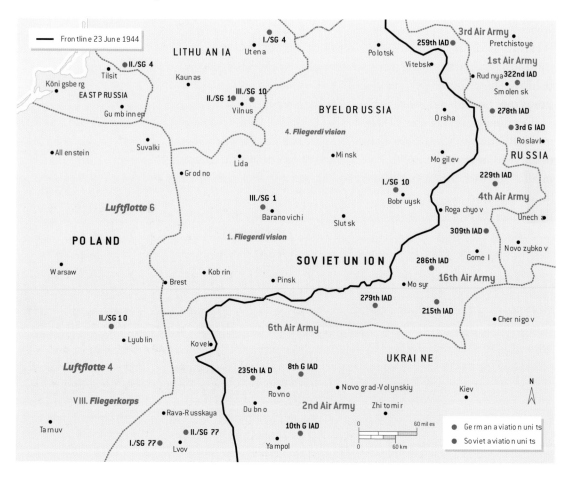

With all but the *Stabsstaffel* of JG 51 having converted back on to the Bf 109 in May, JG 54's two *Gruppen* were now effectively the sole Fw 190 fighter presence on the Eastern Front – albeit already bottled up in Courland. They also now underwent Defence of the Reich style reorganization, a fourth *Staffel* being added to each *Gruppe*. In theory, this translated into an official total establishment of well over 130 aircraft. The reality, as of mid-October, was that they could muster just 56 serviceable aircraft between them. And a new spectre was also beginning to make itself felt: the increasing scarcity of aviation fuel. With everything having to be ferried into Courland by air or sea, the fuel situation would soon reach crisis proportions. Before the end teams of oxen would move aircraft to and from dispersals to prevent unnecessary taxiing.

Within weeks of the commencement of the Central Front summer offensive, German Army Group Centre had been routed – 17 divisions and three brigades had been destroyed, with a further 50 divisions missing more than half of their complement. Huge casualties had been inflicted on troops that had been transferred in from the West and other sectors of the Soviet–German front. Throughout this period senior officers in the Wehrmacht complained to the Luftwaffe that the VVS-KA had total control of the skies. This was because JG 54's enforced retirement into Baltic isolation meant that the only Fw 190s on the main Eastern fighting fronts during the latter half of 1944 were ground-attack machines.

Despite a significant increase in numbers (the seven *Schlachtgruppen* of mid-1944 had grown to 12, plus several independent *Staffeln*, by the end of the year), it was still a pitifully small force – some 300 serviceable aircraft in all – to place in the path of the greatest concentration of armour in military history as it erupted through the Vitebsk–Dnieper gap, the traditional 'gateway' for invading armies in, and out of, Russia.

Although their principal targets were the advancing Soviet ground forces, some *Schlacht* pilots still managed to add to their list of aerial kills. The heady days of the Crimea were long past, but II./SG 2, for example, tasked with escorting the Ju 87-equipped components of their parent *Geschwader* during the long retreat back across Romania and Hungary, continued to take a toll on Russian fighters, including La-5s. And it was not only the VVS-KA that was inflicting casualties on the *Schlachtflieger*. As 1944 gave way to 1945, and the Germans were pushed steadily back – and the distance between their Eastern and Western Fronts diminished – so the danger posed by marauding USAAF and RAF fighters grew.

Some weeks prior to the final cessation of hostilities, however, the Eastern Front had at long last witnessed an influx of Fw 190 fighter reinforcements. Less than a month after Operation *Bodenplatte*, the ill-advised and costly

A bulged-canopy Fw 190F-9 from II./SG 2, based in Hungary in January 1945, taxis through snow and slush while armed with an AB 250 missile container. The latter's deadly load consisted of 30 SD 4 anti-personnel bomblets. (From archives of D. Khazanov and A. Medved)

New Year's Day attack by the Jagdwaffe on Allied-occupied air bases in northwest Europe, elements of some ten *Jagdgeschwader*, including 11 Fw 190-equipped *Gruppen*, began transferring eastwards. In mid-January 1945, with Russian armour already encroaching on German soil and Berlin soon to be directly threatened, fighter reinforcement came to the hard-pressed *Schlacht* units in the east. By then it was too late.

With the Eastern and Western powers drawing ever closer together, and the Reich within weeks of being cut in two by American and Russian forces linking up on the River Elbe, it is arguable whether these latecomers can be classed as true 'Eastern Front' units. Although committed against the Soviets on paper, the majority also had to contend with the marauding Western Allies at their backs.

Ordered to East Prussia on 14 January, for example, I./JG 1 lost some dozen pilots killed or wounded to British fighters, arriving at Jürgenfelde only ten strong. Although claiming several Soviet aircraft destroyed, the unit suffered five more casualties before its withdrawal in early February to retrain on the He 162 Volksjäger. II. *Gruppe*'s introduction to Eastern Front conditions was little better. Losing two pilots killed in a clash with Yaks on the day of its arrival, the unit was then forced to blow up ten of its own aircraft in hasty retreats before the week was out.

Equipped with heavily armed and armoured Fw 190A-8/R8s, IV./JG 3 'Udet' was a Defence of the Reich *Sturmgruppe*, a dedicated anti-bomber unit. But it too was rushed eastwards and pressed into service bombing and strafing Soviet forces advancing along the Oder front towards Stettin and Berlin. Although even more impervious to ground fire than the normal A-8, the '*Sturmbock*' was no match for Russian fighters.

III./JG 11 also returned to the East in late January 1945, this time accompanied by the *Geschwaderstab* and I. *Gruppe* as well. Together they operated primarily along the Oder front and beyond, towards Posen. II./JG 300 was another A-8/R8 *Sturmgruppe* sent to the Eastern Front. Together with elements of JG 301 (a *Geschwader* that also possessed some Fw 190D-9s, plus the only examples of the Ta 152H – the final development of the wartime Focke-Wulf fighter family – known to have entered operational service), it was ordered to the scene of the Russian breakthrough along the Oder on 1 February. But the danger of having to wage war on two fronts was graphically demonstrated eight days later when the combined *Gruppen* were recalled to combat US bombers over western Germany and lost 11 of their number in the process. By April III./JG 301 was attacking American ground forces along the River Elbe, only to be ordered to about-turn once again. It ended the war in the defence of Berlin.

While the majority of these 'new' Fw 190 *Gruppen* fought over the northern and eastern approaches of Berlin, others were being despatched to the southern sectors. JG 6's destination was lower Silesia. At Görlitz, as part of the *Gefechtsverband* Rudel, its II. *Gruppe* took on the unenviable task formerly performed by II./SG 2 – protecting a handful of obsolete anti-tank Ju 87s of SG 2 that were somehow still flying on a daily basis. *Stab.* and I./JG 6 shared their Reichenberg base with a small tactical reconnaissance unit.

While the newcomers from the West were learning the harsh realities of Eastern Front air warfare, the campaign veterans, JGs 51 and 54, were now both cut off with their backs to the Baltic Sea. By mid-March German forces in East Prussia had been pushed back into two pockets either side of Danzig Bay, one around the state capital Königsberg and the other around Danzig itself. They also held the 'Frische Nehrung', the long spit of land between the two. In mid-March JG 51's *Stabsstaffel* was based at Neutief out along this narrow spit. Once operations from this base became completely untenable, the *Staffel* moved east into the shrinking Königsberg pocket. But its new base, Littausdorf, was soon under constant air attack, and on 28 April the *Stabsstaffel* was disbanded.

Elsewhere, IV./JG 51 had re-equipped with brand-new Fw 190A-8s, and even a few D-9s, at Garz, further west along the coast. Compared to the painstaking transition from Bf 109 to Fw 190 back in the winter of 1942–43, the *Gruppe's* recent 'conversion' could best be termed rudimentary. A civilian employee from the Focke-Wulf factory explained the cockpit layout to the veteran pilots, described the Fw 190's handling characteristics, warned them never to lift the tail on take-off ... and that was it. After a few practice flights they were transferred south to the Berlin area. It says something about the men, or the machines – or both – that in three weeks they claimed 115 kills for the loss of just five of their own.

On 29 April Major Heinz Lange was involved in his last dogfight, with four La-7s over Neubrandenburg, but it fell to Oberfeldwebel Alfred Rauch to claim JG 51's final Fw 190 victory of the war on that same date. On 2 May the unit retired to Flensburg and British captivity. For the Fw 190s of JG 51 the war was over.

This left just JG 54, which was fighting a private war on the Courland peninsula. But despite – or perhaps because of – their sense of isolation, I. and II./JG 54's scores continued to mount during their final months of conflict. The comparative lull in the ground fighting between each Soviet offensive aimed at seizing the peninsula offered some semblance of a respite for the weary Courland army. But for JG 54's two *Gruppen* there were no such let-ups. The Russian air force attacked the peninsula's supply and evacuation ports without pause. The main harbour in particular, Libau, suffered raid after heavy raid. II./JG 54 based at nearby Libau-Grobin, and I. *Gruppe* some 40 miles inland at Schrunden, took a steady toll of the attackers. When not defending the supply ports, they were protecting the ships themselves as they ran the gauntlet of Soviet air and sea attack. They also provided fighter escort for Courland's few 'Mausis' – lumbering Ju 52/3ms, each with a large dural hoop beneath fuselage and wings – as they swept the sea approaches to the peninsula for enemy mines.

The pressure never eased. On 24 January 1945 the Russians launched their fourth offensive; on 20 February their fifth. The following month, on 18 March, the sixth and final Soviet onslaught began. Once more it was blunted and stopped. But when Adolf Hitler – the one man at whose insistence the Courland peninsula had been held for all these months – committed suicide in Berlin on 30 April, there died with him all thoughts of using the 'fortress' of Courland as the jumping-off point for a last-minute counter-attack.

The capitulation of Germany, and the surrender of all its armed forces, was only days away. For the Luftwaffe units in Courland this meant one thing: escape to the West, taking as many of their comrades with them as they could. The 'Mausis' repaid JG 54's previous services by loading their departing Ju 52/3ms with fighter groundcrew in addition to their own. The Fw 190 pilots also helped their own. Some 50 aircraft left Courland, stripped of equipment but packed with up to four occupants. The faces of those who watched one Fw 190 land safely in the West and saw *five* people emerge – two squashed behind the pilot, one from the rear fuselage radio compartment and one from each wing ammunition bay – were, by all accounts, something to behold.

Ranking Allied ace Maj Ivan Kozhedub (left) is congratulated by fellow pilots from 176th GIAP soon after claiming his 62nd, and last, victory over Berlin on 17 April 1945. Flying an La-7, he had downed two Fw 190s during the mission – Kozhedub had destroyed 11 Focke-Wulfs since swapping his La-5FN for the La-7 in September 1944. (From archives of D. Khazanov and A. Medved)

A few 'Green Hearts' made for their home towns. One or two opted for neutral Sweden, less than 200 miles away across the Baltic. But the majority followed orders directing them to fly to British-held Flensburg, or Kiel, in Schleswig-Holstein, where they surrendered.

During the final months of the war in Europe losses among Fw 190 units reached 80–90 per cent (some Soviet aviation units had suffered approximately the same loss rate in the summer of 1941). Losses among La-5 and La-7 units for the whole of 1944, by comparison, totalled 1,044 aircraft. Apart from that, a further 760 fighters were written off in operational accidents and another 704 due to the exhaustion of their airframe hours. Meanwhile, the Soviet aviation industry delivered 4,286 La-5s in 1944 (85 per cent of them fitted with ASh-82FN engines, and the rest with ASh-82Fs), and 1,044 La-7s. Therefore, losses of Lavochkin aircraft during this period did not exceed 50 per cent of the total number of aircraft manufactured.

On 12 January 1945, when the Red Army launched the first in its final series of offensives that would culminate in the bloody Battle of Berlin, its armies were supported by 6,719 aircraft divided between 17 Air Corps and eight individual auxiliary air divisions. Among this number were 517 La-5s (479 serviceable) and 227 La-7s (189 serviceable).

As previously noted, the Fw 190 *Schlacht* units were kept busy trying to slow down the advance of the Red Army as it closed on Berlin. Indeed, according to VVS-KA records, 13,950 sorties were noted by the 1st Byelorussian Front alone in the first ten days of February, and most of these were made by Fw 190 attack aircraft. During battles with Soviet fighters that month the Luftwaffe endured exceptionally high loss rates, with 25–30 Fw 190s being downed on a number of days. In March, in the wake of these unsustainable losses, Luftwaffe activity in the East reduced by almost half in comparison with the previous month. Acute shortages of fuel and of pilots with experience were taking their toll.

Realising that the loss of Berlin to the Red Army would signal the end of the Third Reich, the German military leadership ordered the Luftwaffe to concentrate the bulk of its remaining combat aviation – around 2,000 aircraft – in a ring around the capital in April 1945. They were opposed by 7,500 Soviet aircraft split across four air armies. On the morning of 25 April forces from the 1st Byelorussian and 1st Ukrainian Fronts met up to the southwest of Berlin, thus completing the encirclement of the city. Later that day forces from the Soviet 5th Guards Army made contact with units from the American 1st Army advancing from the west in the Torgau region. Soon, the battle for the Reichstag began, but on 2 May the enemy's resistance in Berlin collapsed.

During the battle for the city the Luftwaffe had lost some 4,500 aircraft, many of them Fw 190s. On 8 May 1945 the German High Command signed the act of unconditional surrender.

THE MEN
Soviet Pilot Training

On the eve of the Great Patriotic War, aircrew training in the Red Army Air Force was carried out by 29 initial training schools, 21 fighter pilot and 22 bomber pilot schools and 12 bomb-aimer (navigator) schools. Konotop Aviation College, the officers' training courses at Lipetsk and the Military Academy of Commanders and Navigators (open to pilots of squadron commander rank and above) instructed flight, squadron and regimental commanders, respectively.

Up until the autumn of 1940, the selection of candidates to become pilots was made from volunteers who met the selection criteria pertaining to their levels of health, education and political training. All candidates had to first complete a course at either the Osoaviakhim Flying Club or a Special Air Force School. From 1940 the Flying Clubs would only accept recruits that had completed at least nine years of education at the highest possible level, as confirmed by a recommendation from the candidate's school.

The programme taught by the Flying Club assumed two forms of study for students – either in parallel with tertiary studies (or work) or 'day release training'. Pupils could expect to spend a year completing the Flying

The venerable Polikarpov U-2 (redesignated the Po-2 in 1944) served as the Soviet Air Force's elementary trainer throughout World War II, some 13,500 examples having been built by June 1941. Praised for its positive longitudinal stability and reluctance to spin, the pedestrian U-2 was the ideal tool for the hundreds of Flying Clubs charged with training pilots for the VVS-KA. (From archives of D. Khazanov and A. Medved)

Club course. La-5 pilot Yakov Boreyko commenced lessons at the Flying Club while in his ninth year of studies at secondary school:

> Following the entrance exams, all of your free time was devoted to practical flying. Your aim was to fly the U-2 biplane solo, and to achieve this the flying training course dictated that you complete 18–20 hours in the air with an instructor. On 15 June 1940, after ten introductory and two check flights with the head of the Flying Club, a bag of sand replaced the instructor in the front cockpit – this maintained the correct centre of gravity in the U-2 – and I duly made two solo flights in a box-pattern. My flying career began from that moment.
>
> The final exam on flying technique was a serious matter. I was required to complete one simple circuit around the airfield and a second that included some manoeuvring. For the latter I had to make two shallow turns using 30 degrees of bank, two steep turns using 60 degrees of bank, perform an inside loop (which at that time was known as a dead loop), a roll, a combat turn, a spin with an exit in a given direction, a spiral, a side-slip to both sides and a glide. After I had landed my instructor told me that I had successfully completed the exam. By the time I left the Flying Club I had 40 hours in my logbook.

In 1939 the duration of the flying training course at the military pilots' school had been increased to 18 months, during which time students would complete 80 hours of flying on training types and 30 hours in a front-line combat aircraft. Gunnery and altitude training were excluded from the programme, as it was envisaged that the student would learn this immediately upon his arrival in an operational unit.

In 1940 the People's Commissariat for Defence, Marshal S. K. Timoshenko, decreed that the duration of study at the pilots' school be reduced to 12 months. In December of that year he made a decision to radically change the way pilots were trained. Voluntary involvement was abandoned, with flying schools now recruiting students from army draftees. Secondly, graduates would no longer automatically be accorded the rank of officer upon graduation. Up until then all those completing the pilots' course would be commissioned as junior lieutenants, the chance to become an officer having attracted a large number of volunteers in peacetime USSR.

Now, a graduate of the flying school would be given the rank of sergeant, and he would have to remain a non-commissioned officer for a period of no less than three years following the conclusion of his studies. This move by the Red Army leadership was driven by a desire to increase combat readiness among front-line aviation units and reinforce discipline in their ranks. However, it had the opposite effect as the number of recruits fell sharply and a significant percentage of the students who were enrolled in flying schools were not actually interested in becoming pilots. Finally, discipline in the front line did not improve either.

To further compound the problem, the winter of 1940–41 was snowy, cold and overly long, thus delaying the onset of spring. Flying training was badly affected, slowing the conversion of aircrew through flying schools. Many of these recruits also found it difficult to come to terms with the new generation of fighter types – MiG-3, Yak-1 and LaGG-3 – then entering service, and in the first days of the German invasion in June 1941 it was these poorly trained pilots who accounted for the lion's share of victories among the Luftwaffe *Experten*.

LA-7: IN THE COCKPIT

1. Armoured plate windscreen
2. PBP-1B gunsight
3. Hydraulics pressure gauge
4. Landing flaps indicator
5. Brake pressure gauge
6. Air system pressure gauge
7. Electrical switches
8. Landing gear indicator
9. Clock
10. Cannon air charging
11. Altimeter
12. Cannon manual charging handles
13. Compass
14. Course indicator
15. Current reversing switch
16. Amp meter
17. Fuel gauge
18. Cockpit light
19. Radio compass dial
20. Cylinder head temperature gauge

21. Radio frequency switch
22. Vertical speed indicator
23. Combined fuel and oil pressure and oil temperature gauge
24. Turn and bank indicator
25. Tachometer
26. Supercharger boost pressure
27. Airspeed indicator
28. Ignition switch
29. Landing flaps control
30. Oil cooler flap control
31. Rudder trim wheel
32. Elevator trim wheel
33. Manual bomb release handle
34. Cockpit vent control handle
35. Compressor boost control handle
36. Propeller pitch control handle
37. Engine stop handle
38. Throttle
39. Cold start valve

40. Main hydraulic valve
41. Oxygen regulator
42. Map case
43. Electric bomb release button
44. Brake lever
45. Cannon trigger
46. Control wheel for intake louvres
47. Control wheel for fuselage-mounted cooling air exit louvres
48. Rudder pedals
49. Primer and air starter
50. Oxygen pressure gauge
51. Pilot's seat
52. Control column and grip
53. Emergency canopy release handle
54. Cockpit illumination control dial
55. Undercarriage control lever

(Artwork by Jim Laurier, © Osprey Publishing)

Although the VVS-KA did not experience a shortage of pilots during the first year of the conflict in the east, many aviators were classified as 'horseless' (in the early 20th century, a Russian peasant who had insufficient money to buy even an impoverished horse was dubbed 'horseless') due to a lack of aircraft to replace the thousands destroyed or abandoned during the retreat eastward. Such pilots were sent to auxiliary aviation regiments (ZAPs) and century brigades, and one of the latter was deployed to the Arzamas region, where it was intended to train and reform aviation regiments equipped with the LaGG-3 and, subsequently, the La-5.

Formerly a standard La-5F, this La-5UTI trainer was created by the removal of a fuselage fuel tank and the fitment of a second seat and extra cockpit glazing. 28 two-seat Lavochkin fighters were produced by Factory No. 21 at Gorkiy, despite the fact that would-be La-5 pilots often found the aircraft's high landing speed and excessive propeller torque difficult to handle in the early stages of their conversion onto the fighter. However, the VVS-KA desperately needed single-seat La-5 fighters, rather than trainers, so they took priority. The La-7UTI enjoyed more success, with 584 examples being built in 1945–47. (From archives of D. Khazanov and A. Medved)

On 16 October 1942 the new Red Army Air Force commander, Gen A. A. Novikov, ordered the reintroduction of more advanced training for would-be fighter pilots. In January 1943 the pre-December 1940 order returned, with graduates of military flying schools and aviation colleges becoming junior lieutenants upon the completion of their training course, which was to be of at least nine months duration.

In the first 18 months of the war in the east, Red Army Air Force flying schools and aviation colleges trained more than 40,000 pilots and navigators. The ZAPs also played their part in the training of pilots in World War II. Indeed, in 1941–42, when front-line aviation regiments had trouble replacing their lost aircraft, aircrew were sent to ZAPs to regroup and re-equip. They often converted to new aircraft types while here too. Flying school graduates coming into front-line units had limited experience, so the ZAPs tried to give them the chance to accrue up to ten hours of flying time in a combat aircraft. During this time tyro pilots would learn aerial gunnery and how to fly in a two-ship formation or as part of a flight or larger sub-division. Following a month of such training, the aviation regiment, using its previous designation, but with up to 70 per cent of its pilots new to the unit, was sent to the front.

As a rule, new pilots who survived in the front line for an extended period were promoted to become leaders of two-aircraft formations or larger flights, and the more outstanding among them could even achieve command of a squadron.

From June 1943 the practice of withdrawing entire regiments to the rear to re-equip was stopped. ZAPs now switched to training individual pilots who were flying school graduates. By now the recruitment of pilots from front-line units in the Red Army had also commenced. Separate flying training aviation regiments, staffed by experienced instructors, were also deployed among air armies. It was their job to act as 'entry control', assessing the quality of pilot training and bringing them up to the minimum standard required if deemed necessary.

From early 1944 ZAP graduates were sent to Separate Training Aviation Regiments (OUTAPs), which were tasked with supplying front-line units with pilots that were thoroughly familiar with the idiosyncrasies of the fighter aircraft type they had been assigned to fly, had an understanding of the enemy's tactics and had experience of group flying and aerial gunnery. To achieve this level of preparedness for the front line, pilot training was extended to one year (including time spent at a ZAP or OUTAP) during the final 18 months of the war. The total number of flying hours for a new pilot reaching a front-line fighter regiment was more than 100 hours (30–40 hours in a combat aircraft). The time spent by students at academies, aviation colleges and schools had also been significantly increased during this period.

In the opinion of Major Günther Rall, who claimed 271 victories against the VVS-KA flying Bf 109s, in the second half of the war in the East Soviet pilots had 'closed ranks':

> They learned unbelievably quickly. Already by the middle of 1943 their tactics were close to matching those of the Luftwaffe, and modern Yakovlev and Lavochkin fighters started to appear – both powerful, agile aircraft. I tried repeatedly to better different types of La-5s and Yak-9s in horizontal manoeuvres in my Bf 109G, but this proved to be practically impossible, even when the throttle was pushed forward against the stop.

Such comments are borne out by the improving victory-to-loss ratio enjoyed by Soviet fighter regiments from late 1943 through to the end of the war. During the Battle of Stalingrad in the winter of 1942–43, Soviet units struggled to achieve parity between losses and victories, and this negative ratio remained throughout the Battle of Kursk. However, by the autumn of 1944

A typical La-5 formation from late 1943 through to war's end consisted of two pairs of aircraft loosely formed into a four-fighter flight. Mirroring the German 'finger four' formation that had been successfully used by the Jagdwaffe since its creation during the Spanish Civil War, Soviet pilots would either fly at the same altitude or the second pair (the first two La-5s from the left) would position themselves slightly higher or lower than the 1 lead pair.

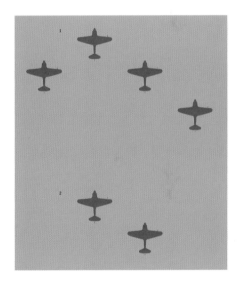

Soviet fighter regiments would also occasionally employ this six-aircraft formation, particularly during the latter stages of the war. Known as the 'binding four', the pilots in Formation 1 would be the first to engage the enemy. Formation 2, or the 'striking pair', would fly behind the 'binding four' at a higher altitude, the distance between the two formations being dependent on the weather. These two fighters would engage enemy aircraft that had evaded the first formation.

Major Ivan Kozhedub. (From archives of D. Khazanov and A. Medved)

The top-scoring Allied ace of World War II and a three-time Hero of the Soviet Union (HSU), Ivan Kozhedub, was born on 8 June 1920 in Obrazhievka, in the Sumy region of the Ukraine. Having learned to fly with the Shostkinsk Flying Club pre-war, he joined the Red Army in 1940 and graduated from the Chuguyevsk Military Aviation Pilots' School in February of the following year. Achieving excellent results during his time at the school, Kozhedub was lucky enough to be retained as a flight instructor, thus avoiding the wholesale slaughter of his contemporaries at the hands of the Luftwaffe in the wake of the German invasion in June 1941.

After Kozhedub's repeated requests to join a front-line regiment were turned down due to the urgent need to train replacement pilots, he was finally posted to 240th IAP in November 1942 shortly after it had received La-5s. A sergeant pilot, Kozhedub joined his regiment with 500 flying hours to his name. Despite this flying experience, he had a lot to learn about combat flying and was almost shot down by a Bf 110 on his first mission. Kozhedub finally claimed his first victory (a Ju 87) on 6 July 1943 over the Kursk salient – this was his 40th combat sortie. By now flying the improved La-5F, he had claimed eight victories by month-end. 'During the long, hot July days we literally did not get out of our aircraft', Kozhedub subsequently recalled. 'We did not feel tired, so great was our nervous tension. However, occasionally, fatigue would overwhelm you, and you would have to catch up with your sleep in a nearby dugout between sorties.'

Soon promoted to squadron commander, Kozhedub was awarded his first HSU on 4 February 1944, having completed 146 combat sorties and claimed 26 victories – he was also promoted to captain. In late June Kozhedub was ordered to fly immediately to Moscow, having by then completed 256 sorties and scored 48 victories. There, he was informed that he was being transferred as deputy commander to 176th GIAP, which had just been classified as a 'free hunt' unit. Kozhedub spent August converting from the La-5FN to the La-7, and on the 19th he received his second HSU.

Between 22 September 1944 and 17 April 1945, Kozhedub would increase his tally to 62 victories, 19 of which were Fw 190s – he claimed 13 Focke-Wulf fighters during this period, including a solitary Fw 190D-9.

Kozhedub maintained that he had actually downed more than 100 German aircraft, but many remained unconfirmed because they were claimed deep within enemy territory. He also never bothered including group kills within his tally. Kozhedub received his third HSU on 18 August 1945, a feat equalled only by Marshal Georgy Zhukov and fellow ace Aleksandr Pokryshkin.

From March 1951 to February 1952 Kozhedub commanded the MiG-15-equipped 324th IAD in combat over North Korea, although he was forbidden by Stalin himself from undertaking combat missions. Kozhedub continued to fly fighters until 1970, and he retired from active duty in 1978 with the rank of marshal. The greatest Allied ace of World War II passed away on 8 August 1991.

La-5/7 regiments sometimes downed as many as ten German aircraft for every Lavochkin fighter lost to enemy action. By then, of course, the majority of Soviet fighter pilots in the front line were combat veterans who were masters of their now superior aircraft, while newer pilots were better trained than their German counterparts.

German Pilot Training

There are many aspects of German pilot training that are interesting to explore. This section will focus specifically on the conversion process that Bf 109-equipped *Gruppen* undertook when transitioning to the Fw 190.

The first unit to make the switch in the East was I./JG 51 in August 1942. The conversion course itself comprized a series of technical lectures on the handling and flight characteristics of the Fw 190. The most obvious difference between this aircraft and the familiar form of the Bf 109 was the pugnacious size of the powerplant. Ideally suited to the Eastern Front, the BMW 801D possessed two important advantages over the Daimler-Benz fitted to the Bf 109 – its very bulk offered a degree of head-on protection for the pilot, and it could absorb a tremendous amount of damage; qualities that were quickly appreciated in the low-level arena of the Russian Front where ground fire was a constant hazard. Whereas the Bf 109 could be downed if nicked in the cooling system by a single rifle bullet, tales would soon be told of Fw 190s staggering back to base with one or more complete cylinder heads shot away.

One word of warning was sounded, however. If, for any reason, the Focke-Wulf's engine did stop, the advice was to get out – quickly. Powerless, the fighter had 'the gliding characteristics of a brick. As soon as the engine faltered, the nose pointed earthwards, followed by the rest of the airframe in close formation'. Opinions were to vary as to the advisability of trying to land with a dead engine. Some pilots swear they never witnessed a single successful attempt at a deadstick landing. Others claim to have actually done so, with varying degrees of damage to themselves and their aircraft. All are agreed, however, that such action was a course of last resort and not one to be recommended on a regular basis.

Belly landings, on the other hand, offered the pilot a reasonable chance of walking away from the resultant mayhem. The forward momentum of the BMW, ensconced behind its armoured ring, tended to brush aside all but the most immovable of obstacles. The trick, one pilot discovered, was to set the propeller blades to as fine a pitch as possible immediately prior to impact. As soon as they hit the ground, they bent backwards and doubled as makeshift skis. Some future ground-attack pilots would even profess to being able to make smoother wheels-up landings on their

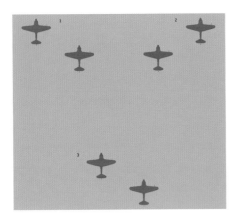

When large areas of German-held territory needed to be swept for enemy aircraft, the 'binding four' could be split into pairs (Formations 1 and 2). The 'striking pair' (Formation 3), however, would again fly behind the 'binding four' at a higher altitude.

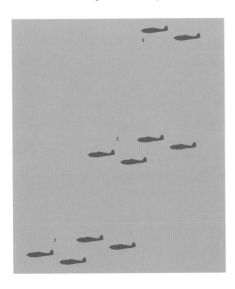

This is a vertical profile of a typical Fw 190 fighter formation during 1942–43. The bottom 'finger four' formation (1) would have been used to initially engage the enemy, or attract the attention of Soviet fighters, after which the second flight (2) (usually positioned 'up sun') would bounce the enemy formation. Flying above them all would be a pair of 'free hunting' Fw 190s (3), the lead machine usually being flown by the *Staffel's* ranking ace. It was their job to pick off any Soviet aircraft that attempted to flee the fight.

fuselage and wing weapons-racks than they ever did by performing a normal three-pointer.

The width of the undercarriage track also proved a distinct boon to Eastern Front flyers. Where the Bf 109 skittered perilously, the Fw 190 ploughed its way splay-legged and tail-down through the worst surfaces the Soviet winter could throw at it – snow, slush, rain or mud – 'like a bullfrog on water skis'. Taxiing and take-off could, however, pose a problem. Despite the near all-round vision from the cockpit (there was a 15-degree blind spot immediately to the rear occasioned by the pilot's head armour), the large cowling precluded a full forward view until airborne. For unlike the Bf 109, the pilots were told, the Fw 190 had to take off the same way as it landed: on all three points. Raise the tail too early and there was every danger that the propeller would dig in and flip the aircraft onto its back.

On the subject of flight characteristics, it was tacitly acknowledged that the Fw 190's performance did fall away at altitude. Although this was currently posing a problem on the Channel Front (and was to assume greater proportions in Defence of the Reich operations in the years to come), it played no part in Eastern Front operations where, experience had shown, the Soviets tended to swarm at low-level over the scene of any ground action 'like a plague of gnats at a picnic'. For the Russian Front, therefore, the Fw 190 was to prove the ideal machine, combining ruggedness with manoeuvrability and stability. In short, it was a superb dogfighter – in all but the tightest of horizontal turns – and an excellent gun platform. The Bf 109 could only match the Fw 190A-3's formidable armament of two 7.9mm machine guns and a quartet of 20mm cannon by bolting on two performance-sapping underwing gondolas.

The tactic evolved in the West of fighting the Fw 190 in the 'vertical plane' – in other words, a quick diving pass and rapid zoom recovery – rather than mixing it on the horizontal, was also suited to the East, where the enemy seldom sought the advantage of height and tended to pay scant regard to his rear. In fact, one of the Luftwaffe's major opponents on the Russian Front, the

AIR WAR IN THE EAST

rugged Il-2 ground-attack aircraft, was all but impervious to anything but a stern attack. While bullets bounced harmlessly off its thickly protected underside and flanks, a well-placed burst of fire into the tail unit could often bring about its demise. If, however, the pilots of I./JG 51 found themselves embroiled in a twist-and-turn dogfight, they were strongly warned of the Fw 190's one basic, and potentially lethal, flaw. In clean configuration the stall was sudden and vicious. Let the speed fall below 127mph and, virtually without warning, the port wing would drop so violently that the Fw 190 all but turned on its back. Pull into a G-stall in a tight turn and it 'would flick over into opposite bank and you had an incipient spin on your hands'.

But a virtue could be made even of this vice, as pilots were told. It was a manoeuvre no pursuer could emulate. 'Be prepared to control the spin, and it is one sure way of shaking Ivan off your tail. Just don't try it at low level. The initial movement eats up too much vertical airspace!'

With this caveat ringing in their ears, the next stage of the course was cockpit familiarization. There was, as yet, no dual-seat trainer variant of the Fw 190 available, and it was crucial that each pilot be made conversant with his new 'office' before his first flight. Pressing the button high on the fuselage side which released the retractable stirrup step buried aft of the port wing root, the pilot climbed aboard by means of a further spring-loaded handhold and step. Once in the semi-reclining seat, vertically adjustable over a range of some four inches, it was immediately apparent just how much of a quantum leap the Fw 190 represented over the Bf 109.

The basic instrumentation could, of course, be recognized from old, but there was also an impressive array of new electric instruments and indicators, for the Fw 190 was equipped with a revolutionary and ingenious

Kommandogerät — variously described as an 'early form of computer' or, more basically, a sort of 'brain box' – which relieved the pilot of such mundane tasks as the setting and controlling of the propeller pitch, mixture, boost and rpm. The Fw 190 was also a nest of electrics, which, with the punch of a button, allowed the pilot to lower or retract the undercarriage (a separate electric motor for each gear leg), set the flaps and adjust trim.

Pilots from I./JG 54 are introduced to the Fw 190A-4 in late 1942. Note the 'Green Heart' on the cowling and the III. *Gruppe* vertical bar on the fighter's rear fuselage – perhaps this was a machine on loan from JG 51 specifically for use in the familiarisation of pilots from I./JG 54? (From archives of D. Khazanov and A. Medved)

All this and more had to be explained, including the arming of the guns. First the fuselage machine guns and wing root cannon had to be switched to live, then a three-second wait before arming the outer wing cannon – forget that delay in the heat of the moment, it was said, and you risked overloading the battery.

Finally, all was ready. One last check under the watchful gaze of the mechanic standing on the wing alongside the cockpit – shoulder straps, parachute harness, oxygen supply, run a not-yet-quite-practised eye over the still unfamiliar banks of switches and buttons. The mechanic then jumped down off the wing and took station off to the left. 'All clear ahead?' 'All clear ahead'. 'Contact'. The BMW 801 was fired up via an inertia starter, which was energized either by an acc trolley or the aircraft's own battery. A stab at the starter, and the BMW roared into life in a cloud of blue smoke. Twelve degrees of flap at the touch of another button, brakes released and the fighter started to roll. Unstick at 112mph, punch the undercarriage and flap retraction buttons as, one by one, the pilots of I./JG 51 forsook theory and returned to their natural element.

Fw 190A-6: IN THE COCKPIT

1. FuG 16ZY communication, homing
2. FuG 16ZY receiver fine-tuning dial
3. FuG 16ZY homing range switch
4. FuG 16ZY frequency selector switch
5. Tailplane trim switch
6. Undercarriage and landing flap actuation buttons
7. Undercarriage and landing flap position indicators
8. Throttle
9. Throttle-mounted propeller pitch control thumb switch
10. Tailplane trim indicator
11. Instrument panel lighting dimmer dial
12. Pilot's seat
13. Throttle friction knob
14. Control column
15. Rudder pedals
16. Wing gun firing button
17. Fuel tank selector lever
18. Engine starter brushes withdrawal button
19. Stopcock control lever
20. FuG 25a IFF control panel
21. Undercarriage manual lowering handle
22. Cockpit ventilation knob
23. Altimeter
24. Pitot tube heater light
25. MG 131 'armed' indicator lights
26. Ammunition counters
27. SZKK 4 armament switch and control panel
28. 30mm armoured glass windscreen panels
29. Windscreen spray pipes
30. 50mm armoured glass windscreen
31. Revi 16B reflector gunsight
32. Padded coaming
33. Gunsight padded mounting
34. AFN 2 homing indicator (FuG 16ZY)
35. Ultraviolet lights (port/starboard)
36. Turn and bank indicator
37. Airspeed indicator
38. Tachometer
39. Repeater compass
40. Clock
41. Manifold pressure gauge
42. Ventral stores and manual release handle
43. Fuel and oil pressure gauge
44. Oil temperature gauge
45. Windscreen washer operating lever
46. Fuel warning light
47. Engine ventilation flap control lever
48. Fuel contents gauge
49. Propeller pitch indicator
50. Rear fuel tank switchover light
51. Fuel content warning light (red)
52. Fuel gauge selector switch
53. Propeller switch (automatic-manual)
54. Bomb fusing selector panel and external stores indicator lights
55. Oxygen flow indicator
56. Fresh air intake
57. Oxygen pressure gauge
58. Oxygen flow valve
59. Canopy actuator wheel
60. Canopy jettison lever
61. Circuit breaker panel cover
62. Battery connected light
63. Map holder
64. Operations information card
65. Flare box cover
66. Starter switch
67. Flare box cover plate release latch
68. Fuel pump circuit breaker switches
69. Compass deviation card
70. Circuit breaker panel cover
71. Armament circuit breakers

(Artwork by Jim Laurier, © Osprey Publishing)

After a few cautious circuits and bumps, they were soon revelling in the superb control harmony of their new mounts, the lightness of the ailerons, the incredibly high rate of roll. Before long, they were practising dummy attacks on one another and staging mock dogfights, during which they found themselves pulling aileron turns that would have wrenched the wings off their old Bf 109s.

The conversion course was at an end. It had been brief, but intensive. For the unit's pilots – the majority of them products of the Luftwaffe's excellent and exhaustive pre- and early-wartime training programmes, and many already veterans of nearly three years of combat flying – there was neither the need, nor the time, to teach them anything more of combat tactics at this late stage.

The transition of Eastern Front fighter *Gruppen* from the Bf 109F to the Fw 190 took place shortly after the early-war pilot conversion system had been abandoned in 1942. Previously, a pilot, upon the successful completion of his formal training programme, would be posted to the subordinate *Ergänzungsgruppe* (replacement wing) of the particular front-line unit he was scheduled to join. Instead of each *Jagdgeschwader* operating what was, in effect, its own personal operational training unit to prepare its newly assigned pilots for front-line combat, henceforth this task would be taken over by the official *Ergänzungsjagdgeschwader* (replacement fighter group), a unit intended to supply the entire fighter arm with combat-ready pilots.

This new EJG was divided into two *Gruppen*, 'Ost' and 'West', and these in turn were composed of a number of *Staffeln*, each of which was responsible for supplying the requirements of a particular *Jagdgeschwader*. Front-line pilots from these *Jagdgeschwader* were rotated back to their specific *Ergänzungsstaffeln* to help prepare the trainees for the conditions they would face when posted to their operational unit. Although the basic training programmes were gradually curtailed as the war progressed (a result of the growing demand for quick replacements, allied to declining fuel stocks), the *Ergänzungs* system continued. The front-line pilots did what they could with the ever more youthful and sketchily trained material passing through their hands, but the outcome was predictable. In the face of overwhelming enemy strength, many young pilots, however eager and willing, failed to return from their first mission.

Despite the official increase in complement experienced by fighter *Geschwader* in the final months of the war, it also meant that there were more pilots available than there were machines to fly. This problem had plagued the Fw 190 *Gruppen* throughout their time on the Eastern Front, which is why few pilots, other than the higher-ranking formation leaders,

Fw 190 PILOT: WALTER NOWOTNY

Major Walter Nowotny. (From archives of D. Khazanov and A. Medved)

One of many Austrians to rise high in the ranks of the wartime Luftwaffe, Walter Nowotny flew almost exclusively against the Russians – indeed, 253 of his 258 victories were VVS-KA aircraft, including an estimated 50 La-5s.

Born on 7 December 1920 in Ceske Velenice/Gmünd on the Czechoslovak/Austrian border, Nowotny joined the Luftwaffe on 1 October 1939. His flying training was completed at *Jagdfliegerschule* 5 at Schwechat, near Vienna, and he was posted to III./JG 54 on 23 February 1941. His first two victories (a pair of I-153s claimed over the Baltic Sea on 19 July) were very nearly his last, as his Bf 109E-7 was in turn shot down by future Russian ace Alexandr Avdeev. Forced to ditch, Nowotny

survived the following 72 hours in an open dinghy before being washed ashore. By the autumn of 1942 his score had topped the 50 mark, he had been awarded the Knight's Cross and he was *Staffelkapitän* of 1./JG 54.

In December 1942 I./JG 54 swapped its Bf 109Gs for Fw 190A-4s, and it was the arrival of the latter that really allowed Nowotny's career as a fighter ace to take off. In June 1943 he claimed 41 kills, including ten on one day, and in August he was promoted to *Gruppenkommandeur* of I./JG 54. Nowotny celebrated his promotion by scoring 49 victories during this month alone – 21 of these were La-5s.

In September Nowotny's tally reached 200, and on 14 October 1943 he became the first fighter pilot to pass the 250-victory mark, making him the top-scoring fighter ace of the Luftwaffe at that time. Nowotny was honoured with the Diamonds to the Oak Leaves with Swords for his Knight's Cross.

By then the Nazi propaganda machine had turned Nowotny into a 'superstar', and fearing his loss in action the Luftwaffe High Command removed him from combat duty shortly after he had claimed his 255th victory on 12 November 1943. During the following months Hauptmann Nowotny's main role was to perform propaganda and morale-boosting duties before, on 1 April 1944, he was made *Kommodore* of JG 101, an operational fighter-training unit based at Pau in France. Five months later he was put in charge of the experimental Me 262 jet fighter unit *Kommando* Nowotny. On 8 November he engaged a formation of B-24 Liberators and their P-51 Mustang escorts, and after claiming two victories he was almost certainly shot down by another Mustang from the 357th Fighter Group. Pilots from Nowotny's unit, watching from their Achmer base, saw their leader's Me 262 emerge from solid cloud and dive vertically into the ground. After flying more than 442 missions and claimed 258 victories, Walter Nowotny had been killed in action.

What the well-dressed Fw 190F wore in the depths of winter on the Eastern Front. Heating trolleys and tents were available only for the lucky few! Tents were often reserved for aircraft undergoing in-the-field maintenance, as conditions were usually too bitter in the depths of winter for the groundcrew to work outdoors for any period of time. (From archives of D. Khazanov and A. Medved)

had individual aircraft permanently assigned to them. They were simply allocated a machine prior to a mission, the groundcrew adjusted the rudder pedals and seat height accordingly, and off they went.

INTO COMBAT

By the time the La-5 and Fw 190 met for the first time in combat, over the Karelian Front, in October–November 1942, the Focke-Wulf fighter had seen more than a year of front-line service with the Luftwaffe on the Western Front. This in turn meant that the numerous teething problems usually associated with a new type had by then been pretty much solved. However, the same could not be said for the La-5, the first production examples of which had been urgently rushed to the Stalingrad front to help defend the beleaguered city. Assigned to 287th IAD (as well as 49th IAP on the Western Front), these machines had shown promise but also revealed numerous problems.

As previously noted, pilots complained that the aircraft was more difficult to fly than a Yak-1 or LaGG-3 due to its heavy weight and poorly balanced control surfaces, although they were impressed with the survivability of the M-82 engine and the protection it offered during frontal attacks. Pilots from 287th IAD also stated that the La-5 was inferior to the Bf 109F and, especially, the new Bf 109G-2 in both speed and vertical manoeuvrability. A report submitted at the time stated, 'We have to engage only in defensive combat actions. The enemy is superior in altitude and, therefore, had a more favourable position from which to attack'.

The fighter's lack of speed was of particular concern, as it barely attained 316mph at low level and 332mph when at its augmented rating – the latter was only available for short periods due to excessive engine overheating. The poor quality of the early airframes also created excessive drag, which in turn slowed the La-5 down. Furthermore, Soviet pilots traditionally flew with their canopies open, cowling side flaps open and retractable tailwheel extended, all of which shaved a further 25mph off the top speed.

Early encounters with the Fw 190A-3/4s of JGs 51 and 54 revealed that the German fighter had the edge on the La-5, but only just. Soviet pilots reported that the Lavochkin could stay with – but not overtake – an Fw 190 in horizontal flight at low altitude, and their performance was similar when manoeuvring in the same plane. When chasing or evading an Fw 190 in a climb, the La-5 (which was half a ton lighter) enjoyed some advantage. However, its manoeuvrability at speeds in excess of 250mph left a lot to be desired in comparison with the Fw 190. Most pilots felt that the ailerons and elevators were particularly heavy when turning tightly at higher speeds and when exiting a dive. This in turn meant that only physically strong pilots could hope to get the best out of the early La-5s when engaging enemy fighters.

The Fw 190 was also more heavily armed, especially the A-3 variant with its quartet of 20mm cannon and two synchronized 7.9mm machine guns. And even without MG/FF cannon in the wings, the Focke-Wulf still packed more of a punch than the La-5. While Soviet pilots rarely complained about the effectiveness of their weaponry, the two synchronized ShVAK cannon occasionally proved insufficient to knock down well-armoured Fw 190 fighters (not to mention the seemingly invulnerable Fw 190F/G *Schlacht* aircraft). The A-3 could also unleash a weight of fire per second that was almost three times greater than that achievable in the La-5.

However, despite the Fw 190 boasting better firepower and performance than the Lavochkin, the principal advantage enjoyed by the Luftwaffe over the VVS-KA in late 1942 centred on the combat experience of its fighter pilots. The men taking the early Fw 190s into combat on the Eastern Front at this time were, in the main, hardened veterans who had been flying fighters since the beginning of the war in September 1939. Most had been fighting the VVS-KA for more than a year, and many of them had already claimed numerous victories. Their counterparts, on the other hand, had often only just completed their flying training, and all of them were new to the La-5. A typical Luftwaffe pilot from this period was Hauptmann Heinz Lange, who had scored his first kill in October 1939. A *Staffelkapitän* with I./JG 54 on the Leningrad front from late 1941, he had been given command of 3./JG 51 on 26 October:

Overleaf
On 28 August 1943, Capt Ivan Kozich and his wingman Jnr Lt Storozhko of 721st IAP were performing an aerial reconnaissance sweep west of Orel when they were attacked by eight Fw 190s split into two formations of four aircraft. The first group approached them from behind at their altitude of 12,000ft, while the second was off to the right some 2,000ft higher. Kozich turned towards the rear four Fw 190s and fired a burst into the lead aircraft. His aim was poor, so he switched targets to the Fw 190 to the left of the leader, which crashed. By now the second German formation had arrived, and Kozich throttled back and performed a tight diving turn that placed him immediately behind all four Fw 190s. Firing from a distance of just 150ft, he quickly downed the Focke-Wulf to the left of the formation leader. The remaining Fw 190 pilots succeeded in downing Storozhko after a period of violent manoeuvring. Kozich made good his escape, however. (Artwork by Gareth Hector, © Osprey Publishing)

I first flew the Fw 190 on 8 November 1942 at Vyazma, in the Soviet Union. I was absolutely thrilled. I flew every fighter version of it employed on the Eastern Front. Because of its smaller fuselage, visibility was somewhat better out of the Bf 109. I believe the Focke-Wulf was more manoeuvrable than the Messerschmitt – although the latter could make a tighter horizontal turn, if you mastered the Fw 190 you could pull a lot of Gs and do just about as well. In terms of control force and feel, the Bf 109 was heavier on the stick. In the Fw 190 aerobatics were a pleasure!

Structurally, it was distinctly superior to the Messerschmitt, especially in dives. The radial engine of the Fw 190A was also more resistant to enemy fire. Firepower, which varied with the particular series, was fairly even in all German fighters. The central cannon of the Messerschmitt was naturally more accurate, but that was really a meaningful advantage only in fighter-versus-fighter combat. The Bf 109's 20mm cannon frequently jammed, especially in hard turns – I lost at least six kills this way.

In the development of our fighter operations, the most significant step was our transition from the closed Kette of three aeroplanes to the four-aeroplane 'finger-fours' Schwarm. This innovation was developed during the Spanish Civil War with considerable help by Werner Mölders. I attribute to this tactic the high number of kills attained by German fighter pilots.

Lange eventually became the sixth, and last, *Kommodore* of JG 51, ending the war with 70 kills (including a handful of La-5s), all bar one of which came in the East. Commenting on the 'free hunt' tactics favoured by the great pilots of this period, 36-victory ace (and HSU recipient) Maj Andrei Baklan of 32nd GIAP remarked:

They would cross the front line at high altitude in their Fw 190s and then turn around and bounce us from above. The Germans always tried to attack us from the rear while we were still over friendly territory, hoping to catch us off guard. During my four years of fighting the Luftwaffe, I failed to discern any particular pattern to the tactical formations and tactics employed by enemy aces. There was no set form of combat that they followed, hence the fact that they were so dangerous.

After service testing and combat experience revealed numerous defects with the La-5, Lavochkin set about rectifying these problems with the follow-on La-5F of early 1943. Incorporating aerodynamic improvements, reduced weight (achieved by losing two of the five fuel tanks), reshaped and larger flight controls and a more powerful (and reliable) M-82F engine, the new fighter started to reach front-line units in March 1943.

Engine reliability had been of great concern with the original La-5, as the M-82 had a tendency to suffer from spark plug failure and exhaust pipe burn-through. The fighter's boost system had also proven difficult to operate, as had the cowling side flaps – the engine routinely overheated as a result.

With the number of Fw 190s appearing on the Leningrad Front dramatically increasing in January 1943 following the arrival of I. and II./JG 54, it was only a matter of time before the Soviets managed to get their hands on a near-intact example. On the 16th of that month Unteroffizier Helmut Brandt of 2./JG 54 shot the blades of his own propeller when the interruptor mechanism failed while he was strafing enemy vehicles on the Lake Ladoga ice highway. 3rd GIAP-KBF 28-victory ace, and HSU recipient, Capt Igor Kaberov recalled what happened next:

The engine howled, the machine shook and the pilot could do nothing except make a belly landing right beside the road. Of course, the Fascist was taken prisoner. His aircraft was delivered to the Leningrad commander's aerodrome. During the evening of 4 February fighter pilots were brought to the aerodrome to acquaint themselves with the enemy's technical novelties. The prisoner, speaking through an interpreter, gave an explanation. He readily answered our questions concerning the characteristics of the machine.

We each in turn sat in the cockpit of the Focke-Wulf and examined the equipment. It must be said the machine was not bad, possessing a high undercarriage and electrically controlled radial engine. Armour-plated glass in front of the gunsight and thick armour behind the back protected the pilot extremely well. But when the hood was closed the field of vision from the cockpit was rather limited.

'It's a high-speed machine', insisted its former master. 'It's not possible to shoot down this aircraft'. 'We'll see about that!' laughed the lads. As time passed, in aerial battles against Fascist aviators, the Soviet pilots demonstrated the vulnerability of the Fw 190.

Although the improved La-5F allowed Soviet pilots to achieve parity with German fighters during the spring of 1943, Lavochkin was fully aware that more still needed to be done. For example, engine reliability was still not what it should have been, with the La-5 suffering a failure rate three times greater than its contemporaries in the VVS-KA at that time. Pilots were also finding the aircraft difficult to recover from inverted spins due to the heaviness of the controls. Indeed, front-line aviators continued to abandon La-5s in an inverted spin until they were shown how to recover the aircraft by Lavochkin test pilots. As previously mentioned, the fighter's handling improved with the advent of the La-5F thanks to the fitment of larger flying surfaces.

The new Lavochkin fighter also had improved survivability due to the installation of self-sealing fuel tanks and an inert gas system, as well as the adoption of central fuel tanks of greater capacity. This in turn meant that the more exposed wing tanks could be removed, thus shortening the vulnerable fuel and oil lines.

31st IAP pilot Leonid 'Lyosha' Maslov (who destroyed six aircraft, four of which were Fw 190s, and shared in nine more victories) saw action in the La-5 on the Southwest Front over Stalingrad in late 1942 and then flew La-5Fs over the Kuban River and Kursk in 1943:

The La-5 and La-5FN were good aircraft, both as fighters and as ground attack machines. In our regiment, division leaders would be equipped with the better performing La-5s, with wingmen having to make do with older and less powerful machines. My aircraft was not as fast as some in my regiment due to the reduced performance of its engine. This was not a big issue, however, as the La-5 was both light and manoeuvrable. Nevertheless, I usually fell behind my flightmates when on operations, much to the annoyance of my flight commander. He would routinely ask me over the radio 'Lyosha, why are you falling behind?', to which I would reply, 'Unfortunately, I'm not riding your horse, sir!'.

When our flight engaged Fw 190s in combat, we would follow our leader into the break and then take the enemy fighters on individually. On one occasion I spotted a Focke-Wulf attempting to flee, so I set off in pursuit. This aircraft was flown by the formation leader, and I soon shot him down. I then saw another Fw 190 fleeing at low-level. I immediately chased after him.

Our division commander told us 'If you can see the rivets, fire'. The gunsight in the La-5 was not very good, so we either fired a trial burst when close enough to our quarry or when we could indeed see 'the rivets'. My foe was heading westward at high speed, and when I got close enough to him I fired a burst. I saw the enemy pilot turning his head in my direction. He then attempted to clip me with his wingtip so as to send me crashing into the forest. I dropped back and opened fire once again, and this time the fighter fell away and crashed into trees. I gained height and headed home. A local artillery battery later confirmed this victory for me.

4th GIAK of the Baltic Fleet Air Force also saw plenty of action with the La-5 and La-5F in the early months of 1943, prompting the unit's commanding officer, Capt Vladimir Golubev (subsequently an HSU), to table the following recommendations:

> The Fw 190, whilst it has powerful weaponry, seeks head-to-head combat, and the rest of the tactics employed remain the same (using the sun, cloud cover etc.) as when fighting the Me 109. You can only break off combat in a dive. When we first encountered the enemy, we found that we climbed more rapidly in the La-5, and when we gained an advantage in speed the Fw 190 rolled onto its back and dived away. After a few vertical attacks the Focke-Wulf fighters always ended up beneath us. When fighting in the horizontal plane, the La-5 has the better performance in a combat turn, and we were not afraid of engaging an Fw 190 at slow speeds.
>
> If you find an Fw 190 on your tail, never attempt to break away from it by diving. You need to disengage either by climbing or side-slipping. Frontal attacks on the Fw 190 are not to be recommended either, as the aircraft has a small cross-section and is heavily armed. It is best to attack from the rear, as accurate fire from this direction will damage the fighter's fuel tanks. You need to direct your fire at the cockpit and along the right hand side of the fuselage, where the wiring for the fighter's electrical system is located. If this is destroyed the Fw 190 pilot will have to quickly force-land.

By July 1943 the first examples of the definitive La-5FN had started to reach 32nd GIAP just as the Battle of Kursk erupted. Featuring the direct

Three Fw 190A-4s of 5./JG 54 bask in spring sunshine at Siverskaya in the late spring of 1943. 'Black 5' was the mount of Austrian Oberleutnant Max Stotz, who became *Staffelkapitän* of 5./JG 54 later that same summer, only to be reported missing in action near Vitebsk on 19 August 1943. All bar 16 of his 189 kills were gained with II. *Gruppe*. (From archives of D. Khazanov and A. Medved)

fuel injected 1,850hp M-82FN engine, lowered rear fuselage decking and myriad other changes, the fighter soon made its mark in combat. One of the pilots who took the aircraft into combat at this time was HSU Capt Vladimir Garanin, who noted:

> Combats were fought at altitudes up to 13,000ft with obvious advantages over the Fw 190 and Bf 109, both in speed and in horizontal and vertical manoeuvring. The La-5FN with an open canopy overtakes hostile fighters, albeit slowly, gets on their tails during banked turns and in vertical combat always turns to get above the enemy.

The La-5FN was not perfect, however, pilots complaining that their ability to train their guns onto a target was made more difficult by the enlarged air intake atop the cowling. The gunsight was also positioned too high as a result, thus preventing pilots from using it with the canopy shut. The cockpit, which could often be excessively hot due to poor ventilation, was routinely filled with noxious exhaust gases in flight. Finally, the radio fitted to the La-5FN was unreliable at best. Nevertheless, the new fighter proved a handful for the Fw 190, as La-5 ace Vladimir Orekhov (who was credited with 19 and two shared victories, including ten Fw 190s – he claimed four Focke-Wulfs during the Kursk battles) of 32nd GIAP reported in late 1943:

> The aircraft as a whole is not bad. It's best not to make a frontal attack on the Fw 190, as it has very powerful weaponry – four cannon. It is very good in a dive and breaks off combat well if the pilot is engaged at medium to high altitude. An experienced Fw 190 pilot practically never fights in the vertical plane. If you were to compare the Fw 190 to the Me 109G, the 'Messer' would be slightly stronger overall when employed as a fighter, possessing greater speed and better manoeuvrability in a vertical fight.

This viewed was shared by Pavel Boykov of 113th GIAP:

> The Fw 190's powerful engine guaranteed high speed, but in combat it could be both heavy and inert. In an effort to offset these disadvantages the fascists created mixed groups. The Focke-Wulfs, as a rule, flew lower, and willingly pressed our fighters in combat head-on, but the Me 109s overhead preferred to dive on us from above and behind.

The Luftwaffe believed that the La-5FN posed the greatest threat to its fighters and bombers from mid-1943, and when an example force landed relatively intact in German-held territory, it was quickly returned to airworthiness. The task of flight testing the fighter was given to Hans Werner Lerche, who performed his first flight in the La-5FN at the Rechlin test centre in the late summer of 1943. As part of his evaluation, he flew the aircraft against an Fw 190A-8 and a Bf 109G, noting:

> The La-5FN represents significant progress in both performance and operational characteristics when compared to early Soviet fighters. Its performance at altitudes up to 3,000m [9,840ft] warrants special attention. However, its maximum speed at any altitude is less than that of German fighters. The fighter's best rate of climb at low level compares favourably with that achieved in the Fw 190A-8 and Bf 109G. The La-5FN's rate of climb and rate of turn at 3,000m [9,840ft] is comparable to the Fw 190A. This is because the efficiency of the fighter's ailerons is truly outstanding. At an air speed of 450km/h [280mph], a roll can be performed in less than four seconds. However, at 600km/h [375mph] pressure on the ailerons becomes excessive. At 1,000m [3,280ft] a maximum rate 360-degree horizontal turn can be performed in 25 seconds using engine boost.
>
> In view of the merits of its engine, the La-5FN is more suited to low-altitude combat. Its maximum speed at low level is comparable with that of the Fw 190A-8 and Bf 109G on boost. Acceleration characteristics are balanced. The La-5FN is bettered by the Bf 109G with MW 50 both in terms of its top speed and rate of climb at any altitude. The Russian fighter is superior to the Fw 190A-8 up to 3,000m [9,840ft].
>
> You should dive in order to escape an attack from a La-5FN.

Although most sources have linked this famous La-5 (seen here near war's end) with 46-victory ace Georgii Kostylev and his service with 3rd GIAP, he in fact flew only older aircraft whilst with the regiment. In reality, the ace flew this La-5 after joining 4th GIAP-KBF in late August 1943. (From archives of D. Khazanov and A. Medved)

Lerche emphasized the fact that the La-5FN was slower than its German fighter rivals. However, when a captured Fw 190A-8 was tested against an La-5FN at an altitude of 13,120ft in the USSR in 1944, the opposite appeared to be true. This was not surprising, as the Lavochkin used in the tests was a factory-fresh machine, while the La-5FN test flown by Lerche was almost certainly a combat-weary example.

As Leonid 'Lyosha' Maslov recalled earlier, the power output of the M-82FN could vary greatly from engine to engine depending on how they had been used in the front line. For example, if one had been flown on boost for a very long time without adequate cooling, the engine would expand and overheat. VVS-KA mechanics quickly recognized when this had happened as the heat generated by the engine would blister the paint on the cowling, causing it to peel away. Engines that suffered regular overboosting soon lost power, and they remained in this state even after being overhauled. It is possible that Lerche had tested just such an aircraft. Conversely, captured German fighters had defects too, which explains why the flight performance figures for the various Fw 190As flown at Soviet test centres seemed so poor.

Lerche noted in his report that the La-5FN was highly manoeuvrable in the horizontal plane at medium to low altitudes. German pilots soon learned through bitter experience not to initiate combat turns in an effort to shake off a Lavochkin.

Despite the improved performance of the La-5FN, fighter regiments continued to suffer heavy losses to Fw 190-equipped fighter units on the Eastern Front until the end of 1943. Most of the high-scoring Luftwaffe aces claimed the majority of their Fw 190 kills during the large-scale battles fought in the summer and autumn of that year, with men such as Walter Nowotny, Otto Kittel and Emil 'Bully' Lang cutting a swathe through Soviet fighter ranks as the latter attempted to defend Il-2 and Pe-2 bombers

On 14 October 1943, while flying this Fw 190A-6, Hauptmann Walter Nowotny, *Gruppenkommandeur* of I./JG 54, scored his 250th victory, thus making him the Luftwaffe's leading ace of the time. Seen at Vitebsk a short while later, Wk-Nr. 410004 had its standard grey camouflage finish heavily overpainted in two shades of green. Note the small 'white 8' in the angle of the command chevrons (believed to be a reference to an earlier favourite aircraft) and Nowotny's additional 'lucky 13' below the cockpit sill. (From archives of D. Khazanov and A. Medved)

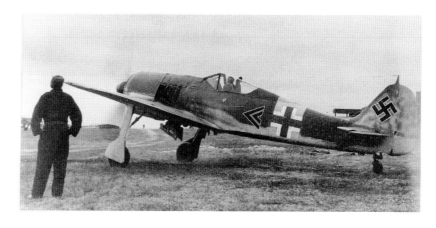

attacking German front-line positions. Indeed, 5./JG 54's Leutnant Lang was to set a new record on the Eastern Front when, on 3 November, he was credited with the destruction of 17 aircraft in one day during fighting in response to the Soviet offensive to recapture Kiev. Having already claimed 35 La-5s destroyed since 13 July 1943, Lang added three more to his tally during his 3 November haul. *Staffelmate*, and fellow ace, Leutnant Norbert Hannig witnessed the destruction of two of them:

The Soviet assault on Kiev commenced with artillery barrages from both north and south, together with a mass of bombers and ground-attack aircraft supported by hordes of La-5 and Yak-7 fighters. Wherever you looked Soviet aircraft filled the sky, undisturbed by German flak or fighters. They seemed oblivious to the fact that our fighters were operating in the area and scoring successes. In one of the few quiet moments Leutnant Lang took off for his third mission of the day, having already claimed nine victories during two morning patrols. He and his wingman, Unteroffizier Paschke, disappeared off to the west. Wave after wave of Soviet Il-2s were coming in, dropping their bombs on our positions ringing Kiev and then immediately turning back eastwards. The *Shturmoviks*, operating from a forward landing ground on the eastern bank of the river Dniepr, barely 15km [9 miles] away from us, were passing almost directly overhead, wheels down, in unbroken procession.

Sixty minutes after taking off, Lang and Paschke came back in to land. We had been standing in a hangar doorway watching the approach of more Il-2s, and their fighter umbrella, when we spotted our two Fw 190s diving in behind them from the east. Lang closed right in on one of the La-5 escorts, fired a short burst at a range of 50 metres [165ft], banked quickly left, got on the tail of a second Lavochkin fighter and gave it the same treatment. Both aircraft broke up in the air, a wing snapping off one and pieces of another crashing down to the ground near where we stood. Neither pilot stood a chance.

The sheer number of aircraft available to the VVS-KA, most of which were flown by better-trained pilots, eventually carried the day. For example, some 1,500 La-5FNs had been delivered to front-line units by the end of 1943.

In early 1944 most Fw 190 fighter units on the Eastern Front were transferred west to help defend Germany from daylight bombing raids. *Schlachtgruppen* now became the principal Fw 190 operators engaged by Soviet fighter regiments, and these proved to be tricky opponents. Leutnant Fritz Seyffardt served with II./SchlG 1, and he would end the war with 30 victories to his name, a number of which were La-5s:

This tactical formation was adopted by La-7-equipped regiments during the final months of the war in Europe. Dubbed the 'front-line formation', it was employed when searching for increasingly elusive German fighter-bombers (primarily Fw 190s) targeting Red Army positions at low altitude. As enemy aircraft became more and more scarce, La-7 units employed the 'front-line formation' to target German troop columns and panzers, as well as hidden weapons emplacements.

I flew the Fw 190A, F and G models, and also the Bf 109. The difference between the Fw 190 and the Bf 109 was that there was more room in the Focke-Wulf's cockpit and the controls were simpler – for example, landing flaps and trim were electric. Another pronounced difference was the stability of the Fw 190. Thanks to its through-wing spars and wide landing gear, the machine was far more stable in flight, and especially in landing on rough fields. At higher altitudes, engine performance was inadequate, however.

Normal range of the later F-models was approximately 375–425 miles. The average mission on the Russian Front lasted 45–60 minutes. Firepower was very good. As a rule we had two 20mm cannon and two machine guns. There was also provision for two additional 20mm cannon in the outer wing panels.

As a flying tactic, we had the greatest success when we flew in open formation, in other words with approximately 80 to 100 metres [260 to 330ft] separation between aircraft. In the target area we split into two-plane Rotte elements for the attack, only re-assembling into larger formations on the return flight. During my 500+ missions, I made several belly landings – something that could be easily done in the rugged Fw 190.

With the Fw 190 possessing a superior speed to the La-5FN in a dive, *Schlachtflieger* would usually drop their bombs and then push the noses of their aircraft towards the ground and escape westward at high speed. A report from 322nd IAD illustrated the problem now posed by Focke-Wulf fighter-bombers:

Fw 190 attack aircraft usually hit targets in groups of six to nine. They release their bombs from a dive, which allows them to accelerate to high speed and depart for their own territory at low level. They don't enter into battle with our fighters, choosing to depart like serpents when they come under attack. Enemy pilots never fight in the vertical plane, where the La-5FN is stronger, preferring to break off combat by rolling away – a tactic long employed by conventional Fw 190 fighters.

Having received numerous complaints from the VVS-KA that its units were having trouble catching Fw 190F/Gs and bomb-toting Fw 190A-8s, Lavochkin responded with the accelerated development of the La-7. Although it was powered by the same ASh-82FN engine as the La-5FN, the La-7 featured numerous aerodynamic improvements and effective weight saving that ultimately boosted its top speed to 373mph at low-level and 425mph at 20,000ft.

The La-7's arrival in the front line from August 1944 also coincided with the VVS-KA's adoption of 'free hunt' tactics as employed by German fighter units from the start of the war. Special 'free hunt' regiments were specifically formed and equipped with the new fighter, the most effective of these being 176th GIAP. Its pilots were ordered not to engage in long battles with the enemy, but to conduct sudden strikes, using the sun or cloud cover, and then break away from the engagement.

Following the regiment's conversion from the La-5FN to the La-7, its commander, Col P. F. Chupikov, organized effective reconnaissance missions over local Luftwaffe airfields and chaired tactical conferences that saw Soviet fighter tactics compared with those of the enemy. He also made sure that a radio compass (to improve pilot orientation in poor weather conditions) and a combat camera (to confirm aerial victories) were installed in each La-7.

Among the aces to see combat in the new type was Capt Nikolay Skomorokhov (who personally destroyed 46 enemy aircraft, including 18 Fw 190s, and was twice a Hero of the Soviet Union) of 164th IAP. A veteran LaGG-3 and La-5/5FN pilot who had been in the front line since November 1942, he first took the La-7 into action in March 1945:

Another formation used by La-7 regiments at war's end saw the lead 'binding four' flight (1) trailed by a second 'striking formation' of four fighters (2), the latter machines being stepped up at a higher altitude.

Having initially sat in the cockpit and familiarised myself with the aircraft's idiosyncrasies, I then took off, with Fillipov as my wingman. I performed a few rolls and vertical climbs – this aircraft was a beast! My conversion ended there.

A short while later our ground-based fighter controller directed us to the Kapolnash–Nieka region, where we spotted ten Fw 190s in front of us that were about to attack our troops. There was no time to waste. I immediately despatched an aircraft that was flying on its own and then opened fire on a second machine. This caused panic to set in among the surviving Focke-Wulf pilots, who scattered in different directions and raced back home at low altitude. Eight more Fw 190s then appeared, and when they tried to commence a bombing run Fillipov and I again managed to shoot down a fighter apiece. Having seen the loss of their comrades, the remaining fascist pilots abandoned their attacks and fled.

La-7: THROUGH THE GUNSIGHT

As this artwork clearly shows, Soviet gunsights were considerably smaller in size than those fitted in German and Western Allied fighters. The La-7 was equipped with the new PBP-1B gunsight, which was an improved version of the PBP-1 fitted in the La-5F/FN. Soviet gunsights were strongly influenced by the equipment fitted to Lend-Lease British and American fighters flown by the VVS-KA.

Victory claims made by Soviet pilots were thoroughly scrutinized by both the squadron intelligence officer/adjutant and an officer of the NKVD (political and military police).

The process of accreditation for an aerial victory is described here by La-5 ace Capt Vladimir Orekhov of 32nd GIAP.

After the mission, pilots gathered together and each one would talk about how many aeroplanes they had personally shot down and how many they had observed their comrades shooting down. The squadron adjutant made notes based on these verbal accounts, which he would then compile into an official document known as the 'Combat Report of the Fulfilled Mission'. Such a document had to be created after every mission, and it contained data detailing the results of the mission, and the pilots who claimed kills. At the end of the day, all such reports were collected and sent to the regimental HQ, where the regiment's combat report was completed.

Kills were usually confirmed by the commander of the regiment. To get confirmation, one of the following 'proofs' had to be available – confirmation from at least two other pilots who took part in the action; confirmation from ground troops; or confirmation from partisans. These forms of verification were equal, but sometimes – especially if the fight took place over enemy territory, or there were other fighters involved – the last two 'proofs' were obligatory.

(Artwork by Jim Laurier, © Osprey Publishing)

Fw 190-equipped *Schlacht* and fighter units targeting Red Army units as they closed on Berlin soon came to fear the La-7, for it was the only Soviet machine that could catch fleeing Focke-Wulf fighter-bombers after they had performed their so-called 'surprise pirate raids' on vehicle columns supporting troops in the front line. Capable of outrunning Yak-3s, Yak-9Us and La-5FNs at low-level thanks to the BMW 801D-2's MW 50 boost, the elite La-7 pilots of the 'free hunt' regiments of the VVS-KA found the Fw 190s easy pickings in the final weeks of the war in Europe.

ANALYSIS

Exactly when and where the La-5 and Fw 190 first clashed remains something of a mystery, although it seems likely that the two fighter types met over the Kalinin Front towards the end of October or the beginning of November 1942. As of 19 November, 78 La-5s were concentrated in that very location – they made up 70 per cent of the total number of Soviet fighters fielded by 3rd Air Army regiments on that day. Fw 190A-3s from I./JG 51 were also active in the region during this period.

However, the leading German Fw 190 aces on the Eastern Front did not start claiming La-5s (initially identified as 'LaGG-5s' by Luftwaffe pilots) until January 1943. For example, the highest scoring La-5 killer, Walter Nowotny, downed the first of his estimated 50 Lavochkin fighters on 7 March. Emil 'Bully' Lang got the first of his 45 La-5s on 13 July, while Otto Kittel, who was credited with 30 Lavochkin fighters, first destroyed an 'LaGG-5' on 24 January 1943. Of the highest-scoring

159th IAP's Vladimir Serov was yet another famous ace to fly an La-5 inscribed with *'Valerii Chkalov Eskadrilya'* titling. This aircraft was one of 13 identically marked Lavochkin fighters issued to the regiment, which was then in action over the northern Ukraine, in the spring of 1943. These machines were also used by fellow 159th IAP aces Pyotr Likholetov and Ivan Kozhedub. (From archives of D. Khazanov and A. Medved)

Fw 190 killers, the first to achieve a recorded victory over the Focke-Wulf fighter was Nikolay Skomorokhov of 164th IAP, who received credit for the first of his 16 Fw 190s on 14 June 1943.

The battle for the Kursk Salient in July–August 1943 was the first time that La-5s and Fw 190s met each other in large numbers. At the start of this epic clash there were around 300 Fw 190 fighters and fighter-bombers assigned to units committed to the battle. They were opposed by more than 500 La-5s split between three air armies.

Lavochkin losses to all causes (including non-combat) totalled 484 aircraft for July–August, while the Luftwaffe had 368 Fw 190s destroyed (again, this number includes operational write-offs) on the Soviet–German front during the same period. The outcome of aerial battles on the Eastern Front often depended more on the skills of the pilots strapped into the opposing fighters, rather than the technical superiority of their respective machines. This was particularly the case over the Kursk Salient, where veteran German aces at the very zenith of their abilities as fighter pilots fought massed ranks of Lavochkin and Yak fighters manned by young aviators fresh from flying training schools. This in turn meant that during July and August 1943 more than 85 per cent of the La-5 pilots posted as killed or missing in combat were junior lieutenants who had only recently graduated from military flying schools. For example, on 5 July all 12 La-5Fs lost by 286th IAD's 265th and 721st IAPs were flown by junior lieutenants. That day JG 51 claimed 26 LaGG-5s and JG 54 18, while many more were credited to Bf 109G-equipped JGs 3 and 52.

As noted earlier, despite suffering terrible losses through to the end of 1943, Soviet fighter regiments began to enjoy the upper hand in combat during early 1944 after Fw 190 fighter units were pulled back to defend Germany from USAAF daylight bombing raids. Focke-Wulf fighters remained in-theatre, however, but they were in the main flown by *Schlachtflieger* who were, first and foremost, ground attack pilots. This meant that veteran VVS-KA aviators who had survived the carnage of 1941–43 now began to prevail in the skies over the Eastern Front in their significantly improved La-5FN fighters. 322nd IAD was heavily involved in operations against Fw 190 fighter-bombers in the Vitebsk region at this time, and between 1 October 1943 and 1 March 1944 its pilots claimed 81 German aircraft destroyed, including 52 Focke-Wulfs, for the loss of 26 La-5FNs in aerial combat.

Large-scale battles similar to those fought over Kursk in July 1943 took place once again from 22 June 1944 when the Red Army launched its summer offensive against German forces in the Central Sector. The only fighter units equipped with Fw 190s in the East at this time were I., II. and

IV./JG 54 with 121 Fw 190A-8s, although seven *Schlachtgruppen* shared close to 200 Fw 190F/Gs between them. Ranged against them were more than 750 La-5FNs split between four fighter divisions.

Unlike the previous year, when the Lavochkin regiments suffered terrible losses at the hands of the Fw 190 fighter *Gruppen*, this time it was the Focke-Wulf units (principally the *Schlachtgruppen*) that were decimated. JG 54 lost 115 aircraft to all causes in July–August 1944, while the fighter-bomber units lost 498 aircraft. Although a number of these machines were downed by flak or destroyed on the ground in Soviet airfield attacks, many Fw 190s fell victim to marauding La-5FNs. The four fighter divisions lost 76 Lavochkins to all causes in return. In fact, according to VVS-KA records, losses for La-5/7s in combat in 1944 totalled 785 aircraft, of which just 167 were classified as downed in aerial combat.

By early 1945, the Luftwaffe was such a spent force in the East that unserviceability rates posed a greater threat to the effectiveness of Lavochkin units – particularly those equipped with the somewhat temperamental La-7 – than the enemy. For example, as of 1 January 1945, of 97 La-7s in 3rd Air Army, 63 were unserviceable.

A cherished exhibit in the Russian Air Force's Monino Museum, this La-7 was issued new to Ivan Kozhedub when he was transitioning to the fighter in August 1944. He duly took it with him when he was transferred to 176th GIAP that same month. Kozhedub initially had 48 victory and two HSU stars marked beneath the cockpit, but by the time Berlin fell his tally of victory stars had increased to 62. A third HSU star would also be added on 18 August 1945. (From archives of D. Khazanov and A. Medved)

LEADING Fw 190 La-5/7 KILLERS			
Ace	La-5/7 kills	Final score	Unit(s)
Major Walter Nowotny	49	258	*Stab.* and I./JG 54
Hauptmann Emil Lang	45	173	I. and II./JG 54
Oberleutnant Otto Kittel	31	267	I./JG 54
Hauptmann Karl-Heinz Weber	19	136	III./JG 51
Major Erich Rudorffer	10+	224	*Stab.* and II./JG 54
Hauptmann Günther Schack	10+	174	III./JG 51
Major Horst Ademeit	10+	166	I. and II./JG 54
Hauptmann Robert Weiss	10	121	I./JG 54

As more La-7s reached the front line and serviceability improved, so the number of victories credited to pilots flying the fighter also grew in the final weeks of the war. Leading aces of the calibre of Ivan Kozhedub, Nikolay Skomorokhov and Aleksandr Kumanichkin were particularly prolific, claiming multiple Fw 190 victories, as both *Schlacht* and fighter units attempted to slow the Red Army advance on Berlin. Fittingly, the last victory claimed by the VVS-KA in World War II fell to La-5FN pilot Capt Konstantin Novikov of 40th GIAP when he downed a lone Fw 190 near Liewarts on 9 May 1945. This was Novikov's 29th success.

LEADING La-5/7 Fw 190 KILLERS			
Ace	Fw 190 kills	Final score	Unit(s)
Snr Lt Vladimir Serov	21	39+6sh	159th IAP
Maj Ivan Kozhedub	19	62	240th IAP and 176th GIAP
Capt Nikolay Skomorokhov	16	46+8sh	164th and 31st IAPs
Capt Nikolay Rudenko	15	26+2sh	240th IAP and 176th GIAP
Capt Kirill Yevstigneyev	12	52+3sh	240th IAP and 178th GIAP
Capt Vasiliy Markov	11	29	116th and 148th IAPs
Maj Aleksandr Kumanichkin	10	27+2sh	41st and 176th GIAPs

AFTERMATH

Production of the Fw 190 abruptly ended with Germany's unconditional surrender on 8 May 1945. According to records kept by the Luftwaffe, some 21,884 examples had been completed by 31 March, and it is not known how many more were built in the final five weeks of the war.

Airfields across Germany and the remaining countries still occupied by the Wehrmacht were littered with abandoned Fw 190s of all variants that were still perfectly serviceable. Soviet forces captured vast quantities of Luftwaffe aircraft, but most of these were simply reduced to scrap in due

The end on the Central Front. Fw 190 carcasses litter the apron of Berlin's huge Tempelhof airport, which was used throughout the war as a storage and repair facility for all manner of Luftwaffe aircraft. (From archives of D. Khazanov and A. Medved)

course. However, the various jet types such as the Me 262, Me 163 and Ar 234 were of great interest to the VVS-KA, as were the Fw 190D-9 and Ta 152 – the ultimate German piston-engined fighters. Six airworthy Fw 190D-9s were seized at a Focke-Wulf repair and maintenance depot at Marienburg, in East Prussia, by 322nd IAD's La-5FN-equipped 2nd GIAP shortly after VE Day. The regiment reportedly kept one or two for identification training while based in Germany post-war. All of these aircraft were re-marked with Soviet national markings, and at least two machines were extensively flight tested by VVS NII KA pilots from the airfield adjacent to Focke-Wulf's Sorau factory in western Poland. Fw 190D-9s were also evaluated at VVS NII KA airfields in the USSR. In 1948–49, photographs published in the official US government publication *Military Review* showed a pair of Fw 190D-9s apparently in service with a Soviet unit stationed at Görden, southwest of Brandenburg. According to the publication the two German fighters remained in the Red Air Force inventory as advanced fighter trainers until late 1949, when one of them was lost in a crash in Latvia.

The veracity of reports that captured Fw 190D-9s were impressed into the ranks of the VVS-KA in the final weeks of World War II and used against their former owners cannot be verified.

What can be confirmed, via counter-intelligence reports unearthed after the collapse of the USSR in the early 1990s, is that the Soviet leadership tried to enlist the services of Focke-Wulf chief designer Professor Kurt Tank after the war. He was living in the western zone of occupation at the time, and it was hoped that Professor Tank could be persuaded to work for the Scientific Production Organisation in the eastern zone.

In early 1946 a meeting was held between the head of Scientific Production Organisation, I. Olekhnovich, and Professor Tank in a Berlin building occupied by the Soviet counter-intelligence organization Smersh. The German expressed an interest in cooperating with the Soviet authorities, and he asked for money to attract other aviation specialists who were well known to him. At the next meeting it was agreed by both parties that Professor Tank, who had been give an advance of around 10,000 marks, and eight to ten of his colleagues should come across to the Soviet zone of occupation no later than 20–23 September 1946. However, having received his cash, Professor Tank failed to turn up for further meetings with his Soviet 'employers' in September and October.

There was speculation at the time that the British authorities had made the German a more lucrative offer, but it subsequently became clear that they had in fact turned down his services. In late 1946 Professor Tank left West Germany for Argentina, where he participated in the development of military jet aircraft for the government of Juan Peron. When this programme proved a failure, Professor Tank worked with the Indian government from 1956 on construction of the elegant HF-24 Marut fighter. Production of this machine commenced in November 1967. Professor Kurt Tank returned to West Germany three years later, and died in 1983.

While the Fw 190 was rendered obsolete following the collapse of the Third Reich, the La-5FN and La-7 continued to see service with the Red Air Force well into the late 1940s. Indeed, both fighter types would play a small part in the war against Japan too, for on 9 August 1945 significant

Six airworthy Fw 190D-9s were seized at Marienburg by 322nd IAD's La-5FN-equipped 2nd GIAP shortly after VE Day. (From archives of D. Khazanov and A. Medved)

numbers of Lavochkins were being flown by regiments within the 9th Air Army on the 1st Far Eastern Front, the 10th Air Army on the 2nd Far Eastern Front and the 12th Air Army on the Trans-Baikal Front. The handful of engagements fought between Soviet and Japanese aircraft in the final weeks of the war revealed the total superiority of the La-5FN and La-7 over their Japanese Army Air Force counterparts. In fact, not a single Soviet fighter was lost in aerial combat, although three La-7s and a single La-5FN fell to Japanese flak.

Although production of the La-5FN ended shortly after the cessation of hostilities in Europe, La-7s would continue to be built until early 1946. By then 5,733 examples had been completed, following on from 10,002 La-5/5F/5FNs. The last La-7s were withdrawn from VVS-KA service in 1947, although the fighter soldiered on with the Czech air force until 1950. By then the improved, all-metal, La-9, armed with four ShVAK 20mm cannon, had entered service. Although based on the La-7, the new machine had a frameless canopy, deeper rear fuselage, larger vertical and horizontal tail surfaces and revised wingtips.

The near identical La-11, which had only three cannon but increased range, replaced the La-9 on the production line after some 1,630 examples of the latter machine had been delivered to the VVS-KA and several Eastern Bloc countries. Seeing action in the Korean War with the North Korean and Chinese air forces, the last examples were finally retired by the latter country during the early 1960s.

The all-metal La-9 of 1946 could trace its lineage to the La-7, but had increased range, a frameless canopy, deeper rear fuselage, larger vertical and horizontal tail surfaces, revised wingtips and four ShVAK 20mm cannon. (From archives of D. Khazanov and A. Medved)

PART IV

BY EDWARD M. YOUNG

ILL-FATED DEFENCE OF THE HOME ISLANDS

F4U Corsair vs Ki-84 'Frank'

World War II was a conflict of industrial production on a massive scale. The Allies and the Axis powers converted their economies to unprecedented levels of war production, building aircraft, ships and weapons in prodigious quantities to cope with the demands of attrition in modern war. A significant proportion of this effort went to the production of aeroplanes. Concurrently, there was an equally significant

Opposite

On 4 May 1945, Maj Michiaki Tojo led a formation of 30 Ki-84s as escorts for a mixed formation of Special Attack aeroplanes. Near the island of Iheya Shima, the *kamikaze* aircraft began their final dives on US vessels. Flying above and monitoring the attack, Tojo suddenly saw two F4U Corsairs below him. One turned to the right and came into firing range. Apparently unseen, Tojo opened fire and sent the F4U down smoking. The leading Corsair also turned to the right and failed to notice the Ki-84s above. Tojo's fire hit the Corsair's engine, and it was forced to ditch. (Artwork by Gareth Hector, © Osprey Publishing) emphasis on developing newer, more capable aircraft with improved speed, capacity, armament and protection to give a nation's pilots an advantage over their enemies in the battle for air superiority. Development was a never-ending process; if one side introduced a superior aeroplane, the other side had to develop one that would at least meet, if not surpass, its capabilities. The duels between the Vought F4U Corsair and the Nakajima Type 4 Ki-84 Hayate (Gale) in the final months of the Pacific War were a product of this battle of development and production.

The American aviation industry was ahead of Japan in the development of high-powered, air-cooled radial engines. Pratt & Whitney made the first test runs of its 18-cylinder R-2800 engine in 1939, initially at 1,800hp but with the potential for 2,000hp with further development. The Vought Corsair was the first American fighter to be powered by the R-2800, and the first to exceed 400mph. For the US Navy, the Corsair represented a leap in performance over its first generation of monoplane carrier fighters, the Brewster F2A and the Grumman F4F. The Corsair was ruggedly built, with excellent speed, rate of roll and heavy armament of six 0.50-in machine guns. Its weaknesses – limited visibility over the nose on approach, poor stalling characteristics and directional instability on landing – initially made it unsuitable for carrier operations, but as a land-based fighter with the US Marine Corps in the Southwest Pacific it established a formidable reputation in battles against the vaunted Japanese Zero-sen.

Seeking a replacement for its Type 1 Fighter (the Nakajima Ki-43 Hayabusa), which entered service shortly before the start of the Pacific War, the Japanese Army Air Force (JAAF) turned to the Nakajima Aircraft Company to develop a successor. The JAAF was probably aware that the fighter would have to go up against this new second generation of American and British fighter aeroplanes, namely the Vought Corsair, the Lockheed P-38 Lightning, the Republic P-47 Thunderbolt and the latest models of the Supermarine Spitfire.

The JAAF also realized the need to combine the manoeuvrability of its 'light' fighter aircraft, such as the Ki-43, with the more powerful armament of its 'heavy' interceptor aeroplanes, such as the Nakajima Type 2 Shoki (Ki-44) in a fighter with superior performance and greater protection for the pilot, engine and fuel. Fortunately, Nakajima had begun working on its own 18-cylinder, air-cooled radial engine, the Ha-45 Homare (Honour), which offered 1,800hp. This would power the company's Type 4 Fighter Ki-84 Hayate, an exceptional design incorporating superior performance that exceeded other JAAF fighters. It had more powerful armament, boasted outstanding manoeuvrability and had greater structural strength and armour protection. This was an aeroplane that could take on the best of the

The Nakajima Type 4 Fighter Ki-84 Hayate ('Frank') went from design to combat in a little over two years. It combined a powerful engine with structural strength, heavier armament and better protection for the pilot and fuel. The Hayate was the JAAF's answer to the second generation of Allied fighter aeroplanes. (Peter M. Bowers Collection, Museum of Flight)

Allied fighters. It is remarkable that the first flight of the Hayate took place only a little over a year after the JAAF approved Nakajima's design.

In designing a fighter aeroplane of the Hayate's calibre, the JAAF can be said to have won the development part of the battle. However, in the production battle, despite Herculean efforts, the JAAF fell well short. The Japanese aviation industry had no realistic hope of ever matching America's productive capacity. During the war Japan devoted an ever-greater amount of resources to aircraft production, doubling output during 1943 and nearly doubling it again during 1944. This was an impressive achievement, but during 1943 alone the American aviation industry built more aircraft than Japan did during the entire war.

The US Navy had the luxury of allocating production of the Corsair to two other companies besides Vought, the Brewster Aeronautical Corporation and the Goodyear Aircraft Company. Between them, they built three times as many Corsairs as Nakajima built Hayates. Production of the Ki-84 began to ramp up during 1944, just as the Japanese aviation industry reached its peak production levels and began an inexorable decline. The US Navy's submarine campaign against Japanese merchant shipping sharply reduced supplies of critical raw materials, especially the metals needed for high-powered aeroplane engines, leading to poorer quality engines and consequent maintenance problems. Although the Hayate was the most numerous JAAF fighter in the final months of the Pacific War, there were never enough to equip all of the JAAF's fighter regiments.

More critical to the outcome of duels between the Corsair and the Hayate was the poor quality of JAAF fighter pilots during the last year of the war. As fuel stocks declined, flying training was drastically curtailed. Indeed, by early 1945 JAAF pilots were receiving as little as 150 hours of flight training. While the Ki-84 was generally considered a straightforward aircraft for neophyte fighter pilots to fly, few had the experience needed to get the best out of their aircraft in combat with US Navy, US Marine Corps and US Army Air Force fighters. The appalling attrition of the air battles over the Philippines in late 1944 deprived the JAAF of hundreds of its more experienced fighter pilots.

The Corsair's higher speed, excellent acceleration and rate of roll gave US Navy and US Marine Corps pilots an advantage in combats with the Ki-84, but the lighter weight Hayate's superior manoeuvrability and rate of climb, coupled with its heavy armament, made the Nakajima fighter a dangerous opponent in the hands of an experienced pilot. In the air battles over the Japanese homeland and over Okinawa, well-trained US Navy and US Marine Corps Corsair pilots most often encountered Hayate pilots who were not up to their level of experience, leading to one-sided victories in these encounters.

THE MACHINES
Vought F4U Corsair

In February 1938, with the Brewster XF2A and Grumman XF4F-2 then undergoing flight tests to determine which would be the US Navy's first monoplane carrier fighter, the Bureau of Aeronautics sent out a request to the American aviation industry for the next generation of carrier fighters with performance significantly in advance of the Brewster and Grumman prototypes. The Bureau wanted a fighter with a level speed of at least 350mph and armed with four machine guns, but with a low stalling speed of only 70mph for safe operation from carrier flightdecks.

Among the companies that responded was the Chance Vought Corporation, a subsidiary of the United Aircraft Corporation. A team under Vought's chief engineer Rex Beisel began working on two single-engined designs to meet the US Navy's request. In April 1938 Vought submitted its designs to the Bureau of Aeronautics. The V-166A featured the Pratt & Whitney R-1830 Twin Wasp engine of 1,000hp. The more ambitious design was the V-166B with the new Pratt & Whitney XR-2800 Double Wasp engine providing 1,850hp – the most powerful American air-cooled radial engine then available.

In June 1938, the Bureau of Aeronautics awarded a contract to Vought to build a prototype of its V-166B design as the XF4U-1. Rex Beisel and his team had created a fighter that combined the most powerful air-cooled radial engine then available with a carefully streamlined design. To accommodate the large, 13ft diameter Hamilton Standard propeller needed

to take advantage of the XR-2800's power, the design team came up with the ingenious solution of using an inverted gull wing, with the landing gear placed at the lowest point of the wing. The wing root sections attached to the fuselage accommodated the oil cooler for the engine and air inlets for the XR-2800 engine's two-stage supercharger.

The prototype XF4U-1 had two 0.30in. Browning AN/M2 machine guns in the nose firing through the propeller and one 0.50in. Browning M-2 machine gun in each wing. Small bomb-bays under each wing held fragmentation bombs, and a window beneath the pilot's seat gave him a view downward for dropping ordnance on formations of enemy bombers below. The forward position of the cockpit provided its occupant with good views over the inverted gull wing. Two fuel tanks in the wing centre sections and two tanks in the outer wing held 273 US gallons of fuel.

The XF4U-1 made its first flight on 29 May 1940, with Vought test pilot Lyman Bullard Jr at the controls. Bullard demonstrated the prototype to the Bureau of Aeronautics on 1 October 1940. During the demonstration the XF4U-1 attained a speed of 405mph, thus becoming the first American fighter aeroplane to surpass 400mph in level flight. After the Bureau of Aeronautics had conducted its own tests on the prototype, the US Navy awarded Vought a contract on 30 June 1941 for 541 F4U-1s. Choosing to assign names to its aircraft, the US Navy christened the new fighter the Corsair. With the increasing likelihood of war, and the need for substantial numbers of new fighter aircraft, the US Navy arranged for the F4U-1 to be built under licence at the Brewster Aeronautical Corporation plant in Long Island as the F3A-1 and at the Goodyear Aircraft Plant in Akron, Ohio, as the FG-1.

The Vought XF4U-1 Corsair in April 1941. The prototype featured two 0.30in. machine guns in the nose firing through the huge Hamilton Standard propeller and a 0.50in. machine gun in each wing. (NARA)

With construction of the new *Essex*-class fleet carriers under way, and production of the F4U-1 beginning, the US Navy appeared well placed to have a new, powerful carrier fighter ready to serve on its new carriers. The only discordant note came from simulated carrier landings conducted in August 1941 where the prototype XF4U-1 demonstrated a disturbing tendency to drop the port wing suddenly when approaching stalling speed on landing.

Based on reports detailing aerial combat in Europe and the results of flight testing, the Bureau of Aeronautics requested that Vought make a number of changes in the production version of the F4U-1. For example, its armament was enhanced to three 0.50in. machine guns in each outer wing in place of the nose-mounted 0.30in. weapons and the single 0.50in. wing guns, with substantially more ammunition totaling 2,350 rounds. The small wing bomb-bays were removed and the outer wing fuel tanks reduced in capacity. The fuel tanks in the wing centre sections were also removed to accommodate the three 0.50in. machine guns and a much larger fuel tank installed in the fuselage between the engine and the cockpit. This required the fuselage to be lengthened by 17 inches and the cockpit to be moved 32 inches to the rear. More armour plate was fitted in and around the cockpit for greater protection of the pilot and the engine oil tank. The span of the ailerons was increased by 20 inches to improve the rate of roll.

An improvement in the performance of the Pratt & Whitney R-2800-8 engine, which now produced 2,000hp, ensured that the fighter's speed and rate of climb did not suffer from the additional weight of fuel, armour and armament. With the newer engine, a production F4U-1 could attain a speed of 417mph at 20,000ft.

The first production aircraft emerged in June 1942, and three months later the seventh production aeroplane undertook carrier landing trials onboard USS *Sangamon* (CVE-26) in Chesapeake Bay. The trials were a disappointment. Moving the cockpit rearward significantly reduced forward visibility in the landing approach to the carrier and on take-off. The most disturbing and dangerous problem was the tendency of the port wing to stall suddenly and unexpectedly without warning. A torque stall on landing approach could be fatal. The oleo struts proved to be too stiff, leading to a pronounced bounce on landing aboard the carrier. After landing, the Corsair was directionally unstable.

Capt Eric Brown, the renowned Royal Navy Fleet Air Arm test pilot, judged the Corsair's landing characteristics as 'really bad'. An experienced pilot could cope with the early F4U's idiosyncrasies, but newly minted pilots would have their hands full landing a Corsair on a carrier. The US Navy had no choice but to disqualify the Corsair for carrier operations until these problems had been addressed. In the interim, production aircraft went to the US Marine Corps to replace the F4F-4 Wildcat for operations from land bases. 'Marine Air' squadrons were delighted to receive an aircraft with superior performance to the Mitsubishi A6M Zero-sen, and the outstanding achievements of US Marine Corps fighter pilots in the fierce aerial battles over the Solomon Islands has been well documented.

The technical development of the F4U Corsair is a story of the continued and ultimately successful effort to qualify the aeroplane for carrier operations, improve its capabilities and performance and increase production, all of which were achieved by the end of the war. Turning the Corsair into an acceptable carrier fighter involved numerous incremental changes, and took nearly two years. Despite its deficient landing characteristics, the Fleet Air Arm accepted the Corsair for carrier duty nine months before the US Navy. Fleet Air Arm pilots developed a curving approach to landing on a carrier, which kept the flightdeck in view for a longer period, facilitating better landings – US Navy and US Marine Corps pilots later adopted this technique.

A change to a bubble canopy improved visibility for landing, and for combat. An extended tail-wheel improved visibility on landing and directional stability on the ground. Further improvement in visibility came from raising the pilot's seat seven inches and increasing the vertical

After disappointing carrier-landing trials in late 1942 the US Navy declared the Corsair unsuitable for carrier operations. Lieutenant Commander 'Swede' Vejtasa, an experienced pilot and F4F Wildcat ace, tested the Corsair onboard USS *Enterprise* (CV-6) and was less than pleased, coming up with a list of 18 concerns. (NARA)

adjustment. Vought spent considerable effort working on modifications to the Corsair's oleo struts. The struts were redesigned with improved oil valves and increased air pressure to reduce the tendency for the fighter to bounce on landing. The solution to the stalling problem was a simple fix – a small wooden spoiler was attached to the leading edge of the starboard wing outboard of the machine guns. This affected the airflow over the starboard wing, allowing both wings to stall at the same time. With these improvements, the Corsair's landing characteristics were judged acceptable, and in April 1944 the US Navy approved the Corsair for carrier operations. The F4U-1D model incorporated a number of improvements to enhance the capabilities of the Corsair as a fighter-bomber. Modifications in the field enabled the aeroplane to carry bombs under the wing centre sections, allowing US Marine Corps Corsair squadrons to commence flying close air support and strike missions during the Southwest and Central Pacific campaigns. Vought developed streamlined pylons that fitted under the wing centre sections and could carry a 1,000lb bomb or a 150-US gal drop tank, or combinations of the two. Later, zero-length rocket launcher stubs were installed in the wings, allowing the aeroplane to carry four folding-fin aerial rockets (FFARs) or high velocity aircraft rockets (HVARs) under each outer wing section. These weapons considerably enhanced the Corsair's capacity for ground attack. A new cockpit canopy with a bubble hood and the frames removed improved visibility. The F4U-1D became the first Corsair to serve onboard US Navy carriers in significant numbers.

Pratt & Whitney, in the meantime, had continued work on the R-2800 Double Wasp engine to gain more power. A major redesign produced the R-2800-18W version, producing 2,100hp on take-off and 2,380hp in War Emergency Power with water-menthol injection. A standard F4U-1A was converted to the prototype XF4U-4 with the newer engine, and this aeroplane made its first flight on 19 April 1944. With more power, the XF4U-4 achieved a top speed of 446mph – some 30mph faster than the F4U-1D. The increase in performance was so impressive that the US Navy decided to reserve production of the R-2800-18W for the F4U-4 and the new Grumman XF8F Bearcat, rather than re-engine the Grumman F6F

Opposite
Although Vought built only 200 examples of the 20mm-cannon-armed F4U–1Cs, this model of the Corsair featured in several combats with the Ki-84 during the Okinawa campaign. The F4U-1C depicted here flew with the US Marine Corps squadron VMF-311, the only cannon-armed Corsair unit serving with the MAGs on Okinawa. VF-85 onboard USS *Shangri-La* (CV-38) used a mix of F4U-1C and F4U-1D Corsairs interchangeably with its sister squadron, VBF-85. Two VF-85 pilots made claims for 'Franks' with the F4U-1C on 28 May 1945. (Artwork by Jim Laurier, © Osprey Publishing)

F4U-1C CORSAIR

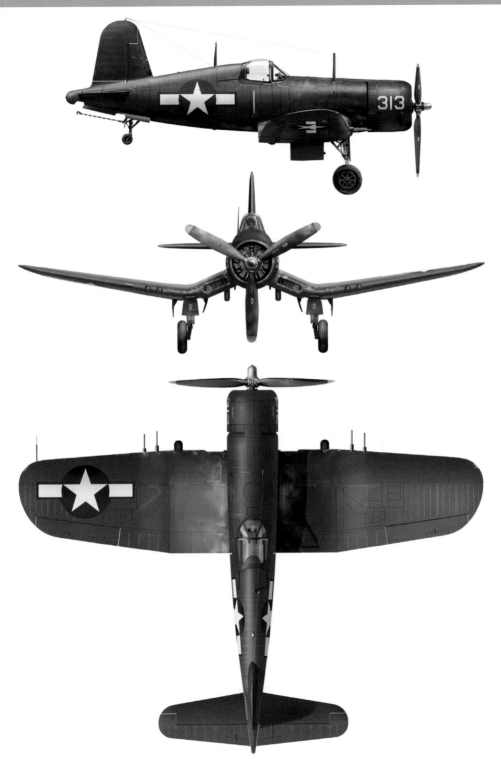

Hellcat. The F4U-4 also featured a redesigned cockpit for greater pilot comfort and easier workload, introducing a cockpit floor. The first production version of the F4U-4 flew in September 1944.

Technical improvements would have meant little during the war without the capacity to produce aircraft in quantity, and in this area the American aviation industry proved superior to Japan. The US Navy had wisely decided before the outbreak of the Pacific War to expand production of the Corsair through licence production. While its experience with the Brewster Aeronautical Corporation proved disappointing – the company suffered from chronic mismanagement that resulted in just 735 F3A-1 aircraft being produced, leading the US Navy to cancel its remaining contracts in July 1944 – the Goodyear Aircraft Corporation became a major builder of the Corsair. Vought delivered 2,814 F4U-1 and -1A aircraft, with Goodyear building an additional 2,010 similar FG-1s. Both companies then switched to the -1D model, Vought building 1,685 F4U-1Ds and Goodyear 1,997 FG-1Ds. Vought shifted to producing the F4U-4 in early 1945, building nearly 2,000 before the end of the war. In total, Vought, Brewster and Goodyear built 11,484 Corsairs before the war ended on 15 August 1945 – more than three times the number of Type 4 Fighters delivered to the JAAF by Nakajima.

The XF4U-4 Corsair had the more powerful Pratt & Whitney R-2800-18W engine. Vought ceased production of the F4U-1D in February 1945 and switched to the F4U-4. Orders for 3,900 'Dash Fours' were cancelled at the end of the war. (NARA)

During the summer of 1945 the F4U-4 Corsair began to replace the F4U-1D/FG-1D in US Marine Corps and US Navy fighter squadrons. The three units of MAG-14, VMF-212, VMF-222 and VMF-223, flew F4U-4s from Okinawa during the final months of the Pacific War, as did VBF-6 on board USS *Hancock* (CV-19), VBF-86 embarked in USS *Wasp* (CV-18) and VBF-94 on board USS *Lexington* (CV-16).

Nakajima Type 4 Fighter Ki-84 Hayate

The Hayate emerged from the evolution of the Rikugun Koku Hombu's (Army Air Headquarters) requirements for JAAF fighter aeroplanes and the availability of more powerful air-cooled radial engines. Over several years, based on combat experience and reports on the aerial engagements of other air forces, the Koku Hombu revised its thinking on the qualities required in fighter aircraft. Although lagging behind American aircraft engine development, Japanese engine manufacturers were beginning to produce aeroplane engines with the greater power needed to meet the demands of more advanced fighter designs by the outbreak of the Pacific War.

In 1938 the Koku Hombu implemented a policy of developing light and heavy single-seat fighters. The light fighter was to be exceptionally manoeuvrable, but lightly armed with two rifle-calibre machine guns. The light fighter reflected JAAF pilots' obsession with manoeuvrability – they believed the ability to manoeuvre in close for a kill reduced the need for heavy armament. The heavy fighter was to have multiple machine guns and cannon, with less emphasis on manoeuvrability and more on speed and rate of climb.

The Nakajima Hikoki K.K. was then developing a replacement to its successful Type 97 Fighter. The Type 1 Fighter Ki-43 Hayabusa (Falcon) was a light single-seat aircraft, with the intended armament of two 12.7mm Type 1 Ho-103 machine guns. In the summer of 1939 the company began work on a heavy fighter design as a specialized interceptor fighter. Designated the Type 2 Fighter Ki-44 Shoki (Devil-Queller), this aeroplane was both faster than the Ki-43 and fitted with heavier armament of two 7.7mm Type 89 Model 2 machine guns and two 12.7mm machine guns. The heavier fighter would intercept enemy bombers while the light fighter achieved air superiority over the battlefield.

After battles against the Soviet Red Air Force over the Nomonhan region during the summer of 1939, some JAAF pilots questioned the emphasis on manoeuvrability. The Type 97 fighters had difficulty coping with the climb and dive tactics and higher speeds of the Polikarpov I-16 and its superior armament of four 7.7mm machine guns, as well as the fast, all-metal SB-2 bombers. A number of JAAF pilots returned from combat over the Nomonhan region demanding fighters with higher speed and heavier armament. Western fighter designs were demonstrating a move towards these elements. Still, the preference for manoeuvrability remained, and the concept of light and heavy fighters continued to influence fighter design in the form of the Kawasaki Ki-60 and Ki-61 with inline liquid-cooled engines.

Towards the end of 1941 as the Type 1 Fighter was entering service, the Koku Hombu began considering the need for its replacement. If the JAAF was to combat the advanced Allied fighters then under development, an aeroplane with considerably better performance than the Type 1 Fighter was required. The development staff within the Koku Hombu realized that in the confusion of combat it would be difficult to separate the mission of a pure air superiority fighter from that of a pure interceptor fighter. Inevitably, a lightly armed air superiority fighter would encounter enemy heavy bombers and an interceptor fighter would face enemy fighters. What the JAAF needed was a multi-purpose fighter combining the manoeuvrability of the Type 1 Fighter with the speed and heavier armament of the Type 2 Fighter.

To survive in combat with advanced Western fighter planes the new JAAF fighter would need self-sealing fuel tanks and greater armour protection for the pilot and systems, items the Type 1 Fighter had sacrificed in pursuit of lighter weight and greater manoeuvrability. Higher speed, heavier armament and better protection for fuel and the pilot meant an aeroplane of greater size and weight, and that would require the development of a more powerful engine.

The Japanese aviation industry lagged behind its American counterpart in the development of high-power engines. Japan's two principal aeroplane manufacturers, the Nakajima Aircraft Company and the Mitsubishi Aircraft Company were also the principal designers and builders of aircraft engines for the JAAF and the IJNAF.

Both companies had started out producing foreign engines under licence to gain experience. Nakajima's first air-cooled radial engine was the licence-built Bristol Jupiter, which it built for both civil and military uses, before developing its own air-cooled radial designs in the early 1930s. Nakajima designed and built the JAAF-designated Ha-1, a nine-cylinder engine of 780hp for the Type 97 Fighter. The company went on to create air-cooled radial engines of progressively greater power. Its first 14-cylinder engine, the famous 'Sakae' (Prosperity), initially of 990hp, was pushed to 1,130hp in later models. This engine powered the JAAF's Ki-43 as the Ha-115 and the IJNAF's Type 0 Fighter Zero-sen. For the Ki-44, Nakajima developed the more powerful 14-cylinder JAAF Ha-109 engine that

The Nakajima Type 2 Fighter Ki-44 Shoki ('Tojo'), designed for the 'heavy fighter' role to intercept enemy bombers, boasted heavier armament and emphasized speed and rate of climb over manoeuvrability. These Type 2 Fighters were assigned to the 47th Hiko Sentai in October 1943. (Peter M. Bowers Collection, Museum of Flight)

produced 1,440hp in its first versions. In 1940, as the Pratt & Whitney R-2800 was just commencing flight trials with the Vought XF4U Corsair, Nakajima began work on its own design for an 18-cylinder engine that would provide greater power than the Ha-109. This became the Homare, certified in 1941 and used by the JAAF as the Ha-45 and the IJNAF as the NK9. The Homare was an exceptional design, with a small frontal section – its diameter was only 1.5 inches greater than the Sakae. The engine produced nearly 700hp more than the Sakae in its early versions for a modest increase in weight. Thus, when the Koku Hombu began to consider its requirements for a new JAAF fighter, there was an engine available that could provide 1,800hp, with the potential for more power with further development.

In late December 1941, the Koku Hombu issued its requirements for a new fighter to Nakajima. The specification called for a fighter with good manoeuvrability, but with greater speed and heavier armament than either the Type 1 or Type 2 Fighters. Specifically, the Koku Hombu wanted a top speed of 400–420mph, the ability to climb to 15,000ft in under five minutes, good range and an armament of two 12.7mm machine guns in the nose and two 20mm Type 1 Ho-5 cannon in the wings. The new fighter was to be strongly built, with armour protection for the pilot and self-sealing fuel tanks, but the Koku Hombu insisted it had to take fewer hours to build than the Type 1 Fighter. The powerplant was to be the new Ha-45 Homare engine.

Nakajima assigned Yasushi Koyama, who had experience with the design of the Type 97, Type 1 and Type 2 Fighters, as chief designer. By the spring of 1942 Koyama and his team had completed a design for an all-metal, low-wing monoplane with the specified armament, an enclosed cockpit providing good all-round visibility for the pilot and widely spread, retractable, landing gear and a retractable tail-wheel. In late May the Koku Hombu approved the design as the Ki-84.

By November 1942 the company had built a full-scale wooden mock-up for the JAAF to evaluate. At the review meeting at the Nakajima plant in Ota, the design team asked the JAAF representatives how many test aeroplanes the company should plan on building. Maj Yoshitsugu Aramaki, from the Koku Hombu's Experimental Division responsible for the Ki-84, stunned the design team and his colleagues by recommending that Nakajima produce 100 test examples. This number was unheard of. Nakajima had built only 13 test aeroplanes for the Type 1 Fighter and ten for the Type 2. However, Maj Aramaki's reasoning was sound. It had taken Nakajima nearly two and a half years to develop the Hayabusa and two years to develop the Shoki. Aramaki knew that by the autumn of 1942 Japan did not have that amount of time. As he explained in a post-war interview:

> We test pilots flew test airplanes and we'd say 'this needs fixing or that needs fixing'. The company worked to meet our demands, but it took many months to fix one thing. During that time the inspection process stopped there and didn't move on. That was fine in peacetime, but this was during the war. We'd already seen the limits of the Hayabusa, the Shoki and Hien [Kawasaki Type 3 Fighter Ki-61]. We needed to get the Ki-84 on the front line of the battle as soon as possible. If we had 100 test airplanes, we could make revisions while we used it for training. If we could work on these multiple tasks at the same time, we could shorten the time it took from trial period to approval. I also thought the factory could better prepare for its mass production.

The Koku Hombu agreed with Maj Aramaki's recommendation, taking the unprecedented step of ordering 125 test and pre-production aeroplanes in two batches. Nakajima completed the first prototype of the Ki-84 towards the end of March 1943 at its main plant at Ota, using the Ha-45 Model 11 version of the Homare engine rated at 1,900 hp. In April the new fighter made its first flight with Tsuruhisa Yoshizawa, Nakajima's test pilot, at the controls. The flight lasted 40 minutes, encountering only minor problems with the extension of the battle flaps – easily remedied that same day. Yoshizawa was more than satisfied with the results of the first test flights. After the war he recalled his first impressions of the Ki-84:

It felt very similar to the Ki-43. I thought this was a bigger horsepower version of the Ki-43. Other than it was a larger airplane than the Ki-43, it didn't seem particularly different, but when I got inside the cockpit, it was very spacious from being equipped with the larger engine.

Nakajima sent the prototype to the JAAF's flight-test centre near Tokyo, where the Ki-84 soon demonstrated a maximum speed of 387mph – the first JAAF fighter to achieve such a figure in level flight. While the Ki-84 prototype failed to meet the JAAF's requirements for rate of climb, its general handling qualities and performance were impressive. The Ki-84 demonstrated better harmony between speed and turning ability than the Hayabusa, and it was also faster, had heavier armament and enjoyed superior performance at higher altitudes than the Shoki. However, as more prototypes entered testing, problems emerged with the Homare engine that would plague the Ki-84 throughout its life.

The engines of the first few prototypes were effectively hand-built and apparently worked well. But later prototypes with mass-produced Homare engines encountered increasing problems with excessive cylinder temperatures at full power. The cylinders functioned smoothly when operating at less than full power, but this prevented the Ki-84 from attaining peak performance. Although these issues appeared to be caused by the carburetor system, extensive testing over the summer of 1943 failed to provide a solution. There were additional problems with the oil pressure dropping at high altitude and a malfunctioning fuel system that were not resolved until later versions of the Homare engine were introduced near the end of the war. Testing did reveal that the engine problems went away when the Ki-84 used higher octane gasoline, as Nakajima test pilot Yoshizawa recalled:

The Ki-84 used 92 octane gasoline. When we used 100 octane gasoline that the Navy stored in Taiwan, all the engine problems stopped. It was obvious that the troubles were caused by the fuel, but it was not easy to obtain such high octane fuel then. So we kept using low octane fuel. We revised the carburretor. One hot cylinder would function normally when it was up in the air, but then other cylinders' temperatures would start to rise. It was like playing cat and mouse.

The Ki-84 also developed problems with the main landing gear, which were thought to have insufficient strength, although Yoshizawa believed that any perceived weakness in the undercarriage was due more to pilot ability:

Later, in the battle area, the Ki-84 gained a reputation for having fragile landing gear that broke easily. Unfortunately, this was mostly related to the pilots' lack of flying skills. It is understandable that they were flustered by an airplane with such large horsepower, after only having a short amount of time being taught in training airplanes such as the Type 95 [Tachikawa Type 95 Ki-9 Medium Grade Trainer]. The situation made it difficult to fly calmly, and as you got frustrated you made basic mistakes. On top of that, it was hard for the Ki-84's tail-wheel to make contact with the ground even after you landed, so it always landed with a thump. This was hard to handle, so pilots just got frustrated and ended up breaking the landing gear. But problems like these we could manage. We truly suffered from the engine issues, however. The Ki-84's weak point was the engine, which we had the most difficult time with, and it never worked properly right until the end. It was really disappointing that we could only operate it by tricking the engine to work, and to gain speed that way.

With the JAAF anxious to get the new fighter into production as quickly as possible, these problems were overlooked and, in April 1944 – just a year after its first flight – the Ki-84 was accepted for service by the Koku Hombu as the Type 4 Fighter Model A (Ki-84 Ko, or Ki-84a). Ordered to commence full-scale production, Nakajima had by then built 83 Ki-84s in the first pre-production batch. In addition to supplementing the test programme, a number of these aircraft went to a special operational test unit formed at the end of 1943. Another 42 aircraft in the second pre-production batch had been completed by June 1944.

Three months earlier, the 22nd Hiko Sentai had become the first JAAF air regiment to re-equip with the Type 4 Fighter, taking its aeroplanes to China in August for the Ki-84's successful combat debut against the USAAF's Fourteenth Air Force. In April three more fighter *sentai* were established with the Ki-84, followed by a further three in May and three more in August. Older established *sentai* such as the 25th and 85th Hiko Sentai in China and the 50th Hiko Sentai in Burma also converted to the Ki-84 during the summer and autumn. The Type 4 fighter found its way to the Rensei Hikotai (Operational Training Units) and other JAAF flying schools too. At last the Japanese had a fighter that could, in experienced hands, match the performance of its Allied counterparts. However, while the Ki-84 showed a definite qualitative improvement over other JAAF fighters, at this stage of the war it was quantity and pilot skill that mattered almost as much, and here the JAAF fell short.

It was unfortunate for the JAAF that production of the Type 4 Fighter began just as Japan's wartime industrial production was peaking, and about to enter an irreversible decline. The Japanese aviation industry's increase in production from 1942 until the middle of 1944 was an impressive achievement. Aircraft production grew nearly three-fold and aircraft engine production nearly doubled in two years, with a tripling of the work force, but production peaked in June 1944 and declined thereafter. The Japanese aviation industry had not fully mastered the techniques of mass production, so that in many factories handwork methods predominated. As the war went on, shortages of skilled workers hampered production. Increasing American air attacks on Nakajima's factories in the autumn of 1944 forced the company to begin dispersing its production away from its main plants, further disrupting the delivery of aircraft.

The majority of Type 4 Fighters were built at Nakajima's Ota plant in Gunma prefecture, northeast of Tokyo. In May 1944 a second production line opened at Nakajima's factory at Utsonomiya, in Tochigi prefecture. Production of the Ki-84 peaked in December 1944, and although the 1,904 aircraft built by Nakajima during 1944 were less than the Koku Hombu had planned, it was still a remarkable achievement. In total, Nakajima completed approximately 3,416 Ki-84 aircraft from November 1943 to the end of the war, compared to 5,919 Type 1 Fighters built from 1941 to 1945. Production at Ota suffered when the plant was severely damaged in an air raid on 10 February 1945. A third source of production was the Manshu Hikoki Seizo K. K. plant in Manchuria, which began building the Ki-84 in 1945 – it had completed just 95 aircraft by VJ Day.

What affected production of the Ki-84 most of all in the final months of the Pacific War was the decline in engine production and engine quality. The

Kı-84-I HAYATE

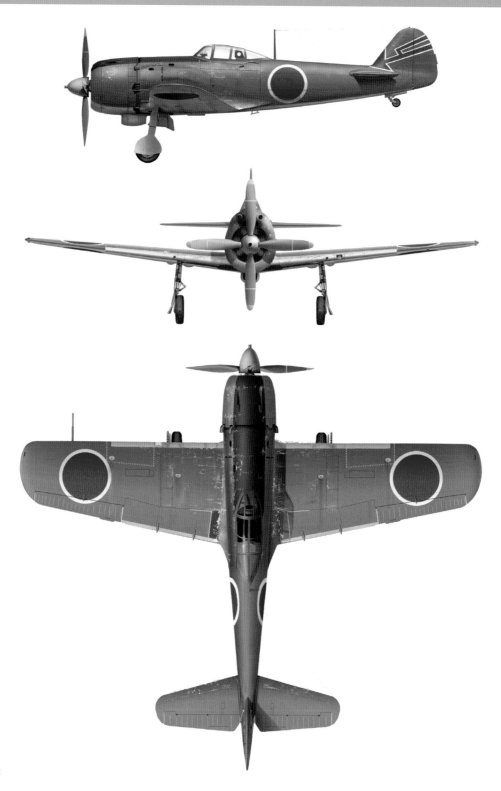

catastrophic shipping losses cut Japan off from sources of the critical metals used in engine manufacture, such as molybdenum and nickel. Engine production fell sharply during 1945. In the month of June 1945, Nakajima produced 168 Ki-84 aircraft but only 150 Ha-45 Homare engines.

In the production models of the Ki-84 Ko, the Ha-45 Model 12 replaced the earlier Ha-45 Model 11 engine, providing a small increase in power to 1,825hp. Late production aircraft had the more powerful Ha-45 Model 21, which was rated at 1,990hp for take-off, or the Ha-45 Model 23 of slightly less power (1,900hp) that finally solved some of the problems associated with the fuel system. The next version of the Ki-84, the Type 4 Fighter Model B (Ki-84 Otsu, Ki-84b) featured heavier armament, with the Ho-5 20mm cannon replacing the fuselage-mounted Ho-103 12.7mm machine guns. The Type 4 Fighter Model C (Ki-84 Hei, Ki-84c) had even heavier armament, with the Ho-5 20mm cannon in the wings exchanged for the 30mm Ho-155-II cannon. Nakajima built a few prototypes of the Type 4 Fighter, possibly as the Model D, with four Ho-5 20mm cannon in the wings and fuselage and a fifth Ho-5 mounted obliquely behind the cockpit to fire at bombers from below. The last production aeroplanes featured the Ha-45 Model 25, this version of the Homare engine finally reaching the elusive rating of 2,000hp.

Serviceability and maintenance remained a problem throughout the Ki-84's operational life. The Homare would function well with regular and careful maintenance, but problems with the engine became even more pronounced in the field, where operating conditions, shortages of skilled groundcrew and a lack of spare parts made regular maintenance problematic. As confidence in engine quality and maintenance declined, worries about the powerplant increased. Difficulties with the hydraulic system and the landing gear, especially when less-experienced pilots flew the Ki-84, resulted in many operational accidents.

The Koku Hombu had hoped that the Nakajima Type 4 Fighter would redress the balance in performance with the second generation of American fighter aeroplanes. While the Hayate went a long way towards achieving this ambitious goal, the American aviation industry made another leap in engine power with the Pratt & Whitney R-2800-18W, providing the F4U Corsair with an even greater margin of performance over its Japanese rival.

Opposite
This three-view shows a Ki-84-I Hayate from the 103rd Hiko Sentai. This unit was formed during August 1944 and initially served on home defense duties, countering the B-29 raids from Okinawa. After the invasion of Okinawa, the unit flew patrols in defense of airfields on Kyushu and escorted the Shimbu-Tai Special Attack units. On an escort mission on 4 May 1945, Maj Michiaki Tojo, Sentai commander, claimed two F4U Corsairs shot down. (Artwork by Jim Laurier, © Osprey Publishing)

TYPE HISTORY
The F4U Corsair

F4U-1D/FG-1D

The F4U Corsair was a large and heavy aeroplane designed and built to withstand the stresses of operating from aircraft carriers. The fuselage was constructed from aluminium panels, with internal ribs and stiffeners for added strength, that conformed as closely as possible to the diameter of the Pratt & Whitney R-2800 engine. The main 217-US gal self-sealing fuel tank was placed between the engine and the cockpit. The Corsair's distinguishing inverted gull wings were built of aluminium panels and spars, but the outer wing panels were fabric-covered and the ailerons were built from fabric-covered plywood. The rudder and horizontal stabilizers were also fabric-covered.

The Corsair had eight main sections, namely the engine, three fuselage assemblies (forward, centre section and rear), inner and outer wing assemblies, landing gear and the tail assembly. The outer wing sections contained the armament and internal fuel tanks in the early F4U-1A, and they could be raised hydraulically to minimize the aircraft's footprint on the carrier deck.

Later production models of the F4U-1D/FG-1D featured four zero-length rocket launchers under each wing for FFAR or HVAR rockets. Here, a pilot from VBF-84 walks to his aeroplane prior to flying a mission over Kyushu in March 1945. (NARA)

F4U-1D CORSAIR MACHINE GUNS

Like its Grumman F6F stablemate, the Corsair was armed with a battery of excellent, reliable Browning M-2 0.50in. machine guns. Three weapons were placed in each outer wing panel, with the ammunition containers located outboard of the guns. Access to the guns and ammunition containers was through panels on the upper wing. The inboard and middle guns were provided with 400 rounds of ammunition, while the outboard gun had 375 rounds. The guns were charged hydraulically with controls located in the cockpit. The high muzzle velocity of the 0.50in. round gave it good range and accuracy and the use of a single calibre of weapon with a single trajectory made sighting easier for the pilot. (Artwork by Jim Laurier, © Osprey Publishing)

The F4U-1D and the similar Goodyear-built FG-1D featured numerous improvements over the F4U-1A. The -1D model incorporated the many changes necessary to make the Corsair a suitable carrier aircraft. The starboard wing had the small wooden spoiler on the leading edge that improved the Corsair's stall characteristics, while changes to the oil valves and air pressure in the shock absorbers reduced the aircraft's tendency to bounce on landing. A lengthened tail-wheel and a reduction in the maximum deflection angle of the tail hook were additional refinements to improve the Corsair's landings on carrier decks. The -1D also incorporated the adjustable pilot's seat for better visibility. Late production models had a bubble canopy with the overhead frames of the F4U-1A removed. All the F4U-1D/FG-1D models had the R-2800-8W engine with water injection that provided 2,250hp at sea level in the War Emergency Power setting. About midway through the production run a new, slightly smaller diameter, Hamilton Standard propeller was introduced.

The F4U-1D/FG-1D had several features designed to enhance the Corsair's ability as a fighter-bomber, the most obvious of which were two streamlined pylons mounted on the underside of the inner wing between the fuselage and the landing gear. Each pylon could carry a 1,000lb bomb or a 150-US gal fuel tank. The -1D retained the centreline mounting for a bomb or drop tank as well, allowing for combinations of drop tanks and bombs to be carried. The provision for additional drop tanks allowed the wing fuel tanks to be removed. Later production models added four zero-length rocket launchers under each outer wing section to carry four 5in. FFARs or HVARs.

F4U-1C

Although the US Navy adopted a battery of six 0.50in. machine guns as standard armament for its fighter aircraft, the Bureau of Aeronautics retained an interest in more powerful 20mm cannon and requested that Vought develop a suitably armed version of the Corsair. In August 1943 the XF4U-1C made its first flight armed with two AN-M2 20mm cannon (a licence-built development of the Hispano-Suiza HS.404 autocannon) in each wing, with 231 rounds per gun. The -1C wing could also be fitted with four zero-length rocket launchers to carry four rockets, but they were not always present as standard equipment. In all other respects, the -1C was similar to the -1D model.

The -1C served with three US Marine Corps squadrons (VMF-311, VMF-314 and VMF-441) on Okinawa in 1945 and with US Navy squadrons VF-84, VBF-84, VF-85 and VBF-85 onboard the carriers USS *Bunker Hill* (CV-17) and USS *Shangri-la* (CV-38) during the final year of the war. These units experienced operating problems with the AN-M2 20mm cannon, which was plagued by misfires. Many pilots also preferred the 0.50in. machine gun for aerial combat because of its more rapid rate of fire and greater quantity of ammunition.

F4U-4

The F4U-4 featured a significant improvement in performance over earlier models thanks to its more powerful Pratt & Whitney R-2800-18W engine. In an attempt to get even more power, reliability and durability out of the R-2800 engine, Pratt & Whitney engineers undertook a major redesign of the engine that became the C-series. It featured forged cylinders in place of cast cylinders, which were reaching the limits of their performance at 2,000hp, with greater cooling fin area. A new strengthened crankcase centre section and a redesigned crankshaft were fitted, designed to accommodate the increase in horsepower. The R-2800-18W had a two-stage, two-speed supercharger and water-menthol injection. The -18W engine gave 2,100hp on take-off and 2,380hp at War Emergency Power.

The demands of the new engine required a larger air scoop for the supercharger at the bottom of the cowling. The cowl flaps were redesigned

and reduced in number to five on each side of the cowling in place of the 15 cowl flaps on earlier models. With the R-2800-18W and a four-bladed Hamilton Standard propeller, the F4U-4 Corsair had a maximum speed of 446mph at 26,200ft – some 30mph faster than the earlier F4U-1D. The more powerful engine improved the Corsair's rate of climb as well, with the F4U-4 capable of reaching 20,000ft in 5.9 minutes (without bombs or drop tanks) compared to 7.7 minutes in the F4U-1D.

Vought took the opportunity to make changes in the cockpit for added pilot comfort and to increase the Corsair's armour protection. To the delight of pilots, Vought replaced the foot rails of the earlier models, which allowed dirt and whatever else might have been dropped in the fuselage to join the pilot whenever the aeroplane was inverted, with a cockpit floor. The pilot's seat was redesigned, and featured armrests, the control column was shortened and the rudder pedals revised. For greater protection, a bulletproof laminated glass plate was placed under the front windshield and an armour plate fitted in front of the instrument panel, with armour plates behind the pilot's seat widened to the width of the fuselage. Additional armour plating was placed underneath the engine.

The -4 model retained the two underwing pylons for drop tanks or bombs, but removed the centreline attachment points. All four of the

The majority of Corsairs were armed with six Browning M-2 machine guns. Three weapons were housed in each outer wing panel, with the ammunition containers located outboard of the guns. Access to the guns and ammunition containers was through access panels on the upper wing. The inboard and middle guns were provided with 400 rounds of ammunition, while the outboard gun had 375 rounds. Here, an armourer from VMF-511 tends to the guns of an F4U-1D on the flightdeck of the escort carrier USS *Block Island* (CVE-21). (Courtesy of Tailhook Association)

273

zero-length rocket launchers under each outer wing were retained. Armament remained the standard six 0.50in. Browning M-2 machine guns with 2,400 rounds.

The Ki-84 Hayate

Type 4 Fighter Model A (Ki-84 Ko) Hayate

The first model of the Type 4 Fighter to enter service, the Model A (Ki-84 Ko) was larger and heavier than the Type I Fighter (Ki-43) it replaced – its maximum take-off weight was some 2,700lb greater than the Hayabusa. A stronger and more robust aircraft than the Type 1, the Hayate had a higher diving speed and could execute more demanding manoeuvres than the earlier fighter.

The relatively small diameter of the Ha-45 Homare engine enabled Yasushi Koyama and his team to design a superbly streamlined oval-shaped fuselage, with the engine enclosed in a tight-fitting cowling. The fuselage and wing were all-metal, with a light alloy stressed-skin covering. The fuselage held a 35-US gal water-menthol tank ahead of the cockpit, with a fuel tank mounted behind. This main tank and two tanks in each wing held 162 US gallons of fuel. The cockpit sat above and just behind the low wing. An adjustable seat allowed good visibility for take-off out of the three-piece canopy. A 65mm armoured glass block behind the windscreen in front and 13mm armour plate behind the pilot's seat provided protection for the pilot.

With its two fuselage-mounted Ho-113 12.7mm machine guns firing through the propeller and two wing-mounted Ho-5 20mm cannon (considered one of the best 20mm aircraft cannon fielded by either side during the war), the Type 4 Fighter had a much heavier weight of fire than the Type 1 Fighter – vitally necessary for engaging strongly built American

The Nakajima Ha-45 Homare engine was only one inch wider than the Ha-115 Sakae, allowing Nakajima to keep the width of the fuselage to the dimensions of the engine. This particular Ki-84 was tested at Wright Field after the end of the war. USAAF pilots found the 'Frank' to be only slightly less manoeuvrable than the Mitsubishi A6M Zero-sen, with lighter control forces than comparable American fighters. (NARA)

fighters. The belt-fed Ho-113 machine guns had a rate of fire of 800–900 rounds per minute, with 350 rounds for each gun. The Ho-5 cannon had a slightly lower rate of fire of 750–850 rounds per minute. The wings of the Type 4 held 150 belt-fed rounds for each Ho-5 cannon.

In common with many other Japanese fighters, Nakajima built the wing of the Type 4 integral with the central fuselage. A strongly built heavy main spar contributed to the aircraft's strength. An auxiliary spar supported the metal-skinned wings, which had fabric-covered ailerons. The flaps could be lowered 15 degrees to improve manoeuvrability in combat. Racks under the wings could carry 44-US gal drop tanks or 250kg bombs. The wings held two more fuel tanks, with self-sealing protection, inboard of the landing gear and two smaller tanks in the wing leading edge.

The first production models of the Type 4 Fighter used the Ha-45 Model 11 engine, providing 1,800hp for take-off. Later versions changed to the Ha-45 Model 12, Model 21 and Model 23, which gave slightly greater horsepower in each model. Although the prototype Ki-84 could reach 5,000m (16,405ft) in 5 min 54 sec, this still did not meet the Koku Hombu's demanding specification. With full armament and armor protection, the time to 5,000m slipped to 6 min 26 sec, leading some pilots to state that the Type 4 lacked sufficient power on account of the Homare engine producing less than 2,000hp. As with so many other fighters, extra equipment in the form of weaponry, armored protection and fuel, with little additional horsepower to offset them, reduced performance. The difficulty of getting the Homare engine to operate reliably at full power only compounded the problem.

During 1944 the JAAF established several new fighter *sentai* to be equipped with the Ki-84, as well as re-equipping several existing units. The 73rd Hiko Sentai, shown here, was formed in May 1944 and fought in the home defence role after seeing combat in the Philippines campaign. (Peter M. Bowers Collection, Museum of Flight)

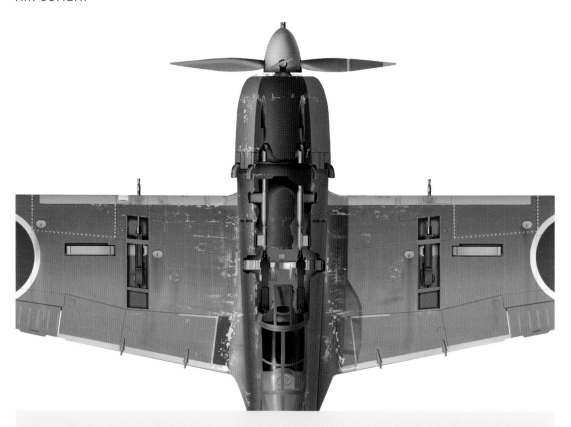

KI-84 HAYATE COWLING/WING GUNS

The Type 4 Fighter was equipped with two 12.7mm Ho-103 machine guns in the nose, synchronized to fire through the propeller. Ammunition for the nose guns consisted of belts of 350 rounds stored in ammunition containers beneath the guns in the fuselage. Based on the Browning machine gun, the Ho-103 had a higher rate of fire than its American counterpart, but fired a lighter-weight cartridge. The wings held two Ho-5 20mm cannon, which had a superior rate of fire to the IJNAF's Type 99-2. Like the Ho-103, the Ho-5 was belt-fed, with containers in the wings for the ammunition holding 150 rounds. These containers were accessible through panels in the upper wing surface. (Artwork by Jim Laurier, © Osprey Publishing)

Type 4 Fighter Model B (Otsu)

The main differences between the Type 4 Model A (Ki-84 Ko or Ki-84a) and the Type 4 Model B (Ki-84 Otsu or Ki-84b) centred on armament and engine fitment. The Model B featured four Ho-5 20mm cannon, with two cannon replacing the Ho-113 12.7mm machine guns mounted in the fuselage. This was intended to give the Type 4 more powerful armament for attacking USAAF B-29 bombers over Japan. The Model B was built in fewer numbers than the Type 4 Fighter Model A, production probably amounting to only several hundred aircraft. The last aircraft to be built were fitted with the final version of the Homare engine, the Ha-45 Model 25 rated at 2,000hp.

F4U-ID AND Kɪ-84 COMPARISON SPECIFICATIONS		
	F4U-1D	**Ki-84**
Powerplant	2,000 hp Pratt & Whitney R-2800	1,900hp Nakajima Homare Ha-45-21
Dimensions		
Span	40ft 11in.	36ft 10 7/16in.
Length	33ft 4in.	32ft 6 9/16in.
Height	16ft 1in.	11ft 1 1/4in.
Wing Area	314 sq. ft	226 sq. ft
Weights		
Empty	8,982lb	5,864lb
Loaded	11,962lb	7,955lb
Performance		
Max Speed	417mph at 19,000ft	392mph at 20,080ft
Range	1,015 miles	1,053 miles
Climb Rate at Sea Level	2,890ft/min at military power	3,790ft/min at military power
Service Ceiling	36,900ft	34,450ft
Armament	6 x 0.50in. Browning M-2 machine guns	2 x Ho-103 12.7mm machine guns 2 x Ho-5 20mm cannon

THE STRATEGIC SITUATION

In January 1945, Japan's strategic military and economic situation was dire. With the invasion of Luzon on 9 January, American forces had effectively gained control over the Philippines, and could now threaten Japan's sea links to the vital raw materials of Southeast Asia. US Navy submarines had already inflicted crippling losses on Japanese merchant shipping, leaving the country dependent on its remaining stocks of fuel and metals. Imports of oil stopped in December 1944, and by the spring of 1945 aircraft production had dropped by one-third and aircraft engine production by two-thirds. The Japanese economy was failing.

The defence of the Philippines had cost the JAAF and IJNAF thousands of aeroplanes and pilots, the bulk of the Imperial Japanese Navy's remaining capital ships and tens of thousands of troops. Japan's Imperial General Headquarters realized that the next stage of the American advance would be an attack on the nation's inner defensive ring – most likely an attempt to capture Okinawa, in the Ryukyu Islands, to use as a base for the invasion of Japan. Imperial General Headquarters decided to prepare Japan for what were likely to be intensive air attacks from USAAF B-29s in the Marianas as a prelude to invasion. Japan's only hope of survival was to inflict such punishing losses on Allied forces that they would be forced to withdraw. Formosa, the Bonin Islands and Okinawa were to be held to the last man.

For the defence of Okinawa, designated Operation *Ten-Go*, Imperial General Headquarters reorganized Japan's air defences. Responsibility for countering American air raids on the main island of Honshu fell to the Tokyo-based 1st Kokugun (1st Air Army) with the 10th, 11th and 12th Hiko Shidan (Air Divisions) and the IJNAF's Home Defence Force, with some 500 aircraft in total. To protect the approaches to the Home Islands, the 6th Kokugun and 3rd, 5th and 10th Koku Kantai in Japan and the 8th Kokugun and 1st Koku Kantai in Formosa had approximately 4,600 aircraft.

Because of insufficient numbers of advanced fighters such as the Type 4 Fighter Hayate and the IJNAF's Navy's N1K2-J Shiden-Kai, the lack of experienced pilots following losses in the Philippines and the impossibility of completing training of the new intake of pilot trainees before the probable date of an American attack, the JAAF and IJNAF decided to rely on mass *kamikaze* attacks to destroy the invasion fleet. Both services converted entire training classes into Tokubetsu Kogeki Tai (Special Attack Units), the 10th Koku Kantai becoming almost exclusively a Special Attack force.

American military planners believed that the only way to force Japan to accept unconditional surrender was through the invasion of the Home Islands. With the seizure of the Philippines to provide a base for the fleet, the need to invade Formosa diminished. To save time and resources, the American Joint Chiefs of Staff decided instead to move forward with the capture of Iwo Jima, in the Bonin Islands, as an advanced base for fighters to escort the B-29s over Japan, and then to take Okinawa as a base for the planned invasion of Kyushu, scheduled for November 1945. Fighters and medium bombers could reach Kyushu from Okinawa to soften up Japanese defences prior to the invasion.

Designated Operation *Iceberg*, the invasion of Okinawa would involve a massive force of 541,000 men in four US Army and three US Marine Corps divisions. They would be supported by the US Navy's Fifth Fleet, with an invasion covering force and Task Force (TF) 58 – the Fast Carrier Task Force – providing air cover until land-based US Marine Corps and USAAF units could take over using captured Okinawan airfields. For the initial invasion, TF 58 had 11 *Essex*-class fleet carriers and six *Independence*-class light carriers. Waiting in the wings were the squadrons of the 2nd MAW.

To counter the *kamikaze* threat, the US Navy increased the number of fighters aboard the *Essex*-class fleet carriers from 54 to 73, cutting back bomber and torpedo aeroplanes to 15 apiece. These enlarged fighter squadrons proved too difficult to administer, so on 2 January 1945 the US Navy divided these squadrons into two – a fighter squadron (VF) and a fighter-bomber squadron (VBF). This gave the carrier groups more aeroplanes for combat air patrols (CAPs) to protect the fleet, while the fighter-bombers made up for the cuts in the number of bomber aeroplanes. More critically, the US Navy needed fighters that were faster and had a better rate of climb than the F6F-5 Hellcat. Fortunately, the Corsair, some 30mph faster than the Hellcat, was available. For the Okinawa campaign, TF 58 had five US Navy and six US Marine Corps Corsair squadrons.

The battle for Okinawa lasted 11 weeks. Operation *Ten-Go* proved to be a failure, the JAAF and IJNAF launching ten Kikusui (Floating Chrysanthemum) attacks that saw 1,465 Special Attack aircraft and their crews lost. In total, the JAAF and IJNAF had approximately 3,000 aeroplanes destroyed attempting to defeat the American invasion of Okinawa. The JAAF used its more experienced pilots and better aircraft on sweeps to clear a path for the Special Attack units making their way to

Only the engines remain of more than 20 Corsairs from VF-84, VMF221 and VMF-451 following a *kamikaze* attack by two bomb-laden Zero-sens on USS *Bunker Hill* (CV-17) on 11 May 1945 that killed 393 men and knocked the vessel out of the war. In the expectation of more attacks during the Okinawa campaign, the US Navy increased the number of fighters aboard its fleet carriers to 72, leading to additional US Marine Corps Corsair squadrons joining the fleet. (NARA)

Okinawa, where the Tokubetsu Tai sought out transport vessels, while their IJNAF counterparts went after the US Navy's fleet units. The carrier air groups of TF 58 (and, belatedly, B-29s from the Marianas) flew repeated strikes against the Special Attack bases on Kyushu and CAPs in defence of the fleet. Land-based US Marine Corps Corsair squadrons flying from Okinawa joined them as soon as airfields were secured.

With the loss of Okinawa, Japan now faced invasion. The American strategy was to undertake an air and sea blockade of Japan, cutting the nation off from all imports of fuel, raw materials and food to weaken its capacity to make war. The B-29s of the Twentieth Air Force would continue their campaign against industrial cities, aircraft factories and oil refineries, adding mining the waters of the Inland Sea to their missions. A steady build-up of US Marine Corps and USAAF tactical units on Okinawa would undertake missions against targets in Kyushu. The US Navy's Fast Carrier Task Force (supported by the British Pacific Fleet), initially under the command of Admiral William Halsey as TF 38 (as TF 58 was designated when under his leadership), would undertake strikes along the Japanese coast, attacking airfields, shipping and industrial plants and wearing down JAAF and IJNAF air strength through attrition. Operation *Olympic* – the invasion of Kyushu – was planned for 1 November 1945, involving more than 50 US Army and US Marine Corps divisions and aircraft from the Far East Air Force (Fifth, Seventh and Thirteenth Air Forces), a Commonwealth air component and MAWs.

In the face of such overwhelming force, Imperial General Headquarters had few options for Operation *Ketsu-Go* – the defence of Japan. A joint JAAF–IJNAF air agreement signed on 13 July 1945 outlined the principal objectives of the air plan. The most important mission was to destroy the American invasion force while it was still on the water in the first stages of landing. For this the JAAF had amassed around 1,600 Special Attack

The intent in capturing Okinawa was to provide a base for tactical air support for the invasion of the home islands, set to begin in November 1945 with the invasion of Kyushu. By July 1945 the US Marines Corps had four MAGs on Okinawa with twelve squadrons of Corsairs. Here, 'Marine Air' Corsairs taxi out at Kadena prior to flying a mission. (NARA)

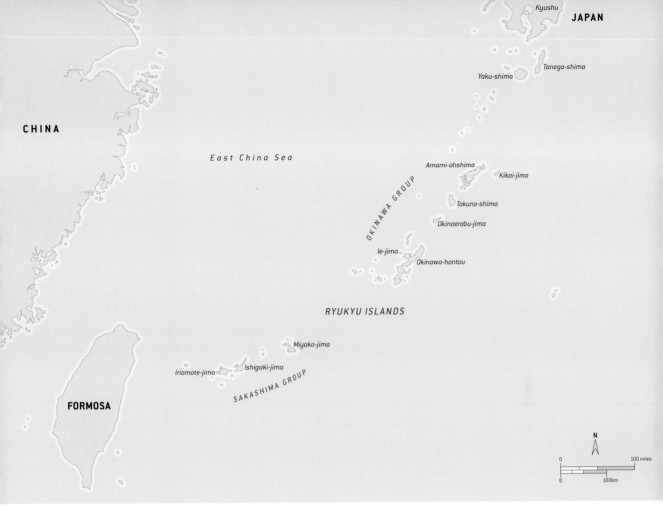

The battleground for the Okinawa campaign stretched from Kyushu, in the Home Islands, to Formosa, off the China coast. The Shimbu-Tai units were based in Kyushu and on Formosa. Their targets were the American transports anchored off the west coast of Okinawa and the carriers of TF 58 steaming to the east of the island. The Special Attack units and their escorts followed the Ryukyu Islands chain to their targets.

aircraft in the 1st and 6th Kokugun, with the expectation of preparing an additional 1,000 Special Attack aircraft from obsolete aeroplanes by the end of August. The IJNAF's 3rd, 5th and 10th Koku Kantai could muster nearly 4,000 Special Attack aircraft.

The secondary missions for both the JAAF and the IJNAF were to provide for the air defence of Japan and to disrupt American pre-invasion operations with their regular air units. For this role the 1st and 6th Kokugun had some 900 aircraft nominally available, including eight fighter *sentai* equipped with the Type 4 Fighter and five *sentai* re-equipping with the new Type 5 Fighter (Kawasaki Ki-100), while the IJNAF's air fleets had approximately 1,200 aircraft available.

As the air attacks on Okinawa petered out in June, Gen Masakuzu Kawabe, commander of the Japanese Army's Koku Shogun (General Air Army), formed in April to better coordinate the operations of the 1st and 6th Kokugun, ordered his forces to refrain from combat with intruding American fighter and bomber formations in order to rebuild the JAAF's air strength following the devastating losses over Okinawa. But USAAF air raids on Japanese aircraft factories had such a serious impact on production that Imperial General Headquarters instructed Kawabe to stop trying to conserve his aircraft and instead respond aggressively to American attacks with the forces he had available.

THE MEN
US Navy and US Marine Corps Pilot Training

For a young American university graduate hoping to be a US Navy or US Marine Corps fighter pilot during 1944, the experience of training was qualitatively different than that which his Japanese counterpart received. By this stage of the war the US Navy's training system was operating efficiently and providing a comprehensive programme covering flying skills, combat tactics and gunnery. In contrast to the JAAF, the US Navy's training programme benefited from an adequate number of experienced instructors, unlimited fuel for flying and a steady supply of training aeroplanes and first-line operational aircraft. With production at high levels, there were now enough first-line fighters to provide both combat units and operational training units. The number of aircraft in the US Navy's training command peaked in 1944 at 9,652.

At the end of 1943, Naval Air Training Command was established to control all phases of training at the three subordinate commands – Primary, Intermediate and Operational Training Command. During 1944, this system trained 21,067 naval aviators for the US Navy and the US Marine Corps.

The North American SNJ Texan fulfilled the advanced training role. Trainee fighter pilots would move on to the SNJ in the second phase of their intermediate training, practicing formation flying, aerial gunnery and basic fighter tactics in the machine. (Museum of Flight)

An aviation cadet began his training with three months at Flight Preparatory School, where he took classes in the basic elements of flight, navigation, maths, physics and aircraft and ship recognition. He also undertook intensive physical training. From there the aviation cadet went to a War Training Service school for three months of elementary flying training with civilian flight instructors on light aeroplanes such as the Piper J-3 Cub, accumulating around 40 hours of dual and solo flight time. If successful, the aviation cadet then moved to a primary training school for up to 14 weeks of flight instruction in the Naval Aircraft Factory N3N or Boeing N2S Stearman primary training biplane. The emphasis in primary training was learning to fly the aircraft with precision, individually and as part of a formation. During primary training the aviation cadet would accumulate another 90 to 100 hours of flying time.

During the intermediate training phase the aviation cadet learned to fly heavier and more powerful aeroplanes in anticipation of moving on to operational aircraft. At Pensacola in Florida, or Corpus Christi in Texas, cadets would spend 14 to 18 weeks gaining another 160 hours of flying time. During the first part of intermediate training the cadet would fly the Vultee SNV Valiant, moving on to the North American SNJ Texan in the advanced stage. Here, a cadet selected for training as a fighter pilot would begin working on more advanced formation flying, elementary combat tactics and aerial gunnery. On completion of intermediate training the cadet would be given his wings and a commission as an ensign in the US Navy or as a second lieutenant in the US Marine Corps. By this time a cadet would have acquired around 300 hours of flying time before moving to an operational training unit to become a fully qualified service pilot.

US Navy and US Marine Corps pilots destined for fighter squadrons went to one of several operational training units at fields on the southeast coast of the USA. Here, they were introduced to service aeroplanes, learning to fly the F4F and FM-2 Wildcat, the F6F Hellcat and the F4U Corsair. Operational training was an intensive course in fighter tactics and gunnery, combining ground school classes and flying practice that added a further 100 flying hours to a trainee fighter pilot's logbook.

The goals of operational training were to ensure that the neophyte fighter pilot learned to fly a high-performance aeroplane with confidence, and practised basic fighter manoeuvres until they became second nature. The trainee learned to fly as part of a division of four aeroplanes – the US Navy's basic fighting formation – being taught how to fly as a wingman in support of his element leader. There was intensive practice in aerial gunnery and gunnery approaches, learning the mechanics of deflection shooting until this too became automatic. US Navy pilots would practise carrier

Capt William Snider of VMF-221 claimed two 'Franks' shot down over Kyushu on 18 March 1945, and his wingman claimed a third. Another division of VMF-221 claimed two more during the same mission. (NARA)

William Snider is representative of the experienced US Navy and US Marine Corps division leaders who fought during the final months of the Pacific War. Snider was born in December 1918 in Cairo, Illinois. He appears to have entered US Navy flying training before Pearl Harbor, receiving his commission as a second lieutnant in the US Marine Corps on 22 May 1942. In December he reported to VMF-221, stationed in Hawaii. Equipped with the F4F-4 Wildcat, the squadron was shipped to the Solomon Islands in February 1943, arriving on Guadalcanal in March. It would fly two combat tours from Guadalcanal, and a third tour based at Vella Lavella. On 1 April 1943, VMF-221 had its first encounter with Japanese aircraft, claiming seven shot down over the Russell Islands. 1Lt William Snider claimed

three Zero-sens destroyed in his F4F-4 in the space of just 90 seconds.

VMF-221 converted to the F4U-1 Corsair in May, but Snider did not score again until 17 October when he claimed two 'Zekes' shot down and a third probably destroyed over Bougainville, making him an ace. Snider received a Distinguished Flying Cross and an Air Medal for his actions on his first combat tour, duly being promoted to captain. VMF-221 returned to the USA in January 1944.

Snider remained with the squadron, helping to train new pilots as the unit prepared for its second combat tour. Combat-experienced pilots like Snider were instrumental in passing on tactics and helping replacements hone their combat skills.

At the end of the year VMF-221 was chosen as one of the US Marine Corps Corsair squadrons to be assigned to a fleet carrier, joining VMF-451 in Carrier Air Group 84 assigned to USS Bunker Hill (CV-17). Snider made the first claim of his second combat tour on 16 February 1945 during TF 58's strike on Tokyo when he and a squadronmate shot down a G4M 'Betty' bomber. A month later Snider participated in the carrier strikes on airfields on Kyushu, claiming two 'Franks' and a 'Zeke' shot down in an intense aerial battle. For this action he was awarded the Silver Star.

Snider claimed a 'Tony' shot down on 6 April during the Kikusui Operation No. 1. Ten days later he was credited with destroying a 'Tojo' and a 'Zeke' during Kikusui Operation No. 3, but there is a possibility that the Ki-44 he claimed was actually a 'Frank' from the 35th Sei – a Special Attack unit operating from Formosa that day. This would make Snider one of the leading US Navy and US Marine Corps scorers against the Type 4 Fighter. These were Snider's final claims of the war, bringing his total to 11.5 Japanese aircraft destroyed. On 11 May Bunker Hill was severely damaged in a kamikaze attack, after which Snider and the other surviving pilots of VMF-221 returned home and saw no further combat. Snider left the US Marine Corps after the war and died in March 1969.

landings and complete eight recoveries either on an escort carrier or one of the two converted passenger liners used for carrier landing practice in Lake Michigan off Chicago. By the time he completed his operational training, a US Navy or US Marine Corps pilot would have accumulated 400 to 500 hours of flying time – nearly double what his Japanese counterpart would have accrued during the same period.

Young naval aviators accumulated more flying hours and went through additional intensive combat training once they joined a squadron. By this stage of the war the US Navy and US Marine Corps had enough combat squadrons in their carrier air groups and MAGs to be able to rotate units out of the front line for periods of rest and rebuilding. Pilots fresh from operational training would join their squadrons, where they would undergo more training in combat flying under the experienced eyes of veterans who had served one or more combat tours and were preparing their squadrons for their next deployment.

New pilots would be assigned to a division, where they would fly as wingmen to more experienced pilots, who would train them in aerial combat, bombing, strafing and the other skills they would need when engaging the enemy. There would often be opportunities for practice dogfights with other US Navy or US Marine Corps squadrons or cooperative USAAF squadrons flying different types of fighters – invaluable experience for the beginner. In contrast to a newly trained JAAF pilot, a US Navy or US Marine Corps fighter pilot going off to combat in early 1945 would have had not just more flying hours, but better and more comprehensive practice in controlling his aeroplane, in air combat tactics and in aerial gunnery.

By 1944 there were more than enough Corsairs to equip front-line squadrons and Stateside training units. These F4Us were stationed at MCAS El Toro, California, which was home to a Fighter Training Unit and facilities for squadrons training to return to combat. (Peter M. Bowers Collection, Museum of Flight)

JAAF Pilot Training

During the course of the Pacific War, JAAF pilot training underwent significant changes in both organizational structure and duration as a result of attrition and growing shortages of aircraft and fuel. As the war went on, shortened flying training courses and inadequate flying practice led to a steady deterioration in pilot quality. When the JAAF was finally able to introduce a superior aeroplane in the Type 4 Fighter, its training system was not able to produce pilots with the skills needed to take advantage of its flying and fighting qualities.

As with most air forces, the JAAF's training scheme was divided into segments providing for progressive advancement in flying skill. After a period of ground instruction, pilot trainees would begin flight training at an elementary flying training school (*hiko gakko*), where they would be taught basic flying skills in the Type 95 Basic Trainer (Tachikawa Ki-17) and the Type 95 Medium Trainer (Tachikawa Ki-9). Over a six-month period trainees would receive up to 70 hours of dual instruction and solo flying.

Moving to advanced flying training schools (*kyoiku hikotai*), trainees would begin flying the Type 99 Advanced Trainer (Tachikawa Ki-55). They practised formation flying, more aerobatics and elementary combat tactics. Those selected to become fighter pilots flew aircraft such as the Type 97 Fighter (Ki-27) and Type 1 Fighter (Ki-43). During his advanced training a trainee pilot would receive 120 hours of dual instruction and solo flying over six to eight months.

From an advanced flying training school a pilot moved to an operational fighter regiment for operational training. Ideally, over six months, the neophyte fighter pilot would receive an additional 200 to 300 hours of training in combat tactics and gunnery from experienced combat pilots, usually when a unit had been withdrawn from the front line for rest and re-equipment.

Although the JAAF's training organization was expanded during 1941–42, it still could not produce the number of fighter pilots needed to replace growing losses in combat. Nor

JAAF pilot trainees learned to fly on the Tachikawa Type 95-1 Medium Grade Trainer (Ki-9 'Spruce'), which served as the primary trainer throughout the Pacific War. (Edward M. Young Collection)

Tachikawa Type 95 trainers at the Koku Shikan Gakko (Army Air Academy), which trained officer pilots, prepare for take-off. Officer pilots underwent a separate training programme from enlisted aviators. (Edward M. Young Collection)

could the system of operational training at unit level function well as Hiko Sentai increasingly remained in combat for extended periods. This meant that new pilots were often thrown into combat before completing their training. To provide more pilots for the JAAF and IJNAF, the Japanese government authorized the conscription of university and secondary school students in the autumn of 1943. To cope with this influx of pilot trainees, the JAAF increased the number of Kyoiku Hikotai from 18 to 50 in the spring of 1944, establishing many of these new units overseas in China, Korea, Manchuria, Malaya, French Indochina and Java so that they were closer to supplies of aviation fuel.

At the same time, the JAAF removed the training burden from operational units and created specialized operational training units (Rensei Hikotai), which were placed overseas as well as in the Home Islands. Instructors for the Rensei Hikotai were drawn from the advanced training schools and from experienced pilots who had been withdrawn from combat, often after being badly wounded. The Rensei Hikotai were equipped with operational aircraft, including the Type 1, Type 2, Type 3 and Type 4 Fighters. These units were made responsible for converting graduates of the advanced flying training schools to the operational aircraft they would fly in combat and teaching them combat techniques, in addition to conversion training for experienced pilots. In some cases the Rensei Hikotai provided local air defence and flew convoy patrols to relieve regular fighter regiments of these duties, providing a supplement to operational training.

The Tachikawa Type 99 Advanced Trainer (Ki-55 'Ida') acted as a bridge between the Ki-9 and the more demanding operational fighter aircraft a young pilot would fly in his last stage of training. This photograph shows Ki-55s from the Koku Shikan Gakko practising formation flying. (Edward M. Young Collection)

The rapid expansion of pilot trainees created problems because of a shortage of training aircraft and instructor pilots. These shortages led to disruptions and delays in the training programme. The more critical factor was the growing shortage of aviation fuel as US Navy submarines sank more and more Japanese tankers. The influx of trainees at the same time that fuel supplies were dwindling meant fewer training hours per trainee. The shortage of fuel forced the JAAF to cut back pilot training to nine months during 1944, and to four months in early 1945. Whereas pilots previously would have accumulated 400 to 500 hours of flying time before entering combat, by early 1944 the average had dropped to around 300 hours, and it continued to decline as the year went on. With fewer flying hours allocated to them, JAAF pilot trainees had less and less chance to build up their fundamental flying skills and gain the experience they would need for air combat. Training in combat tactics and gunnery had to be cut back too.

With the expectation of American bombing raids from the Mariana Islands, from the autumn of 1944 much of the operational training new pilots received was devoted to intercepting bomber formations at high altitude, and less time was allocated to fighter-versus-fighter combat beyond some basic fighter manoeuvres.

For a newly trained fighter pilot, however, the Type 4 Fighter's flying characteristics were considered to be superior to other JAAF fighters. Conversion to the Type 4 was thought to be straightforward, although neophyte pilots did have problems landing the more powerful fighter. The Ki-84 was not as instantly manoeuvrable as the Type 1 Fighter, but its heavier weight and heavier control response made it easier to fly. It had superior handling to the Type 2 Fighter, which some experienced pilots considered to be 'twitchy and unstable', especially at higher altitude, and

Ace WO Katsuaki Kira survived six years of aerial combat over China, New Guinea, the Philippines and Okinawa, having progressed from Ki-27s to Ki-84s during his remarkably long career in the front line. This photo of Kira was taken at the time of the Nomohan Incident in 1939, when he was fighting with the 24th Hiko Sentai. (Courtesy of Yasuho Izawa)

By 1945 JAAF pilots with as much experience as WO Katsuki Kira were unfortunately all too rare. Born in Kumamoto Prefecture, on the island of Kyushu, in 1919, Kira completed his military and flight training in July 1938 and was transferred to the Akeno Army Flying School, where he trained to be a fighter pilot. On completing his training, Kira was promoted to corporal (prior to 1941, two-thirds of JAAF pilots were enlisted men), and went to join the 24th Hiko Sentai in northeast China.

Not long after he joined the unit, Kira had his first experience of combat flying the Type 97 Fighter (Ki-27 'Nate') during the Nomonhan Incident of 1939, when on the 22nd June, he downed an I-16 over the Khalka River. By the end of the conflict, he had claimed eight further victories against Soviet aircraft and amassed a wealth of valuable combat experience.

Kira also participated in the invasion of the Philippines with the 24th Hiko Sentai, but he did not claim any victories during this conflict. In September 1942 the unit transferred to Sumatra, where it converted to the Type 1 Fighter (Ki-43 'Oscar'). From there, the 24th Hiko Sentai went to New Guinea in May 1943. Kira spent six months in-theatre, and he claimed seven victories against American aeroplanes, including a B-17 and a B-24.

The *sentai* returned to Japan in October 1943, and that same month Kira was assigned to the new 200th Hiko Sentai, which was made up of instructors from the Akeno Army Flying School and experienced combat veterans flying the new Ki-84 exclusively. Kira fought with the unit throughout the Philippines campaign and scored several more victories. On one mission Kira attacked a formation of P-38s, claiming two shot down. For this feat he received a promotion to warrant officer.

Returning to Japan, Kira was assigned to the 103rd Hiko Sentai in March 1945 and participated in air combat over Okinawa, scoring the last of his 21 victories during the fighting. He survived six years of aerial combat over China, New Guinea, the Philippines and Okinawa – a remarkable achievement that not many equalled. After the war Kira joined the Japanese Self-Defence Force, and eventually retired as a major.

At a Rensei Hikotai or another Army Flying School, neophyte fighter pilots would fly their first operational fighters, beginning with the Type 97 Fighter (Ki-27 'Nate') or the Type 1 Fighter (Ki-43 'Oscar'), shown here, before moving on to the more demanding Type 2 Fighter (Ki-44 'Tojo') and the Type 4 Fighter (Ki-84 'Frank'). (Peter M. Bowers Collection, Museum of Flight)

benefited from a lower landing speed than the Type 2. Commenting on converting from the Type 2 to the Type 4 Fighter, a pilot from the 47th Hiko Sentai recalled, 'the hachi-yon [Ki-84] was much easier to control than the yon-yon [Ki-44], which had a higher landing speed. It only took me a few days to get used to it since the changeover. Everyone said it was an easy aeroplane to fly'.

But while learning to fly the Ki-84 was straightforward, as with their IJNAF counterparts, fewer and fewer JAAF fighter pilots trained in the final year of the war had the skills to get the most out of their new fighter, as good as it was.

INTO COMBAT
US Navy and US Marine Corps Combat Tactics

Through hard-won experience, the US Navy had refined its basic fighter combat tactics to four key principles:

- Superiority of Position
- Superiority of Disposition
- Superiority of Concentration
- Superiority of Marksmanship

Superiority of position referred to the necessity of maintaining superior altitude over enemy aircraft and staying between an enemy force and its objective, while superiority of disposition spoke to arranging formations so that all sections and divisions could be employed efficiently. Superiority of concentration was perhaps the most important element in fighter combat – the vital necessity of pilots keeping together to maintain air discipline and mutual protection. The US Navy stressed over and over again the need for mutual support and coordinated action. Its combat doctrine clearly stated that 'each aeroplane is part of an invisible chain. Any aeroplane which breaks the chain by diving away, either to avoid an enemy or in pursuit of a target, subtracts from the overall strength of the group'. If fighters remain concentrated, and fight together as a team, 'they will command the air where they are concentrated'.

Superiority of marksmanship was itself based on four principles:

- Ability to hit with the first burst.
- Ability to make effective runs in the heat of battle on manoeuvring targets.
- Cool selection of the point of aim – engine, pilot or tanks, rather than spraying the whole target.
- Conservation of ammunition.

The division of four aircraft, in two elements, was the basic combat formation for the US Navy and US Marine Corps fighter units. Pilots were drilled to fight as a team both offensively and defensively, and never to break off to engage in combat on their own. A division of four Corsairs from VBF-84 are shown here flying in formation in the final months of the Pacific War. (Robert Lawson Collection, National Naval Aviation Museum)

CAPs were usually under the direction of a Fighter Director Officer. Fighters would stay closed up in one of four formations as they approached the intercept point to avoid confusing the radar. The formations were designed to place the main intercepting force some 2,000–3,000ft above the estimated height of the enemy formation to give superiority of position, with a part of the formation flying above to provide high cover. Formations varied based on visibility and the probable composition of the enemy formation.

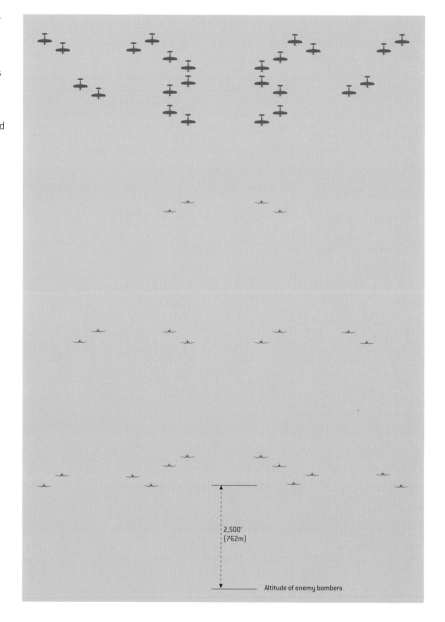

2,500'
(762m)

Altitude of enemy bombers

Beginning in intermediate training, and continuing through operational training and initial squadron service, these principles were drummed into new fighter pilots. From a trainee pilot's first gunnery runs to his introduction to combat, the US Navy and the US Marine Corps stressed the importance of marksmanship and the fundamentals of aerial gunnery. As the US Navy's gunnery manual put it, 'the intelligent combat pilot knows his responsibilities and he strives for perfection in fundamentals in order to achieve a cool, smooth, machine-like precision in action. He corrects his mistakes in practice, for in actual combat the smallest individual error may cause the loss of a battle.'

Superiority of position, disposition, concentration and marksmanship were vital in defending against the *kamikaze* attacks during the Okinawa campaign. To protect the carrier task force and the many transports bringing supplies for the ground battle, US Navy and US Marine Corps fighter squadrons spent hours on CAPs under fighter direction from controllers on board radar picket ships or manning land-based portable radar stations. Successful interceptions required excellent cooperation between fighter squadrons and the Fighter Direction Officer who directed the intercept.

Approaching the intercept point, fighters would shift to one of four formations – designated 'Victor', 'William', 'X-ray' or 'Yoke' – depending on visibility, the accuracy of the estimated altitude of the enemy formation and whether or not it was escorted. These formations would attempt to bring the fighters in at an altitude above the enemy formation, with the flight leader's division flying above other divisions to ensure accurate direction of the engagement. The flight leader would deploy his divisions to obtain superiority of disposition and concentration, always trying to attack with an altitude advantage and, if possible, to engage escorting fighters while other divisions went after the Special Attack aeroplanes, although it appears that identifying escorts from Special Attack aeroplanes was not always straightforward.

It was accepted that in an attack the principle of concentration might have to be violated, but doctrine stressed the importance of maintaining tactical concentration at the section and, if possible, division level. Pilots were admonished not to break away from their leader to engage an enemy aeroplane, as mutual support would break down, leaving one or both aeroplanes unprotected. The US Navy wanted an 'organized melee' instead of a general 'melee', where there was greater risk. Doctrine stated that in attacking a large formation of enemy aircraft 'success will depend largely on the ability of pilots to follow the leader, maintain effective tactical concentration, preventing straggling and the pursuit of individual enemy aeroplanes'.

JAAF Combat Tactics

During the Pacific War, JAAF air combat tactics evolved as commanders came to recognize that they were less effective against an enemy employing coordinated formations and air discipline, aeroplanes with superior performance and well-trained pilots. In the years leading up to the Pacific War, and in the conflict's early stages, JAAF fighter pilots were obsessed with manoeuvrability. They retained the belief that air combat would continue to be a battle between two combatants in a whirling, turning dogfight, with the aircraft with superior manoeuvrability inevitably the victor. Japanese pilots believed that a light armament of two 7.7mm machine guns was adequate because of their ability to place their fighter in an advantageous position for a 'single-shot' that resulted in the 'certain death' of an enemy pilot.

The Type 97 Fighter exemplified this approach to close-in air combat and the emphasis on agility above all other characteristics. The Type 1 Fighter made a concession to the trend towards heavier fighter armament by switching to two 12.7mm machine guns, but retained the emphasis on manoeuvring into a superior position for the kill.

JAAF fighter tactics in the first part of the war aimed at drawing an opponent into manoeuvring combat, where the superior agility of Japanese aircraft could be brought to bear. Like their IJNAF counterparts, JAAF regiments used the three-aeroplane *shotai* as their basic formation, although this was a more fluid scheme than the standard V formation of most other air forces. The No. 2 and No. 3 pilots in the *shotai* were not rigidly attached to the *shotai* leader, but had more flexibility in manoeuvre. In an attack, the No. 2 and No. 3 pilots often followed their leader in when engaging an enemy aeroplane, or lagged behind to catch an enemy fighter as it tried to manoeuvre away from the leader's attack.

When attacked from behind, a *shotai* formation would often split up, the leader pulling up in a loop to use superior manoeuvrability to come down behind an Allied fighter, while the No. 2 and No. 3 pilots executed a chandelle or an Immelmann turn to gain an advantageous position to counter the attack. These tactics proved highly effective in the early months of the Pacific War before Allied pilots learned to avoid manoeuvring combat with the more nimble Japanese fighters and adopted

JAAF pilots receive a briefing from their commanding officer before heading off on a mission. Once in the air, the poor quality of Japanese aerial radios made communications between a leader and his formation difficult. (Edward M. Young Collection)

dive-and-zoom, hit-and-run tactics instead. Using their superior speed and diving ability, Allied pilots could initiate an attack from higher altitude, then break away and climb back above a Japanese formation to launch another attack. In their lighter and slower aircraft, Japanese pilots found these tactics difficult to counter.

During 1943 JAAF air leaders recognized the need to revise fighter tactics. They conducted extensive research, drawing on their experiences of combat with Allied fighter pilots and their knowledge of German combat tactics. A report issued towards the end of the year highlighted the need for greater air discipline and mutual support. In combat, the JAAF had found that the three-aeroplane *shotai* formation proved difficult to coordinate and provided weaker protection. Training had emphasized individual over coordinated action in combat. Once engaged with an enemy formation, JAAF fighter pilots had a tendency to conduct individual attacks, with

Three young JAAF enlisted pilots pose for a photograph. By early 1945 pilot training had been cut back to the extent that young pilots were joining their units with around 200 flying hours and only the most basic training in aerial combat. (Edward M. Young Collection)

little thought given to mutual support. Often, the formation broke up into one- and two-aeroplane groupings, leaving the single fighter isolated and vulnerable to attack.

Following German and Allied practice, the JAAF belatedly switched to a two-aeroplane element as its basic combat formation, increasing the *shotai* to four aeroplanes in two sections (*buntai*) of two aeroplanes for greater mutual support. There was also a greater emphasis on seeking a more advantageous position prior to engaging in combat, especially the need to attack with an altitude advantage as the Allies did. Pilots were strictly instructed not to engage in combat on their own.

In aerial combat over Japan and Okinawa during 1945, US Navy and US Marine Corps pilots noted an improvement in Japanese tactics. Pilots would climb for altitude before attacking, and would try to maintain an altitude advantage. They would attack when there was an opportunity – a wingman out of formation, a pilot straggling after a low-altitude strafing run, or a pilot who went too far out in a weave. However, effective use of the two-aeroplane element and four-aeroplane formation did not appear

The escorts had three objectives to fulfill when protecting the Special Attack unit formations. Because so many of the *kamikaze* pilots were inexperienced, the escorts would guide them to their targets. The direct escort force would fly alongside or among the Special Attack aircraft as guides. The intermediate escort force and the direct escort force would attempt to clear a path for the Special Attack aircraft through the American CAPs. Assuming the Special Attack aircraft made it through to their targets, the escort force was instructed to observe and report on the results achieved, before returning to base.

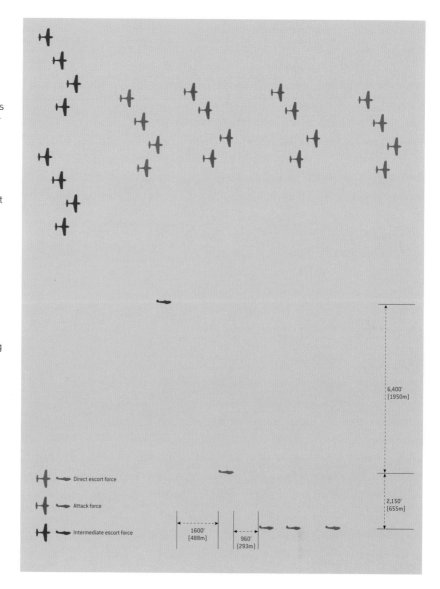

Direct escort force

Attack force

Intermediate escort force

1600'
(488m)

960'
(293m)

6,400'
(1950m)

2,150'
(655m)

to be the case in all JAAF fighter units. US Navy and US Marine Corps pilots continued to comment on the failure of their Japanese foes to provide mutual support.

A great handicap to improved air discipline and formation tactics was the poor quality of Japanese airborne radios. It was often difficult, and sometimes impossible, for a formation leader to maintain voice contact with the pilots in the formation. This problem was never satisfactorily addressed before the end of the Pacific War. A pilot who flew the Type 5 Fighter (Ki-100) late in the conflict recalled the problems bad radios caused. 'The aeroplane's radio equipment was very poor,' he remembered.

'This defect was common to all Japanese aircraft. I had heard that the enemy aeroplanes had very good communications equipment, and that they had no difficulty in calling for reinforcements while in combat. In the case of Japanese aeroplanes, radio communications were of no use, and no plane came to our assistance on such occasions.'

The switch to the four-aeroplane formation and hit-and-run tactics towards the end of 1943 and early 1944 coincided with the introduction of the Type 4 Fighter into the JAAF's front-line regiments. The Type 4 Fighter was ideally suited to the newer hit-and-run tactics. Heavier, sturdier and faster in the dive than the Type 1 Fighter, with more power at altitude and manoeuvrablity than the Type 2 Fighter, the Hayate had the ability to dive down on American fighter formations at speed, fire a burst from its machine guns and cannon and climb back to altitude with a rate of climb superior to the F4U Corsair, F6F Hellcat, P-47 Thunderbolt or P-51 Mustang. And if the combat broke up into a turning fight, the Hayate was more manoeuvrable than the American fighters and could execute the standard split-S evasive manoeuvre more readily.

The Type 4 Fighter gave its pilots confidence. An aviator who flew the Hayate with the 47th Hiko Sentai in the defence of Japan towards the end of the war recalled that he went into combat thinking 'it will work out as long as the battle is fought one-on-one, and the skills and conditions of the enemy pilot were equivalent. I thought the Hachi-yon was superior'.

During 1944, the Japanese government began conscripting university and high school students to train as pilots. Since many of these classes would not complete their training before the likely invasion of the homeland, large numbers of students were trained as *kamikaze* pilots for the Tokubetsu Kogeki Tai. (Edward M. Young Collection)

The difficulty for the Type 4 Fighter *sentai* in these final aerial battles of the war was that on many of the missions they flew the Hayates were mostly on the defensive. Hit-and-run tactics required altitude, and gaining sufficient altitude for the defence of the airfields on Kyushu required adequate warning, which did not always happen. As one Hayate pilot put it, 'if the battle was fighter against fighter, usually the one who had the higher position won. When you take off into skies where the enemy is waiting, you might as well take off into Hell.' In some units at least, one *chutai* would be assigned to fly cover over the airfield to protect the other squadrons as they took off to intercept and returned for landing.

While escorting the *kamikaze* formations to Okinawa, the Type 4 Fighter *sentai* often found themselves at a disadvantage, tied to the Special Attack formations. The escort force usually flew in two types of formation – direct and intermediate escort. The direct escort force would either fly intermixed with the Special Attack aeroplanes, acting as guide aircraft, or as a separate force flying ahead and behind the Special Attack force, with the rear escorts flying slightly above. The intermediate escort force would fly above and behind the direct escort and Special Attack aeroplanes to give them room to manoeuvre against attacking American fighters.

First Encounters

Following the fall of the Philippines, Imperial General Headquarters began preparations for the defence of the Home Islands against an expected American invasion, likely to begin with an attack on the Ryukyu Islands to establish a base for air support of the invasion force. On 20 January 1945, Imperial General Headquarters issued an outline of JAAF and IJNAF operations, a key component of which was a joint plan for the air defence of the Ryukyu Islands and the homeland. Given shortages of more capable aeroplanes, fuel and especially experienced pilots, the emphasis in the air plan was the mass employment of Special Attack units, the Tokubetsu Kogeki Tai (also called Shimbu Tai, Special Attack Units, known to Americans as the *kamikaze*), using partly trained pilots and, in the main, obsolete aircraft.

In December 1944 the JAAF had established the 6th Kokugun as a reserve force to counter the planned invasion of the Ryukyus and the Home Islands, operating both regular and Special Attack units. With the invasion of Okinawa, the 6th Kokugun became responsible for conducting Special Attack missions under Operation *Ten-Go*, the defence of Okinawa, and for protecting the JAAF's airfields on Kyushu, operating under the control of the IJNAF's Rengo Kantai (Combined Fleet). The JAAF's contribution to the air defence of the Home Islands remained with the 1st

Kokugun, with its 10th, 11th and 12th Hikoshidan (10th, 11th and 12th Air Divisions).

The Type 4 Hayate served with fighter *sentai* in both air armies. In general, the Hayate units serving with the 1st Kokugun were responsible for the air defence of Japan's industrial areas against attacks from B-29 bombers and American carrier aircraft. The 6th Kokugun's Hayate units had responsibility for defending the Special Attack unit airfields on Kyushu from marauding US Navy carrier aircraft, as well as being given the unenviable task of escorting the Tokubetsu Tai on their missions to attack American shipping off Okinawa. Although most of the JAAF's Shimbu Tai units were equipped with obsolete Type 97 (Ki-27) and Type 1 (Ki-43) fighters, Type 99 Assault aeroplanes (Ki-51) and training aircraft, a few units were assigned Type 3 (Ki-61) and Type 4 Fighters for their Special Attack missions.

US Navy and US Marine Corps Corsair pilots flying off carriers or from airfields on Okinawa would encounter the Type 4 fighter in all three roles during the initial carrier strikes against the Home Islands, throughout the Okinawa campaign and in the final few combats of the last months of the Pacific War.

One difficulty in looking at engagements between the Corsair and the Hayate is the problem of aircraft recognition. The speed and intensity of aerial combat, often against large formations of different types of Japanese aircraft, made it hard to identify positively the aeroplane being attacked. During this late-war period the JAAF fielded four radial-engined fighters – the Type 1 Hayabusa (Ki-43 'Oscar'), the Type 2 Shoki (Ki-44 'Tojo'), the Type 4 Hayate (Ki-84 'Frank') and the Type 5 (Ki-100, which had no Allied code name). The IJNAF fielded three – the A6M Zero-sen ('Zeke'), the J2M Raiden ('Jack') and the N1K2-J Shiden-Kai ('George').

For many Allied pilots the 'Frank' was a relatively new aeroplane that few would have seen before. While it had gone into combat during the late summer of 1944 over China and Burma, it was not until the Philippines campaign in October of that same year that US Navy pilots encountered the 'Frank' in any significant numbers, and not until US forces captured several examples that the fighter's features and outlines could be clearly defined. As a Technical Air Intelligence Center report on the Type 4 from January 1945 noted, the 'Frank 1 does definitely resemble both Oscar 2 and Tojo 2. The wing structure is similar to that of Oscar and the fuselage and tailplane closely resemble Tojo'.

It is not surprising, therefore, that US Navy and US Marine Corps pilots often mistook 'Franks' for the more familiar 'Tojos' – although during the Okinawa battles the Ki-44 units were in fact committed to air

Overleaf
On 25 February 1945, Lt Cdr Roger Hedrick, CO of VF-84 flying off *Bunker Hill*, led four divisions on a fighter sweep east of Tokyo. In poor weather, with a solid overcast above, Hedrick spotted eight Japanese fighters he identified as 'Franks' circling over an airfield below his flight level, with two more 'Franks' flying beneath the Japanese formation. He dove down with his division and came in behind a 'Frank' at the 'seven o'clock' position, firing and getting hits in the wing roots and the fuselage. The Japanese fighter started burning and went down. On his second pass, Hedrick came in directly behind another 'Frank' and opened fire from close range. This 'Frank' exploded. Hedrick's wingman, Ens Thomas Mitchell, claimed a third 'Frank', while his element leader, Lt William Gerner, claimed a probable and a damaged. The Corsairs demonstrated superior speed to their opponents at this low altitude. (Artwork by Gareth Hector, © Osprey Publishing)

defence over Japan – or mistook 'Franks' for 'Georges' because of their superior performance, or saw any brown-coloured Japanese fighter aeroplane as an 'Oscar' or a 'Zeke'. Understandably these young fighter pilots had more on their minds than identifying properly the aeroplane they were shooting at. Therefore, Aircraft Action Reports have to be approached with a degree of caution. It is sometimes possible to link combats between American Corsair units and Japanese Hayate units, but not in every case.

As no US Marine Corps Corsair unit claimed a 'Frank' over the Philippines, and the US Navy Corsair units were not involved in that campaign, the first apparent clash between F4Us and Ki-84s took place on 25 February 1945 during the carrier strikes TF 58 had launched against airfields and aircraft factories in the Tokyo area in support of the landings on Iwo Jima. Flying off USS *Bunker Hill* (CV-17), Lt Cdr Roger Hedrick, commander of VF-84, was leading 16 F4U-1D Corsairs on a morning fighter sweep over airfields east of Tokyo.

On the first two days of attacks on 16 and 17 February, JAAF and IJNAF interceptors rose up in force to challenge the American aeroplanes, the Type 4 pilots of the 47th Hiko Sentai claiming 14 F6F Hellcats shot down and US Navy pilots submitting claims for six 'Franks' destroyed in return.

On the 25th the weather was overcast at 5,000ft, with snow falling over some areas, limiting interceptions. Hedrick was an experienced fighter

Rocket-armed Corsairs prepare for take-off from *Bunker Hill* for the 18–19 March strikes on airfields on Kyushu. VF-84, VMF-221 and VMF-451 flew Corsairs from the vessel at this time. (NARA)

pilot, having claimed nine 'Zekes' destroyed in F4Us with shore-based VF-17 in the Solomons. Flying at the base of the overcast, the Corsairs spotted eight Japanese aircraft they identified as 'Franks' flying below them, with two more 'Franks' flying below and ahead of the Japanese formation. Leaving two divisions as top cover, Hedrick came down on one of the 'Franks', closing in and firing from the 'seven o'clock' position. He hit the fighter in the fuselage and wing roots, sending the aeroplane down on fire. His wingman, Ens Thomas Mitchell, claimed another 'Frank' in the same pass. Lt William Gerner fired at a third 'Frank', but could not get it to burn – it went down smoking and was credited as damaged. Hedrick made a second pass on the formation, claiming another 'Frank' shot down from directly astern.

The Corsair pilots were then jumped by a mixed formation they identified as 'Oscars', 'Zekes' and 'Franks'. Gerner fired on another 'Frank', getting hits and sending the aeroplane down smoking and seemingly out of control. The VF-84 pilots noted that the Japanese fighters appeared to have a high 'rate of zoom', pulling quickly up into the overcast to avoid combat in a lack of aggressiveness that Hedrick contributed to poor training or inexperience. These aeroplanes, if they were indeed Hayates, were probably from the 47th Hiko Sentai, based nearby.

A month later, on 18 March, carrier-based Corsair squadron VMF-221, also flying off *Bunker Hill*, ran into a formation its pilots identified as 'Franks' and 'Zekes' while on a fighter sweep over central Kyushu as part of TF 58's strikes against airfields in the area. Here, too, there is a question about aircraft identification, as in the normal course of operations JAAF and IJNAF squadrons rarely flew together. However, on this day, both JAAF and IJNAF fighters were scrambled in an effort to counter the American raids. The 6th Kokugun had on Kyushu the 100th Hikodan (Air Brigade) with the 101st, 102nd and 103rd Hiko Sentai equipped with the Type 4 fighter. The 'Franks' VMF-221 encountered may have been from one of these units.

Three divisions of Corsairs from VMF-221 attacked an aircraft factory at Kumamoto, in central Kyushu, on the 18th. After expending their rockets on buildings, the F4U pilots were heading east towards the coast when they ran into a formation of 25 Japanese fighters. Capt William Snider, leading a division, attacked at once, firing at a fighter he identified as a 'Frank' approaching him head-on from '11 o'clock level'. Snider was an experienced pilot on his second combat tour, having claimed six 'Zekes' over the Solomons flying Wildcats and Corsairs. Snider continued firing until nearly colliding with the 'Frank', setting it on fire. He then attacked a second 'Frank' from above, coming in from the 'seven o'clock' position.

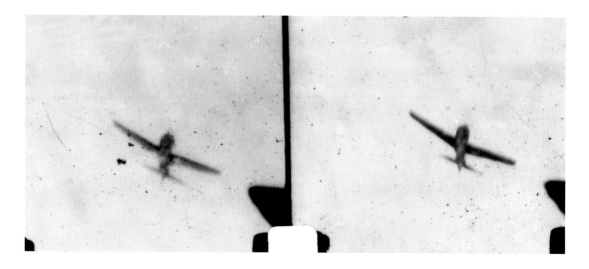

Gun camera film of a Ki-84 'Frank' under attack from a Corsair off *Bunker Hill* during one of the carrier strikes on Kyushu. The 'Frank' was longer than the 'Oscar,' with broader wings and a wider rear fuselage. (NARA)

He set this 'Frank' on fire too, and the pilot bailed out. Snider's wingman, 1Lt Donald McFarlane, claimed a third 'Frank' shot down, while 1Lt Neylon Murphy was credited with two damaged. In the third division, 1Lt Joseph Brocia Jr and 2Lt Richard Wasley both claimed 'Franks' shot down.

In what had been only a short combat, three VMF-221 divisions claimed eight 'Zekes' and five 'Franks' shot down. In the Aircraft Action Report the pilots observed that '"Franks" and "Zekes" did not use their natural advantages to any extent – even their turns were wide and sloppy. Their speed and dives were inferior, and their only manoeuvre seemed to be the split-S. The "Franks" seemed to absorb more lead than the "Zekes" and be harder to burn. Both types executed head-on attacks, however.'

What emerges from these two early actions is a paradox that would be repeated in the majority of combats between the Corsair and the Hayate in the months to come. Here was a fighter aeroplane with significant performance, armament capable of engaging American fighters in head-on attacks and improved armour protection, the latter making the Ki-84 much harder to set on fire than earlier Japanese fighters like the 'Oscar' and the 'Zeke'. Yet many of the Japanese pilots flying the Hayate seemed incapable, through lack of training or experience, of getting the best out of their fighters and using their capabilities to their advantage. For those pilots designated for Special Attack missions, the options for using their fighters to their full potential were limited.

Okinawa Campaign

The JAAF and IJNAF air plan for Operation *Ten-Go* was to launch ten mass *kamikaze* attacks against the American invasion force off Okinawa and the fleet units of TF 58. These attacks, dubbed Kikusui, began with

Kikusui Operation No. 1 on 6 April 1945 and continued until the last attack, Kikusui Operation No. 10, on 21–22 June 1945. Spread over one to three days, the strikes involved Special Attack units from both the JAAF and the IJNAF. The former had gathered its remaining experienced pilots into regular fighter regiments to act as escorts for the Special Attack units, hopefully clearing a path to enemy ships through the CAPs.

Although most of the Special Attack aircraft were obsolete fighter and trainer types, the JAAF did assign more capable Type 3 Hien (Ki-61 'Tony') and Type 4 Hayate to some of the Special Attack units. During the Okinawa campaign, for example, the Type 4 fighter equipped the 26th, 57th, 58th, 59th, 60th and 61st Shimbu-Tai units flying out of Kyushu and the 33rd, 34th, 35th and 120th Sei squadrons based on Formosa. The three Hayate Sentai of the 100th Hikoshidan (101st, 102nd and 103rd) regularly flew as escort. The losses suffered by the 100th Hikoshidan's units were considerable – during the aerial battles over the homeland and Okinawa in 1945 the three *sentai* lost more than 70 pilots in combat.

Following the invasion of Okinawa on 1 April 1945, carrier-based US Navy and US Marine Corps Corsair squadrons (VF-5, VF-10, VBF-10, VBF-83, VF-84, VF-85, VMF-112, VMF-123, VMF-221 and VMF-451) flew regular CAPs over US Navy shipping in the anchorages off Okinawa

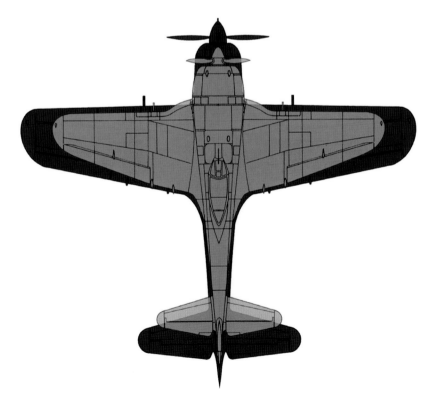

This artwork shows the outline of a Ki-44 'Tojo' laid over the outline of a Ki-84 'Frank' to illustrate the problem of aircraft recognition. In the aerial battles around Okinawa, US Navy and US Marine Corps pilots appear to have often mistaken the 'Frank' for the more familiar 'Tojo'. It seems that no Ki-44s were used as either Special Attack aircraft or as escorts for Shimbu-Tai units heading for Okinawa. (Illustration courtesy P. J. Muller, Museum of Flight)

and over TF 58. Land-based Corsair units began flying CAPs on 7 April when MAG-31 arrived at Yontan airfield, on Okinawa, with VMF-224, VMF-311 and VMF-441. Two days later MAG-33 began operating from Kadena airfield, also on Okinawa, with VMF-312, VMF-322 and VMF-323 (MAG-22, with VMF-113, VMF-314 and VMF-422, arrived in May and MAG-14, with VMF-212, VMF-222 and VMF-223, equipped with the newer F4U-4 Corsair arrived in June).

During the series of Kikusui attacks these squadrons intercepted many formations of different types of Special Attack aircraft – and their escorts – attempting to sink US Navy transports or the all-important radar picket ships off Okinawa. Formations of Type 4 Fighters were included in this number.

Again, the problem of aircraft recognition makes it difficult to determine with any degree of precision exactly which combats were between Corsairs and 'Franks', and how many of either type were shot down by the other. In some cases US Navy and US Marine Corps pilots would identify 'Franks' as their opponents, but often claims for 'Franks' would be mixed with other types, notably 'Tojos', 'Oscars' or 'Zekes'. Since none of the Shimbu-Tai units was equipped with the Ki-44, it is probable that many, but not all, of these combats where US Navy and US Marine Corps pilots claimed 'Tojos' actually involved the 'Frank'. The dates on which US Navy and US Marine Corps Corsair squadrons claimed 'Franks" and 'Tojos' do correspond fairly closely with the dates on which the

F4U-ID: IN THE COCKPIT

1. Armoured glass
2. Mk 8 reflector gunsight
3. Gun switch box
4. Bomb switch box
5. Water injection quantity warning light
6. Stall warning light
7. Carburetor air temperature warning light
8. Engine speed indicator
9. Auxiliary drop tank fuel control switch
10. Altimeter
11. Manifold pressure gauge
12. Directional gyro
13. Airspeed indicator
14. Compass
15. Turn and bank indicator
16. Artificial horizon
17. Rate of climb/descent indicator
18. Elapsed time clock
19. Cylinder temperature indicator
20. Oil temperature indicator
21. Oil pressure gauge
22. Fuel pressure gauge
23. Instrument panel lights
24. Flap control/indicator
25. Ignition switch
26. Alternate air control
27. Throttle lever
28. Supercharger control
29. Landing gear and dive brake control lever
30. Gun charging control
31. Mixture control lever
32. Propeller control lever
33. Aileron trimming tab control wheel/indicator
34. Fuel tank selector
35. Hydraulic hand pump
36. Elevator trimming tab control wheel
37. Elevator trimming tab indicator
38. Rudder trimming tab control
wheel/indicator
39. Tail wheel locking handle
40. Rudder pedals
41. Control grip with gun-firing button
42. Control column
43. Cockpit ventilator
44. Signal pistol cartridge container
45. Rocket station distributor box
46. Main tank fuel contents gauge
47. Hydraulic pressure gauge
48. Voltmeter
49. Fuel tank pressure gauge
50. Accelerometer
51. Radio control box
52. Cooling flap control levers
53. Pilot's distribution box
54. Map case
55. Pilot's seat
56. Pilot's seat adjustment lever
57. Gunsight reflector glass

(Artwork by Jim Laurier, © Osprey Publishing)

Shimbu-Tai units equipped with the Type 4 Fighter were active, and they usually had Ki-84s from the regular fighter *sentai* as escort.

The first of these combats with multiple Ki-84-equipped Shimbu-Tai units took place on 28 April during Kikusui Operation No. 4, when VF-84 claimed four 'Franks' and one 'Tojo'. That day, the 61st Shimbu-Tai unit sent seven Ki-84s to attack shipping west of Okinawa, as did several Shimbu-Tai units equipped with Type 97 Fighters, with an escort of Ki-84s from the 101st Hiko Sentai, which lost two fighters that day. VF-84 had four divisions on CAP, and after spotting the Japanese formation they attacked it from above and behind. Lt(jg) Cyrus Chambers claimed two 'Franks' shot down, while Lt(jg)s Willard Rempel and Harvey Matthews were credited with one each. Lt(jg) R. E. Miller claimed a 'Tojo', which was no doubt a 'Frank', noting that it took five bursts to shoot down the Japanese fighter.

On 4 May pilots of VF-84 claimed a further three 'Franks' shot down during Kikusui Operation No. 5. The Corsairs of VBF-83 also ran into several Ki-84s, Ens Roy Rechsteiner claiming two shot down. He also noted that neither of his opponents carried any bombs, indicating that they were possibly part of the escort force. That day the 60th Shimbu-Tai unit sent out six Ki-84s to attack shipping, while the 36th and 120th Sei squadrons from Formosa dispatched nine Ki-84s to Okinawa. Several hours later a pilot from VMF-323 claimed a 'Tojo' during a combat with a large force of Special Attack aircraft. On 7 May VMF-323 claimed two 'Tojos' shot down, with VBF-83 being credited with a third. It is possible that these were in fact 'Franks', not 'Tojos'.

The greatest number of claims came on 25 May during Kikusui Operation No. 7. On this day the JAAF sent 100 Special Attack aircraft to Okinawa, including 23 Ki-84s from the 26th, 57th, 58th, 60th and 61st Shimbu-Tai. The 102nd Hiko Sentai, and possibly other units of the 100th Hikoshidan, flew as escort, the 102nd losing at least two pilots that day. The Corsairs of VMF-312 appear to have been the first to run into these formations. Capt Herbert Valentine's division, having just been relieved from their CAP, saw a formation of what they identified as 15 'Zekes' approaching and attacked it, claiming ten shot down. 2Lt Malcolm Birney was lost to one of the 'Zekes', however.

Immediately after this combat Valentine observed what he identified as three 'Tojos' and three 'Vals' (Type 99 Carrier Bombers). It is more likely, given the units involved that morning, that this was a formation of 'Franks' escorting several Type 97 Fighters or Type 2 Advanced Trainers (Ki-79s), both of which were active that day – the latter machines also had fixed undercarriages like the 'Val'. Valentine initially climbed and then dived on the formation, shooting down two of the 'Tojos' with hits in the engine and the cockpit – his wingman Lt William Farrell dispatched the third fighter. Valentine also claimed two 'Vals' shot down for his fifth and sixth kills of the day.

Shortly thereafter VMF-322 engaged another Japanese formation, claiming seven 'Tojos' shot down – 2Lt James Webster was credited with three kills and a fourth as a probable. A division from VMF-323 was next, attacking a formation the division identified as seven 'Tojos', one 'Tony' and two 'Zekes' flying in loose formation, noticing that two of the 'Tojos' were carrying bombs. 1Lt John Strickland claimed a 'Tojo' and a 'Zeke', while 1Lts Charles Allen and James Feliton were credited with two 'Tojos' each, 2Lt Thomas Blackwell claiming the sixth. Some 30 miles away, 2Lt Stuart Alley claimed another 'Tojo' shot down following an intense duel.

On 28 May, during Kikusui Operation No. 8, a division from VF-85 came across four Ki-84s flying in formation. These may have been from the 58th and 59th Shimbu-Tai, which sent out four Hayates that day. Lt(jg) Kennard Moos, flying an F4U-1D, claimed two 'Franks' shot down, while Lt(jg)s James Egolf and David Lawhon claimed one each flying cannon-armed F4U-1Cs.

Despite the Ki-84 units suffering terribly at the hands of US fighters, there were several combats during this period that show the capabilities of the Hayate to advantage. On 4 May, Maj Michiaki Tojo, commanding

The pilots of VMF-323 sit on the wing of one of the squadron's Corsairs on Okinawa. VMF-323 claimed seven 'Tojos' shot down on 25 May 1945, but these were more likely to have been Ki-84 'Franks' from several Shimbu-Tai units that sortied that day with their Ki-84 escorts. (Jack Lambert Collection, Museum of Flight)

the 103rd Hiko Sentai, led a formation of Hayates from his own unit and the 102nd Hiko Sentai charged with escorting a mixed Special Attack aeroplane formation consisting of Ki-27 'Nates', Ki-43 'Oscars', Ki-84 'Franks' and two Ki-45 'Nicks' (Type 2 Two-seat Fighters) to Okinawa. More 'Oscars' from the 65th Hiko Sentai also participated in the mission. That same morning VF-85 sent up three divisions on CAP north of Okinawa.

Flying at 20,000ft, Ens E. L. Myers, wingman to Lt(jg) Saul Chernoff, saw a formation of what he identified as 12–16 'Zekes', and Chernoff ordered him to take the lead. The other members of the division found that the 20mm cannon in their F4U-1Cs had frozen and had to break off the attack. Chernoff continued, seeing that the Japanese aircraft were in two formations, one higher and one lower. He decided to attack the higher formation on his own in order to protect Ens Myers, even though he would be attacking from below. Another division of VF-85 was climbing rapidly to help.

Chernoff came in on what he identified as a formation of 'Zekes' and opened fire with his cannon, knocking the port wing off one aeroplane. He fired on a second, which blew up under his fire, then came down to make a run on two more fighters, firing three bursts at one, which also blew up (these may well have been 'Franks', as the 60th Shinbu-Tai lost three that day and the escort force lost eight). As he tried, and failed, to follow the second fighter through a turn, Chernoff noticed three 'Zekes' coming down on him from above.

A VF-85 Corsair attacks a 'Frank' during the combat of 28 May 1945. VF-85 pilots claimed four Ki-84s shot down this day, two with the F4U-1D and two with the cannon-armed F4U-1C. (NARA)

Maj Tojo had been watching the Special Attack aeroplanes targeting what he thought was a group of US Navy cruisers and destroyers when he saw two Corsairs come into view below him, one behind the other. They were firing on the Special Attack aeroplanes, and apparently did not see him. The second Corsair, apparently flown by Lt(jg) F. S. Siddell, came within range and Tojo immediately opened fire and sent it down smoking. Chernoff did not see Tojo closing behind him, the Ki-84 pilot opening fire and hitting the Corsair's engine, which began to smoke badly and covered the windscreen with oil. Chernoff did a split-S to escape, but his Corsair was finished. Major Tojo was not sure how badly he had damaged the two Corsairs, but wisely did not follow them down. Chernoff and Siddell were badly hit, but both made water landings and were rescued. With an experienced pilot at the controls and an altitude advantage, the Hayate had shot down two Corsairs in under a minute.

2Lt Stuart Alley had the good fortune to survive a dogfight with an experienced Japanese fighter pilot during this same encounter, as VMF-323's Aircraft Action Report recorded:

> Lt Alley, at 500ft, sighted a single Tojo flying in the opposite direction at 4000ft. When sighted the Tojo was making a run on Lt Alley from above at 11 o'clock, Lt Alley pulling up his nose and firing back at the approaching Tojo. A burst or two was exchanged and Lt Alley noticed the Tojo's engine slightly smoking and pieces flying off the Tojo's fuselage. Both overshot the termination of this first pass, and both then scrambled to get altitude advantage. Lt Alley managed to get above the Tojo and initiated his second pass from above at 12 o'clock. A few scattered hits were noticed, hitting around the Tojo's engine cowling, before Lt Alley passed by the Tojo on this run. Lt Alley recovered fast and again got an altitude advantage. A third pass was then made slightly above at 6 o'clock. Lt Alley opened fire at 350 yards and closed fast. The Tojo jinked violently but was smoking badly. The Tojo dove for the water, crashed and exploded.

2Lt Stuart Alley of VMF-323, who encountered an experienced and determined Japanese fighter pilot during the 25 May combats around Okinawa and fortunately came out the winner of the duel. (NARA)

Commenting on comparative performance between the 'Tojo' (almost certainly one of the escorting Hayate fighters from the 102nd or 103rd Hiko Sentai), the report said, 'The Tojo Lt Alley destroyed was very aggressive, and very fast. The pilot displayed excellent airmanship – the Tojo proved to be an equal match for the Corsair in both dives and turns'.

One of the last encounters between the Corsair and the Hayate occurred during Kikusui Operation No. 10. This was the first combat with a 'Frank' involving the latest model of the Corsair, the F4U-4, which had significantly better performance. On that day, 21 June, 1Lt Martin Tiernan was leading a division from VMF-223 on a barrier CAP over the islands north of Okinawa. VMF-223 had arrived on Okinawa earlier in the month, missing out on the intense air combat of April and May. By June, the JAAF and IJNAF were running out of Special Attack pilots. For this last Kikusui attack the JAAF sent out just 15 Special Attack aircraft over two days and the IJNAF only 30. On the first day of the attack the 26th Shimbu-Tai unit sent out four Ki-84s to attack shipping west of Okinawa, apparently with an escort force.

Flying at 10,000ft in the late afternoon, Tiernan was following a vector from the Fighter Director when he spotted a formation of 12 aircraft flying

Ki-84: IN THE COCKPIT

1. Wing-mounted Ho-5 20mm cannon arming cock
2. Exhaust temperature gauge
3. Cylinder temperature gauge
4. Overboost control lever
5. Model 1 ignition switch
6. Landing gear position indicator
7. Propeller speed control
8. Type 1 oil temperature gauge
9. Type 100 tachometer
10. Type 2 boost pressure gauge
11. Type 3 speed indicator
12. Type 98 compass
13. Type 98 turn indicator
14. Artificial horizon cock
15. Type 98 artificial horizon
16. Cockpit airflow control lever
17. Army Type 3 reflecting gunsight
18. Main instrument panel
19. Type 97 vertical speed indicator
20. Type 97 altimeter
21. Type 100 aeronautic clock
22. Oxygen flow gauge
23. Type 95 fuel gauge
24. Data table
25. Type 1 fuel gauge

26. Two-speed compressor oil pressure gauge
27. Tank pressurization fuel pressure gauge
28. Turn indicator adjustment
29. Oil gauge selector
30. Airspeed indicator rain remover
31. Tank pressurization selector
32. Electric box
33. Type 95 oil gauge
34. Ho-103 12.7mm machine gun loading cock
35. Rudder pedal position adjustment handle
36. 'Hi' Mk 3 wireless receiver
37. Type 94 oil pressure gauge
38. Rudder pedals
39. Ultraviolet cockpit light
40. Cannon firing switch
41. Main power switch
42. Starter switch
43. Oil cooler shutter control
44. Cowl flap control lever
45. Seat light
46. Dust filter control lever
47. Air warmer control lever
48. Five-way cock control lever

49. Manual oil pressure pump lever
50. Control column
51. Three-way cock control lever
52. Seat
53. Elevator trim tab control
54. Canopy open lever
55. Throttle lever
56. Manual propeller pitch control lever
57. Radio remote control
58. Supercharger zero-speed selector lever
59. Supercharger automatic high-altitude valve selector lever
60. Supercharger two-speed selector lever
61. High altitude valve adjustment lever
62. Flap control
63. Landing gear control
64. Tail wheel lock control
65. Ho-103 12.7mm machine guns
66. Seat height adjustment lever

(Artwork by Jim Laurier, © Osprey Publishing)

abreast at 8,000ft, with two divisions in the middle and a section of two aircraft on either end. In the fading light Tiernan thought they were P-47s, but as the division closed in he identified them as 'Tojos'. Tiernan and his wingman, 1Lt John Groot, took on the section on the right, while his element leader, 1Lt Arthur Evans, took the section on the left. Tiernan closed to within 50 yards of the Japanese wingman and apparently killed the pilot with a burst into the cockpit. Turning to take on the leader, he saw tracers going past his right wing – the Japanese pilot had apparently seen the attack and reacted with speed and manoeuvrability to whip around and come in on Tiernan's Corsair. Fortunately, Tiernan's wingman was in position to fire on the attacking fighter, sending it down smoking. Evans and his wingman, 2Lt Roy McAlister Jr, shot down the two aircraft in the other section on the left of the formation. While this combat was going on, the remaining eight aircraft used their speed to reach a cloud layer and escape.

On the same day the 47th Hiko Sentai lost a Type 4 Fighter over Okinawa, and since these were the only aircraft claimed on 21 June in that area, it seems probable that the 'Tojos' VMF-223 ran into were 'Franks' from the 26th Shimbu-Tai unit, with an escort from the 47th Hiko Sentai. This unit had been transferred to Kyushu on 27 May to defend the Kyushu airfields and to provide escorts to the Special Attack units. It was a quick and one-sided encounter, giving evidence of the F4U-4's superiority. As VMF-223's Aircraft Action Report stated, 'the enemy airplanes were outclassed by the F4U-4s, which closed on them from above and showed superior speed.'

The next day the 27th Shimbu-Tai and the 179th Shimbu-Tai sent out 11 Type 4 Special Attack aircraft to attack American vessels west of

F4U-1C and F4U-1D Corsairs onboard USS *Shangri-La* (CV-38), with the Royal Australian Navy destroyer HMAS *Napier* (D15) keeping station alongside the carrier. VF-85 and VBF-85 used these Corsairs interchangeably, flying missions using both models in the same division. (NARA)

Okinawa. That morning 2Lt Duncan Urquhart with VMF-322 claimed a 'Tojo' southwest of Okinawa, which may have been one of the 'Franks' from the Shimbu-Tai units.

The last combat between the Corsair and the 'Frank' almost certainly took place on 25 July 1945, and it proved to be an uneven contest. Early that morning ten Corsairs from VF-85, consisting of eight F4U-1Cs and two F4U-1Ds, joined 12 F6F-5s from VF-88 on a fighter sweep over the Japanese airfields of Miho and Yonaga, on the southwest coast of Honshu. The Corsairs of VF-85 struck Yonaga while VF-88 attacked Miho, dropping 260lb fragmentation bombs and firing 5in. rockets. Coming in on a strafing run Ens Loyd Miller caught a Japanese fighter he identified as a 'Frank' just as it was taking off. A burst from the four 20mm cannon in Miller's F4U-1C hit the Ki-84 in the engine, sending it crashing near the airfield. In the final weeks of the Pacific War neither US Navy nor US Marine Corps Corsair squadrons appear to have met 'Franks' in the few remaining clashes fought over Japan.

On 21 June a division from VMF-223 was flying a combat air patrol when they spotted 12 Japanese fighters flying in near line abreast. Using the superior speed of their F4U-4s, 1Lt Martin Tiernan and his wingman, 1Lt John Groot, closed on a section flying on the right side of the formation. Tiernan quickly shot down the wingman, but another 'Frank' turned to pursue him. As Tiernan pulled up to evade the fighter, Groot came in on the 'Frank' from above and behind and shot it down with two short bursts. (Artwork by Gareth Hector, © Osprey Publishing)

ANALYSIS

The aerial engagements between the Corsair and the Hayate took place from February to July 1945. The two fighters met in combat perhaps 20 times, taking into account the confusion over aircraft recognition in the heat of battle and the lack of available JAAF records. Since many of these combats appear to have involved Corsairs attacking Ki-84s from the Shimbu-Tai Special Attack units that were flown by less-experienced pilots, it can be argued that these actions are not representative of the capabilities of the Hayate versus the Corsair. But even if the superior performance of the Ki-84 improved the odds for all pilots regardless of their level of experience, the introduction of the Type 4 fighter in the defence of Japan did little to alter the outcome of the battle.

In the duels between the Corsair and the Hayate, the F4U won handily, although it was not without effort. Fortunately for the US Navy and US Marine Corps Corsair pilots, the Hayates were too few in number with too few experienced pilots to change significantly the outcome of the aerial battles waged against superior numbers of American fighters flown by better-trained pilots.

Determining the number of Corsairs that fell to the Type 4 and the number of Type 4s that fell to the Corsair with any degree of precision is an exercise in frustration because of the problems of aircraft recognition and the paucity of information currently available from the Japanese side. After World War II, the US Navy published *Naval Aviation Combat Statistics – World War II*, which gives a listing of claims against different types of Japanese aircraft from 1 September 1944 to 15 August 1945. This report states that US Navy and US Marine Corps Corsairs shot down 28 'Franks' during this period, but also 53 'Tojos' and seven 'Georges'.

The historical information available today indicates that several encounters between what US Navy and US Marine Corps pilots identified as 'Franks' were actually combats with 'Georges' from the IJNAF's 343rd Kokutai, while many of the claims for 'Tojos' were in all likelihood actually the 'Franks' of the Shimbu-Tai units and their escorts. If one looks at the combats during the period in which the US Navy or US Marine Corps pilots specifically claimed 'Franks' (excluding the combats that can be attributed to battles with the 343rd Kokutai), and adds the combats that took place during the Okinawa campaign and the Kikusui attacks in which US Navy and US Marine Corps Corsairs claimed 'Tojos' that can be linked with the Shimbu-Tai units flying the Type 4 (admittedly, a somewhat subjective exercise), one comes up with the total of approximately 67 fighters shot down that were probably, but not certainly, Type 4 Fighters.

Corsair losses to the Hayate are equally difficult to attribute with any degree of certainty, particularly in the absence of Japanese records of claims against the American fighter. As the US Navy's statistical study commented, 'the errors in identification which may normally be expected in the action reports results in a decrease of accuracy which leaves something to be desired, but permits comparisons which are believed to be sufficiently near the truth to be of considerable value and interest, and are in any event the best available.' The US Navy listed four Corsairs lost against claims for 'Franks', and four lost against claims for 'Tojos'. In addition, the US Navy listed three losses to 'Jacks' and, oddly, no losses to the 'George'.

When comparing claims to losses, the US Navy added one unidentified loss of a Corsair to losses against the 'Frank', 'Jack' and 'George'. The US Navy reported a ratio of six late-war Japanese fighters ('Frank', 'Jack' and 'George') destroyed for each Corsair lost. Adding in claims for 'Tojos' that may have been 'Franks' takes the ratio up to around seven-to-one, giving the Corsair a clear superiority. But this contrasts with the Corsair's twelve-to-one record against the 'Zeke' during this period, clearly indicating that the more capable Japanese fighters were in fact more difficult to shoot down.

For the US Navy and US Marine Corps Corsair pilots, the 'Frank' was just one of many Japanese fighters they encountered in aerial battles over Kyushu and Okinawa. They were far more likely to encounter the 'Zeke'.

Although this VBF-85 Corsair was damaged in combat with the N1K2-J 'George', this photograph illustrates the destructive power of the 20mm cannon that equipped JAAF late-war fighters like the Ki-84 and the Ki-100. (NARA)

Given the intensity of the fighting over Okinawa and the relatively few encounters between the Corsair and the 'Frank', spread over three US Navy and nine US Marine Corsair squadrons, not to mention the positive outcome of almost all of these combats, it is not surprising that the Ki-84 did not make a dramatic impression.

It is possible, however, to detect a degree of respect for the Japanese fighter from comments in the Aircraft Action Reports. These remarks relate to speed, manoeuvrability and protection. Some reports, but not all, noted that the 'Frank' was nearly as fast as the Corsair. On a mission to Kyushu on 14 May, the Corsairs of VMF-112 ran into a formation of Hayates from the 100th Hikoshidan flying a patrol and went in pursuit. As the Aircraft Action Report noted:

> This was the first time the Corsairs had battled a number of the new Jap Franks. When the Franks were first sighted they were approximately three miles away in a slight dive. The Corsairs started after them from level flight. The leading Franks were able to maintain their distance advantage, but the Corsairs did manage to close on the last three Franks. It was evident from this performance that the Franks had every bit as much speed as the Corsairs although Maj Andre thought in a prolonged chase the Corsair might catch the Frank.

After fighting with Ki-84s during a CAP on 28 May, the pilots of VF-85 commented that the 'Frank' was 'more manoeuvrable than the F4U-1C' and 'could easily turn inside it'. From the same combat, VF-85 pilots added that the '"Frank" had very good protection. After being hit in the wings it burned a very short while then smoked slightly. Very hard to explode'. Other squadrons had similar experiences, VMF-221 noting that 'armour appears to be definitely present, as none burned and all hit many times'.

Summarizing the experiences of VF-84 against the 'Frank' and the 'George', Lt Cdr Roger Hedrick probably reflected the views of most US Navy and US Marine Corps pilots who encountered these fighters when he stated that 'the F4U-1D was found to be superior to the latest Jap models. The edge over the Frank and the George is not large but is ample to gain victory by aggressive attack'. But in so many combats, the level of pilot experience was the most telling factor. The comments of VMF-441 on this score are representative:

> In each case the enemy pilots appeared to ours to be inexperienced and not aggressive. None of the enemy aircraft fired on our planes and they did not take advantage of their superior manoeuvrability.

KI-84: THROUGH THE GUNSIGHT

The JAAF developed its own gunsights separately from the IJNAF. Most Ki-84s used the Army Type 3 gunsight, a replacement for the earlier Type 100 reflector gunsight. The Type 3 was based on the German Revi 12C gunsight and featured a larger reticule than the Type 100.

The Ki-84's mixed armament of Ho-103 12.7mm machine guns and Ho-5 20mm cannon presented its pilots with a mix of trajectories, but the two weapons had the benefit of similar rates of fire and muzzle velocities. The Ho-103 round had a muzzle velocity of 760 metres a second, while the Ho-5 round travelled at 700 metres a second. The Ho-103 put out 15 rounds a second, while the Ho-5 could fire off 14 rounds. The Ho-103's 12.7mm round was similar in effect to the American 0.50in. round, but the 20mm round of the Ho-5 had nearly double the

destructive power. The projectile weight of the Ho-5's 20mm round was three times heavier than the 12.7mm round of the Ho-103 machine gun. A few rounds could do significant damage to a Corsair. There were several examples where an F4U that made it back to the carrier after receiving 20mm hits in the wing had to have the latter entirely replaced. It was fortunate for American pilots that Nakajima produced only limited numbers of the Ki-84 Otsu (Ki-84b) armed with four Ho-5 cannon.

Once again, pilot experience was a factor. Most Japanese pilots at this stage of the war had only limited experience with aerial gunnery. Knocking down a Corsair required hits in a vital area such as the engine – not an easy target for a beginner in fast-moving combat. (Artwork by Jim Laurier, © Osprey Publishing)

Pilot experience appears to have been the Achilles heel of the Type 4 Fighter Sentai in the final battles of the Pacific War. With its superior flying characteristics and performance over the Type 1 and Type 2 Fighters, the Hayate was well-liked by JAAF fighter pilots, and as one aviator who survived the war said, 'I'm sure there's no need for me to comment on the advantages of its high speed and Ho-5 20mm cannon'. While the Type 4 was easier for the young pilots coming out of training in 1944 and 1945 to adjust to, it is not surprising that it was the more experienced pilots who were able to take advantage of the Hayate's performance.

Among the more successful Ki-84 pilots in the final months of the war was WO Katsuki Kira, who scored nine victories during the battles over the Nomonhan region, claimed seven more over New Guinea, several in the Philippines and achieved the last of his 21 victories fighting over Okinawa with the 103rd Hiko Sentai. Maj Hyoe Yonaga was another Nomonhan veteran who fought in the Okinawa battles as commander of the 101st Hiko Sentai, ending the war with 16 victory claims. As described earlier, Maj Michiaki Tojo, another experienced pilot, shot down two Corsairs in the Okinawa battles. It is also important to note that three pilots from the 103rd Hiko Sentai, Capt Tomojiro Ogawa and 1Lts Yasushi Miyamotobayashi and Shigeyasu Miyamoto, were all awarded the *Bukosho* medal, Japan's highest award for gallantry, for their actions during the Okinawa air battles. But there were far too few pilots of this calibre to make a difference in these final battles, particularly against American numerical superiority.

Maj Tojo's experience following his combat with Navy Corsairs on 4 May is perhaps representative of the frustrations many of the JAAF's fighter pilots felt at the time. In a post-war interview he recalled what happened as he led his formation of Hayate fighters back to base:

On our way home we took the course on the island's line [following the Ryukyu Island chain back to Kyushu]. When we flew at an altitude of 4000m [13,124ft] west of Yaku-shima, I saw some hundreds of enemy carrier-based planes flying at an altitude of 3000m [9,840ft] in tight formations like a military review. There were also fighter squadrons in fighting formation above them, flying grandly back to the south. I thought the possibility if our 30 planes could attack them from behind, but I decided no, 'We have many young birds [with] less than 300 hours. I should be patient.' We continued to fly north. I thought the enemies were the same. Both didn't want a fight. The situation was greatly different from that when we had combats in the south years earlier. Skills of fighter pilots [had gone] down.

CORSAIR PILOTS' 'FRANK' VICTORY CLAIMS			
Pilot	Unit	Claims	Date
Ens Roy Rechsteiner	VBF-83	2 'Franks'	5 April 1945
Lt(jg) Cyrus Chambers	VF-84	2 'Franks'	28 April 1945
Lt Cdr Roger Hedrick	VF-84	2 'Franks'	2 February 1945
Lt(jg) Kennard Moos	VF-85	2 'Franks'	28 May 1945
2Lt Wendell Browning	VMF-112	1.5 'Franks'*	14 April 1945
Capt William Snider	VMF-221	2 'Franks'	18 March 1945
2Lt Raymond Barrett	VMF-311	2 'Franks'	8 June 1945
Capt Herbert Valentine	VMF-312	2 'Franks'*	25 May 1945
2Lt Jay Allen	VMF-322	1.5 'Franks'*	25 May 1945
2Lt James Webster	VMF-322	3 'Franks'*	25 May 1945
1Lt Charles Allen	VMF-323	2 'Franks'*	25 May 1945
1Lt James Feliton	VMF-323	2 'Franks'*	25 May 1945
* These were claimed as 'Tojos' during the Kikusui attacks			

AFTERMATH

Following the fall of Okinawa, the JAAF ordered all of its air units to conserve their strength for the expected invasion of the Home Islands – they were not to respond to American raids. It lifted this restriction when it realized that American bomber and fighter attacks were severely disrupting aircraft production. The order does explain the dearth of combats between the Corsair and the Hayate following the loss of Okinawa. Towards the end of the campaign the 6th Kokugun had been returned to Army control. The General Air Army, formed in April to command and control all JAAF air units in the Home Islands, now commanded the 1st Kokugun and the 6th Kokugun. Together these two formations had eight *sentai* equipped with the Type 4 Fighter covering Honshu, Shikoku and Kyushu. Serviceability was a problem. At the end of the war the JAAF reported to Allied authorities that there were 267 Type 4 Fighters in Japan, but only 162 were operational.

Production, or lack of it, was also a continuing problem. With the Type 4 Fighter, it peaked in December 1944 at 373 aeroplanes, and declined thereafter. In July Nakajima built 184 Type 4 Fighters at its two plants, but as previously mentioned production of the Ha-45 Homare engine lagged behind aircraft construction. The bombing of Nakajima's aircraft factories, the move to start production in dispersed underground facilities and the impact of raids on urban areas around the factories reduced productivity. Production of the Type 4 at the Mansyu Hikoki Seizo K. K. (Manchurian Aeroplane Manufacturing Company Ltd) factory in Manchuria had begun in early 1945, but less than 100 aeroplanes were built.

The Tachikawa Aircraft Company undertook the development of a wooden version of the Type 4 Fighter to conserve resources. Designated the Ki-106, this effort did not go beyond a few prototypes. (Peter M. Bowers Collection, Museum of Flight)

To conserve diminishing supplies of critical aluminium, the Tachikawa Hikoki K. K. (Tachikawa Aircraft Company) undertook the design and development of an all-wood version of the Type 4 as the Ki-106. Three prototypes were built and were under test when the war ended. Nakajima worked on a Ki-84 built with carbon steel components and sheeting (as the Ki-113), but this proved to be significantly overweight. Even if Nakajima had been able to increase production of the Hayate, there was insufficient fuel for major operations, and pilot training had been limited almost exclusively to training pilots for Special Attack missions. Given all the constraints on resources, it is doubtful that the JAAF could have overcome the problem of inexperienced pilots.

There were several advanced designs of the Ki-84 undertaken at Nakajima during the last year of the war, drawing on the company's experience with the Ki-87 experimental high-altitude fighter. These were intended as interceptors to combat the B-29s. The first was the Ki-84-III, which simply replaced the Ha-45 Homare with the Ha-44 12Ru engine of 2,450hp and added a turbo-supercharger under the fuselage. This aeroplane did not progress beyond the design stage. The Ki-84R exchanged the turbo-supercharger for a mechanically driven device and incorporated a wing of larger area. More ambitious designs were the Ki-84N and the Ki-84P, featuring the Ha-44-13Ru engine giving 2,500hp, a turbo-supercharger and increased wing area. The Koku Hombu decided to pursue the Ki-84N and assigned it the designation Ki-117, but this, too, remained only a design.

Vought undertook no further development of the Corsair during World War II, concentrating instead on production. It stopped building the F4U-1D in February 1945, switching to production of the more capable F4U-4. By the end of the Pacific War Vought had completed 1,850

F4U-4s, compared to 1,485 Type 4 Fighters built during the same period. Goodyear Aircraft undertook development of the F2G-1 Corsair, using the Pratt & Whitney R4360 Wasp Major giving 3,000hp. Although the F2G-1 had a terrific rate of climb, its performance was not sufficiently greater than the F4U-4 or the newer F8F-1 then coming into service. The Bureau of Aeronautics cancelled the F2G-1 production order in May 1945.

By early August 1945, the US Navy had 11 squadrons of F4U-4s with the Fast Carrier Task Force either in the Pacific or preparing for combat on the west coast. Ten of these were fighter–bomber squadrons, as the Corsair had proved to be more capable in this role than the Hellcat. MAG-14 remained the only Marine Air Group on Okinawa with the F4U-4, the other US Marine Corps squadrons retaining the F4U-1D/FG-1D/F4U-1C. Had the war continued, it is likely that more 'Marine Air' Corsair squadrons would have converted to the F4U-4, as Vought had contracts for an additional 3,900 that were cancelled after the war.

In the last few months of the Pacific War the US Navy converted more Corsair squadrons to the F4U-4, particularly the fighter-bomber units. These examples were assigned to VBF-89 onboard USS *Antietam* (CV-36) in July 1945. (NARA)

FURTHER READING

PART I
Books

Bishop, Patrick, *Fighter Boys* (Harper Perennial, 2003)

Caldwell, Donald J., *The JG 26 War Diary* Vol. 1 (Grub Street, 1998)

Caygill, Peter, *Spitfire Mark V in Action* (Airlife, 2001)

Dundas, Hugh, *Flying Start* (Stanley Paul, 1988)

Fernandez-Sommerau, *Messerschmitt Bf 109 Recognition Manual* (Classic Publications, 2004)

Foreman, John, *Battle of Britain – The Forgotten Months* (Air Research Publications, 1988)

Foreman, John, *RAF Fighter Command Victory Claims of World War 2 Part Two* (Red Kite, 2005)

Franks, Norman, *Fighter Command's Air War 1941* (Pen & Sword, 2016)

Franks, Norman, *RAF Fighter Command Losses of the Second World War Vols 1 and 2* (Midland Publishing Ltd, 1997 and 1998)

Galland, Adolf, *The First and the Last* (Fontana, 1971)

Jefford, C. G., *RAF Squadrons* (Airlife, 2001)

Johnson, AVM J. E. 'Johnnie' and Wg Cdr P. B. 'Laddie' Lucas, *Winged Victory* (Stanley Paul, 1995)

Mathews, Andrew Johannes and John Foreman, *Luftwaffe Aces* Vols 1–4 (Red Kite, 2014)

Michulec, Robert, *Messerschmitt Bf 109F* (Stratus/MMP Books, 2013)

Mombeek, Eric, with David Wadman and Martin Pegg, *Jagdwaffe Volume 2 Section 3 – Battle of Britain Phase Three* (Classic Publications, 2002)

Mombeek, Eric, with David Wadman and Martin Pegg, *Jagdwaffe Volume 2 Section 4 – Battle of Britain Phase Four* (Classic Publications, 2002)

Morgan, Eric B. and Edward Shacklady, *Spitfire – The History* (Key Publishing, 1993)

Murawski, Marek J., *Messerschmitt Bf 109F* Vol. 1 (Kagero, 2007)

Nijboer, Donald, Duel 60: *Spitfire V vs C.202 Folgore* (Osprey, 2014)

Price, Dr Alfred, Aircraft of the Aces 12: *Spitfire Mark II/III Aces 1939–41* (Osprey, 1996)

Price, Dr Alfred, Aircraft of the Aces 16: *Spitfire Mark V Aces 1941–45* (Osprey, 1997)

Prien, Jochen, *Jadgeschwader 53* Vol. 1 (Schiffer, 1997)

Ross, David, Bruce Blanche and William Simpson, *The Greatest Squadron of Them All,* Vol. 1 (Grub Street, 2003)

Shores, Christopher and Clive Williams, *Aces High* (Grub Street, 1994)

Sims, Edward H., *The Fighter Pilots* (Corgi Books, 1967)

Thomas, Andrew, Aircraft of the Aces 131: *Spitfire Aces of the Channel Front 1941–43* (Osprey, 2016)

Turner, John Frayn, *The Bader Wing* (Airlife, 1999)

Wadman, David and Martin Pegg, *Jagdwaffe Volume 4 Section 1 – Holding the West 1941–1943* (Classic Publications, 2002)

Weal, John, Aircraft of the Aces 29: *Bf 109F/G/K Aces of the Western Front* (Osprey, 1999)

Weal, John, Aviation Elite Units 1: *Jagdgeschwader 2 'Richthofen'* (Osprey, 2000)

Weal, John, Aviation Elite Units 22: *Jagdgeschwader 51 'Mölders'* (Osprey, 2006)

Wellum, Geoffrey, *First Light* (Viking, 2002)

Websites

Aces of the Luftwaffe – www.luftwaffe.cz

Luftwaffe Wartime Aerial Victory Credits – www.aces.safarikovi.org

PART II

Aviation History Unit, *The Navy's Air War – Mission Completed* (Harper Brothers, 1946)

Carl, Maj Gen Marion E., USMC (Ret.) with Barrett Tillman, *Pushing the Envelope – The Career of Fighter Ace and Test Pilot Marion Carl* (Naval Institute Press, 1994)

Ewing, Steve, *Reaper Leader – The Life of 'Jimmy' Flatley* (Naval Institute Press, 2002)

Ewing, Steve, *Thach Weave – The Life of 'Jimmy' Thach* (Naval Institute Press, 2004)

Foss, Joe and Donna Wild Foss, *A Proud American – The Autobiography of Joe Foss* (Pocket Books, 1992)

Frank, Richard, *Guadalcanal* (Random House, 1990)

Greene, Frank L., *History of the Grumman F4F Wildcat* (Grumman Aircraft Engineering Corporation)

Hata, Ikuhiko, Yasuho Izawa and Christopher Shores, *Japanese Naval Air Force Fighter Units and Their Aces 1932–1945* (Grub Street, 2011)

Horikoshi, Jiro, *Eagles of Mitsubishi – The Story of the Zero Fighter* (University of Washington Press, 1981)

Lundstrom, John B., *The First Team – Pacific Naval Air Combat from Pearl Harbor to Midway* (Naval Institute Press, 1984)

Lundstrom, John B., *The First Team and the Guadalcanal Campaign – Naval Fighter Combat from August to November 1942* (Naval Institute Press, 1994)

Mikesh, Robert C., *Zero – Combat and Development History of Japan's Legendary Mitsubishi A6M Zero Fighter* (Motorbooks International, 1994)

Miller, Thomas G. Jr, *The Cactus Air Force – The Story of the Handful of Fliers Who Saved Guadalcanal* (Harper & Row, 1969)

Minora, Akimoto, *Reisen Ku Senki – Vol. 1: Reisen no Eiko (Chronicle of the Reisen Battles: Vol. 1 – Glory of the Reisen)* (Kojinsha, 2010)

Minora, Akimoto, *Reisen Ku Senki – Vol. 3: Fukutsu no Reisen (Chronicle of the Reisen Battles: Vol. 3 – The Invincible Reisen)* (Kojinsha, 2010)

Okumiya, Masatake and Jiro Horikoshi with Martin Caidin, *The Zero Fighter* (Cassel & Co., 1958)

Peattie, Mark R., *Sunburst – The Rise of Japanese Naval Air Power, 1909–1941* (Naval Institute Press, 2001)

Sherrod, Robert, *History of Marine Corps Aviation in World War II* (Combat Forces Press, 1952)

Wilmott, H. P., *The War with Japan – The Period of Balance May 1942–October 1943* (SR Books, 2002)

Wilmott, H. P., *Empires in the Balance: Japanese and Allied Pacific Strategies to April 1942* (Naval Institute Press, 1982)

PART III

Aders, G. and W. Held, *Jagdgeschwader 51 'Mölders'* (Motorbuch Verlag, 1985)

Caldwell, D., *The JG 26 War Diaries Vols 1 and 2* (Grub Street, 1996 and 1998)

Campbell, J. L., *Focke-Wulf Fw 190 in Action* (Squadron Signal Publications, 1975)

Gordon, Y. and D. Khazanov, *Soviet Combat Aircraft of the Second World War, Vol. 1* (Midland Publishing, 1998)

Green, W., *Warplanes of the Third Reich* (Doubleday & Company, 1970)

Griehl, M. and J. Dressel, *Focke-Wulf Fw 190/Ta 152 – Jäger, Jagdbomber, Panzerjäger* (Motorbuch Verlag, 1997)

Hannig, N., *Luftwaffe Fighter Ace* (Grub Street, 2004)

Kaberov, I., *Swastika in the Gunsight* (Sutton Publishing Ltd., 1999)

Khazanov, D. G. and V. G. Gorbach, *Aviation in Battle over Orel-Kursk Salient* (Moscow, 2004)

Kriegstagebuch des Oberkommandos der Wehrmacht 1940–1945. Bd. 3. Teil 1 (Bernard & Graefe Verlag für Wehrwesen, 1963)

Medved, A. N., *Focke-Wulf Fw 190* (Moscow, 1995)

Mellinger, G., Aircraft of the Aces 56: *LaGG & Lavochkin Aces of World War 2* (Osprey, 2003)

Mombeek, E., *Defending the Reich (JG 1)* (JAC Publications, 1992)

Mombeek, E., *Sturmjäger – Zur geschichte des Jagdgeschwaders 4 und der Sturmstaffel. Bd. 1, 2.* (Privately published, 1997 and 2000)

Nowarra, H. J., *Focke-Wulf Fw 190 & Ta 152* (G. T. Fowlis & Co. Ltd., 1988)

Obermaier, E., *Die Ritterkreuzträger der Luftwaffe. Bd. 1.* (D. Hoffman, 1966)

Polak, T. and C. Shores, *Stalin's Falcons* (Grub Street, 1999)

Prien, J., Rodeike. *Jagdgeschwader 1 und 11. Bd. 1–3* (Struve Druck, 1994 and 1996)

Prien, J., *IV/Jagdgeschwader 3 – Chronik einer Jagdgruppe 1943–1945* (Struve Druck, 1996)

Scutts, J., *Jagdgeschwader 54* (Motorbooks, 1992)

Smith, J. R. and A. L. Kay, *German Aircraft of the Second World War* (Putman, 1972)

Weal, J., Aircraft of the Aces 6: *Focke-Wulf Fw 190 Aces of the Russian Front* (Osprey, 1995)

Weal, J., Aircraft of the Aces 9: *Focke-Wulf Fw 190 Aces of the Western Front* (Osprey, 1996)

Weal, J., Aviation Elite Units 6: *Jagdgeschwader 54 'Grünherz'* (Osprey, 2001)

Weal, J., Aviation Elite Units 13: *Luftwaffe Schlachtgruppen* (Osprey, 2003)

Weal, J., Aviation Elite Units 22: *Jagdgeschwader 51 'Mölders'* (Osprey, 2006)

PART IV

Akimoto, Minoru, Yoshio Ikari, et al., *Yon-Shiki Sentoki Hayate (Nakajima Army Type 4 Fighter Hayate (Ki-84)), The Maru Mechanic No 33* (Ushio Shobo, 1982)

Brown, Capt Eric 'Winkle', RN, *Wings of the Navy – Testing British and US Carrier Aircraft.* Rev. Edn (Hikoki Publications, 2013)

Cea, Eduardo, *Japanese Military Aircraft No 8: Tokubetsu Kogeki Tai. Special Attack Units* (AF Editions, 2011)

Condon, John Pomeroy, *Corsairs and Flatops – Marine Carrier Air Warfare 1944–1945* (Naval Institute Press, 1998)

Dean, Francis H., *America's Hundred-Thousand – US Production Fighters of World War 2* (Schiffer, 1997)

Ferkl, Martin, *Nakajima Ki-44 Shoki* (Revi, 2009)

Green, William and Gordon Swanborough, *World War II Fact Files – Japanese Army Fighters, Part 2* (Macdonald and Janes, 1977)

Guyton, Boone T., *Whispering Death – The Test Pilot's Story of the F4U Corsair* (Orion Books, 1990)

Harvey, Ralph, *Developing the Gull-Winged F4U Corsair and Taking it to Sea* (Privately published, 2012)

Hata, Ikuhiko, Yasuho Izawa and Christopher Shores, *Japanese Army Air Force Fighter Units and Their Aces 1931–1945* (Grub Street, 2002)

Ikari, Yoshiro, *Sentoki Hayate (Hayate Fighter)* (Shirogane Shobo, 1976)

Japanese Monograph No. 157, *Homeland Air Defense Operations Record* (Office of the Chief of Military History, 1952)

Model Art No. 451, *Special Issue – Imperial Japanese Army Air Force Suicide Attack Unit* (Model Art Co., 1995)

Nohara, Shigaru et al., *Hayate Rikugun Yon-Shiki Sentoki (Hayate Army Type 4 Fighter Ki-84)* (Model Art No. 283, 1986)

Nohara, Shigaru et al., *Nakajima Rikugun Yon-Shiki Sentoki Hayate (Ki-84) (Nakajima Army Type 4 Fighter Hayate (Ki-84)* (Model Art No. 493, 1997)

O'Brien, Phillips Payson, *How the War was Won – Air-Sea Power and Allied Victory in World War II* (Cambridge University Press, 2015)

Rielly, Robin L., *Kamikaze Attacks of World War II – A Complete History of Japanese Suicide Strikes on American Ships, by Aircraft and Other Means* (McFarland & Co., 2010)

Sakaida, Henry, Aircraft of the Aces 13: *Japanese Army Air Force Aces 1937–45* (Osprey, 1997)

Sakaida, Henry and Koji Takaki, *Genda's Blade – Japan's Squadron of Aces – 343rd Kokutai* (Classic Publications, 2003)

Szlagor, Tomasz and Leszek A. Wieliczko, *Kagero Monographs No. 52 – Vought F4U Corsair,* Vol. I (Kagero, 2013)

Szlagor, Tomasz and Leszek A. Wieliczko, *Kagero Monographs No. 56 – Vought F4U Corsair,* Vol. II (Kagero, 2014)

Tillman, Barrett, *Corsair – The F4U in World War II and Korea* (Naval Institute Press, 1979)

Tokkotai Senbotsusha Irei Heiwa Kinen Kyokai, Interview with Maj Michiaki Tojo (Tokko, 2004) available at: http://cs.iupui.edu/~ateal/Ingraham/May4/Tojo.html (last accessed 18 November 2015)

Watanabe, Yoji, *Kessen no So-ku-e – Nihon Sentoki Retuden (To the Blue Skies of Decisive Battles – Japanese Fighter Plane Biographies)* (Privately published, 2010)

Wieliczko, Leszek A., *Kagero Monographs No. 53 – Nakajima Ki-84 Hayate* (Kagero, 2013)

Yon-Shiki Sentoki Hayate (Pacific War No. 46) (Bunshan Bunko, 2004)

INDEX

References to images are in **bold**.